The Buddhist Revival in Sri Lanka

Studies in Comparative Religion
Frederick M. Denny, *Editor*

The Holy Book in Comparative Perspective
Edited by Frederick M. Denny and Rodney L. Taylor

Dr. Strangegod: On the Symbolic Meaning of Nuclear Weapons
By Ira Chernus

Native American Religious Action: A Performance Approach to Religion
By Sam Gill

Human Rights and the Conflict of Cultures:
Western and Islamic Perspectives on Religious Liberty
By David Little, John Kelsay, and Abdulaziz A. Sachedina

The Munshidīn of Egypt: Their World and Their Song
By Earle H. Waugh

The Buddhist Revival in Sri Lanka:

Religious Tradition, Reinterpretation and Response

By George D. Bond

*University of
South Carolina Press*

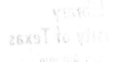

Published in Columbia, South Carolina, by the
University of South Carolina Press

First Edition

Manufactured in the United States of America

LIBRARY OF CONGRESS
Library of Congress Cataloging-in-Publication Data

Bond, George Doherty, 1942–
    The Buddhist revival in Sri Lanka : religious tradition,
reinterpretation, and response / by George D. Bond. — 1st ed.
        p.   cm. — (Studies in comparative religion)
    Bibliography: p.
    Includes index.
    ISBN 0-87249-557-4
    1. Buddhism—Sri Lanka—History—20th century.   I. Title.
II. Series: Studies in comparative religion (Columbia, S.C.)
BQ376.B66 1988
294.3'09549'3—dc 19   88-14788
                                                                                                CIP

CONTENTS

Editor's Preface

There is a sense in which this series of books provides its readers with opportunities to compare scholarly approaches to different religious traditions, and this is one aim of the project. There is another sense in which unity and variety within single traditions are discerned and analyzed. Finally, there is the major aim of the series: to provide a global, integrative approach to the study of religions and religious dimensions of human experience through a scholarship that makes sense regardless of the specific tradition being examined, and thus becomes accessible to thoughtful readers from a wide variety of interests and backgrounds. But such scholarship also requires very specific kinds of mastery of the religious symbol and action system being examined: its texts and contexts, its doctrines, practices, and community forms.

George Bond's *The Buddhist Revival in Sri Lanka: Religious Tradition, Interpretation and Response,* amply fulfills all the aims listed above—and then some. On one level, this study can be read as an epitome of recent Western scholarship on Theravada Buddhism, especially in Sri Lanka, a country that has both produced and attracted the highest caliber of scholars, whether in humanistic or social scientific studies of Buddhism. On another level, *The Buddhist Revival* permits the reader to place the Sri Lankan developments in this century within the entire history of Buddhism, partly because that island nation and the ancient tradition are almost coterminous. Indeed, the Pali language texts of Theravada in Sri Lanka can be traced back to the Buddhism of the early centuries in southern Asia. The most important level at which this book will be appreciated is in its arresting comparisons between colonialist modernizing of education and Christian missionizing in religion and their unplanned and unforeseen results in inspiring and empowering a new Sri Lankan Buddhist elite in one of the most far-reaching reforms in Buddhist history. Ironically, yet perhaps inevitably, the Protestant Reformation in Europe provided, through its English-speaking missionary legatees, several key elements of the Sri Lankan revival: an emphasis on scripture and related literacy; individual decision making in spiritual and ethical matters; a lay focus that translated Luther's "priesthood of all believers" into a sophisticated and widely appealing lay meditation movement: the *Vipassanā Bhavānā*; and a "this-worldly asceticism" that minimizes hierarchy, preaches universalism, and cultivates social action as meritorious activity that takes literally Buddha's final admonishment to: "Work out your own salvation with diligence," with the tacit understanding that personal salvation is not a matter of classical, elitist *arhantship*, only, but an altruistic vocation suited to an urban laity that has the freedom and learning to take charge of their lives.

Modern Buddhist reform in Sri Lanka is by no means uniform nor unilinear in its development, as the author demonstrates in his wide-ranging, yet focused survey which contains, among other valuable elements, the most extensive treatment of the *Vipassanā* meditation movement currently available. It is now almost trite to speak of bringing together both the "text and context" of a tradition for balanced scholarship. Yet it is still all too unusual to read a solid example of fieldwork based scholarship on Theravada Buddhism whose author is also a seasoned specialist in the Pali tradition and the history of religions. *The Buddhist Revival in Sri Lanka* is thus an example of the new, integrative scholarship that this series is designed to publish, both for its intrinsic interest and value and for its anticipated impact on comparative studies in religion generally.

Frederick Mathewson Denny
Series Editor

Acknowledgments

A word of thanks is in order to those in Sri Lanka who helped me in my field research. I carried out research in Sri Lanka for this book during three periods from 1983 through 1985. Many people gave generously of their time and knowledge to help me understand the revival of the Buddhist tradition. Among them I should thank particularly the *Sangha* who granted me interviews and hospitality, and Mr. D. C. P. Ratnakara, who shared his wisdom with me and allowed me to participate in his Saddhama Friends Society. I should thank also the hundreds of Buddhist meditators who shared their experiences and beliefs with me. I interviewed over one hundred and fifty meditators, and have been able to include only a few of their stories in chapters four through six, but I learned from them much more than I can convey in those chapters: I learned about the effectiveness and peace of *vipassanā*. I cannot thank these people personally here as I would like and still preserve their anonymity, but I am very grateful nonetheless.

I am particularly grateful also to Dr. A. T. Ariyaratne, the founder of Sarvodaya, for all his assistance in studying his movement. The leaders of the lay Buddhist societies—the All Ceylon Buddhist Congress, the World Fellowship of Buddhists, and the Young Men's Buddhist Association—including Dr. Ariyapala, Mr. Albert Edirisinghe, and Mr. L. Piyasena, also generously and patiently tolerated my questions and allowed me to participate in their activities and use their archives. The assistance of a Fulbright-Hays grant, the United States Educational Foundation in Sri Lanka, and its director, Mr. Bogoda Premaratne, also facilitated the research for this study. I should also like to thank Dr. K. J. Perera and Dr. Kingsley de Silva for their assistance and Professors Richard Gombrich and Gananath Obeyesekere, who shared with me some of their ideas on the reinterpretation of Buddhism, on which topic they too have been doing research for a book.

Abbreviations

References to the Buddhist canonical and commentarial writings have in most instances, been placed in parentheses in the text rather than in the footnotes. The abbreviations employed in these references are, primarily, the standard abbreviations for Pali works as given in the Pali Text Society's *Pali-English Dictionary*. The most frequently used abbreviations are listed below:

A.   Aṅguttara-Nikāya
AA.   Aṅguttara-Nikāyaṭṭhakathā (Manorathapūraṇī)
D.   Dīgha-Nikāya
DA.   Dīgha-Nikāyaṭṭhakathā (Sumaṅgalavilāsinī)
DAT.   Dīgha-aṭṭhakathā-Ṭīkā
Dh.A.   Dhammapada-aṭṭhakathā
Dhs.   Dhammasaṅgaṇī
Dhs.A.   Dhammasaṅgaṇī-Aṭṭhakathā (Atthasālinī)
Dpv.   Dīpavaṃsa
JA.   Jātakaṭṭhakathā
Kh.   Khuddakapāṭha
KhA.   Khuddakapāṭha-aṭṭhakathā (Paramatthajotikā I)
Kv.   Kaṅkhāvitaraṇī
Kvu.   Kathāvatthu
M.   Majjhima-Nikāya
MA.   Majjhima-Nikāyaṭṭhakathā (Papañcasūdanī)
Mhv.   Mahāvaṃsa
N.   Netti-Pakaraṇa
P.   Peṭakopadesa
Pu.   Puggala-Paññatti
S.   Saṃyutta-Nikāya
SA.   Saṃyutta-Nikāya-aṭṭhakathā (Sārattha-ppakāsinī)
Smp.   Samantapāsādikā (Vinaya aṭṭhakathā)
Sn.   Suttanipāta
Sn.A.   Suttanipāta-aṭṭhakathā (Paramatthajotikā II)
V.   Vinaya Pitaka
Vbh.   Vibhaṅga
Vism.   Visuddhimagga

The Buddhist Revival in Sri Lanka

Introduction

This book represents a study of tradition and interpretation, the dialectical process by which religions live. Typically, studies of the process of tradition and interpretation focus on the texts of a religion which reveal how succeeding generations received, reinterpreted, and transmitted the traditional heritage. My own previous work has, for the most part, also focused on this process in the texts. The process of tradition and interpretation is not restricted to texts, however; in living religions it interfaces with the present context. Thus, this study of tradition and interpretation examines the ways that Theravada Buddhists have reinterpreted their ancient tradition in order to revive and re-present it in the modern context.

Rediscovering and reinterpreting their tradition, the Theravadins of Sri Lanka have generated a revival of Buddhism that began in the late nineteenth century and has intensified since the independence of that country. Although Buddhism has undergone a similar revival or resurgence in many countries in the twentieth century, the case of Theravada Buddhism in Sri Lanka has particular significance because it represents a case study in the history of religions of how a people who had almost lost their tradition along with their identity under colonialism rediscovered and reinterpreted both. From the standpoint of the history of religions this revival of Buddhism is interesting also because it represents something of a continuity in the Theravada tradition. As Tambiah has pointed out, the attempt to renew and purify Theravada by reinterpreting it and "returning to the canon is a recurring phenomenon in the Buddhist societies, not just a feature of the modern renaissance."[1]

We can view this most recent reinterpretation and revival of Theravada as a Buddhist response to the revolution of modernization, a revolution that has confronted all of the major religions but has had a special impact on the religions of the Third World. The revolution of modernization has posed for these religions the problem of identity and responsiveness: How is it possible to maintain one's tradition, one's identity, and at the same time to reinterpret or re-present that

3

tradition in ways that respond to the modern situation? Another way of viewing this dilemma, employing the approach of Mary Douglas, is to see it as a dilemma of cosmology and context.[2] Cosmologies arise in particular contexts because the context establishes a "cost structure" that permits or requires certain value systems and interpretations of the meaning of existence, and at the same time renders implausible other values and interpretations. Whenever the context changes, and especially when it changes radically, as in the case of modernization, a new cost structure, or cultural and cosmological bias, replaces the old one and requires a reinterpretation of traditional beliefs and values.

In the specific case of Theravada Buddhism in Sri Lanka, modernization and the creation of a new context came with colonialism. The colonial powers that ruled Sri Lanka, particularly the British, created a new cost structure by instituting changes in all areas, including the political, economic, social, educational, and religious spheres. Although the immediate effect of these changes was to suppress Buddhism, the long-term effect was to compel Buddhists to respond by reinterpreting their tradition.

Since the revival of Buddhism constitutes a broad subject with many dimensions, I have not attempted a comprehensive survey. This study focuses on aspects of the reinterpretation of Buddhism by the laity, especially the contributions of the urban, educated laity who had been profoundly affected by the Western influences of the colonial period. To be sure, the rural laity have also played a significant role in this revival, and, as we shall see, they have come into the picture more in the post-Jayanti or post-independence period. However, the major focus in a study of the Buddhist revival must be upon the group identified loosely as the new elite, or the emerging urban middle class, for as Swearer and others have shown, "the most important changes in Buddhism have undoubtedly come about through the inspiration and direction of urban, educated Buddhist laity."[3] Although the *Sangha*, the monastic order, has also experienced a resurgence in recent times, the reinterpretation and reformation of the tradition among the laity represents a significant subject in its own right. Some of the most innovative reinterpretations of the tradition have been effected by and on behalf of the laity. Laity-originated reforms have changed the face of contemporary Theravada for laypersons as well as monks. Thus, although we shall touch on other dimensions of the Buddhist revival, such as the reemergence of the *Sangha*, the political uses of Buddhism, and the rejuvenation of *deva* worship, we shall do so only as these developments bear upon our central topic, the evolution of a new understanding of Buddhism among the Sinhalese laity.

In analyzing the revival of Theravada brought about by this new understanding, I have tried to give an accurate picture of both its diversity and its unity. Regarding diversity, this movement should not be understood in monolithic terms but rather as a series or spectrum of interpretations of the tradition. These interpretations constitute what Bardwell Smith has described as "a broad spectrum of responses to the modern scene."[4] From the beginning of the revival in the nineteenth century up to the present day, Theravada lay persons have re-presented their tradition in diverse ways. Within this diversity, or spectrum, four major crystallizations or patterns of interpretation and response can be identified. These four patterns represent variations on the two kinds of interpretation that Bellah has shown to be the main alternatives for religious traditions confronting modernity: neotraditionalism and reformism.[5]

Although these four response patterns naturally overlap to some extent, they represent definite and discernible modes of interpretation. To be sure, as we note in chapter one, these patterns of interpretation are not carved in stone, and other interpreters might classify them differently. I have classified the interpretations under these four patterns, however, because each of the four has distinctive features and constitutes a somewhat different approach to the reinterpretation and revitalization of the Theravada tradition. Positing these four patterns enables us to recognize the diversity and the dynamic nature of this living process of reinterpretation. Since we cannot, in a short book, examine all the manifestations of the revival among the laity, I have sought to examine important examples of these four approaches to re-presenting the tradition.

The four patterns of reinterpretation and response are:

1. Protestant Buddhism:[6] the response of the early reformers who began the revival by both reacting against and imitating Christianity.
2. The return to traditionalism or neotraditionalism during the Buddha Jayanti period (c.1956).

3. The Insight Meditation (*vipassanā bhāvanā*) Movement: the reinterpretation and resurgence of meditation among the laity.
4. The social ethical interpretation of Buddhism: the reinterpretation that regards social development and social equality as the fulfillment of the Buddhist ideal.

Defining the parameters of the lay reformation, these four patterns of interpretation and response constitute the organizing framework for this book. Viewed diachronically, these four responses represent the development of the Theravada revival over time. Thus, one of my purposes is to examine the origins and evolution of the revival, showing how earlier reforming responses eventually lost vitality but brought into being other responses that have carried the revival into the present. In addition to this diachronic approach, I also show that all four responses must be viewed synchronically to some degree, since the earlier solutions to the problem of interpretation have not disappeared but have tended to survive in certain areas and on certain levels of society.

To indicate the unity as well as the diversity of the revival I have identified some basic motifs that are expressed in varying ways and varying degrees in these patterns. To some extent these motifs serve to distinguish the reformist interpretations from the neotraditionalist interpretations. On another level, however, the motifs show the ways that the differing perspectives are linked by common concerns and common issues in responding to the modern context. Among these motifs are the following: a strong appeal to the Buddhist scriptures for authority; the rationalization of all or part of the Buddhist symbol system; an emphasis on the role of the laity and on universalism; a world-affirming or at least world-accommodating bent; and an emphasis on pragmatic achievement.[7] Thus, by analyzing examples of each pattern of response historically, structurally, and philosophically, we may come to understand how the revival of Buddhism among the laity has reshaped the tradition.

I approach this subject by examining first, in chapter one, the backgrounds of the Buddhist revival: the changes during the colonial period that produced a new social context and set the stage for the reinterpretation of traditional Theravada. This chapter also considers the nature of Buddhism's response to modernization and the motifs and outlines of the four patterns. The second chapter explores the pivotal events that began the revival and established Protestant Buddhism. Here we note the early stirrings of reform in the mid-eighteenth century by Venerable Välivita Saraṇaṃkara, the confrontation between Buddhists and Christians in the debates held in the late nineteenth century, and the two key figures of the early lay revival, Colonel Henry Olcott and Anagārika Dharmapāla. These two giants not only developed influential interpretations of Buddhism but also organized the lay Buddhist associations that became the major vehicles of the revival. Thus, chapter two discusses also these lay Buddhist groups, their importance for the revival, and their drift toward neotraditionalism. Examining the crucial Jayanti period when the Buddhist revival blossomed in the postindependence winds of freedom, the third chapter argues that the events of this period produced the clearest expression of the neotraditional reinterpretation of the tradition, which contrasted sharply with the optimistic, reformist viewpoint of the early Protestant Buddhists such as Dharmapala. In chapter three we study the emergence of this neotraditional outlook among the laity who sought "to restore Buddhism to its rightful place" in Sri Lanka. I analyze the key document for understanding this period, the report of the Buddhist Committee of Enquiry, and trace the effects that both the Jayanti and the report have had on the Buddhist revival during the three decades since that period. Although many articles were written about the Jayanti period and the promise its proposals held for reforming the tradition, little has been written on the outcome of these proposals and this period. Thus, I have sought to follow up the proposals and programs that arose from the Jayanti period with the promise of renewing Buddhism. To summarize my findings, we can say that the events of the Jayanti period have shaped the subsequent revival, but not always in the ways that the reformers anticipated. Many of the programs and proposals for reviving the religion and the society have had disappointing results; but the conservative, neotraditional orientation has nevertheless endured and has influenced the outlook of many Buddhist householders, monks, and, significantly, government leaders. Whereas at the outset of the Buddhist revival Dharmapala and others summoned the laity to new roles and new optimism about achieving the Buddhist ideals of wisdom and liberation, the neotraditionalists reverted to traditional roles and traditional goals without any expectations of wisdom or liberation in this lifetime.

Neotraditionalism, however, has not been the only interpretation of the tradition in the post-Jayanti period, and the remaining chapters examine two reformist interpretations that have emphasized two divergent but complementary Buddhist themes: meditation and social development. These two approaches constitute the vitality of the revival today. Based upon field research, interviews, participant observation and textual research, chapters four, five, and six explore various aspects of the insight meditation movement; and in chapter seven, the recent social development responses are examined. With regard to the insight meditation movement, these chapters trace its origins, examine its reinterpretation of traditional Buddhist ideas, notably its rationalization and universalization of the virtuoso practice of meditation, and discuss the opposition and conflict that the meditation reformers have encountered from traditionalist Buddhists. To indicate the depth and breadth of the meditation reform and its significance as a movement that has enabled Buddhists genuinely to employ their tradition to cope with modernity, chapter five examines case studies of individuals who represent this movement, and chapter six analyzes two lay Buddhist associations that have evolved from this movement.

Turning to the other side of this modern dichotomy within the reformation, the final chapter considers reinterpretations that have emphasized a socially relevant understanding of the tradition. Giving prominence to the motifs of world affirmation and this-worldly asceticism, these interpretations have played an important role in the modern period. The Sarvodaya Shramadāna Movement, which is the best known but not the only instance of this reform, serves as the primary focus of this chapter. We shall examine both the approach that these interpreters employ to derive a "social gospel" from the Buddhist texts and the practical ways that they have implemented this interpretation in society.

One matter not discussed in detail is the current ethnic conflict between the Sinhalese and the Tamils. Although I indicate in chapter three that the revival, and particularly the neotraditional viewpoint, played a significant role in creating some of the conditions for this terrible confrontation, to examine this conflict and the grievances of the

Sinhalese and Tamils adequately would have required going too far beyond the scope of the religious revival, into the history of events in politics, economics, education, and other areas that could be better studied by political scientists and others. In a real sense the conflict is not an integral part of the revival of Buddhism but a tragic distortion or exploitation of it. After Sinhalese nationalism combined with the neotraditional interpretation of Buddhism, politicians and political elements among the Sinhalese capitalized on the sentiments of the Buddhists for restoring their tradition. By taking too literally the symbols and the mythology linking Buddhism with the Sinhalese people, the politicians and others rendered authentic neotraditionalist interpretations inauthentic. It is one thing to believe that the Buddha prophesied that his religion of wisdom and compassion would flourish in Sri Lanka; it is quite another, however, to use this belief to gain power by insisting that one has a divine mandate to restore to prominence not only Buddhism but also all Buddhists, to the exclusion of others.

The disastrous consequences of this exploitation of the neotraditionalist interpretation are plainly seen in Sri Lanka today. What was once a land of peace and *Dharma*, both for Sinhalese and Tamils, has become a battleground. No easy solutions have been found. To their credit, however, many Buddhists, in the wake of the 1983 riots, have disavowed the integral connection between nationalism and religion. Others have noted that such incidents indicate that much remains to be done to revive Buddhism and its values in the hearts of the people.

The neotraditional interpretation that has been distorted by politicians and fundamentalists is not the only or even the most significant development in the revival of Buddhism. Unfortunately though, because of the ethnic conflict, it has attracted the most attention in recent times. If, however, the current attempts to resolve the conflict succeed, I believe that the two reformist interpretations examined in chapters four through seven will provide more viable ways for Buddhists to respond to the modern context. These reinterpretations of the tradition are more inclusive and less nationalistic. They develop new roles for Buddhists that allow them to live with wisdom and compassion in a pluralistic modern society. These interpretations stress the possibilities of the future, not the golden age of the past. Let us hope that the proponents of both *vipassanā* and social ethics can somehow persuade the Buddhists and the Tamils to live in loving-kindness.

Notes

1. S. J. Tambiah, *World Conqueror and World Renouncer* (New York: Cambridge University Press, 1976), 433.
2. Mary Douglas, *Natural Symbols: Explorations in Cosmology* (London: Barrie and Rockliff, 1970).
3. Donald K. Swearer, "Lay Buddhism and the Buddhist Revival in Ceylon," *Journal of the American Academy of Religion* 38 (1970): 259-60.
4. Bardwell L. Smith, Introduction, *Tradition and Change in Theravada Buddhism*, ed. Bardwell L. Smith (Leiden: Brill, 1973), 2.
5. Robert Bellah, Editor. *Religion and Progress in Modern Asia* (New York: Free Press, 1965), 204-15.
6. This term was coined by Gananath Obeyesekere. See chapter 1, n. 101, for a more complete reference to his use of it.
7. For further explanation of these motifs and references to the ways that others have analyzed them, see chapter 1.

1

The Theravada Tradition and the Background of the Buddhist Revival

In 1956 Theravada Buddhists in Sri Lanka and throughout Southeast Asia celebrated the Buddha Jayanti, the 2,500th anniversary of both the Buddha's entrance into his *Parinibbāna* and the establishment of the Buddhist tradition in Sri Lanka. For the Sinhalese Buddhists of Sri Lanka this celebration marked the flowering of what has been called a "reformation,"[1] a "revival,"[2] or a "revolution"[3] in Theravada Buddhism. In a key article on this movement Michael Ames observed in 1963 that "now, perhaps for the first time in its long history, Sinhalese Buddhism appears to be facing a fundamental transformation or 'reformation.'" He went on to say that with regard to the changes then taking place, "it is too soon to assess their importance for the future of Sinhalese religion."[4] Now, however, three decades after the Buddha Jayanti and the emergence of the Sinhalese Buddhist revival, it is possible to assess the changes that occurred and that are continuing to occur.[5]

Religion and the Problem of Modernization

The reformation in Theravada Buddhism represents a Buddhist response to what has been described as the "revolution of modernization"[6] or the transition to a postcivilized society, a revolution that has confronted all of the major world religions. Bellah has pointed out that "modernization, whatever else it involved, is always a moral and a

11

religious problem."[7] A complex phenomenon, modernization eludes precise definition. One writer has described it as "the totality of the influence of the unprecedented increase in man's knowledge of and control over his environment that has taken place in recent centuries."[8] Bellah defines modernization as the rationalization not only of the means, as in technology, but also of the ends: "Modernization involves the increased capacity for rational goal-setting."[9] These definitions indicate that the revolution of modernization has to do with the interweaving of continuity and change. In one sense there is nothing new in this, for all history represents an interweaving of continuity and change. In another sense, however, modernization is revolutionary because of the nature and rapidity of the changes it has brought. As Bardwell Smith has observed, "The extent and severity of dynamic forces termed 'modernization' and 'modernity' have no exact parallel."[10] Modernization, as a revolution in knowledge, has brought sweeping and continuing changes in science and technology, and consequently in society and culture. Manfred Halpern writes that "the revolution of modernization involves the transformation of all systems by which man organizes his society—the political, social, economic, intellectual, religious and psychological systems."[11]

Modernization with its rapid, systemic change poses problems for participants in religious traditions in general because it creates a radically different context. Bellah describes the function of religions as "cultural gyroscopes" or "cybernetic control mechanisms" that serve both to identify the ultimate reality and principle of order and meaning in the universe, and to project guidelines or "limit images" of "what sorts of action by individuals make sense in such a world."[12] But when the context changes dramatically, the old religious symbols no longer serve to provide these guidelines for meaning and motivation, and must be reinterpreted. Mary Douglas analyzes this dilemma as a dialectic of context and cosmology.[13] The beliefs and values that constitute the cosmology of a group arise in a particular social context. Because the context establishes a "cost structure," a distribution of advantages for social action, a pattern of rewards and punishments, it renders plausible certain values and interpretations of existence and, at the same time, it renders implausible other values and interpretations. When the context changes, a new cost structure, or "cultural and cosmological bias," arises and necessitates a reinterpretation of beliefs and values.

Religious traditions such as Buddhism have always lived by the dynamic of tradition and interpretation. In W. Cantwell Smith's terms, they represent cumulative traditions interacting in each generation with the faith of individuals whose personal responses become part of the tradition to be handed on to the next generation.[14] Thus, it is in the nature of cumulative religious traditions to respond to change. Modernization, however, represents a serious challenge to the ability of religious traditions to accommodate to change. Modernization poses the dilemma, for religious traditions and their members, of identity and responsiveness. Joseph Allen describes this dilemma by asking, "How is it possible in the midst of revolutionary change to maintain both one's identity, that which makes him what he really is, and his responsiveness, his capacity to be fitting to the occasion, to changing conditions around him?"[15] Others have perceived this dilemma as that of how a religion can "alter its normative symbols without losing its coherence and internal integrity,"[16] or as a search for both "timeless truths" and "situational truths."[17] However it is expressed, it is the problem of tradition and interpretation intensified. Since modernization has changed the context radically, religions have an urgent need to respond by reinterpreting, re-presenting the essence of their tradition, their central truth, in a way that provides meaning both within and for the new context. Bardwell Smith has pointed to the complexity and importance of religious reinterpretation in the contemporary context:

> If the task for religious institutions and their membership were simply to apply old teachings to new situations, the dilemma would be real enough. Instead, they are confronted with what is essentially a religious task, namely the question of identity, in an age where the tension between sacred and secular is shattered or unperceived, or where the sacred is allowed one room in a mansion seen as secular.[18]

The Colonial Context and the Setting for the Buddhist Reformation

In the specific case of Theravada Buddhism in Sri Lanka, modernization and the creation of a new context came with colonialism. The colonial powers that ruled Sri Lanka, then Ceylon, from the sixteenth century to the middle of the twentieth century created a new "cost structure" that challenged the identity of the Buddhists and eventually led to the reinterpretation of the Theravada tradition. Since much has been written on the colonial period in Sri Lanka and on the relationship between Buddhism and the colonial powers,[19] we need not rehearse that in detail, but only identify some of the major factors in the new context or cost structure, factors that both created the situations to which the Buddhists eventually responded and, at the same time, shaped the kinds of responses that the Buddhists found plausible. These new factors can be described as changes in the political, economic, social, and educational spheres, all of which together brought about changes in the religious sphere.

The most important political and economic changes resulted from the shift in the center of power during the colonial period from the Kandyan highlands to the low country. The Portuguese and Dutch governed only the low country, and the British, even after they consolidated their control of the entire island, had their centers of government and commerce in the coastal regions. The British especially changed the political context by ending the system of patrimonial kingship entirely and introducing the first stages of parliamentary democracy. Since Buddhism had traditionally maintained a close relationship with the monarchy, receiving both support and protection from the kings, the overthrow of the last king of Kandy by the British had far-reaching consequences for Buddhism.

In the economic sphere, the changes introduced by colonial governments had equally radical effects. The traditional economy of Sri Lanka was a village-centered, subsistence-agriculture economy. Traditional Sinhalese society had no caste of traders, and the agriculturalists, or *Goyigamas*, occupied the highest place in the caste system.[20] The colonial era, especially the British period, saw sweeping changes in this traditional economic system through the introduction of estate agriculture and a plantation economy. The plantation economy, based on export crops such as coffee, tea, and rubber, required urban centers for commerce and networks of transportation and communication. These factors unified the island and shifted the center of power and society away from the villages.

The growth of a plantation economy and its commerce provided new avenues for social mobility that led to the emergence of a new elite. Before the colonial period Sinhalese society corresponded to Singer's description of a traditional society that was not achievement oriented but primarily "ascriptive."[21] The rise of commerce introduced changes by establishing wealth rather than caste and kinship as the means of gaining status and power.[22] In the early part of the nineteenth century the British instituted reforms abolishing *rājakāriyā* and the "feudal system of service obligations and land tenure."[23] Although the impact was not felt immediately, this set the stage for social mobility. Unlike the traditional village system that rewarded group conformity and cooperation, the new plantation economy encouraged competition and placed a premium on individual ambition. This new social context produced a new elite "who based their claims to prestige and influence on personal achievement, as opposed to the authority of the traditional elite which was based on caste and lineage."[24]

The new elite came from the low country where the three successive colonial regimes were centered. Singer has shown that more or less the same high-caste, low-country families constituted the indigenous leadership that served the Portuguese, Dutch, and British.[25] Although these families had high status in the coastal areas, they were, for the most part, lower in the caste hierarchy than the *Goyigamas*. These relatively lower castes of *Salagama, Karava,* and *Durava* produced many of the new leaders who, taking advantage of the new economic opportunities, rivaled the old, established Sinhalese elite.[26] The headmen among the *Salagamas,* for example, experienced social mobility during the Dutch period when they had opportunities to facilitate the cinnamon trade.[27]

The British as well as the other colonial governments encouraged the growth of this new elite both because it was necessary to the commercial success of the colony and because its emergence undercut the power and status of the traditional elite. This emerging middle and upper class found a place in the colonial system not only as traders and landholders but also as civil servants manning the vast bureaucracy that the British colonial administration spawned.

To equip these emerging classes for these roles, the Europeans established schools. Two streams of education were set up during the colonial period: one developing literacy in the Western languages and the other instructing students in the vernacular. The former schools had the greatest impact on the new elite, since during the British period they made an English education the primary key to social mobility and success. To serve in commerce or government one needed a knowledge of English, and the newly emerging elite, who understood the ground rules of the new context, eagerly sought admission to English schools. Some wealthy families sent their sons off to England to prepare them for professional careers, but most families were content with gaining admission for their children in one of the more prestigious English curriculum schools in the island. An English education represented both a necessary training for participation in the new economic structure and a status symbol. The dowry value of a man who had both an English education and a post in the government service was high.[28]

The English educational system had two important effects on the new context and on the place of Buddhism in it. First, the new schools established by the British displaced the traditional Sinhalese educational system that had been largely controlled by the Buddhist monks. The village schools had always had small classes that received a personal and traditional education. At higher levels the temple schools and the *pirivenas,* or monastic colleges, were staffed by monks who instructed the future elite and literati in Buddhist philosophy, as well as astrology, medicine, and other traditional arts and sciences. The British saw no value in these schools, however, and replaced them with government and missionary schools. As one British education director observed with regard to the temple schools, "The education given in them is worse than useless, consisting mainly of learning to read almost by heart a number of sacred books on olas (palm leaves) . . . while the astrological teaching given is not only useless but absurd, and arithmatic is almost entirely neglected."[29] Thus, the British gave their support to the Protestant mission schools that had a Western curriculum and taught in English, and the monks lost one of their most important ways of influencing the leaders of the society. Wriggins observed that the majority of village monks considered this alienation of the *Sangha* from the laity to be "the most deleterious result of the colonial period."[30]

The second effect of these educational policies, closely related to the first, was the alienation of the new English-educated laity from their Sinhalese and Buddhist heritage by the Western and Christian curriculum of the new schools. The British during the nineteenth century regarded both Westernization and an introduction to Christianity as necessary to the process of education and civilization. Lord Acton wrote that "the pioneer of civilization has to get rid of the religion of India to enable him to introduce a better culture, and the pioneer of Christianity has to get rid of the Indian culture before he can establish his religion."[31] The missionary societies ran their schools with a deep faith both in the superiority of Western civilization and in Christianity as the underlying cause of that superiority. Ames observes that "scientific progress and mechanical skill represented to the Victorian English proof of their advance of 'civilization' over the superstitious and speculative mystical philosophies of the East: to teach science was thus to impart both the moral and practical benefits of civilization."[32] With a thoroughly Western curriculum stressing European history and literature, mathematics, Western science and Christianity, the mission schools indoctrinated the young Ceylonese elite with an Anglicized version of the rationalistic humanism of the Enlightenment. Even in the vernacular schools the students were exposed to a curriculum of modern science, liberal arts, and Western values, but it was in the English-language schools that these subjects had the greatest impact. To be sure, many of the colonial administrators and educators probably sincerely desired to assist the Sri Lankans. One writer observed that their aim was "to associate the natives with European civilization and gradually raise them to a higher social level."[33] Nevertheless, these administrators lacked the sensitivity to be able to distinguish between what Ames has termed modernization and Westernization.[34] To the avid colonial administrator, "to be civilized was to be Western, preferably English middle class, and the only real hope would be for the Ceylonese to develop according to this English pattern."[35]

The students subjected to this Western and Christian curriculum, believing with good reason that it held the key to their success in the colonial system, inevitably fell under the sway of Western ideas that set them apart from their heritage and from the rest of the society. In gaining the key that opened the door to the new society, the new elite lost the key to their traditional culture. An observer remarked that "in the colonial period, the Sinhalese upper middle class was more Westernized than any other Asian group outside of the Philippines."[36] Similarly, Leach has commented that "by the second decade of this century the whole of the Ceylonese middle and upper classes had been very thoroughly Anglicized."[37] Although it is difficult to assess the exact extent of the Westernization of Sri Lankan society,[38] clearly the English-educated elite, who came to occupy influential positions in society, became very Westernized. They adopted eagerly the Western fashions of dress and Western style of living. As time went on, many of them could no longer speak the language of their relatives in the village, and those who could still speak the language now found that they had nothing to say to villagers. Living in the cities, reading English books and newspapers, the new elite enjoyed a different intellectual climate from their village cousins. Michael Ondaatje has beautifully documented the life style of some of the people who were among this Anglicized elite during the early decades of this century. He depicts a world of social occasions, dances, horse races, trips to England, bridge parties, tennis championships, tea estates, and church services. His grandparents, he writes, "spent most of the year in Colombo and during the hot months of April and May moved to Nuwara Eliya. . . . Books and sweaters and golf clubs and rifles were packed into trunks, children were taken out of school, dogs were bathed and made ready for the drive."[39] This was the life style of the English, being lived by upwardly mobile Ceylonese.

Undoubtedly this class of people had entered a different world, where the emphasis fell on the future rather than the past, where people were optimistic about the potential for both individual and social improvement, and where the old ways were just that. Many of these people converted to Christianity, at least nominally, while others remained Buddhist, but again only nominally. The Buddha Sāsana Commission Report referred to these English-educated laymen as "a class of so-called Buddhists who did not go to the temple, did not know Buddhism, did not know the *bhikkhus,* and considered Buddhist customs and practices as something to be looked down upon."[40] It became something of a mark of status among this lay elite to say, if they acknowledged themselves as Buddhists at all, that they were not "temple Buddhists," which meant that they saw Buddhism as a philosophy and not as a religion—a distinction they learned from their Western mentors. These people who became the leaders in the new political, economic, and social spheres, having lost their traditional identity as Sinhalese Buddhists, now identified with the cosmopolitan English culture.

The final factor to note in the new context of colonial Sri Lanka represented the corollary to the rise of the Westernized lay elite: namely, the decline of the traditional Buddhist elite, the *Sangha,* and the suppression of Buddhism. We have seen that all of the European powers sought to replace Buddhism with Christianity. Since the monks were not only the most visible representatives of the "Boodhoo superstition," but also one of the main forms of traditional elitism, the erosion of their prestige suited the purposes of both the missionaries and the colonial administrators. Singer observes that "the power of the Buddhist *Sangha* in Ceylon rested on two main pillars—deference and wealth."[41] The colonial administrations attacked both of these pillars. They undermined the respect that the monks received by edging them out of their traditional roles as teachers who had an influence on the youth. Concomitantly, the entire ethos of the new Western education curriculum further discredited the wisdom of the monks and the rituals that they performed.

The other source of the *Sangha*'s power, its wealth, came from extensive landholdings donated to the temples over the centuries by kings and laypersons. From the start, the European powers recognized the need to reduce these lands in order to strike at the prestige of the monks. The Portuguese openly seized temple lands in the low country and gave them to the church. The net effect of British policies was to disestablish Buddhism by ceasing to protect the *Sangha* and its landholdings. When the British acquired control of the Kandyan region in 1815, they signed the Kandyan Convention. In this treaty they agreed that "the religion of the Budhoo professed by the chiefs and inhabitants of these provinces is declared inviolable and its rites, ministers and places of worship are to be maintained and protected."[42]

Although many of the British administrators seem to have entered into this treaty sincerely, intending to offer some government protection and toleration to Buddhism, they clearly never understood the treaty to imply that they would provide the kind of far-reaching protection and support that the Kandyan Buddhists expected. The Buddhists believed that the British had essentially taken over the duties of the kings to support Buddhism in every way possible, especially by legalizing and confirming the appointment of the monks to head the major temples, by providing some stipends to presiding monks, by protecting and administering the tooth relic and all the associated property, and by enforcing the temples' rights to their property and wealth.

The British, however, seem to have been of several minds about the treaty, with most believing that they had agreed only not to interfere with the Buddhists and to provide protection under the law. To the administrators who desired to keep the peace in the region, this attitude seemed most useful. Other British administrators, however, came under what was termed "very strong pressure from the missionary bodies" and from politicians at home who were outraged at the thought of "our Christian Government" supporting "heathenism." The colonial governor, Robert Brownrigg, wrote letters to the British Parliament assuring them that he did not mean to patronize Buddhism and that his greatest desire was the "propagation of the Gospel."[43] He professed that he never intended to install the government as the head of the Buddhist religion.

In the end, by the third and fourth decades of the nineteenth century, the English, making plain their intentions, enacted legislation that severed "all active participation in practices at once idolatrous and immoral."[44] Withdrawing support for monastic ceremonies, ceasing to legalize monastic appointments, refusing to administer and adjudicate Buddhist temporalities, the British turned both the tooth relic and the governance of Buddhism over to the Buddhists. The result of this shift in the centuries-old relationship between the *Sangha* and the ruling government was disorganization and much loss of landed wealth by the *Sangha*.[45] Having created the chaos surrounding the rights to temple lands, the British themselves seized some of these lands when they expanded their coffee and tea estates. The *Sangha*, deprived of its rule in education as well as its source of wealth and status, went through a period of disarray.

While disestablishing Buddhism in these ways, the colonial administrations gave favored status to Christianity, as Brownrigg's comment above indicates. K. M. deSilva has observed, "Roman Catholicism, Calvinism and Anglicanism have had in succession, a special relationship with the ruling power and with this the prestige and moral authority of the official religion of the day, while converts to the orthodox version of Christianity—especially under the Portuguese and the Dutch—came to be treated as a privileged group."[46] While the Portuguese gained infamy by their persecution of the Buddhists, the Dutch employed subtler means of conversion, requiring anyone who sought to hold land or government office to be baptized a member of the Protestant Church. In addition to economic persuasion, which continued throughout the colonial period, the missionary societies mounted what Ames describes as "a full scale ideological attack on Hinduism, Buddhism and local folk traditions."[47] And, as we have seen, the combination of Christianity, Western values, and modernization exercised a profound influence on many of the English-educated laity.

All of these factors—political, economic, social, educational, religious—taken together set the stage for the Buddhist revival in Sri Lanka. Although the exact causes for the beginning of the revival are difficult to trace, the rise of an educated, Westernized laity and the repression of both the traditional Buddhist elite, the *Sangha*, and traditional Theravada itself proved to be tandem forces that generated the need for reform. On the one hand, the English-educated laity, fitted with a Western world view and trained to participate in the new economy, eventually discovered that the British would never allow them to become full partners in their society. The gulf that separated them from the British and Europeans they found to be as vast as that now separating them from the traditional Sinhalese villagers. Ondaatje writes of the Anglicized elite of the 1920s and 30s: "There was a large social gap between this circle and the Europeans and English who were never part of the Ceylonese community."[48] They had acquired the British viewpoint but were allowed neither to mix socially with the British nor to assume top leadership positions in business and government. One of these Anglicized Sinhalese, James Alwis, observed that "the cant of Exeter Hall—'we are bretheren'—has no influence out of England."[49] Fernando notes the feelings of these people: "To be denied the privileges enjoyed by Europeans after having painfully assimilated one's self to Western values is an obviously embittering experience."[50] Cast adrift and feeling rootless, these educated Ceylonese began to search for their identity and self-respect. They sought, as Ames has described their situation, to be modern without becoming completely Westernized.[51]

On the other hand, the severely depressed and disorganized state of Buddhism and the *Sangha* attracted the attention of the new elite. It was an injustice that demanded redress. Paradoxically, by cutting Buddhism off so sharply, the British had created the necessity for its reform. The Anglicized elite, although estranged from their Buddhist heritage, began to recognize it as the key to their identity. Thus, when the pendulum of reformation began to swing back in the last quarter of the nineteenth century, when the Buddhist monks felt bold enough to challenge the missionaries to debate, when European and American Theosophists arrived to raise the Buddhists' consciousness of their heritage, the English-educated laity emerged as the leaders of the revitalization movement. Their task was that of identity and responsiveness, to reinterpret their Buddhist heritage to suit the modern context. Tambiah writes that they had to accomplish "a revival, because it was an attempt to resuscitate a religion that had declined under British rule."[52] With the *Sangha* having been excluded from the new context, however, the laity had great freedom to reinterpret and "resuscitate" the Theravada tradition. They sought, as Leach wrote, "an evocation of the past, but of what past?"[53] Thus, the Sinhalese Theravada revival arose as an attempt to reinterpret the Theravada Buddhist tradition to provide an identity that would enable the educated Sinhalese to cope with modernity.

Traditional Theravada Buddhism: The Gradual Path

Since the revivalists sought to reinterpret traditional Theravada, we need, before looking at their reinterpretation, some benchmark, some understanding of what traditional Theravada meant. Defining traditional Theravada is necessary yet difficult because cumulative religious traditions such as Buddhism, always developing, contain ambiguities, what

Tambiah has called "dialectical tensions,"[54] that make any definition of "pristine Buddhism" only one possible interpretation. Perhaps the most promising way of approaching this question of identity is the historical approach taken by a number of scholars who have posited several stages in the development of Theravada.[55] Instead of looking for an essential "early Buddhism" to contrast with modern Buddhism, they suggest that Theravada has passed through at least three developmental phases: (1) canonical Buddhism, the early Buddhism reflected in the *Tipiṭaka*; (2) traditional or historical Buddhism, the postcanonical Theravada established during the Asokan period (c.268–233 BCE) and continued by the Pali Commentaries; and (3) modern Theravada, the Buddhism of the revival and reformation.

Ancient, or canonical, Buddhism is perhaps the most difficult to define because of the size of the Pali Canon and because we lack a set of precise criteria for distinguishing early from later material within it. Since Weber's work, the scholarly consensus regarding ancient Buddhism has been that it represented a religion of individual salvation-striving for ascetic monks. Weber argued that early Buddhism accorded the laity a place similar to that of the "tolerated infidels in Islam" who "existed only for the purpose of sustaining by alms" those ascetics who sought the true goal of the religion.[56] Malalgoda describes this phase of Buddhism as "intellectual and contemplative . . . asocial and apolitical in its orientation."[57] Tambiah, however, has properly warned that this picture represents an oversimplification, since the Pali Canon indicates that early Buddhism had well-developed views of social and political matters. Weber undoubtedly overstated the extent to which early Buddhism was limited to ascetics.[58]

Traditional Theravada can be described as the development of the religion after the canonical period, or beginning approximately from the time of Asoka. Our primary source for this important stage is the commentarial literature attributed for the most part to Buddhaghosa, who lived in Anuradhapura during the time of King Mahānāma (409–431 CE). However, we must recognize that as a cumulative tradition traditional Theravada continued to develop, and this development is reflected in postcommentarial texts such as the *Ṭīkās, gatapadas sannayas,* and other subcommentaries as well as the Sinhalese prose religious classics.[59] Although this later literature manifested some new developments in the religion, such as the growth of a devotional emphasis,[60] for our purposes we can take the commentaries' picture of Theravada as a model for understanding traditional Theravada. In doing so, I do not contend that Theravada showed complete continuity from Buddhaghosa's time down to the colonial period. It was not set in amber; it continued to evolve as a cumulative tradition. But the commentaries established the outline and the structures for Theravada, which later works developed in various ways. Richard Gombrich has written that with regard to the Theravada Buddhism he observed in the Kandayan highlands, "Religious doctrines and practices seem to have changed very little over the last 1,500 years,"[61] that is, since the time of Buddhaghosa. I do not think that Gombrich intended to imply—nor do I imply—however, that the tradition ceased to evolve during this period. As our knowledge of medieval Sinhalese literature grows, we shall perhaps be able to say more about the ways that it evolved and the various themes that arose within the tradition. The point Gombrich made was that when anthropologists and others began observing Theravada Buddhists during the modern period, they found these Buddhists espousing a cosmology that had significant continuity with the Buddhist cosmology set out in the commentarial literature. In this context it is worth recalling Tambiah's observation that Theravada has "deep-seated continuities in the form of structures and dialectical orientations" that have persisted through various periods of change.[62] The understandings of religious vocations and ritual systems that Ames found functioning in rural Sinhalese Theravada have much in common with the commentarial literature's conceptions.[63] Thus, since the commentaries established this cosmology, and since it formed the basis for the Sinhalese Theravada that the modern Buddhists of the reformation have sought either to revive or reform, we should examine the outline and structures of this cosmology.

The commentarial as well as other later Buddhist writings indicate that traditional Theravada represented a reinterpretation of early Buddhism made in response to a particular kind of social context. Perhaps the best summary descriptions of both the early Buddhist social context and the process of reinterpretation that characterized traditional Theravada were given by Louis Dumont and Louis De La Valee Poussin.[64] Dumont described the Indian context as having had two kinds of people: "those that live in the world and those that have renounced it." People who lived in the village according to the norms of the caste system he termed "men in the world," and those who went to the forest he styled "renouncers."[65] Poussin also depicted the ancient Indian social context in this way and explained how Indian religious traditions addressed this context. Ancient India, he observed, generated two kinds of religious traditions: one suited for the renouncers and another suited for the people in the world. For the renouncers, "disciplines of salvation" provided paths leading to liberation. Supramundane rather than mundane ends constituted the focus of these disciplines. For the people in the world, however, "religions" arose that differed from the disciplines by providing rituals, deities, moral guidelines, and other accommodations to the mundane plane.[66]

Although I do not contend that ancient and traditional Theravada represented pure forms of a "discipline of salvation" and a "religion," respectively, the outlines of these two types help us to understand how Theravada developed. If ancient Buddhism began as a discipline for renouncers, at some point, probably sooner rather than later, it had to come to terms with the needs of persons in the world. As Buddhism developed, it necessarily began to establish relations with the society in which people in the world lived. Dumont has commented on this process of development in Indian religions, saying that "the secret of Hinduism may be found in the dialogue between the renouncer and the man in the world."[67] Change occurred and the Hindu religious tradition evolved because the renouncers, who were "the agent(s) of development in Indian religion and speculation, the 'creator(s) of values,' " had to address themselves to the larger society.[68] Again Dumont writes, "The true historical development of Hinduism is in the sannyasic developments on the one hand and their aggregation to worldly religion on the other."[69]

For Buddhism also, the interaction between these two contexts and two cosmologies served as the catalyst for developments that shaped the religion. One of the major problems that Buddhism faced as it spread in India and elsewhere was the necessity of validating the role of the man in the world, meeting the social or religious needs of nonrenouncers.

Traditional Theravada Buddhism arose in this clash of contexts as Buddhists sought to interpret the *Dhamma* to meet the needs of all kinds of persons. The hermeneutical strategy employed in the Pali

Commentaries to balance these varying religious needs and goals was the gradual path of purification. This path, given definitive form in Buddhaghosa's *Visuddhimagga*, represents the hallmark of traditional Theravada. As a hermeneutical device, the gradual path enabled the commentators to subsume mundane goals under the supramundane goal in order to develop a religion that had integrity and yet related to all people.

Early expressions of this gradual path can be found in the Pali Canon itself in the explanations of *Nibbāna* and arahantship.[70] The *arahant* concept seems to have developed from an ideal believed to be readily attainable in this life (*ditthe va dhamme*) into an ideal considered to be remote and impossible to achieve in one or even several lifetimes. The immediate availability of arahantship was depicted in suttas that told of the Buddha's followers reaching enlightenment in response to his proclamation of *Dhamma*. One sutta, for example, described the immediate attainment of arahantship by one thousand *bhikkhus* who heard the Buddha deliver his "Fire Sermon."[71]

This picture of arahantship as attainable in this very life gave way fairly early, however, to a view of arahantship as a distant goal at the end of an immensely long, gradual path that the individual had to ascend over the course of many lifetimes. A sutta in the *Anguttara Nikāya*, for example, compares the monk's task in following the path to *Nibbāna* to the farmer's task of planting and preparing his crop. The farmer cannot demand: "Let my crops spring up today. Tomorrow let them ear. On the following day let them ripen." For "it is only the due season that makes these things happen." In the same way, the monk cannot demand that the path be accomplished overnight and the goal be attained immediately, for "it is just the due season that releases his mind as he undergoes the three-fold training (A.I. 239f.)." Another sutta depicts an interesting conversation between Mahā-Kassapa and the Buddha when the Buddha was nearing the end of his life. Mahā-Kassapa asks why formerly there were fewer training rules and more *arahants* but now there are fewer *arahants* and more training rules. The Buddha answers that this situation developed because people had become degenerate and the *Dhamma* had been obscured (S.II.223f.).

For traditional Theravada, *Nibbāna* and arahantship increasingly became transcendent ideals. A number of important suttas in the Pali Canon contrast the *arahant* with the *puthujjana*, the ordinary person.[72]

The Theravada Tradition and the Background of the Buddhist Revival

The *arahant* is described as a perfected being who, by virtue of his or her perfections, transcends the ordinary plane of existence in almost every way. Because a vast gulf of imperfection divides ordinary persons from the *arahant*, they cannot hope to attain enlightenment immediately. The gradual path spanning many lifetimes constitutes the only way for ordinary persons to follow the *arahant*. Thus, in developing the notion of the gradual path, Theravada adhered to the same pattern that Dumont perceives in Hinduism, where the doctrine of *saṃsāra*, rebirth, "establishes the relation between the renouncer as an individual man and the phantom-like men who have remained in the world and support him."[73] Transmigration becomes what Collins terms a "soteriological strategy"[74] making possible a continuum of spiritual stages and abilities linking the ordinary person and the *arahant*. Because of their previous lives ordinary persons have various degrees of wisdom that empower them for diverse purifying disciplines.

Traditional Theravada spelled out the dimensions of this gradual path in texts as early as the *Netti Pakaraṇa*, but Buddhaghosa gave it its distinctive formulation in the *Visuddhimagga, the (Path of Purification)*.[75] Some of the main features of the path are the threefold training, the two levels, and the four noble persons. The threefold training that provides the basic framework of Buddhaghosa's *Visuddhimagga*[76] constitutes three kinds of perfection that must be developed: perfection in higher morality (*adhisīla*), perfection in higher concentration (*adhicitta*, or *samādhi*), and perfection in higher wisdom (*adhipaññā*). Higher morality (*adhisīla*) comprises guidelines covering all aspects of life, from the ordinary precepts governing relationships with people to the higher virtues required for meditation, such as nonattachment and restraint of one's senses. In traditional Theravada's formulations of the path, only this stage was open to laypersons; all of the higher stages necessitated abandoning completely the householder's life. Higher concentration (*adhicitta*) involved the attainment of concentration (*samādhi*) and mindfulness (*sati*) as preparations for going on to higher wisdom and *Nibbāna*. The complexity of the path was increased by Theravada's conception of it as having mundane (*lokiya*) and supramundane (*lokuttara*) levels, both of which had to be traversed. As long as a person practiced these perfections on the mundane level, he remained within the realm of *saṃsāra*, bound to be reborn. With sufficient progress in the perfections, however, the seeker could accomplish a "change of lineage"to the supramundane plane, thereby breaking free from the inevitability of rebirth. This supramundane path (*lokuttara magga*) was structured in terms of the four noble persons, the highest stages of the path: stream-enterer (*sotāpanna*); once-returner (*sakadāgāmin*); nonreturner (*anāgāmin*), and *arahant* (D.I. 156, A.I.233, DIII.107).

When one has advanced sufficiently on the mundane path (*lokiya*), one enters the supramundane path when one attains the stage of the stream-enterer (*sotāpatti magga*) and gains a glimpse of the higher wisdom. Each of the four noble persons or stages results in a fruition (*phāla*) or a complete attainment of that stage of the way. So when a person fulfills the stage of stream-entry, he attains the fruit of stream-entry, which carries assurance of becoming an *arahant* within seven more rebirths. Second is the stage of once-returning (*sakadāgāmi magga*), the fruit of which assures the Buddhist of becoming an *arahant* upon his next rebirth in this world. The stage of nonreturning (*anāgāmi magga*), the penultimate stage, guarantees one who attains its fruit that he will be reborn in a heavenly realm or "pure abode" and there will reach arahantship. Arahantship, of course, stands as the fourth stage or, more properly, the fourth fruition, the completion of the supramundane path and the "flowing into *Nibbāna.*" The descriptions of the four stages or paths with their complex criteria for advancement reinforce the idea that arahantship is a distant goal. In some texts the four are even subdivided into a number of intermediate stages. The stage of stream-entry is subdivided into three grades, and that of the nonreturner into five (Pu.37f.; A.I.233; A.II.133)

Refining this notion of stages on the path, the postcanonical Theravada texts, *Netti-Pakaraṇa* and *Peṭakopadesa,* employed the gradual path as a hermeneutical strategy for sorting out the diverse material in the Pali Canon. These texts viewed the gradual path as a framework that explained the logic of the *Dhamma.* For example, the *Netti* posits four basic types of suttas that the Buddha gave to people in different situations. The four types include suttas dealing with defilement (*saṇkilesa*), suttas dealing with moral living (*vāsana*), suttas on penetration (*nibbedha*) and suttas dealing with the adept or *arahant.*[77] There is a clear progression in these sutta types, indicating the ways that the Buddha was believed to have structured his message. In addition to

The Theravada Tradition and the Background of the Buddhist Revival

the sutta types the *Netti* and *Petakopadesa* set out further classifications of persons to whom these types apply. Here the text lists ordinary persons (*puthujjana*), learners (*sekha*), and adepts (*asekha*), as well as desire-temperament (*taṇhācarita*) and view-temperament (*diṭṭhicarita*) personalities. When the *Netti* multiplies the sutta types by these and other personality types, it demonstrates how long and complex the gradual path had become for Theravada.

The *Netti's* description of the gradual path, although intended as a guide for interpreters of the *Dhamma* to assist them in finding the meaning and application of the *Dhamma*, has significance for our understanding of the path because it shows more clearly than the *Visuddhimagga* the place of the laity on the path. The first two of the *Netti's* four sutta types have reference to the lay life. Suttas dealing with defilement (*saṅkilesa*) and suttas dealing with living (*vāsana*) both have to do with the householder's life. The *Netti* explains that these suttas concern merit (*puñña*) and the way to earn a favorable rebirth (N. 48f). Under this category of sutta the *Netti* lists the traditional components of the merit-making ritual system in Theravada: giving (*dāna*), virtue (*sīla*), and heaven as a goal for rebirth (*sagga*) (N. 49). Suttas dealing with morality do not provide instruction about the higher stages of the path but have to do with virtue as restraint and the rewards of good *karma* (N. 49, 159). The examples given of this type of sutta describe the progress that people made toward the goal as a result of virtuous acts and favorable rebirths. One such example cites the story of a man who gave a flower garland to the Buddha and, as a consequence, the Buddha told Ānanda that the man would have good rebirths for 84,000 aeons, during which, after fulfilling roles as a king and a *deva*, he would go forth as a monk to find the truth (N. 138f). Other examples of suttas of this type mention similar meritorious acts, such as giving four flowers or a measure of rice, that resulted in the person's gaining thousands of delightful rebirths. One sutta declares, "Today these thirty aeons have passed (after my meritorious act) and since then I have not been to a bad destination" (N. 141). Clearly, this classification of suttas sanctions rebirth as an acceptable goal for people in the world. By doing meritorious deeds a person is assured of a "good destination." Favorable rebirths are seen not as ends in themselves, however, but as stages on the path, as stepping stones to a birth in which the person is able to strive for the path. The sutta passages cited in the *Netti*, many of which cannot be traced in the Canon, make it clear that rebirth in good destinations represents a penultimate, not an ultimate goal. One passage, for instance, tells of a man who gave a gift of robes to a *Paccekabuddha* and was reborn in various heavenly realms until finally being born as the son of a wealthy banker in Varanasi. In that lifetime he encountered the Buddha and went forth to find enlightenment. Fortunate births neither represent nor replace the supreme goal, but they constitute a hierarchy of subgoals of the kind needed by persons in the world. Far from being irrelevant or unnecessary for the attainment of *Nibbāna*, these births represent necessary stages on the path of purification and development (N. 143).

The relevance of the mundane path to the supramundane is shown also in the Pali Commentaries that recount the previous lives of the great *arahants* of the tradition. Each *arahant* is said to have begun the path countless aeons ago when he or she was still living as a householder. Just as the concept of the four noble persons lengthened the path by extending it into the future, so these life histories extended the path into the past as well. At the same time these stories resolved the dilemma of how an ordinary person could both venerate and imitate the *arahants*. The good Buddhist could imitate the *arahants*, whom he naturally venerated, by performing the kinds of ethical and meritorious deeds that the *arahants* themselves were said to have performed at the outset of their path of perfection. Mahā-Kassapa, for example, is said to have earned merit by feeding five hundred *Paccekabuddhas* during one of his previous lifetimes (Thag.A.121f.). Other *arahants* perfected their generosity and compassion by building Buddhist monasteries and temples. The female *arahant* Khemā attained her favorable rebirth by giving gifts to an exalted elder and by donating land and buildings to the *Sangha* (Thig.A.126f.). Similarly, the seven daughters of King Kiki of Kasi built seven monasteries for the Buddha, and because of the merit from this gift they all became *arahants* in subsequent lives (Thig.A.17). In general the Commentaries relate that the great saints progressed toward arahantship by "heaping up merit of age-enduring efficacy in this and that rebirth." When this past dimension is added to the path, the present life appears to be only a small part of an immense existential process coming out of the past and running on into the future.

The commentarial literature also stressed that this protracted, gradual path was difficult. Buddhaghosa's view of the path was laid out in his great work, the *Visuddhimagga*. His purpose in the *Visuddhimagga* was to explain in detail the course one must follow to reach perfection. His account reveals the complexity of the path as it was transmitted by the commentarial teachers of his day. As Buddhaghosa understood it, the path to purification comprised seven difficult stages (*satta visuddhi*) that one must master en route to enlightenment. We appreciate the length and complexity of the gradual path as it was understood by Buddhaghosa when we see that he held that the first six stages, the accounts of which require twenty-one chapters in the *Visuddhimagga*, were still on the mundane path, whereas the first stage of the supramundane path, the path of the stream-enterer, was not attained until one reached the seventh stage of purification. On this view even stream-entry was a remote goal lying relatively near the end of an immensely long and gradual path. Buddhaghosa says that few people reach the advanced stages of the path because "only one in a hundred or a thousand is able to reach even the intermediate stage," and of those who attain that much, "only one in a hundred or a thousand" progresses further (Vism.375).

For traditional Theravada, when arahantship and *Nibbāna* became implausible goals in this life, the gradual path provided a means of balancing the path of renunciation with that of accommodation. Early Buddhist world rejection was tempered somewhat by this qualified affirmation of the world, now seen as an integral part of the preparation for higher wisdom. This is not to say that traditional Theravada was thoroughly world affirming, however, but only that it more or less walked a middle path between world-rejecting and world-affirming views. Leach's comment applies fairly accurately to the traditional Theravadin: "A good Buddhist has no vision of a New Heaven or a New Earth. . . . The most he is prepared to hope for is a future existence which is rather less unpleasant than this one."[78]

With the conception of the gradual path established as its central tenet, traditional Theravada manifested other, related ideas and structures. It had a basic pessimism about the potential for both individual and social improvement. The wheel of *saṃsāra* turned very slowly; *Nibbāna* was "a thousand lives away."[79] Time devoured its children. Living in the *Kali yuga*, people could expect only worsening conditions, for the golden age lay in the past. In both its theoretical and actual structures traditional Theravada was hierarchical. Cosmologically its universe exhibited gradations of being, with the *devas* ranked at the top in their tiers of heavens, human beings below them, and other creatures and spirits below humanity, down to the *Niraya* worlds. In addition to being objects of worship or fear, all of these forms of being stood for possible planes of rebirth within the cycle of *saṃsāra*.

This was the cosmology that formed the basis for the development of Theravada in Sri Lanka. Ames has shown that the hierarchical emphasis laid the groundwork for a fourfold system of religious vocations.[80] These four vocations include two for monks and two for laity, differentiated according to their spiritual ability and their level of specialization in Buddhist practice. The monastic vocations include hermit monks (*āraṇyavāsins*) and village monks (*gāmavāsins*), and the lay side comprises lay devotees (*upāsakas*) and ordinary householders (*gihi*). The hermit monks and the lay devotees are the virtuosos in this structure, following the higher ritual system of meditating, while the village monks and ordinary householders accept the lower ritual system of merit-making. Ames demonstrates that on the basis of vocations and ritual systems, these four types constitute a pyramid with the virtuosos at the top and the ordinary monks and laity constituting the base.

In this practical outworking of the path, the vocations and ritual systems all correspond closely to the theoretical formulations of the gradual path in texts such as the *Netti*. In practice as in theory, the lower stages of the path predominate, with most monks and laypersons accepting the lower ritual duties of merit-making. Ames notes that this ritual system was made necessary by the same logic that governed the theoretical formulations of the path: the belief that *Nibbāna* was a remote goal. As Bardwell Smith observed, "The radical separation of the worldly from the sacred leads, ironically, to an ethic of accommodationism."[81] Laypersons who had no hope of *Nibbāna* needed ways of dealing with both the long-range problems of rebirth and the immediate needs of this life. For these purposes merit-making rituals and what Ames terms "magical animism," *deva* and spirit cults, became integral to traditional Theravada.

Although all of the vocations in Ames's model of Sinhalese practice represent the mundane plane according to the textual conceptions of the path, a definite hierarchy of roles emerged, with the monks having elite status in traditional Sinhalese Theravada because they were mediators of the *Dhamma* and representatives of the Buddha. The *bhikkhus* officiated in most rituals where laity earned merit, especially by preaching and receiving the gifts of the laity.[82] As we shall see in chapter four, the village monks in traditional Theravada regarded scholarship rather than meditation as their proper task in this lifetime. Because of these various forms of *Dhamma* meditation the *Sangha* acquired status both with the Buddhist laity and with the Sinhalese kings, who donated to them extensive landholdings and wealth, as discussed above.

To summarize this brief description of traditional Theravada, we can note that it represented an interpretation and socialization of Buddhism for a village-centered or traditional South Asian society. Its gradual path balanced the unity of the *Dhamma* with the diversity of the social contexts of the persons in the world. An organic system in which different persons played different parts, traditional Theravada fit Douglas's description of a corporate religious system where "more honor for public formality allows less pressure on personal sanctity, more tolerance for compromise and lower levels of spiritual aspiration."[83]

The Theravada Reformation: Patterns of Reinterpretation and Response

The third stage in the development of Theravada is the modern period, the Buddhism of the revival that emerged as an attempt to reinterpret and renew the traditional Theravada Buddhist heritage of Sri Lanka. This stage of Theravada actually comprised a series or spectrum of interpretations of the tradition put forward as responses to the modern context.[84] The new elite and others who took up the task of interpreting Buddhism to find their personal and corporate identities, having great freedom, re-presented the tradition in a variety of ways.

Bellah has commented on the general phenomenon of religious change and reformation, noting that the central factor is the "process of rationalization of the religious symbol system" accompanied by reinterpretations on both the social and personal levels.[85] In the confrontation between Asian religions and modernity, Bellah finds four basic types of response: conversion to Christianity, traditionalism, reformism, and neotraditionalism.[86] Of these the two "main alternatives" for reinterpreting and rationalizing religions have been what he terms reformism and neotraditionalism. Reformism represents a rationalization of both the means and the ends of traditional religion. Neotraditionalism, however, rationalizes only the means, preferring to retain the traditional ends or goals. As Bellah defines neotraditionalism, it is "an ideology designed to keep change to a minimum and defend the status quo as far as possible."[87] Reformism, on the other hand, amounts to a thorough reinterpretation of the tradition involving three important moves: an appeal to the early teachers and texts, a rejection of much of the intervening tradition, and an interpretation that advocates social reform and national regeneration.[88]

These two alternatives for reform cut across the spectrum of responses in the Sinhalese Buddhist revival. They constitute the two basic options for people caught in the contextual dilemma of identity and responsiveness. We shall see that contemporary Theravadins have tried both approaches as ways of adapting the tradition to the modern context. Tambiah points out the presence of these two courses of reform in the nineteenth-century Theravada reformation in Thailand under King Rama IV (Mongkut): this movement involved "his attempt on the one hand to purify religion and to adhere to its pristine form and on the other to initiate changes and to champion Buddhist rationalism to meet the intellectual challenges of the nineteenth century."[89] This revival, Tambiah shows, had many similarities to the Sinhalese revival as a quest for both "timeless truths" and "situational truths."[90]

The alternation between the authoritative sources and the world view of the modern context constitutes one of the central dynamics of the Sinhalese Theravada renaissance. One basic theme of all the Sinhalese revivalists, whether neotraditionalists or reformists, has been what Tambiah terms "an accent on scripturalism."[91] No matter what their ideological stance, most reformers have turned to the texts to find authoritative foundations for their reinterpretations. The lack of a strong Buddhist leadership or institutional presence in the late colonial period made this move especially necessary as a basis for reform. However, this was not the only reason that the reformers became scripturalists, for, as Tambiah notes, Theravada has a history of scripturalist purifications of religion going as far back as Asoka's legendary purging of the *Sangha*.[92] This is not to say, however, that the modern interpreters have introduced nothing new. They have been scripturalists responding to a very different context that has required new interpretations. By the same token we should not assume all modern scripturalists to be in agreement, for they have differed in the ways they perceived their particular context, the scriptures they employed and the charters for reform they found in the texts.

In addition to scripturalism, other general themes or motifs can be cited that particularly characterize the reformist viewpoint and distinguish it from traditional Theravada as well as from the neotraditionalist viewpoint. Among such motifs are (1) rationalism and individualism, (2) world affirmation, (3) universalism, minimization of hierarchy, (4) devaluing mediation and ritual, (5) an achievement-centered orientation, and (6) this-worldly asceticism.

These motifs provide an overview of the ways that the reformers have reinterpreted the traditional Theravada system. Rationalism represents the crucial theme here for, as Weber and others have observed, reason constitutes the chief weapon for reforming tradition. The assertion of reason as an authoritative source of truth signifies a shift from a group-centered, custom-bound society to an individualistic one. This kind of shift was precisely what took place in colonial Ceylon. The reformers produced by this new society consequently redefined both the ends and the means of their religion in terms of rationalism and individualism. The aim of Buddhism, on the reformers' interpretation, can be described as a form of world affirmation in contrast to the tendency toward world denial in traditional Theravada. Bechert pointed to this theme when he wrote, "Buddhist modernism consequently does away with the old separation of the supramundane and mundane spheres."[93] The reformers have telescoped the supramundane and mundane paths, central to traditional Theravada, holding that both are available in this life. *Nibbāna*, many reformers believe, is attainable here and now. As Bardwell Smith wrote, *Nibbāna* "is conceived not as limited to a remote future or as something other-worldly."[94] The corollary to world affirmation is the emphasis on universalism. The reformers have a definite optimism about what Douglas has called "the human potential for sustaining great spiritual achievement."[95] The revival in Theravada, carried out in large part by the new laity, the English-educated elite, has stressed the layman's spiritual potential. It has in various ways taught that the layman has both the opportunity and the responsibility for his own liberation. A standard theme in reformist movements, this universalism also implies an opposition to hierarchicalism and clericalism. In contrast to the traditional Buddhist idea that great sanctity is exceptional, and that if it exists at all it is the province of the ordained clergy, the reformers have held that laypersons have at least as good, or perhaps better, chances to attain the goal in this life. We shall see that some groups of reformists have been explicit in their opposition to the *Sangha*, whereas even the neo-traditionalist groups, who have supported the traditional status of the monks, have given the laity new and often controlling roles in the religion.

Having rationalized the ends of Buddhism, the reformists also rationalize the means or the path in various ways. They abandon for the most part the traditional emphasis on the gradual path leading to a remote *Nibbāna* hundreds of lives away. Instead they tend to emphasize ways of achieving *Nibbāna* here and now. Liberation is not mediated through the rituals of merit-making or *deva* worship but is immediately accessible to those who pursue it seriously. This achievement-centered orientation devaluing almost all forms of magic and ritual often results in a Buddhist version of this-worldly asceticism. The shift from an ascriptive status to an achievement orientation has carried over from the social realm to the religious. The reformists feel that they have the freedom as well as the necessity to employ their reason to interpret the religion in ways that address the modern situation and enable people to cope with the changes that are occurring. For the reformists time is no longer a declining spiral; the golden age lies in the present or the future, rather than in the past. Being scripturalists, the reformists take seriously the Buddha's final injunction, "Work out your own salvation with diligence." The path is open to everyone and does not require one to renounce the world. It does, however, require being active rather than passive in seeking to live out this ideal in the modern world.

Optimism about individual potential and this-worldly asceticism translates into optimism about the social plane as well, with reformists advocating social welfare and development as integral goals of Buddhism. Although at first these reforms may have been taken up as a response to the Christian emphasis on them, as the reformation proceeded the Buddhists grounded these motifs in their own heritage and made them significant themes in the reinterpretation of their tradition. One of the most far-reaching aspects of the recent reformation has been the emergence of institutions and movements that seek to apply Buddhist ideals to effect social change and development. This movement has found expression among both neotraditionalists and reformists.

In general, the motifs characterizing the reformist reinterpretation of religion correspond to Douglas's description of a religion's adjusting to a changing or nontraditional social context by becoming "more egalitarian, more individualistic, and more optimistic about the human potential for sustaining great spiritual achievement."[96] The motifs reflect an urban, lay reformation that has as its foundation literacy and a heavy dose of Western humanism inculcated by the British educational system, as we have seen. For as Gellner points out with regard to a similar reform movement, "Literacy makes possible direct access to revelation and hence makes easier the dispensing with intermediaries, whether in this or another world, whether priest or spirit, and hence with hierarchy or cult of personality."[97]

These motifs and other related themes indicate the general direction and ethos of the reformist side of the revival; they should not be regarded, however, as demonstrations of unanimity of viewpoint among the reformers. Different reformers have taken up these motifs in different ways. Although the neotraditionalists, preferring to keep change to a minimum, have been reluctant to adopt fully many of these innovative, reformist interpretations, they have wrestled with the same issues, as we shall see. Their neotraditional understanding of Buddhism, although not as liberal as that of the reformists, has been more rational, more accommodationist, and more pragmatic than that of traditional Theravada. Tambiah, describing various themes in the Thai Buddhist reformation, writes: "At any juncture of time these and other ideological postures may coexist in the same society among differently placed groups or individuals. . . . Moreover, any single school of thought may in practice mix these orientations in diverse ways."[98] Thus, in the Sri Lankan case, when we speak of overall motifs, we must recognize an element of generalization, because these themes have received various degrees and forms of expression. As Ames has said, "It should be understood that the Buddhist reformers never presented a unified front nor a consistent ideology."[99]

Because of this diversity and variety the Buddhist revival among the laity can be characterized as a series or spectrum of interpretations of the Buddhist tradition developed as responses to the modern situation. Although someone could conceivably identify an infinite number of interpretations and responses within this series or spectrum, for purposes of study we shall divide the spectrum into four major crystallizations or patterns of interpretation and response.[100] These four appear as interesting blends of Bellah's two main alternatives, neotraditionalism and reformism, as well as variations on the overall themes of the revival. Although not written in stone, these four response patterns are not simply arbitrary divisions, for each of the four has distinctive features and represents a somewhat different approach to the reinterpretation of the Theravada tradition.

The four patterns of response are:

1. "Protestant Buddhism."[101] The response of the early reformers who began the entire movement by both reacting against and imitating Christianity.

2. The Buddha Jayanti period. An approach that followed Protestant Buddhism, beginning in the 1940s with the independence movement and culminating in the celebrations surrounding the 2,500th anniversary of Buddhism in 1956. This response marked a shift toward traditionalism or neotraditionalism accompanied by a new alliance between Buddhism and politics. The actors in this scene of the revival included not only the Anglicized new elite but also the old elite, especially the monastic leadership of the Siyam Nikāya of the *Sangha* who sought to restore Buddhism to its "rightful" place.

3. The insight meditation (*vipassanā bhāvanā*), movement, a true reformist movement on Bellah's definition and a radical contrast to the neotraditionalism of Jayanti Buddhism. This movement, characterized by the rationalization of *Nibbāna* and the universalization of the virtuoso practice of meditation, represents the most important new direction of the revival today. It expresses the

implications of the rationalization of the religious symbol system for the personal level.

4. Social development as the fulfillment of the Buddhist ideal. The interpretations in this group represent the most serious attempts to derive a socially relevant understanding of the Buddhist tradition. Here the rationalization of the symbol system is applied to the social level. The best known example is the Sarvodaya Shramadāna Movement.

These four responses can be viewed diachronically, to some extent, since they represent the development of the revival over time. There are some clear differences between the earlier responses and the present-day responses. As the context has evolved, so have the interpretations. For example, as Christianity became less powerful, the anti-Christian reactions of Protestant Buddhism became less necessary, and the Buddhists turned to address other problems. The various stages of the revival also developed chronologically by either building upon or reacting against the previous Buddhist responses. Yet despite this diachronic development, the reformation must also be seen synchronically since the various responses all coexist in the present to some degree. The earlier solutions to the problems of interpretation have not disappeared entirely, but have tended to survive in some areas and on some levels of society.

Two important points must be noted about this variety of interpretations of the Buddhist tradition. First, although the proponents of the various interpretations may differ among themselves about the validity of their positions, all of these responses can be defended as legitimate interpretations of the tradition. Since the reformers are all scripturalists, they find their differing charters in the *Tipiṭaka*. The *Tipiṭaka*, however, like the scriptures of other religious traditions, is complex, ambiguous, and rich, containing what Tambiah describes as "parameters, dialectical tensions and even paradoxes."[102] The ambiguity and variety of the Buddhist canonical writings, Tambiah observes, "make for greater continuity between canonical and post-canonical ideas than is usually imagined and make the question of deviance of the latter from the former a vexed issue."[103] The *Tipiṭika* can support almost all of the diverse interpretations that have arisen as responses to modern contexts.

Second, in arriving at these diverse interpretations, the modern Theravadins have more or less instinctively fulfilled a basic Theravada presupposition: the entire reformation can be seen as an exemplification and verification of Buddhism's ancient tenet that the *Dhamma* contains teachings and levels of application appropriate for people at diverse existential and spiritual levels. On this reading the Theravada revival and reformation constitutes a new gradual path with levels and goals adapted for the diversity of modern Buddhist society. As on the traditional gradual path, the stages and viewpoints are different yet interrelated. The four patterns of response have their distinctive constituencies and levels of application, yet they all overlap, to some extent, philosophically and practically. This gradual-path metaphor helps us to understand how the various patterns of response function in Sinhalese society where, although some conflict between interpretations does exist, for the most part the various responses coexist, with each having its appropriate audience. Although the *Dhamma* is one, the reinterpretation and representation of it in the Buddhist revival has manifested its pluralistic potential providing many options for people to define and develop their Buddhist identity.

Notes

1. Michael Ames, "Ideological and Social Change in Ceylon," *Human Organization* 22 (1963): 45-53.

2. S. J. Tambiah, *World Conqueror and World Renouncer* (New York: Cambridge University Press, 1976), 218; Donald K. Swearer, "Lay Buddhism and the Buddhist Revival in Ceylon," *Journal of the American Academy of Religion* 38.3 (1970): 255-75.

3. Donald E. Smith, "The Sinhalese Buddhist Revolution," in *South Asian Politics and Religion,* ed. Donald E. Smith (Princeton: Princeton University Press, 1966), 453-88. Other terms used to describe this movement include "revitalization" and "resurgence" (e.g., Michael Ames, "Westernization or Modernization: The Case of Sinhalese Buddhism," *Social Compass* 20 ([1973]2: 141). Although the different terms convey differing nuances as descriptions of the movement, I prefer the term revival because it allows one to indicate the kind of pluralistic reinterpretation of a tradition that has taken place in Sri Lankan Buddhism.

    While similar and related revivals took place in Burma and Thailand, these movements will not be considered except insofar as they relate to the movement in Sri Lanka. The reader is referred to other studies of these revivals, such as Emanuel Sarkisyanz, *Buddhist Backgrounds of the Burmese Revolution* (The Hague: M. Nijhoff, 1965); Donald K. Swearer, "Thai Buddhism: Two Responses to Modernity," in *Tradition and Change in Theravada Buddhism: Essays on Ceylon and Thailand in the 19th and*

20th Centuries, ed. Bardwell L. Smith (Leiden: Brill, 1973); and the works of S. J. Tambiah, esp. *World Conqueror and World Renouncer.*

4. Ames, "Ideological and Social Change in Ceylon," 46.

5. Although our focus is primarily on the lay Buddhists, the reforms within the *Sangha,* the monastic order, have been treated by several authors, including Michael Carrithers, *The Forest Monks of Sri Lanka: An Anthropological and Historical Study* (Delhi: Oxford University Press, 1983); and Kitsiri Malalgoda, *Buddhism in Sinhalese Society, 1750-1900* (Berkeley: University of California Press, 1976).

6. Kenneth Boulding, *The Meaning of the Twentieth Century: The Great Transition* (New York: Harper, 1965), 12.

7. Robert N. Bellah, *Beyond Belief* (New York: Harper, 1970), 64.

8. Cyril Black, "Political Modernization in Historical Perspective," cited in Robert N. Bellah, ed., *Religion and Progress in Modern Asia* (New York: Free Press, 1965), 170.

9. Bellah, *Religion and Progress,* 195.

10. Bardwell L. Smith, *Tradition and Change in Theravada Buddhism,* 1.

11. Halpern, "The Revolution of Modernization in National & International Society," *Revolution: Nomos VIII,* ed. Carl J. Friedrich (New York: Atherton Press, 1966), 179.

12. *Religion and Progress,* 172.

13. Among her works related to this topic are *Cultural Bias,* Occasional Paper 35 of the Royal Anthropological Institute of Great Britain and Ireland, 1978; and *Natural Symbols: Explorations in Cosmology* (London: Barrie and Rockliff, 1970).

14. See W. Cantwell Smith, *The Meaning and End of Religion* (New York: New American Library, 1964).

15. Joseph L. Allen, "Interpreting the Contemporary Social Revolution: The Revolution of Secularization," unpublished paper, 1968.

16. Donald K. Swearer, "Thai Buddhism: Two Responses to Modernity," 92.

17. Tambiah, *World Conqueror,* 401.

18. Bardwell L. Smith, "Sinhalese Buddhism and the Dilemmas of Reinterpretation," in *The Two Wheels of Dhamma: Essays on the Theravada Tradition in India and Ceylon,* ed. Bardwell L. Smith (Chambersburg, PA: American Academy of Religion, 1972), 84.

19. Among the important works on this are the following: Hans-Dieter Evers, "Buddhism and British Colonial Policy in Ceylon, 1815-1875," *Asian Studies* 2, (1964): 323-33; G. C. Mendis, *Ceylon Today and Yesterday: Main Currents of Ceylon History* (Colombo: Associated Newspapers, 1963); L. A. Mills, *Ceylon Under the British* (Colombo: Colombo Apothecaries, 1948); C. R. deSilva, *The Portugese in Ceylon 1617–1638* (Colombo: H. W. Cave, 1972); K. M. deSilva, "Buddhism and the British Government in Ceylon," *Ceylon Historical Journal* 10 (1961): 91-160; W. Howard Wriggins, *Ceylon: Dilemmas of a New Nation* (Princeton: Princeton University Press, 1960).

20. As Singer observes, however, not all *Goyigamas* have actually been involved in farming, even though that is their hereditary occupation. Marshall R. Singer, *The Emerging Elite: A Study of Political Leadership in Ceylon* (Cambridge, MA: M.I.T. Press, 1964), 12.

21. Singer, *Emerging Elite,* 6.

22. Tissa Fernando, "The Western Educated Elite and Buddhism in British Ceylon: A Neglected Aspect of the Nationalist Movement," in *Tradition and Change in Theravada Buddhism*, 20.
23. Robert N. Kearney, "Politics and Modernization," Chapter in *Modern Sri Lanka: A Society in Transition*, ed. Robert N. Kearney and T. Fernando (Syracuse, NY: Syracuse University, 1979), 58.
24. Fernando, "Western Educated Elite . . .," 19.
25. Singer, *Emerging Elite*, 28.
26. Tambiah, p. 217.
27. D. A. Kotelawele, "Nineteenth Century Elites and their Antecedents," *The Ceylon Historical Journal* 25 (1978): 208.
28. Wriggins, p. 30.
29. Ames, "The Impact of Western Education on Religion and Society in Ceylon," p. 28.
30. Wriggins, *Ceylon*, 188.
31. The Buddhist Committee of Enquiry, *Betrayal of Buddhism* (Balangoda: Dharmavijaya Press, 1956), 2.
32. Ames, "Westernization or Modernization," 152.
33. D. K. Wilson, *The Christian Church in Sri Lanka* (Colombo: Study Centre for Religion and Society, 1975), 12.
34. Ames, "Westernization or Modernization," 140.
35. Ames, "Westernization or Modernization," 152.
36. Fernando, "The Western Educated Elite," 21.
37. Edmund Leach, "Buddhism in the Post-Colonial Political Order in Burma and Ceylon," *Daedalus* 102 (1973): 40.
38. Ames says that in 1914 the English-speaking community was about one percent of the population ("The Impact of Western Education," 31).
39. Michael Ondaatje, *Running in the Family* (London: Pan Books, 1984), 39.
40. Ames, "The Impact of Western Education," 32.
41. Singer, *The Emerging Elite*, 18.
42. Tennakoon Vimalananda, *The State and Religion in Ceylon since 1815* (Colombo: Gunasena & Co., 1970), 89.
43. T. Vimalananda, *Buddhism in Ceylon Under the Christian Powers* (Colombo: Gunasena & Co., 1963), lxvi.
44. Vimalananda, *The State and Religion*, 126.
45. Wriggins, *Ceylon*, 186f.
46. K. M. deSilva, "Buddhism, Nationalism and Politics in Modern Sri Lanka," unpublished paper delivered at South Asia Conference, Madison, Wisconsin, Nov., 1984, p. 1.
47. Ames, "Westernization or Modernization," 153.
48. Ondaatje, *Running in the Family*, 41.
49. Cited in Ames, "Westernization or Modernization," 155.
50. Fernando, "The Western Educated Elite," 22.
51. Ames, "Westernization or Modernization," 141.
52. Tambiah, *World Conqueror*, 218.

53. Leach, "Buddhism in the Post-Colonial Order," 39.
54. S. J. Tambiah, "The Persistence and Transformation of Tradition in Southeast Asia, with Special Reference to Thailand," *Daedalus* 102 (1973): 55.
55. Among those who have analyzed Theravada Buddhism in this way are Tambiah, "The Persistence and Transformation of Tradition," 56; Heinz Bechert, "*Sangha, State, Society, 'Nation': Persistence of Traditions in 'Post-Traditional' Buddhist Societies*," *Daedalus* 102 (1973): 85; K. Malalgoda, "Buddhism in Sri Lanka: Continuity and Change," in *Sri Lanka: A Survey,* ed. K. M. deSilva (London: Hurst, 1976), 383-89; and Bardwell L. Smith, "Toward a Buddhist Anthropology: The Problem of the Secular," *Journal of the American Academy of Religion* 36 (1968): 203-16.
56. Max Weber, *The Religion of India* (New York: Free Press, 1958), 214.
57. Malalgoda, "Buddhism in Sri Lanka," 383.
58. Tambiah, *World Conqueror,* 402, 515.
59. See my book *"The Word of the Buddha": The Tipiṭaka and Its Interpretation in the Theravada Buddhist Tradition* (Colombo: Gunasena and Co., 1983), ch. 3.
60. Charles Hallisey, "Epithets of the Buddha," paper presented at the University of Chicago, November 1985.
61. Richard F. Gombrich, *Precept and Practice: Traditional Buddhism in the Rural Highlands of Ceylon* (Oxford: Clarendon Press, 1971), 40.
62. Tambiah, *World Conqueror,* 525.
63. Michael Ames, "Magical Animism and Buddhism: A Structural Analysis of the Sinhalese Religious System," *Journal of Asian Studies,* 23 (1964), 28.
64. Louis Dumont, "World Renunciation in Indian Religions," Appendix B, in *Homo Hierarchicus: The Caste System and Its Implications* (Chicago: University of Chicago Press, 1980), 267-86; Louis De La Valee Poussin, *The Way to Nirvana* (Cambridge, 1917).
65. Dumont, "World Renunciation," 270.
66. Poussin, *The Way to Nirvana,* ch. 1.
67. Dumont, "World Renunciation," 270.
68. Dumont, "World Renunciation," 275.
69. Dumont, "World Renunciation," 434 n. 21.
70. See G. D. Bond, "The Development and Elaboration of the Arahant Ideal in the Theravada Buddhist Tradition," *Journal of the American Academy of Religion* 52 (1984): 227-42.
71. *Ādittapariyāya-Sutta, Saṃyutta Nikāya,* ed. L. Feer (London: Pali Text Society, 1898), 4: 19f.
72. For example, *Dīgha Nikāya,* ed. T. W. Rhys Davids and T. E. Carpenter (London: Pali Text Society, 1967), 1: 47; *Anguttara Nikāya,* 2: 207; and *Majjhima Nikāya,* ed. R. Chalmers and V. Trenckner (Pali Text Society, 1888), 1: 33.
73. Dumont, "World Renunciation," 276.
74. Steven Collins, *Selfless Persons: Imagery and Thought in Theravada Buddhism* (Cambridge: Cambridge University Press, 1982), 12.
75. Buddhaghosa, *Visuddhimagga,* ed. C. A. F. Rhys Davids (London: Pali Text Society, 1975).

76. The Visuddhimagga's outline of the path has seven stages, but it sees these as falling under the more basic framework of the threefold training. See Visuddhimagga, ch. 1.

77. *Netti Pakaraṇa*, ed. E. Hardy (London: Pali Text Society, 1902), 128-61.

78. Leach, "Buddhism in the Post-Colonial Order," 50.

79. A phrase used by Theravadins traditionally. The concept is discussed by Winston King, *A Thousand Lives Away* (Cambridge, MA: Harvard University Press, 1964).

80. Ames, "Magical-Animism and Buddhism," 28ff.

81. Bardwell L. Smith, "Toward a Buddhist Anthropology," 209.

82. For further discussion of the process of merit-making, see Gombrich, *Precept and Practice*, chrs. 5 and 6.

83. Mary Douglas, "The Effects of Modernization on Religious Change," *Daedalus* 3 (1972): 4.

84. Bardwell L. Smith, "Introduction," *Tradition and Change in Theravada Buddhism*, p. 2.

85. Bellah, *Religion and Progress*, 78. See also Swearer, "Thai Buddhism: Two Responses to Modernity."

86. Bellah, *Religion and Progress*, 215.

87. Bellah, *Religion & Progress*, 213.

88. Bellah, *Religion & Progress*, 210.

89. Tambiah, *World Conqueror*, 251.

90. Tambiah, *World Conqueror*, 401.

91. Tambiah, *World Conqueror*, 219.

92. Tambiah, *World Conqueror*, 429.

93. Bechert, "*Sangha*, State, Society," 91.

94. Bardwell L. Smith, "Sinhalese Buddhism and the Dilemmas of Reinterpretation," 86.

95. Douglas, "The Effects of Modernization," 4.

96. Douglas, "The Effects of Modernization," 4.

97. Ernest Gellner, *Saints of the Atlas* (Chicago: University of Chicago Press, 1969), 7.

98. Tambiah, *World Conqueror*, 402.

99. Ames, "Ideological and Social Change in Ceylon," 48.

100. Ames also pointed out that "there appeared to be several dominant patterns of response." ("Westernization & Modernization," 154). He did not, however, identify the same patterns that we do here.

101. The term "Protestant Buddhism" was applied to the early period by Gananath Obeyesekere in "Religious Symbolism and Political Change in Ceylon," *Modern Ceylon Studies*, 1 (1970): 43-63. Although some writers have applied this term to the entire reformation, I use it to refer primarily to the earliest period and the movements and emphases that began then, some of which continue today.

102. Tambiah, "The Persistence and Transformation of Tradition," 81.

103. Tambiah, *World Conqueror*, 433.

2

The Early Revival and Protestant Buddhism

When did the Buddhist revival begin? Although some have traced its beginnings to the coming of the Theosophists, Colonel Henry Olcott and Madame Helena Petrovna Blavatsky, to Sri Lanka, the origins of this movement to revive Buddhism go much further back in time, receding into the Middle Ages. Malalgoda has correctly noted that the "Buddhists were by no means dormant before the arrival of the Theosophists."[1] This chapter examines those origins and focuses on the early period of the Buddhist resurgence in Sri Lanka. The hallmark of this period was the establishment of a form of Buddhism that Obeyesekere has labeled "Protestant Buddhism" because it both (1) derived many of its viewpoints and organizational forms from Protestantism and (2) represented a "protest *against* Christianity and its associated Western political dominance prior to independence."[2] Protestant Buddhism, both because it mirrored Protestant Christianity and because it attempted to revive Buddhism and make it relevant to a new context, represented a reformist movement. Since much has been written about this early movement, the aim of this chapter will be simply to highlight pivotal events and figures in this period of reformism that set the course for much of the later revival.

Beginnings

Several events and figures can be identified as signaling the origins of the attempt to reform and revive Theravada. When the fortunes of Buddhism had reached a low point in the mid-eighteenth century, a Buddhist monk, Välivita Saraṇaṃkara, persuaded the king of Kandy, Srī Vijaya Rājasiṃha, to bring monks from Thailand to reestablish higher ordination in Sri Lanka.[3] Saraṇaṃkara sought to reform the *Sangha* of his day by insisting on scholarship and monastic discipline. His monks resumed practices such as alms begging, *piṇḍapāta*, and were called the company of pious ones, *silvat samāgama*. Saraṇaṃkara's reforms led to the reestablishment of higher ordination in 1753 and the founding of the Siyam Nikāya with its headquarters in the Kandyan monasteries of Malvatta and Asgiriya. This monastic reform gave new impetus to all aspects of Buddhism, prompting the king to restore ancient temples, encouraging the laity to renew their interest in Buddhist observances and rituals, and checking the Hindu influences in the country.

Saraṇaṃkara's reforms led to a series of other reforms in the *Sangha*, especially in the nineteenth century, as various groups imported monks from Burma to administer higher ordination. Since the Siyam Nikāya prevailed in the hill country and ordained only members of the highest caste, *Goyigama*, the emerging non-*Goyigama* elite in the low country founded monastic fraternities for their members. The resulting Amarapura and Ramañña *Nikāyas* with their various segments and fraternities originated not simply to protest this caste discrimination but also to reform the *Sangha* by returning it to the strict observance of the *Vinaya*.[4] Ames notes that "within a span of about 150 years, beginning in 1802, over thirty new fraternities were established in the coastal areas in opposition to the one controlled by the Kandyans."[5]

Another important event during this period of monastic reform was the founding in 1845 of the Parama Dhamma Cetiya Piriveṇa in Ratmalana south of Colombo. Pupils from this Buddhist institution of higher education established Vidyodaya Piriveṇa at Maligākanda in 1873 and Vidyālankāra Piriveṇa at Päliyagoda in 1875.[6] The monastic founder of Vidyodaya was the influential scholar monk Hikkaḍuvē Sumaṅgala. The work of scholars such as Sumaṅgala and the founding of these educational institutions shifted the focus of Buddhism from Kandy to the low country, where the new elite was emerging under the colonial system. Although the monks bore most of the burden of the reform during the first half of the nineteenth century, some laymen among the new elite also began to involve themselves in reviving Buddhism. For example, two Buddhist businessmen from Colombo, Don Philip de Silva Äpä Appuhämi and Don Velon Vikramatilaka Appuhämi, headed a group that planned and raised the funds to establish a Buddhist college, Vidyodaya Oriental College in 1873.

At the outset the *bhikkhus* who initiated this resurgence of Buddhism responded to Hindu opposition in the Kandyan kingdom, but during the nineteenth century the ongoing movement had to respond to opposition posed by the Christian missionaries under the British. In this context two events stand out as significant in shaping this reinterpretation of the Theravada tradition. First, in 1855 the Buddhists acquired a printing press, which enabled them to respond to the tracts of the Christian missionaries. This event can be said to have opened the way for significant participation by laymen in the reform movement, first as operators of the press for the monks and later as the new spokesmen for Buddhism. The press made the ideas and debates of the reformers available to a wide and receptive audience.

Second, beginning in 1864 and lasting until 1873, the Buddhists engaged the Christian missionaries in a series of historic debates. These debates betokened the flowering of the Buddhist revival that had been growing in the monasteries for over a century. In these debates in low country centers such as Baddēgama, Varāgoda, and, finally, Pānadurā in 1873, the Buddhist laity as well as the monks regained pride in their heritage. For years the Christian missionaries had attacked Buddhism in sermons and through tracts. Although the Buddhist monks had shown great tolerance toward them, the missionaries, regarding Buddhism as paganism and idolatry, continued to challenge the Buddhists to debate. Pushed to the limit, the monks finally accepted the challenge and confronted the missionaries in a series of written and oral debates. The climax of the affair took place at Pānadurā, where, in a two-day debate, the eloquent Buddhist monk Mohoṭṭivattē Guṇānanda refuted the missionaries and defended Buddhism before an audience of ten thousand laymen.[7] Perhaps more than earlier events these debates, publicized by the Buddhist presses, marked the beginning of the lay Buddhist revival and reformation. When Guṇānanda defeated the Christians in debate at Pānadurā, lay Buddhists began to realize anew the potential of their own tradition.

Colonel Olcott and the Theosophists

News of these debates spread widely and came to the attention of Colonel Henry Olcott in America. Olcott and Madame Blavatsky, who had formed the Theosophical Society in 1875, had a great interest in Hinduism and Buddhism, which they saw as prototypes of the true religion.[8] At this time the West in general had just begun to discover Buddhism, and in intellectual and literary circles Buddhism was much in vogue. The publication of Sir Edwin Arnold's *The Light of Asia* in 1879 created a great wave of interest in this noble religion. The discovery of Buddhism by the West thus coincided with the rediscovery of Buddhism in Sri Lanka, and the two movements reinforced each other.

Olcott arrived in Sri Lanka along with Madame Blavatsky on May 17, 1880, to lend the strength of the West to the Buddhists in their struggle. The resounding welcome that Olcott received on his arrival indicated the symbolic importance that this endorsement of their cause by Westerners had for the Buddhists. Greeted by throngs of Buddhists wherever they went, Olcott and Blavatsky, by their interest in the cause of Buddhism, gave a tremendous psychological lift to the Buddhist movement. The *Maha Bodhi* later reported, "No king ever received the homage of a devoted people as these two when they landed on the shores."[9]

Olcott's specific contributions to the Buddhist movement strengthened the role of the laity and influenced their reformist viewpoint. He established the Buddhist Theosophical Society with two divisions, clerical and lay. Olcott thought it significant that the clerical division brought together monks from all the different fraternities, but, as Malalgoda shows, the monks had already been cooperating in the confrontation with the missionaries.[10] The real significance of the BTS, however, lay in its providing an organization for the laity, who until that time had been divided by their loyalties to individual temples and branches of the *Sangha*. As Malalgoda observes, before 1880 the laymen had not been the primary actors in the revival of Buddhism.[11] The lay organization of the BTS not only gave the laymen a new sense of unity in opposing the Christians, but it also gave them independence from the monks to participate in the reform of Buddhism. The Theosophists proved to be powerful allies for the Buddhists because, according to deSilva, "their familiarity with the rationalist and 'scientific' critique of Christianity" gave the Buddhists good intellectual support in opposing the missionaries.[12] The new elite laity, with their activist inclinations, supported by this new freedom and intellectual encouragement, grew in the BTS and laid the foundations for reform.

Olcott provided leadership for these laymen on a number of important issues involving Buddhism. As an outsider, his intercession with the colonial government proved especially useful. In 1883, for example, riots occurred between Catholics and Buddhists because the Buddhists held an elaborate *pinkama* ceremony on Easter Sunday near a church. Olcott was chosen by the Buddhists to present their case to the government. On other occasions also Olcott succeeded in persuading the government to acknowledge the rights of the Buddhists; he gained their recognition of *Vesak* as a national holiday and got the government to appoint Buddhist marriage registrars. Olcott even helped design the Buddhist flag which became a symbol of the rising consciousness of the Buddhist laity.

Recognizing the advantage that the Christian schools gave the missionaries and appalled by the lack of knowledge about Buddhism that he found among Sinhalese children, Olcott began a campaign to raise funds for Buddhist schools. He noted, "The Christians spend millions to destroy Buddhism; we must spend to defend and propagate it."[13] To this end he traveled the countryside in a specially equipped bullock cart, collecting money for the education fund. With this support the BTS began Buddhist Sunday schools to rival the missionaries, and soon afterward began regular elementary and high schools patterned after the mission schools but with a Buddhist rather than a Christian component in their curricula. By 1990 there existed 142 Buddhist-managed schools, with some of them becoming first-class educational institutions equal to the best Christian schools.[14] Mendis observed that these schools brought "into being a new generation of persons educated in Buddhist schools with a greater knowledge of Buddhism . . . to press the claims of Buddhism and see that it was given its rightful place."[15]

Mendis's observation, however, fails to point out that this "new generation" trained in the BTS schools imbibed not traditional Buddhism but the spirit of a new rational and reformed Buddhism. Although viewing himself as a Buddhist, Olcott said his Buddhism "was that of the Master-Adept Gautama Buddha" which represented "the soul of all the ancient world faiths."[16] To be sure, the teachers in the new Buddhist schools would not have been as steeped in the Theosophical interpretation of Buddhism as Olcott was, and most of them probably presented a somewhat more traditional view of Buddhism. Nevertheless, the curriculum of the schools followed a Western, rational model, and the students undoubtedly learned to see Buddhism from this perspective.

Olcott's *Buddhist Catechism*, drawn up to rival the missionaries' catechism and first published in Sinhala in 1881, represents this rational and reformed interpretation of Buddhism. Although the *Catechism*'s exact effect upon the Sinhalese Buddhist students cannot be estimated, it was widely used in the BTS schools and appears to represent the general approach of the new Buddhist education. That this approach created some controversy can be seen from Hikkaḍuvē Sumaṇgala's initial refusal to endorse the *Catechism* until Olcott changed his interpretation of *Nibbāna*. In the end, however, Venerable Sumaṇgala allowed his name to be used on the title page of the *Buddhist Catechism:* "Approved and recommended for use in Buddhist schools by H. Sumaṇgala, Pradhana Nayaka Sthavira, High Priest of Sri Pada and the Western Province and Principal of the Vidyodaya Parivena."

Despite whatever adjustments Olcott made to gain Venerable Sumaṇgala's approval, the *Catechism* depicts Buddhism as a rational, scientific religion that sets out an ethical path to liberation without the necessity of a god or a divine revelation. According to the *Catechism*, the Buddha was not god, for "Buddha Dharma teaches no 'divine' incarnation." The Buddha was a human being, although "the wisest, noblest and most holy being who had developed himself in the course of countless births."[17] The *Catechism* teaches that the goal of Buddhism is accessible: "The nirvānic state can be attained while one is living on this earth."[18] Regarding the viability of the goal of Buddhism, Olcott wrote:

There is in Ceylon a popular misconception that the attainment of Arhatship is now impossible; that the Buddha had himself prophesied that the power would die out in one millennium after his death. This rumor . . . I ascribe to the ingenuity of those who should be as pure and . . . *psychically* wise as were their predecessors, but are not, and who therefore seek an excuse.[19]

The essence of this ideal state is depicted as a rational and ethical purity:

Q.   And what is that which is most valuable?
A.   To know the whole secret of man's existence and destiny . . . so that we may live in a way to ensure the greatest happiness and the least suffering for our fellow men and ourselves.[20]

The path leading to this goal also receives a rational interpretation in the *Catechism*. Although Olcott cites the basic precepts and the traditional guidelines for a Buddhist's conduct, he summarizes it with passages such as this:

Q.   Do these precepts show that Buddhism is an active or a passive religion?
A.   To "cease from sin" may be called passive, but to "get virtue" and "to cleanse one's own heart," or mind, are altogether *active* qualities. Buddha taught that we should not merely not be evil, but that we should be *positively* good.[21]

Or again:

Q.   What other good words have been used to express the essence of Buddhism?
A.   Self-culture and universal love.[22]

The *Catechism*, although not critical of the *Sangha*, clearly states that one does not need to be a monk to tread this path to the goal: "The mere wearing of yellow robes, or even ordination, does *not* of itself make a man pure or wise or entitle him to reverence."[23]

The *Catechism* explicitly states that to arrive at this kind of rational Buddhism requires that one reject aspects of traditional or "popular" Buddhism. It asks, "Does popular Buddhism contain nothing but what is true and in accord with science?" And answers that popular Buddhism "like every other religion that has existed many centuries . . . contains untruth mixed with truth. . . . The poetical imagination, the zeal, the lingering superstition of Buddhist devotees have . . . caused the noble principles of the Buddha's moral doctrines to be coupled with what might be removed to advantage."[24] Among the items that "might be removed to advantage" were all rituals and ceremonies, and especially the worship of the *devas* that played an integral role in the traditional Sinhalese religious system. The *Catechism* asks,

Q.   Did the Buddha hold with idol-worship?
A.   He did not; he opposed it. The worship of gods, demons, trees, etc., was condemned by the Buddha.[25]

It says that "charms" and "devil dancing" are "repugnant" to the fundamental principles of Buddhism.

In sum, the *Catechism* interprets Buddhism as a rational and scientific religion, ideally suited for the modern age. It sounds many of the themes of reformism that were to be raised by the Sinhalese Buddhists in the coming years of the reformation. Its Western and humanistic ideas were undoubtedly influential in shaping the reformers' perspectives. Olcott's one-paragraph summary of Buddhism expresses many of these reformist motifs:

Q.   What striking contrasts are there between Buddhism and what may be properly called "religions"?
A.   Among others, these: It teaches the highest goodness without a creating God; a continuity of life without adhering to the superstitious and selfish doctrine of an eternal, metaphysical soul-substance that goes out of the body; a happiness without an objective heaven; a method of salvation without a vicarious Savior; redemption by oneself as the Redeemer, and without rites, prayers, penances, priests or intercessory saints; and a *summum bonum*, i.e. Nirvāna, attainable in this life and in this world by leading a pure, unselfish life of wisdom and of compassion to all beings.[26]

Anagārika Dharmapāla

The individual who probably was influenced the most by Olcott and who in turn did the most to advance the cause that Olcott began was Anagārika Dharmapāla. When Olcott delivered his first lecture in Colombo in 1880, one of the Buddhists in his audience was a fourteen-year-old schoolboy named Don David Hevavitharana. His family belonged to that group of low-country new elite families who had become both wealthy and ardent lay supporters of Buddhism. Through his family young Hevavitharana came to know well both of the leading figures in the early revival, Hikkaḍuvē Sumaṇgala and Mohoṭṭivattē Guṇānanda, whose temple in Kotahena was near the Hevavitharana home. At the age of ten, David Hevavitharana had seen these two *bhikkhus* debate and defeat the Christians at Pānadurā. Olcott's arrival in the island and the enthusiasm that it generated propelled the boy into the growing Buddhist movement.

Since the details of Dharmapāla's biography have been ably examined by Obeyesekere and others,[27] we shall not rehearse those biographical details except as they enable us to understand Dharmapāla's contributions to the reformation of Buddhism. Dharmapāla's decision to devote his life to the cause and the welfare of Buddhists came as a result of the influence of Colonel Olcott and Madame Blavatsky. Dharmapāla's grandfather served as the president of the lay section of Olcott's Buddhist Theosophical Society in Colombo. In 1884 David Hevavitharana was initiated as a member and became a favorite of Colonel Olcott and Madame Blavatsky. Later in that same year, although his father opposed it, young Hevavitharana accompanied Blavatsky on a trip to India. While in India, she told him that he should not devote himself to the occultism with which he had become fascinated but should "work for the good of Humanity" and that he should take up the study of Pali "where all that is needed is to be found."[28] This advice coincided with the influences from his home, where he had been surrounded by the resurgence of Buddhism with its call to revive the *Dhamma* for the good of the world. He had found his mission.

In the following year Don David Hevavitharana vowed to live as a *brahmacharin* and took the name Anagārika Dharmapāla. He was creating a new role for himself to follow in the renewal of Buddhism for an *anagārika* was neither a monk nor a layman. This new role was perfectly suited to the reform of Buddhism. It allowed him to pursue the religious life while being active in the world. Neither a monk nor a householder, he thought, would have as much freedom and potential to work "for the welfare of humanity" as an *anagārika*. Obeyesekere notes that the new role "is a clear statement of the personal ideals he sets for himself: celibacy (*brahmachariya*) and this worldly asceticism."[29]

Dharmapāla wrote of his life, "I left the family and ever since I have worked with sincere devotion sacrificing all selfish interests for the welfare of humanity. Day and night I worked hard for the welfare of the Theosophical Society and Buddhism."[30] Although he later broke with the Theosophical Society, his early years were both devoted to and shaped by it. He served as Olcott's translator on his tours of Sri Lanka to raise funds for Buddhist education. Later he traveled with Olcott to India and Japan. Dharmapāla's travels to various parts of the world made two significant impressions on him. First, already believing in the need to revive Buddhism in Sri Lanka, he became even more convinced of this need when he visited Bodh Gaya and found the most sacred shrine of Buddhism crumbling under the control of a Hindu. He vowed beneath the Bodhi tree to rescue Buddhism from neglect. Bodh Gaya struck Dharmapāla as a symbol of the degradation of Buddhism. The Mahā Bodhi Society, which he founded in 1891, became Dharmapāla's chief vehicle for working to revitalize Buddhism both in India and Sri Lanka. The second factor that impressed Dharmapāla in his travels both to the West, where he attended the World Parliament of Religions in Chicago in 1892, and to Japan was the progressive nature of these societies. He wrote, "Europe is progressive. Her religion is kept in the background for one day in the week, and for six days her people are following the dictates of modern science. Sanitation, aesthetic arts, electricity, etc. are what had made European and American people great."[31] By contrast, he felt that religion as it was traditionally understood was impeding progress in Asia, where "gods and priests keep the people in ignorance."

These impressions led Dharmapāla to work as a reformer who sought to enable the Buddhists to address the twofold dilemma of recovering their identity and becoming responsive to the modern world with its social, political, and economic problems.

Obeyesekere has examined the importance that the search for identity had for Dharmapāla personally as well as for the Buddhists collectively. He writes, "Dharmapāla initiated the process of identity affirmation which has continued into our day."[32] Dharmapāla explicitly discussed the crisis of identity that had come with colonialization, Westernization, and Christianization. He observed that "with this inception of the modern era the Aryan Sinhalese has lost his true identity and become a hybrid."[33] He had no doubts that this loss of identity resulted from the colonial policies and influences. "After a hundred years of British rule the Sinhalese as a consolidated race is on the decline."[34] "Influenced by the money grabbing, whiskey-drinking, beef-eating, pork-loving European the anglicised Sinhalese does not want to know whether his ancestor was an Aryan from India, or a hybrid foreigner from Portugal . . . or Holland."[35] Like Gandhi, Dharmapāla called on the people to abandon their attachment to a foreign identity in order to reclaim their true identity. When rediscovered, their true identity would be as Sinhala Buddhists.

Dharmapāla linked Buddhism and nationalism, relying on the traditional ethnic myths of the *Mahāvaṃsa* (*The Great Chronicle of Ceylon*). This combination, not new but largely forgotten during the colonial period, was to become a major theme in Sri Lanka both before and after independence. Expounding the rhetoric of reform, Dharmapāla called on the people to become patriots "for the preservation of our nation, our literature, our land, and our most glorious religion at whose source our forefathers drank deep for nearly seventy generations."[36] The manifest destiny of the Sinhala race according to the *Mahāvaṃsa*, he noted, was to be the guardians of the *Dhamma*. The modern Sinhalese must identify himself with King Dutugamunu, "who rescued Buddhism and our nationalism from oblivion."[37]

A powerful orator and writer, Dharmapāla employed these themes of Buddhism and Sinhala nationalism very effectively to motivate Buddhists to search for their identity. He wrote on these themes in the newspaper *Sinhala Baudhaya* (*Sinhala Buddhist*), which he began for the Maha Bodhi Society.[38] He convinced the Buddhists that their own traditional identity was nobler than that of the British whom they now aped. With brilliant wit and sarcasm he observed that "when the ancestors of the present holders of our beloved Island were running naked in the forests of Britain with their bodies painted, . . . our ancestors were enjoying the fruits of the glorious and peaceful civilization whose seeds were sown by the scions of the Sakya house 540 B.C."[39]

Recovering their true Buddhist identity represented what Dharmapāla considered the best response that the Sinhalese could make to the problems of the modern context. Reestablishing Buddhism and Buddhist values would enable them to reestablish the "glorious civilization" of Buddhist antiquity, where "free from foreign influences, . . . with the word of the Buddha as their guiding light," the Sinhalese people enjoyed happiness and prosperity.[40] Dharmapāla regarded Japan as an example of how the Buddhist heritage could contribute to modernization without Westernization. Although Dharmapāla employed the rhetoric of a traditionalist in arguing for the value of reasserting Buddhism and recovering the golden age, the Buddhism that he advocated was not traditional but represented a reformist reinterpretation. He clearly accepted the Theosophists' rational interpretation of Buddhism. Obeyesekere has described Dharmapāla as a champion of Protestant Buddhism.[41]

Dharmapāla based his interpretation of the *Dhamma* on the canonical Pali texts, which Madame Blavatsky had urged him to study. His essays and speeches were filled with allusions to these original texts. He regarded very highly the work of Western scholars such as T. W. Rhys Davids and Henry Clarke Warren, who labored to make the Pali texts available to a wider audience. Early texts such as the *Netti Pakaraṇa* and *Abhidhammattha Saṅgaha*, he observed, "are the books which give the interpretation of the wonderful doctrine; but they are in Pali, and to understand Buddha Vacana a knowledge of Pali is essential." He criticized the *bhikkhus* who knew only "a smattering of Pali" and the youth who were more interested in *kāmayoga*, the yoga of pleasure, than the *Dhamma*.[42] For the revival of Buddhism as well as for the development of humanity, he recommended that people study the early texts as he did.

Basing his own interpretation of the meaning and potential of the Buddhist tradition on the Pali texts, he rejected and criticized some important aspects of traditional Theravada. He rejected, for example, the traditional belief that *Nibbāna* is unattainable in this life, being "a thousand lives away." He noted in the *Mahā Bodhi Journal*, "Bhikkhus in Ceylon are sceptics regarding the realization of Arhatship. They say that Arhatship is passed, and that it is not possible in this age." Likewise he lamented that "most of the *bhikkhus* are indolent, they have lost the spirit of heroism and altruism." A monk "thinks he has done his duty if he goes to the funerals and once a week gives a discourse on the ethical aspects of the Buddhist Religion."[43] This pattern of monastic life that he depicts represented a traditional understanding of the *bhikkhu's* vocation accepted by traditional *bhikkhus* and laymen. Dharmapāla did not accept it, however, for he saw the need to reform the tradition in order to provide the basis for a modern society.

In keeping with his rational interpretation of Buddhism, Dharmapāla also deplored the worship of the *devas*: "No enlightened Buddhist . . . would ever care to invoke a god who is only a step higher in the evolutionary scale of progress than man."[44] In good rationalist fashion Dharmapāla explained his objection to this worship by saying, "Dependence on a god helps to destroy self-reliance."[45] At other times, however, he seems to have accepted at least the existence of the great gods of the Hindu tradition while opposing demon worship, astrology, and other "low and cunning arts."[46] Although these gods and arts constituted part of traditional Sinhalese practice, Dharmapāla, as reformer and a devotee of the original *Dhamma*, proclaimed, "Before the majestic figures of the All Compassionate, gods . . . pale into insignificance."[47]

Dharmapāla's reformist interpretation of Buddhism rationalized both the ultimate goal and the means of achieving it. Unlike the *bhikkhus* who were skeptical of arahantship, he taught that enlightenment can be found in this world. "*Nirvāna* is not a postmortem existence, but it is realizable in perfect consciousness in this earthly body, purified both physically and mentally."[48] He had an optimistic view of life and of the human potential for spiritual and material progress. With what might appear to some traditionalists as un-Buddhistic optimism, he expressed his world-affirming view, saying, "The earth life is one that cannot be called full of misery."[49]

In contrast to traditional Theravada, which was skeptical about anyone's attaining the goal, Dharmapāla opened the supramundane stages of the path to all persons, laity as well as monks. Traditional Buddhists doubted that stream-enterers, *sotāpannas*, could exist today; Dharmapala said, "Any human being may follow the Sotapatti (stream enterer) path, whether a householder or a *Bhikkhu*." Householders could also achieve the states of once-returner and nonreturner, although they would have to become lay *brahmacharins*.[50] By making these states of near-enlightenment available to those living in the world, Dharmapāla radically lowered the barriers separating the layperson from full participation in the religion. Arahantship, however, remained beyond the lay life, Dharmapāla believed, for it could be reached only by "perfect Brahmacari Bhikkhus."[51]

The path to the attainment of this enlightenment and *Nibbāna* is characterized by individualism and pragmatism. The essence of Dharmapāla's Protestant Buddhism can be seen in the rational and pragmatic guidelines that he set out for lay Buddhists. Emphasizing vigorous, direct action to realize the *Dhamma*, he saw the path as this-worldly asceticism.[52] He interpreted the doctrine of *karma* in a positive, not a negative or fatalistic, light, describing it as the "noble ethic of progress."[53] *Karma* inspires people to work for the good of all beings.

Activity more than anything else constituted the means to the goal. Buddhists must not be passive about either their own spiritual progress or the progress of the nation. Dharmapāla pointed to his own active life as an example of what Buddhism demands: "Buddhism teaches an energetic life, to be active in doing good work all the time. A healthy man requires only 4 hours sleep."[54] Sloth, indolence, and indifference represented the chief causes of evil *karma*.[55] He said that the "whole philosophy" of Buddhism was built on activity.[56]

Along with activism Dharmapāla included morality as a key to the path. He showed himself to be a true rationalist with statements such as, "Greater than the bliss of sweet Nirvana is the life of moral activity."[57] In a number of articles and in one important pamphlet entitled "The Daily Code for Laity," Dharmapāla spelled out the moral requirements of the Buddhist path. Obeyesekere has shown that this code included not only religious rules but also rules for manners and deportment, with Western norms placed alongside Buddhist norms.[58] Much of Dharmapāla's teaching pertains to these moralistic prescriptions for Buddhists who were rediscovering their tradition. Since Buddhism applied to all aspects of life—social, economic, and political— the moral code had to be all-encompassing. Prohibitions of indifference to the sufferings of others could, on this logic, be placed alongside prohibitions of "allowing dirt and filth to accumulate."[59] Cleanliness seems to have been an especially important virtue for

Dharmapāla. Its repeated presence in his moral codes points to the emerging middle- or elite-class origin of these ideals.[60] Like the Protestant Christians, Dharmapāla opposed the "drink abomination," and like the traditional Buddhists he urged vegetarianism.

Dharmapāla's emphasis on this moral code pertaining to all aspects of life recalls Weber's conception of urban religion's moving away from ecstatic practices in favor of practices stressing duty and orderliness.[61] Analyzing a contemporary reformist movement in Morocco that represents an example of urban religion, Gellner has noted that such groups, having a high rate of literacy, emphasize the importance of following rules. Literacy frees people from dependence on rituals and intermediaries, but at the same time it creates a need for a new order to replace the old order that had been regulated by the intermediaries—whether priestly or divine. Literacy, Gellner observes, "makes possible insistence on rules and their elaboration and abstention from ritual excess, hence a general puritanism."[62] On this model Dharmapāla's moralism appears to be consistent with his reformist interpretation of the tradition for the emerging elite and middle classes.

Morality alone, however, did not constitute the totality of the path to the goal, although Dharmapāla clearly believed it was a central component. Meditation was also important. In many essays and articles Dharmapāla described the techniques and the psychology of meditation. He was well versed in the *Abhidhamma* psychology and understood the path of meditation. He clearly went against the tradition in encouraging lay Buddhists to practice meditation in order to realize the truth.[63] Serious meditation had not traditionally constituted an option for lay Buddhists. Since, however, on this new interpretation the path to the goal is immediate, not mediated by the monks but accessible to those who would lead a vigorous life in the *Dhamma*, meditation represented a useful practice for lay persons. While he encouraged people to meditate, he did not disparage the traditional practices of merit-making which represented the lower stages of the path. Indeed he saw merit-making to be a valuable aspect of the *karma* doctrine because people seeking merit had developed the great Buddhist civilizations of the past.[64] Of course, merit-making should be disinterested and unselfish, dedicated to the welfare of humanity.

Anagārika Dharmapāla was undoubtedly the most influential individual in the Buddhist revival in Sri Lanka. His teachings enabled Buddhists to rediscover their identity and their heritage that had been obscured during the colonial period. He popularized a reformed Buddhism that suited the rational world view taught first in the Christian and later in the Protestant Buddhist schools. This Buddhism had as its chief characteristics a lay orientation, a this-worldly asceticism, an activistic and moralistic focus, and a strong social consciousness. These and other elements of his interpretation of Buddhism turn up repeatedly in the later reformation.[65] As a corollary to the Buddhist identity Dharmapāla stressed the Sinhalese heritage. This association of Buddhism and Sinhala nationalism also became widely accepted in the later period of the revival. Dharmapāla's teachings about the Buddhist identity had wide appeal because he convinced Buddhists that this heritage provided the solution to their modern problems. Dharmapāla endorsed progress. He did not teach Buddhism apart from social reform and national regeneration. Buddhism could not be compartmentalized, for it related to all of life. Six years before his death Dharmapāla recalled, "It was as much my hope to revive industry and inspire an interest in education of a modern type as to preach Buddhism. After all, this hope was in keeping with the teachings of Gautama."[66]

Dharmapāla was more than a teacher of these values and reformed ideas, however; he was a symbol of them. His status as a symbol undoubtedly accounts for much of the effectiveness of his reforms and the influence of his ideas. He not only taught that lay Buddhists should be active and involved, he showed by his life what must be done. Although he was absent from Sri Lanka during most of the last forty years of his life, when he was traveling abroad and working with the Maha Bodhi Society in India, his work in restoring Buddhism to the land of its birth and carrying the message of the *Dhamma* to the West symbolized to the lay Buddhists in Sri Lanka the value of their tradition and their identity. Paradoxically, he was probably more successful in Sri Lanka because he was absent from the country. He became a national hero who raised the consciousness and pride of the Buddhists by proclaiming that Buddhism was superior to any import the West had to offer. Not only did he proclaim this message, but he was received and accepted by the West for doing so. One man such as Dharmapāla proclaiming the ethics of the *Dhamma* to a receptive audience of Christians at the World Parliament of Religions, or confronting the leading Hindus of India with their own forgotten heritage, was undoubtedly worth more to the success of the Buddhist revival in Sri Lanka than a hundred individuals who merely preached reform in their own temples and to their own countrymen. Dharmapāla himself carried this symbolism one step further by receiving ordination as a *bhikkhu* in the final years of his life, signaling both his total devotion to the *Dhamma* and possibly his having entered a higher stage of sanctity.

Lay Organizations and the Buddhist Revival: 1890–1940

While Dharmapāla was preaching and symbolizing the burning issues of reform, the actual work of reviving and reforming Theravada was being done by several kinds of Buddhists in Sri Lanka. Ames has distinguished two types of people concerned with revival. First there were "those who wished to restore or regain certain privileges which were threatened."[67] This group comprised especially the Kandyan monastic establishment of the Siyam Nikāya who sought to regain their power and control over the religion. The Kandyan *Sangha* resented the attempt by laymen to direct the reform movement. Ames observes that in 1904 the Siyam Nikāya issued a statement, in the context of objecting to lay control of temple lands, that said, "By the laws of the Buddha, the laity form no part of the religion."[68]

The other type of people Ames identifies were the people who were "attempting to secure privileges newly won because of the changing times."[69] This group comprised, of course, the Anglicized elite, the newly emerging laity in the low country. Bechert employs another means of distinguishing these two groups, referring to traditionalists and modernists.[70] While agreeing with both Ames and Bechert about the makeup of the revival, I suggest a third distinction. During the period when Dharmapāla was active, there seem to have been at least three groups of Buddhists interested in reasserting the religion: the Kandyan elite who sought to regain their traditional position; the militant reformists who followed Dharmapāla completely in his attempt to revive both Buddhism and nationalism; and a more moderate group that might be called neotraditionalists who, while admiring

Dharmapāla's high ideals, sought more political and less radical ways of restoring Buddhism in the modern context.

Events in Sri Lanka conspired to give this last group a dominant role during the first four decades of this century. Two events in particular had this result: the temperance movement and the 1915 riots. The temperance movement, as its name indicates, represented an early manifestation of Protestant Buddhism. The Protestant missionary bodies had introduced the temperance crusade to Sri Lanka during the late nineteenth century, and the Buddhists took up the cause during the first two decades of the twentieth. This cause fit neatly into the Buddhist revival, for intoxicants were prohibited by the Buddhist precepts. The advocates of temperance formed in 1912 the Central Total Abstinence Union with Dr. W. A. deSilva as its President.[71] In Buddhist hands, however, the temperance movement took on an additional dimension: it became a protest against the Western and Christian values that introduced alcohol to Sri Lanka as well as a protest against the British government that profited from the excise tax. A prominent Sinhalese describing this movement commented that "the political life of this country began with the Temperance Movement."[72] DeSilva has shown how many of the early political leaders in Sri Lanka got their start in the temperance movement.[73] The British authorities regarded this movement as hostile and potentially dangerous because of its mass rallies and anti-British rhetoric.

The riots of 1915 occurred when Muslims interfered with a Buddhist *perahera* in Kandy and in retaliation the Buddhists attacked Muslims in many parts of the country. The British authorities, already uneasy with the Buddhists because of the temperance agitation, severely punished them for these riots. In particular, the government jailed all of the leading Buddhist temperance leaders because they headed the most visible organizations. Fernando observed that their imprisonment after the riots "brought many Western-educated Buddhist leaders to the political limelight and helped them to emerge as national leaders."[74] Among these leaders were F. R. Senanayake, D. S. Senanayake, D. B. Jayatilaka, D. R. Wijewardene, Arthur V. Dias, and W. A. deSilva. After the riots, when these men were freed and resumed the leadership of the Buddhist movement, they avoided the militant and emotional reformism of Dharmapāla, preferring instead restraint and order. DeSilva notes, "Their approach to the religious problems of the day was in every way a contrast to Dharmapāla's and they it was who set the tone up to Jayatilaka's retirement from politics in 1943."[75]

These leaders worked for the uplift of Buddhism through a number of lay Buddhist organizations. Having their roots in the organizational inspiration that Olcott gave to the lay Buddhist revival, these laymen's groups became the chief vehicles of the revival and reform of Buddhism during this period. They represented important expressions of Protestant Buddhism. Four organizations dominated the scene. The Buddhist Theosophical Society, as noted above, was founded by Olcott in 1880. The Maha Bodhi Society followed in 1891, founded by Dharmapāla to regain the Buddhist sites in India and to revive Buddhism in Sri Lanka. Inspired by these two movements, twenty young men led by C. S. Dissanayake met at the BTS in 1898 to form the Young Men's Buddhist Association. The final organization in this group began in 1919 when the various branches of the YMBA came together to form the All Ceylon YMBA Congress, which later became the All Ceylon Buddhist Congress.[76]

All of these organizations were closely related both in their membership and in their objectives. Drawing on the same constituency of lay Buddhists, the societies' membership rolls overlapped. Their members belonged to the Anglicized elite or emerging classes. A historian of the YMBA has described it as "the first secular society for English speaking Buddhists," and he notes with pride that the YMBA in 1916 possessed the "largest collection of English Buddhist books in the Island."[77] Not surprisingly, the leadership of these organizations also overlapped considerably. A small group of men served as leaders of all of them. The same men who led the temperance movement and served as the political leaders of the Anglicized Sinhalese during the first part of this century also led the lay Buddhist organizations. Among them was D. B. Jayatilaka, who served as the first president of the YMBA in 1898 and continued in that office for forty-six years, until his death in 1944. Jayatilaka had been, with Dharmapāla, an early follower of Olcott and had worked in the BTS. When the ACBC was established, the Congress members chose Jayatilaka as their president. One of the leading politicians in the liberation movement in Sri Lanka, Jayatilaka also became the senior statesman of the Buddhist laity movement.[78]

Other lay leaders included the brothers Senanayake, with the oldest brother, F. R., being an active leader in lay organizations and his younger brothers, D. S. and D. C., following him. Dr. C. A. Hevavitharana, Dharmapāla's younger brother, provided leadership in these groups. Dr. W. A. deSilva, also an early follower of Dharmapāla, served as a president of the BTS, as general manager of the Buddhist schools operated by the BTS, as vice-president of the YMBA for thirty-four years, and as a founding member and president of the ACBC.[79]

These men, who led the lay Buddhists during much of the first half of the twentieth century, had a synoptic vision of Buddhism and its restoration. Their viewpoint was more traditional, or neotraditional, than reformist. Although they rallied to Dharmapāla's cry to revive both Buddhism and their Sinhala identity, they did not share his zeal for reforming the tradition. DeSilva observes that, as political leaders, these men "were committed to the maintenance of the liberal ideal of a secular state" with clear separation of church and state.[80] This moderate stance carried over to their approach to Buddhism. The Buddhism they sought to revive approximated traditional Theravada, with traditional roles for the laity. Unlike Dharmapāla, who had opened the supramundane path to laypersons, these men retained the traditional separation of the mundane and supramundane paths and kept laymen firmly entrenched on the mundane path.

The interpretation that these men gave to Buddhism and their approach to reestablishing it are nicely summarized in an article that D. B. Jayatilaka published in *The Buddhist* in 1901. This article, entitled significantly "Practical Buddhism," describes the layman's path in Buddhism or "the duties and virtues of the household life."[81] Jayatilaka contrasts the household life with the path of renunciation, explaining that renunciation or monasticism "is the nobler and the higher path." Renunciation alone leads to liberation. It is "the golden key" that can open "the gates of immortality." In traditional fashion Jayatilaka affirms the gradual path to enlightenment, noting that liberation cannot be gained by the efforts of one life. The householders' path represents the "preliminary course," the "real training ground" for a future life of renunciation. This "preliminary course," however, has great significance because it represents the essential preparation for a future life when one can fight "the final battle against the foes of *saṃsāra.*"[82] The president of the YMBA here relinquishes the reformist conception of a plausible *Nibbāna* and an immediate path for lay persons. "The teachings of Buddhism, therefore, have for their end the gradual development of man so that in some future life he may be fitted to enter on the higher path of Renunciation which leads to final emancipation."[83]

Thus, rather than following Olcott and Dharmapāla in advocating this-worldly asceticism for the laity, Jayatilaka explains that the householder has a threefold task: to observe the precepts, to support one's family by right livelihood, and to "do good in the world." The layman's primary duty is to follow the precepts and develop good conduct. Presumably this involves merit-making also as one strives for meritorious conduct. Jayatilaka's conception of the second duty, supporting one's extended family, reflects the ethics of the Anglicized, Protestant-influenced elite. He says supporting one's family "presupposes a life of energy and industry devoted to the acquisition of those means requisite for their due performance."[84] Finally, he interprets the notion of "doing good" to mean that one should engage in various forms of social service.

This understanding of the Buddhist tradition found expression in the various activities and programs of the lay Buddhist organizations. The YMBA, for example, sponsored traditional *baṇa* or preaching services on *poya* days, importing leading *bhikkhus* to deliver the sermons. Monks also were brought in to conduct the *Vesak* celebrations as well as *pirit* chantings and almsgivings. Through these activities, these laymen's organizations in effect reestablished the monks, who followed the path of renunciation, as mediators of the *Dhamma* for the laity. The proper role of the layman, however, also included the study of the *Dhamma*, although this ideal might seem somewhat incongruent with their dependence upon the *Sangha*. Conducting *Dhamma* examinations and operating *Dhamma* schools constituted the major project of the YMBA. In 1956, 168,000 students took these voluntary exams.[85] The exams were not held for the reformist purpose of enabling the individual Buddhist to follow the path without the aid of the monks, however; rather, they were understood to have the aim of providing "the youth of the land with the same standard of religious instruction and Buddhist education as was imparted by the *Mahā Sangha* in the temple schools in times before foreigners destroyed the great national institution."[86] The YMBA leaders longed for a time when everyone learned the *Dhamma* from the *Sangha*; but since that seemed no longer possible, they gave the *Sangha* a major role in drafting the content of the exams. The exams represented a new way of asserting the *Sangha*'s traditional supremacy in the religion.

In addition to studying the *Dhamma* and listening to the *Dhamma* sermons of the monks, the lay members of the YMBA engaged in other social and educational activities befitting a neotraditional, Anglicized elite. They held discussions and debates on points of *Dhamma*. *Abhidhamma* classes were organized from time to time to give the members "insight into the deeper realms of Buddhist philosophy."[87] Various lecturers were invited to speak to the society on topics related to Buddhism. In 1927, for example, Mahatma Gandhi, Viscount Saito of Korea, and Annie Besant of the Theosophical Society delivered lectures. The YMBA took up the publication of the English journal *The Buddhist*, originally issued by the BTS, publishing popular articles conveying their understanding of Buddhism.

The All Ceylon Buddhist Congress, having grown out of the YMBA, followed this same pattern of moderate, gentlemanly Buddhism. Malalasekera, recounting the history of the ACBC, said, "Its annual gatherings were largely social events in which members of Buddhist organizations from various parts of the country met one another." As it evolved, the ACBC assumed the role of watchdog of Buddhist interests in the country and sought to lobby the government on behalf of the Buddhists. The BTS meanwhile served as the educational wing of the revival, operating an extensive system of Buddhist schools.

Jayatilaka's third duty for the householder—doing good for the welfare of all, or social service—constituted an important aspect of the programs of the YMBA and ACBC. The laymen in these organizations,educated for the most part in Western-curriculum schools, had learned rational, humanistic ideals. Having heard the Christian missionaries criticize Buddhism for its lack of social concern, they responded by attempting to prove that social service was an integral part of Buddhism, even though this response was not entirely consistent with their desire to reestablish traditional Theravada. They argued that since compassion represented a cardinal Buddhist virtue, social service to alleviate suffering was incumbent upon all Buddhists.

They pointed to the Asokan example of the relation between the *Dhamma* and social welfare.

The social welfare projects begun by these Protestant Buddhists again mirrored the Christian missionary institutions that they opposed. The YMBA had a relief fund that aided victims of floods and other disasters. They built Buddhist shrine rooms at sanatoriums and leper asylums. Clearly one of their motives, whether conscious or subconscious, in starting social service institutions such as these was to respond to the Western criticisms of Buddhism. Another motive, however, was to establish Buddhist institutions for Buddhists because the laymen believed that the Christian orphanages and hospitals had the ultimate aim of converting the Buddhists. The Buddhist Congress established the National Council of Social Services to operate crèches, orphanages, homes for the aged, and other services. In these homes Buddhists could receive the care they required without being coerced into abandoning their own religion.

In some cases, however, these Buddhist laymen had difficulty convincing other Buddhists of the necessity of social service. They tried, for example, to reform and regulate the women who had taken up lives as *sil mātāvas*, or Buddhist nuns. The laymen and their wives felt that these nuns could be trained to engage in useful service similar to that rendered by the Catholic nuns in hospitals and homes.[89] They noted that "such work is done by Christian Sisters and it is high time women of the country work for the welfare of fellow human beings in a selfless way."[90] This noble, and decidedly Protestant Buddhist, aim, however, was not shared by the Buddhist nuns. The laity who sponsored the *aramya* that housed the nuns were frustrated to find that the nuns took no interest in social service, perferring to live lives of pure renunciation and meditation. Advocating the plausibility of the goal and the accessibility of the path, the nuns shared a reformist perspective much like Dharmapāla's. They did not share the activistic, Protestant Buddhist outlook of the lay groups.

Reform Movements Among Monks and Nuns

To complete the picture of the Buddhist resurgence during the first four or five decades of this century, we should note that the nuns represented one of several reform movements taking place within the *San-*

gha.[91] We do not intend to examine these in detail because, first, to do so would carry us too far beyond the scope of our focus on the reformation in lay Buddhism and, second, these movements have been analyzed in competent studies that deal exclusively with them. We should note these movements, however, because they interacted with the lay Buddhists, and their views and actions affected those of the laity.

Three movements for reform were particularly noteworthy in this regard: the nuns, the forest monks, and the "political *bhikkhus.*" Significantly, all three of these movements encountered opposition to a greater or lesser degree from the lay Buddhist groups. The first group was the Buddhist nuns, or *sil mātāvas.*[92] As early as the late nineteenth century, but especially in the first half of the twentieth century, women attempted to take up the *bhikkhunī* vocation. Since the ordination lineage for *bhikkhunīs* had lapsed in Sri Lanka centuries ago, there were no longer any officially ordained Buddhist nuns, although there were elderly laywomen, *upāsikās*, who lived as nuns. As Buddhists began to reawaken to their heritage, some women sought to reform these unofficial nuns and to reestablish a proper vocation for women who wished to live the religious life. One of the pioneers in this cause was Catherine deAlvis, who was from a prominent elite family. During the latter decades of the nineteenth century she went to Burma, obtained ordination, and returned to Sri Lanka as Sister Sudharmachari. Others after her made similar pilgrimages to Burma and returned to establish centers for the nuns. For the most part, the urban Buddhist laity supported these women, admiring their idealism and their desire to aid in the restoration of Theravada. At times, however, as the nuns' refusal to work in the hospitals and orphanges mentioned above indicates, the nuns' interpretation of Theravada clashed with that of these neotraditional laypersons.

A second group comprised the *bhikkhus* who sought to revive the forest monasteries and the monastic life of exclusive meditation. Carrithers has shown how this movement evolved during the first half of this century and up to the present.[93] This movement also received support from the urban laity who marveled at the piety of these monks. The forest monks' interpretation of Buddhism, however, differed substantially from that of the urban lay Buddhists. The forest monks were reformists, optimistic about the attainment of liberation in this life. Their view of Buddhism, like that of the nuns, was more in line with Dharmapāla's. Both the forest monks and the reformist nuns represented an interpretation of the tradition that was to become prominent among the urban laity only when the *Vipassanā*, or insight meditation, movement developed after Sri Lanka's independence (see chapter four).

A third group of monastic reformers were the "political *bhikkhus*" from the Vidyālankāra *piriveṇa*. Although the majority of the monks during this period probably supported the attempts by the *Sangha's* conservative hierarchy to restore the former status and role of the *Sangha*, these "political *bhikkhus*" desired to reinterpret the role of the monks. DeSilva mentions five *bhikkhus* who had pivotal importance in this movement: U. Saraṇankara (1902–1966), N. Dhammaratana (1900–1973), H. Paññāloka (1903–1953), Dr. Walpola Rahula (b. 1907), and B. Siri Sīvali (b. 1908).[94] All of these *bhikkhus* had been to India, several at the invitation of Anagārika Dharmāpala, and had there learned about nationalism and Marxism. On their return to Sri Lanka, they began to write and debate publicly about the merits of *bhikkhus* becoming involved in politics.[95] This position brought them into direct conflict with the moderate, urban lay Buddhist leadership that sought to restore a more traditional Theravada. As deSilva explains, "At issue was the role of the *bhikkhu*. Was he to renounce the world, or to seek to reform it?"[96] The Protestant Buddhist laity felt that *bhikkhus* should renounce the world, leaving politics to the laity. These *bhikkhus*, however, sought to become reformers instead of renouncers.

The specific issue that brought the Vidyālankāra *bhikkhus* to prominence was an education reform proposal debated by the State Council in 1945. This "free education" proposal would have increased the government's, and thereby the Buddhists', control over the schools while decreasing that of the denominational bodies. What is significant for our topic is the confrontation that ensued between these reformist *bhikkhus* and the orthodox Buddhist laity and *Sangha*.

The Vidyālankāra *bhikkhus* clearly understood the need for reform of the tradition. In 1946 they issued a document entitled *"Bhikkhus* and Politics: Declaration of the Vidyālankāra Pirivena." In it they said: "It has to be admitted that the political, economic, and social conditions of today are different from those of the time of the Buddha, and that consequently the life of *bhikkhus* today is also different from that of the *bhikkhus* at that time."[97] The *bhikkhus* also noted that although the *Vinaya* rules had not changed, the entire context of the life of the monk had. They concluded from these premises that if *bhikkhus* today are to fulfill their traditional goal of protecting Buddhism, they must be allowed to employ different means. Especially the *bhikkhus* must be permitted to advocate political causes that pertain to the protection of Buddhism. They declared, "It is nothing but fitting for *bhikkhus* to identify themselves with activities conducive to the welfare of our people."[98]

To support their new interpretation of the *bhikkhu's* vocation, some monks wrote lengthier treatises. Perhaps the most influential work was Dr. Walpola Rahula's historic *Bhikṣuvagē Urumaya,* later translated as *The Heritage of the Bhikkhu.*[99] In it he traced the history of the *Sangha* and the fortunes of Buddhism from its origins through the colonial period. His basic thesis was that although both Buddhism and the life of the *bhikkhus* had evolved, "from the beginning to the end of the history of the Sinhala nation, *bhikkhus* were the custodians of its freedom, culture and civilization, literature, arts and crafts."[100] The *bhikkhus* had historically rendered selfless service and must do so in the present "in consonance with the needs of the modern world."[101]

The urban lay Buddhists, however, opposed these *bhikkhus'* involvement in political issues. The lay board of trustees of Vidyālankāra *piriveṇa,* including D. S. Senanayake, sought to use financial pressure to prevent such involvement. The *bhikkhus,* however, refusing to back down, prevailed and the Free Education Bill was passed. Their courage bolstered by this success, these *bhikkhus* went on to issue another declaration in 1947, "The Kelaniya Declaration of Independence," which called for the freedom of Sri Lanka from British rule. With the emergence of the Vidyālankāra group, *bhikkhus* became an important force in the politics of the country in the decade before and after independence. DeSilva notes, however, that their approach also divided the Buddhists, for these *bhikkhus* "gave every impression of being the nucleus of an 'alternative' religious elite, and for that reason were regarded as a potential threat to the orthodox Buddhist establishment."[102]

Notes

1. K. Malalgoda, *Buddhism in Sinhalese Society 1750–1900: A Study of Religious Revival and Change* (Berkeley: University of California Press, 1976), 256. In this book

The Early Revival and Protestant Buddhism

Malalgoda examines another important aspect of the Buddhist revival: the reformation in the *Sangha* and the reestablishment of higher ordination.

2. Gananath Obeyesekere, "Religious Symbolism and Political Change in Ceylon," in *The Two Wheels of Dhamma: Essays on the Theravada Tradition in India and Ceylon*, ed. Bardwell L. Smith (Chambersburg, PA: American Academy of Religion, 1972), 62.

3. Malalgoda, *Buddhism in Sinhalese Society*, 58ff. Kotagama Vācissara, *Vālivita Saraṇaṃkara and The Revival of Buddhism in Ceylon*, PhD diss., University of London, 1961, 269ff. See also Heinz Bechert, *Buddhismus, Staat und Gesellschaft in den Ländern des Theravāda-Buddhismus* (Berlin: Alfred Metzner Verlag, 1966), 1: 44, and Bechert, "Theravada Buddhist Sangha: Some General Observations on Historical and Political Factors in Its Development," *Journal of the Association of Asian Studies*, Aug. 1970: 767f.

4. Malalgoda, *Buddhism in Sinhalese Society*, 166, 263, shows that the Amarapura Nikāya began in 1803 and the Ramañña Nikāya in 1864, and various other fraternities of all three Nikāyas sprang up throughout the period, all espousing reformist platforms.

5. Michael Ames, "Ideological and Social Change in Ceylon," *Human Organization* 22 (1963): 50.

6. Malalgoda, *Buddhism in Sinhalese Society*, 188. See also G. C. Mendis, *Ceylon Today and Yesterday: Main Currents of Ceylon History* (Colombo: Associated Newspapers, 1963), 162-63, who gives the dates as 1872 and 1876, respectively.

7. Malalgoda, *Büddhism in Sinhalese Society*, 226.

8. Anonymous, *The Theosophical Movement 1875–1925: A History and A Survey* (New York: Dutton, 1925), 16.

9. Carl T. Jackson, *The Oriental Religions and American Thought* (Westport, CT: Greenwood Press, 1981), 163.

10. Malalgoda, *Buddhism in Sinhalese Society*, Ch. 6.

11. Malalgoda, *Buddhism in Sinhalese Society*, 237f.

12. K. M. deSilva, *A History of Sri Lanka* (Berkeley: University of California, 1981), 341.

13. Henry Steel Olcott, *Old Diary Leaves* (Madras: Theosophical Publishing House, 1931), 4: 120.

14. Michael Ames, "Westernization or Modernization: The Case of Sinhalese Buddhism," *Social Compass* 20 (1973): 159.

15. Mendis, *Ceylon Today*, 164.

16. Jackson, *The Oriental Religions*, 163.

17. Henry Steel Olcott, *The Buddhist Catechism* (Madras: Theosophical Publishing House, 1970), 3–4.

18. *Buddhist Catechism*, 81.

19. *Buddhist Catechism*, 64–65-n.1.

20. *Buddhist Catechism*, 35.

21. *Buddhist Catechism*, 43.

22. *Buddhist Catechism*, 54.

23. *Buddhist Catechism*, 45.

24. *Buddhist Catechism*, 61.

25. *Buddhist Catechism*, 55f.

26. *Buddhist Catechism*, 59.
27. Gananath Obeyesekere, "Personal Identity and Cultural Crisis: The Case of Anagārika Dharmapāla of Sri Lanka," in *The Biographical Process: Studies in the History and Psychology of Religion*, ed. Frank E. Reynolds and Donald Capps (The Hague: Mouton, 1976), 221–52. Also see Obeyesekere, "Religious Symbolism and Political Change," 58–78; Bhikkhu Sangharakshita, *Anagārika Dharmapāla: Biographical Sketch* (Kandy: Buddhist Publication Society, 1964); Ananda Guruge, ed., *Return to Righteousness: A Collection of Speeches, Essays and Letters of Anagārika Dharmapāla* (Colombo: The Government Press, 1965); Guruge's introduction to this volume gives biographical details; B. G. Gokhale, "Anagārika Dharmapāla: Toward Modernity Through Tradition in Ceylon," in *Tradition and Change in Theravada Buddhism*, ed. Bardwell L. Smith (Leiden: Brill, 1973), 30–39.
28. Guruge, *Return to Righteousness*, 702.
29. Obeyesekere, "Personal Identity and Cultural Crisis," 235.
30. Guruge, *Return to Righteousness*, 702.
31. Guruge, *Return to Righteousness*, 717.
32. Obeyesekere, "Personal Identity and Cultural Crisis," 244.
33. Guruge, *Return to Righteousness*, 494.
34. Guruge, *Return to Righteousness*, 508.
35. Guruge, *Return to Righteousness*, 639.
36. Guruge, *Return to Righteousness*, 501.
37. Guruge, *Return to Righteousness*, 510.
38. Sangharakshita, *Anagārika Dharmapāla*, 80.
39. Guruge, *Return to Righteousness*, 502.
40. Guruge, *Return to Righteousness*, 489.
41. Obeyesekere, "Religious Symbolism and Political Change," 69f.
42. Guruge, *Return to Righteousness*, 519–20.
43. Guruge, *Return to Righteousness*, 748.
44. Guruge, *Return to Righteousness*, 638.
45. Guruge, *Return to Righteousness*, 194.
46. Guruge, *Return to Righteousness*, 669, 637.
47. Guruge, *Return to Righteousness*, 395.
48. Guruge, *Return to Righteousness*, 287.
49. Guruge, *Return to Righteousness*, 392.
50. Guruge, *Return to Righteousness*, 53.
51. Guruge, *Return to Righteousness*, 54.
52. Obeyesekere, "Personal Identity and Cultural Crisis," 246.
53. Guruge, *Return to Righteousness*, 69.
54. Guruge, *Return to Righteousness*, 669.
55. Guruge, *Return to Righteousness*, 337.
56. Guruge, *Return to Righteousness*, 694.
57. Guruge, *Return to Righteousness*, 737.
58. For a summary of the "Daily Code for Laity," see Obeyesekere, "Personal Identity and Cultural Crisis," 247f.
59. Guruge, *Return to Righteousness*, 337.

60. See Mary Douglas, *Purity and Danger: An Analysis of the Concepts of Pollution and Taboo* (London: Routledge and Kegan Paul, 1966), 7ff.
61. Reinhard Bendix, *Max Weber: An Intellectual Portrait* (Berkeley: University of California Press, 1977) 296f.
62. Ernest Gellner, *Saints of the Atlas*, 7ff.
63. Guruge, *Return to Righteousness*, 281.
64. Guruge, *Return to Righteousness*, 69.
65. Obeyesekere, "Personal Identity and Cultural Crisis," 249, has shown that the people most influenced by Dharmapāla were the "not yet emerged" village elite.
66. Guruge, *Return to Righteousness*, 694.
67. Ames, "Ideological and Social Change," 47.
68. Cited in Ames, "Ideological and Social Change," 47. Also cited in Heinz Bechert, *Buddhismus, Staat and Gesellschaftin den Ländern des Theravāda-Buddhismus*, Band 1 (Berlin: Alfred Metzner Verlag, 1966), p. 67.
69. Ames, "Ideological and Social Change," 48.
70. Heinz Bechert, "*Sangha*, State, Society, 'Nation': Persistence of Traditions in 'Post-Traditional' Buddhist Societies," *Daedalus* 102, 1 (W, 1973): 89f.
71. S. Gunawardene, "Dr. W. A. deSilva: Pioneer Agriculturist, Patriot and Philanthropist," *The Buddhist* 52 (Oct. 1981): 11.
72. Gunawardene, "Dr. deSilva," 11.
73. deSilva, *History of Sri Lanka*, 375.
74. Tissa Fernando, "The Western Educated Elite and Buddhism in British Ceylon," in *Tradition and Change in Theravada Buddhism*, 26.
75. K. M. deSilva, "Buddhism, Nationalism and Politics in Modern Sri Lanka," paper presented at the South Asia Conference, University of Wisconsin, Nov. 1985.
76. Rachaka, "A Short History of the Y.M.B.A. 1898–1958," *The Buddhist* 29 (May 1958): 45.
77. "Short History of the Y.M.B.A.," 43f.
78. deSilva, *History of Sri Lanka*, 430f.
79. Gunawardene, "Dr. deSilva," 11.
80. deSilva, "Buddhism, Nationalism and Politics," 14.
81. D. B. Jayatilaka, "Practical Buddhism," *The Buddhist* 51, 9 (Jan. 1981): 2-17 (repr. from July 1901).
82. Jayatilaka, "Practical Buddhism," 3.
83. Jayatilaka, "Practical Buddhism," 3.
84. Jayatilaka, "Practical Buddhism," 3.
85. "Short History of the Y.M.B.A.," 46.
86. *The Buddhist* 37 (June 1966): 7; cited in Donald K. Swearer, "Lay Buddhism and the Buddhist Revival in Ceylon," *Journal of the American Academy of Religion* 38 (1970): 267.
87. "Short History of the Y.M.B.A.," 50.
88. G. P. Malalasekera, "Fifty Years of Service," *Golden Jubilee Souvenir* (All Ceylon Buddhist Congress, 1969), 20.
89. I am endebted to Professor Lowell W. Bloss for this example. He has presented a part of his extensive studies of the "nuns" in, "Female Renunciants of Sri Lanka:

the *dasasilmattawa,"* *Journal of the International Association of Buddhist Studies* 10.1 (1987): 7-32. Bloss lists the following people as lay supporters of these nuns: D. B. Jayatilaka (trustee), D. D. Wijewardena (patron), A. M. deSilva (president), Mrs. W. A. deSilva, D. L. Wijewardena, Mrs. A. E. deSilva, Mrs. E. Sirimanne, Mrs. W. S. F. Wijegooneratne (vice-president), and Mrs. S. Samarakkodi and Mrs. J. R. Jayawardena (secretaries).

90. Ceylon *Daily News,* Oct. 26, 1936.

91. The term *Sangha* is used loosely here, since the *sil mātāvas* were not actually members of the *Sangha;* they lacked official ordination. They were, however, not ordinary laywomen either in their own opinion or in that of the laity. Thus, it seems proper to include them in this section.

92. Studies of this movement have been written by Bloss (above), Mrs. Kusuma Devendra (Ph.D. Thesis in preparation, University of Sri Jayawardenapura), Nirmala Salgado and C. Thamelo. See below, chapter five, note 22.

93. Michael Carrithers, *The Forest Monks of Sri Lanka: An Anthropological and Historical Study* (Delhi: Oxford University Press, 1983).

94. deSilva, "Buddhism, Nationalism and Politics," 20.

95. See Heinz Bechert, "Theravada Buddhist Sangha: Some General Observations on Historical and Political Factors in its Development," *Journal of the Association of Asian Studies* 29 (A 1970): 775. See also his *Buddhismus, Staat und Gesellschaft,* 1:310ff.

96. deSilva, "Buddhism, Nationalism and Politics," 21.

97. Walpola Rahula, *The Heritage of the Bhikkhu,* trans. K. P. G. Wijayasurendra (New York: Grove Press, 1974), 131.

98. Rahula, *Heritage of the Bhikkhu,* 132.

99. Another influential treatise from this period was a statement arguing that the *Sangha* had the "dual responsibility" of acting as religious and social guides for the nation. Written by Pahamune Sri Sumaṇgala, Mahānāyaka of the Malvatta Fraternity, this statement was published as the foreword to D. C. Vijayavardhana, *The Revolt in the Temple* (Colombo: Sinha Publications, 1953), 11–20.

100. Rahula, *Heritage of the Bhikkhu,* 65.

101. Rahula, *Heritage of the Bhikkhu,* 97.

102. deSilva, "Buddhism, Nationalism and Politics," 28f.

3

The Buddha Jayanti and the Post-Jayanti Period

The Buddha Jayanti, the 2,500th anniversary of the Lord Buddha's entry into *Parinibbāna* or final *Nibbāna* celebrated by Theravada Buddhists in 1956, had significance because the Buddha is believed to have prophesied that his *sāsana* or *Dhamma* would endure for five thousand years, and at the mid-point of that period would undergo a great renewal and resurgence.[1] Since the *Mahāvaṃsa* relates that Vijaya, the legendary patriarch of the Sinhalese, landed in Sri Lanka just as the Buddha achieved *Parinibbāna*, and that the Buddha further prophesied that Vijaya's descendants would preserve the *Dhamma*,[2] the Jayanti marked the anniversary not only of the Buddha but also of the Sinhalese association with and preservation of Buddhism. In the words of one Buddhist writer at the time, "In 1956 will occur the unique three-fold event—the completion of 2500 years of Buddhism, of the life of the Sinhalese race, and of Ceylon's history."[3] This historic event, celebrated on the full-moon day of the month of Vesak (May), 1956, brought together the religious and nationalist sentiments of the Sinhalese Buddhists. As Smith observed, "The land, the race and the faith were intimately associated in the national mystique which the Jayanti helped to elaborate."[4]

This period can be seen as the flowering of the Buddhist revival and particularly as the highpoint of Protestant Buddhism. Coming some eight years after Ceylon had received its independence, it was a time of enormous optimism. The watchword of the Jayanti was, "Let us restore Buddhism to its rightful place." Buddhists believed that doing so would (1) restore their heritage and identity, long eclipsed by colonialism, and (2) resolve the country's problems and ensure a bright future for the new nation. To accomplish these aims the Buddhist organizations and the government put forward many proposals and programs representing the fruition of decades of attempts to revive and restore Theravada Buddhism. This chapter focuses on those proposals and programs attempting to show both how they arose and what their outcome was. Although Protestant Buddhism comprised both reformist and traditionalist or neotraditionalist elements, the drift during the Jayanti period was toward a traditionalist or neotraditionalist understanding of Theravada. The Buddhism they sought to "restore to its rightful place," as reflected in the proposals and programs, was "original Buddhism." The Jayanti in many ways sought to solve the problems of the present by reestablishing the Buddhism of Sri Lanka's glorious past.

Preparations and Expectations for the Jayanti

The initial optimism surrounding the Jayanti began to build long before the actual date arrived. When Sri Lanka attained its independence in November, 1947, the Buddhists had already begun to believe that a renaissance of Buddhism was under way. Attaining freedom after four hundred and fifty years of foreign rule inspired a natural euphoria in the country. During this time success seemed to follow success for the Buddhists. The Sinhalese Buddhists also caught the enthusiasm emanating from India and Burma for the Jayanti. In 1954 the Burmese Theravadins convened the Sixth Council, reviving the ancient tradition of historic councils that rehearsed the *Dhamma* and renewed the religion. Buddhist leaders from all of Asia, including Sri Lanka, were invited to participate in this historic council. Prior to this event, in 1947, the British government had agreed to send back to India the relics of the Buddhist patriarchs Moggallāna and Sāriputta, which had been discovered during archaeological excavations in India.[5] These relics were exhibited in Sri Lanka en route to India and evoked deep religious feelings among the Sinhalese Buddhists. In the same year the All Ceylon Buddhist Congress resolved to invite representatives from all Buddhist countries to meet for a conference. That conference, which finally met in 1950, founded the World Fellowship of Buddhists to unite Buddhists everywhere "to work for the *Dhamma* and for peace."[6]

Against the backdrop of all these propitious signs the Jayanti symbolized to the Sinhalese Buddhists the inauguration of an even greater renaissance for the nation and the religion. The belief that this 2,500th anniversary of the religion would signal the waxing of the *Dhamma*, however, represented a new interpretation of the Buddha's actual prediction according to the texts and commentaries. The texts record that the Buddha predicted that the *Dhamma* would last for only five hundred years after the order of *bhikkhunis* had been established.[7] Since this figure had been exceeded when the commentators wrote, they extended the life span of the *Dhamma* to five thousand years, but noted that the *Dhamma* would undergo a gradual diminution or decline until it finally disappeared at the end of the period.[8]

The transformation of this pessimistic prophecy into an optimistic one could represent either another version of this tradition or possibly another manifestation of Protestant Buddhism and its world-affirming outlook. The beliefs expressed by Buddhists about the Jayanti and its marvelous portents bear a striking similarity to the Christian predictions about the dawning of the kingdom of God. Although the Buddhists would not have consciously and explicitly imitated the beliefs about the kingdom, since Christianity had been a major factor in both the educational and cultural contexts of the elite class that espoused the Protestant Buddhist interpretation, these Buddhists could have unconsciously echoed these eschatological conceptions.

Another possible source for this optimism was posited by a prominent Buddhist at that time who explained the Jayanti in terms of an indigenous Sinhala millennial myth. He pointed out that a "tradition that is current amongst the Sinhalese is that, when Buddhism shall have completed 2500 years, a prince named Diyasena will establish a Buddhist Kingdom in Ceylon. Then, it is said, the faith will shine forth in glory and be a beacon to the whole world, and Lanka itself will be prosperous and joyous."[9]

Whatever their source, millennial expectations characterized the Buddhists' interpretations of the Jayanti anniversary. One Buddhist wrote, "The belief had been long cherished that the Jayanti . . . would herald the dawn of a new era with an unparalleled revival of Buddhist activities all over the world."[10] The report of the Buddhist Committee of Enquiry referred to the momentous significance of Sri Lanka's having been included in "the Buddha's Kingdom of Righteousness."[11] A poem in the Jayanti special issue of *The Buddhist* expressed the Buddhists' desire at that time for renewing this kingdom. It described Sri Lanka as a "thrice Blessed Isle" where "the Master's presence hallowed thy soil" and "Buddhism in pristine purity shines." There, "Buddha Jayanti heralds a new dawn, Plenty and prosperity bloom like a lily in morn."[12]

Essential to the Jayanti outlook was this belief that peace and prosperity would reign in Sri Lanka. Because of it the Buddhists generated the programs we shall consider below as ways of unleashing this reign of plenty. Another important aspect of the myth, however, declared that the *Dhamma* would shine not only in Sri Lanka but also on the rest of the world. One Buddhist explained that the tradition taught that from the Jayanti year "the *Dhamma* would flourish and spread far and wide."[13] As in the time of Asoka, the *Dhamma* would be followed in all corners of the earth. Professor Malalasekera wrote in his introduction to the Jayanti edition of *The Buddhist*, "Now, more than ever before, the world needs the message of the Buddha, his teaching of tolerance and tranquility."[14] Malalasekera also predicted that after the Jayanti, "Buddhism will rise to great heights again and blossom forth once more in Sri Lanka. From there it will spread over the world."[15]

After being made to believe during the colonial period that truth and value emanated only from the West, these ascending Buddhists now felt they had a great treasure to share with the rest of the world. So, in a move that they compared to Asoka, but which might also be seen as another echo of Protestantism, the Buddhists began sending missionaries or *dhammadūtas*, messengers of the *Dhamma*, to other countries. This zeal for sending missionaries became an important part of the Jayanti and its aftereffects. A *Mahāthera* proclaimed, "It is but our duty and birthright to see this unique teaching imbibed by all humanity."[16]

To carry out this duty the All Ceylon Buddhist Congress and the World Fellowship of Buddhists set up a Dhammadūta Activities Committee, which coordinated the sending of monks to other lands. The apparent success of these missionaries substantiated the Buddhists' belief that the time was approaching when the *Dhamma* would prevail everywhere. Buddhists pointed to the growing popularity of Buddhism in the West. Dharmapāla had, of course, been the first *dhammadūita*, and the Buddhists were proud that he had introduced the teachings to India, Europe, and America. "In recent times," one writer commented, "a great deal of interest in Buddhism has been awakened both in Europe and in America."[17] This awakening was seen as further verification of the Jayanti prophecies. As another Buddhist said,

> The history of Buddhism in Ceylon from the closing years of the last century has clear indications that the prophecy, as far as Ceylon is concerned, is coming true. In other parts of the world too it is seen that more and more people who were not Buddhists by birth are becoming interested in Buddhism.[18]

The Jayanti Programs and the Buddhist Committee of Enquiry Report

In a country where the majority of the people were Buddhists (approximately 70 percent), the newly independent government could not ignore the Jayanti and the hopes it inspired among the people. In 1953 the All Ceylon Buddhist Congress urged the government to celebrate the Jayanti as a national festival on the model of the recent Festival of Britain. Malalasekera said, "The event should, therefore, be of significance not only to Buddhists but to all peoples inhabiting this Island."[19] Although the ruling United National Party had always advocated the separation of state and religion, it bowed to the demands of the Buddhists to support the celebration of the Jayanti. The government set up in 1954 the Lanka Bauddha Mandalaya, the Buddhist Council of Ceylon, which outlined a series of celebrations and projects to commemorate the event.[20] The Council sponsored a *sangāyanā*, a council of the monks to recite the Pali *Tipiṭaka*, the scriptures of Theravada Buddhism. This council convened at the end of the Jayanti year, in May, 1957, at Vidyālaṅkāra Piriveṇa. Among other projects of the Lanka Bauddha Mandalaya were the translation of the *Tipiṭaka* into Sinhala, the writing of a Buddhist Encyclopedia as well as a Sinhalese Encyclopedia, and restorations of important Buddhist shrines, such as the Daḷadā Māligāva, the Temple of the Tooth.

The Buddhist Revival in Sri Lanka

The two major long-term projects of this group, the *Tipiṭaka* translation and the Buddhist Encyclopedia, signified important aspects of what can be called Jayanti Buddhism. The *Tipiṭaka* translation, being the first project intiated, symbolized both the importance that the Canon had always had in Theravada and the scripturalism of the Protestant Buddhists. These laymen acknowledged the traditional place of the *Sangha* by entrusting this translation to an editorial board of twenty monks and two lay scholars. The traditionalism of the project was somewhat qualified, however, because the scriptures were being translated into Sinhala in order to make the *Dhamma* available to those Buddhists, especially the laity, who did not read the Pali language of the texts. Thus the project clearly had a Protestant or reformist purpose. The encyclopedia project, on the other hand, was headed by G. P. Malalasekera and was largely a lay rather than a monastic project. Malalasekera, a leading scholar who had already produced an important Buddhist dictionary,[21] saw the encyclopedia as an academic contribution to the world's understanding of Buddhism. He called it "a special contribution Ceylon could make to cultural studies in the world and . . . a permanent memorial to the Buddha Jayanti."[22] This project recalled the great scholarly achievements of Buddhism. Significantly, since laymen were producing it, it was to be issued in English rather than Sinhala, the explicit reason being to make it accessible to the world.

The most important document of the Jayanti period for an understanding of the Buddhist revival was the report of the Buddhist Committee of the Enquiry issued in February of 1956. Sponsored by the All Ceylon Buddhist Congress, this report both documented and expressed the sentiments of the Buddhists about the need to "restore Buddhism to its rightful place." The English version of the report was entitled *The Betrayal of Buddhism*, denoting its charge that the British government had failed to protect the Buddhist religion as it had promised in the Kandyan Convention of 1815. Smith explains that the ACBC, as early as 1951, had petitioned the government to establish a commission "to enquire into the state of Buddhism."[23] When the government refused to do so on grounds of separation of politics and religion, the ACBC itself set up this committee at its annual meeting in 1953.

G. P. Malalasekera, the president of the Buddhist Congress, was the chief architect of both the committee and the report. Serving as head of the ACBC for over twenty years, he was the leading figure of the lay Buddhist revival during the period from 1939 to 1973. He served as president of the ACBC for two terms, first from 1939 to 1957, when he entered the diplomatic service of his country as the first ambassador of Ceylon to the Soviet Union, and again on his return, from 1967 to 1973. Scholar, politician, and devout Buddhist, Malalasekera embodied the spirit of lay Buddhism at the time of the Jayanti. Although he was a member of the English-educated elite, with a PhD from the School of Oriental and African Studies of the University of London, he had close ties to traditional village culture and religion. His father had been an *āyurvedic* physician in a village near Pānadurā. Having become one of the leading Buddhist scholars in the country and dean of the Faculty of Oriental Studies at the Universtiy of Ceylon, Malalasekera gave the lay Buddhist movement credibility in the eyes of laymen and monks alike.[24]

Malalgoda has written of this period, "With independence, due to a new convergence of interests, traditionalist Buddhism became much stronger."[25] Dr. Malalasekera combined in one person both this traditionalism and the reformist legacy of Protestant Buddhism from the time of Dharmapala. His conservatism had brought him to prominence in the 1940s when he had spoken for orthodoxy and against the "political *bhikkhus*." He believed that the Buddha's *Dhamma* constituted timeless truth which needed no change or reinterpretation to apply to the present. "Whether man travels to the moon or to other planets, whether life is found to exist elsewhere than on earth . . . none of these things can affect the validity of the eternal verities of the Buddha's teachings. Their efficacy can meet any challenge."[26] He also believed, however, that Buddhists should be involved in the world: "There are many social problems crying for reform in this country and the Buddhists, who form the majority of the population, must pay heed to them."[27]

Looking ahead to the Jayanti anniversary, Malalasekera called on the Buddhist Congress to set up the Committee of Enquiry "to investigate and report on the present state of Buddhism in Lanka." He already, however, had a pretty clear idea of what the state of Buddhism was and what was needed to revive the religion. His Presidential Address to the ACBC in 1953 dealt with almost all of the main points that were eventually covered in the report.

Having received the approval of the Buddhist Congress, Malalasekera established a committee comprising seven high-ranking *bhikkhus* and seven important laymen with himself as the chairman.[28] The Malvatta and Asgiriya chapters of the Siyam Nikāya were represented by the *anunāyaka,* or deputy supreme chief monk, of Malvatta, and by a senior *bhikkhu* who later became the *anunāyaka* of Asgiriya. The Mahānāyakas of the two chapters refused to give the inquiry their full support, however,.[29] Other important *bhikkhus* on the committee included Venerable Balangoḍa Ānanda Maitreya, who was then the principal of a *piriveṇa* and later a *mahāñāyaka* of the Amarapura Nikāya, and Venerable Maḍihē Paññāsīha, who also became a *mahānāyaka* of the Amarapura Nikāya. The lay members in addition to Malalasekera were leaders in education and in politics. From June, 1954, until May, 1955, this group held hearings in all parts of the country to gather evidence about the current condition of Buddhism.

Before an assembly of over three thousand *bhikkhus* and many more Buddist laymen at Ānanda College, the leading Buddhist educational institution, the committee, which came to be known as the Buddhist Commission, presented its findings in February of 1956, just a few months ahead of both the Jayanti and, as it turned out, new governmental elections. The substance of the report, somewhat like the views of the lay Buddhists at that time, including Malalasekera, reflected a dual orientation: it was reformist in means and methodology but traditionalist in ends and goals. A number of writers have pointed to the report's revolutionary modernist assumptions. Mendis noted that the authors of the report did not follow the traditional Buddhist doctrines "emphasizing the vanity of life and suggesting a withdrawal from the world."[30] Instead, the authors affirmed this world and assumed that action in the world was necessary to improve the condition of Buddhism and the life of the Buddhists. As D. E. Smith wrote, the traditional ideals of renunciation and liberation were "replaced by the conviction that the political, economic and social system of modern Ceylon must be transformed."[31] Wriggins remarked that these Buddhists "assumed that progress could be achieved in the religious and social world through legislative, financial and institutional reforms."[32] In these active and achievement-oriented views, the report reflected "the modern outlook of the English-educated Buddhist laymen who wrote it."[33]

These modernist approaches, however, represented only half of the picture, for they were qualified by strong traditionalist aims. The prevailing intention of the report was traditionalist: "to restore Buddhism to its pristine purity." According to the report, the reason that Buddhism had declined and now required restoring was that "the leaders of our country have forsaken those Buddhist ideals which for centuries were the keystone of the country's greatness and have embraced a shallow and ephemeral materialism."[34] The report blamed colonialism and Christianity for subverting Buddhism and introducing these false ideals, and it looked to the *Dhamma* for solutions to the current problems. "The real and final remedy is the displacement of Western materialistic social and individual values and the establishment of genuine values founded on the Buddha Dhamma."[35]

Like the lay Buddhist organizations, the report held a traditional view of the roles of monks and laymen. In contrast to the universalism and egalitarianism of earlier and later reformers, the report sought to return both the *Sangha* and the laity to their quite distinct and unequal roles. The authors of the report reinstated the *bhikkhus* as the mediators of the *Dhamma* to the laity, and lamented the loss, during the colonial period and after, of "the wholesome influence of the Buddhist monks."[36] By appointing monks to half the places on the committee, these laymen indicated their deference to the orthodox *Sangha*. The laymen wanted to see the monks regain their traditional status and life style. Although this attitude represented, on one hand, a desire to liberate the *Sangha* from oppression and decline, it represented, on the other, a tendency toward a conservative outlook, reluctant to acknowledge the need or right of the *Sangha* to evolve with the times. This view had been the crux of the dispute with the political *bhikkhus*. If the laymen were unwilling to allow the reinterpretation of the monastic role, however, they were equally unwilling to revise their own role. Throughout the report, the layman's role is depicted as the traditional life of the householder on the mundane path. We find here none of the reformism and spiritual optimism for laymen that we found in Dharmapāla and that we shall find again in the insight meditation movement. The report does not convey the idea that *Nibbāna* can be attained here and now by lay persons. It implies the traditional separation of the mundane and supramundane paths.

Swearer recognized that the report reflects a definite moralistic and traditionalistic tendency. "The moralism stems from a critical stance toward the 'materialistic' values of Western society; and the traditionalism is based on an idealization of a Buddhist heritage eclipsed by a long history of colonial domination."[37] To describe the report's combination of modernism and traditionalism we might employ Bellah's category, neotraditionalism. He describes this position as the idea "that one could maintain the traditional orientations as basic but utilize modern technology as auxiliary." This position is attractive because it "taps emotional depths in the masses through its direct use of traditional symbolism" and also because it asserts "the superiority of the indigenous tradition to any other and particularly to Western culture."[38] The Buddhists sought to use modern institutional methods to restore the traditional Theravada ideals. Ames explained the Sinhalese Buddhists' synthesis of traditionalism and modernism as the attempt by the Buddhists to find a compromise between "their recent experience with colonial rule . . . and their ancient heritage."[39] They sought ways to respond to modernity without surrendering their identity to Westernization. That the Buddhists were attempting to balance traditional truth with modern responsiveness becomes apparent in the recommendations of the report.

After a long introduction detailing the history of Buddhism in Sri Lanka up through the colonial period, showing how the Sinhalese had lost "the two things which they most valued, their religion and their distinct nationality," the report presented its findings and recommendations for reform in eight areas.[40] The bulk of the report, however, dealt with four topics: religion and state; education; social conditions; and the *Sangha*. The first chapter, "Religion and State in Ceylon," establishes the basic premise of the report that the *Sangha*, the Buddhist temples, and Buddhism generally had suffered under the British, who showed great favoritism toward Christianity. Indeed, in the view of the Buddhist authors of the report little had changed with independence. "Political Christianity still flourishes as free as ever before while the chains of Colonialism still tie down the Buddhists in Independent Ceylon."[41] Wriggins discerned that "the principal problem as seen by the commissioners was the position of Buddhist institutions in comparison with Christian bodies."[42] Being better organized and having had foreign support, the Christian institutions had an advantage over the Buddhists that should not be allowed to continue, since the Buddhists represented the majority group in the country. The report in many ways identified the Buddhists as a disadvantaged majority and called on the government to restore both Buddhism and Buddhists to their "rightful place" in Lanka. In his Presidential Address in 1953 Malalasekera had raised this issue: "Now with Sri Lanka once more free, the Buddhists, who form more than two-thirds of her permanent population, demand that the elected government of the people shall give its active support and assistance in the rehabilitation of their religion."[43]

Four important recommendations for reforms in Buddhism arose from this section of the report. (1) The committee argued that the government should cease aiding Christianity in various ways and begin to compensate Buddhism for the years of neglect. (2) A Buddha Sāsana Council should be set up to exercise "all the prerogatives of the [ancient] Buddhist kings as regards the Buddhist religion."[44] This was, perhaps, the most revolutionary recommendation of the report, for it called for a new way of conceiving the relations between the *Sangha* and the laity. Donald Smith saw this Sāsana Council as "the creation of a coherent organization which would link together the *Sangha* and laity in an organic relationship."[45] Not only would it give the Buddhists unity in confronting a well-organized Christianity, but it would also provide a structure for regulating and settling disputes within the diverse *Sangha*. (3) A Ministry for Religious Affairs was to be established to "rehabilitate the religions which have suffered under colonial rule." This ministry would help enact the previous two recommendations. (4) Finally, the report urged that the seat of government be moved from Colombo, which was a reminder of the colonial oppression, to a new and truly Sinhalese site. The committee declined to make what was to become one of the most hotly debated proposals: that Buddhism be made the state religion of Sri Lanka. The committee, endorsing the government's policy of separation of state and religion, reasoned that Buddhism should not be the state religion in a country with many religious traditions.[46]

In the committee's opinion, the second topic of the report—education—represented the principal area in which the Buddhists had been disadvantaged. Malalasekera had singled out education as a significant problem when he addressed the ACBC in 1953. He recalled that the colonial powers had utilized Christian education to subvert both Sinhalese nationalism and Buddhism. Not only was that the situation in the past, but it continued in the present: "No one, who has regard for the truth, can deny that the chief purpose of Missionary Education was then, as it is now, the spread of Christianity."[47] Donald Smith contends that the earlier religious motives behind denominational schools no longer applied in 1956 as they had around 1900. He correctly perceives that the report's impact in this area came from the emotional charge "that a great historic injustice had been perpetrated over a century and a half."[48]

The new Sinhalese elite class placed a very high premium on education for their children. The educational system in Sri Lanka in 1956 had two streams, English medium schools and vernacular (Sinhala or Tamil medium) schools. There was a system of state-managed schools and a system of privately managed but state-assisted schools. The Christian denominations controlled only 35 percent of the private, assisted schools, but they controlled 70 percent of the English medium schools in the country.[49] More to the point, the report showed that the Christians controlled thirty-five of the prestigious colleges or high schools while the Buddhists had only nine such schools.[50] These colleges offered the necessary preparation for university education. Thus, the Buddhists argued, the Christians controlled a disproportionate share of the prestige schools and teaching positions. The majority of the students in these Christian-controlled schools were Buddhists because their parents sought to give them an education that would lead to the university and a career. At worst, these schools broke down the Buddhist children's beliefs in their native religion and converted them to Christianity. At best, they imbued them with Western materialist values. In either case the students lost both their contact with their own culture and their reverence for the Buddhist monks who formerly served as teachers.

The report recommended that the state take over all of the private, state-assisted schools. It further proposed that schools should teach the students their own religion. As D. E. Smith accurately observed of these recommendations, "It was clear that the objection was not to denominational schools as such, but to denominational schools controlled by a minority community.[51] The Buddhists, understandably enough, wanted to operate their own schools for their own children, giving them fair opportunities for higher education and eliminating "the 'hybrid education' that takes children from their national and religious roots."[52]

Smith maintains that the report's recommendations were as revolutionary as its assumptions, for it recommended not a return "to the traditional Buddhist *pansalas* [monastery schools] but the establishment of "a modern system of state schools."[53] If the committee's approach to education, however, was modern, its goal, as far as the religion was concerned, was traditional. They wanted a modern educational curriculum, but one in which the *bhikkhus* could teach the ideas and values of the *Dhamma* just as in the *pansalas*, although now alongside other teachers and other secular subjects.

The third chapter of the report, "Contemporary Social Conditions," describes the results of the problems pointed out in the previous two chapters. Because the Sinhalese had lost their culture and their religion, they had accepted the false values and social practices of the West. They adopted materialistic values, believing in "the acquisition of wealth by fair means or foul," rather than Buddhist values such as nonattachment and right livelihood.[54] The only long-term solution, the report notes, lies through rebuilding a Buddhist civilization by education, as outlined in Chapter 2. In the meantime, however, steps could be taken to remove corrupting Western influences and to encourage the adoption of more authentically Buddhist life styles. The recommendations of this chapter recall Dharmapāla's rules for the Buddhists.

The first recommendation was to ban the publication and importation of obscene books and magazines, and to appoint a National Film Board of Censors who would monitor the films that were shown. In addition, the report favored outlawing all forms of alcoholic drinks and enforcing total prohibition, which, although it had been a standard Buddhist cause since the turn of the century, was far from being observed. Horse racing, too, should be banned since the gambling associated with it led to "the greater gain of the wealthy few and the further degradation of the poverty-stricken." Racetracks in Colombo, Nuwara Eliya, and elsewhere should be closed and replaced by more wholesome games and festivals.

To inculate Buddhist mores the report recommended making *poya* days, which were the traditional Buddhist holidays, the national days of rest instead of Sundays.[55] Lay people should be encouraged to attend the temples and observe *sil* regularly. In general the report called on the Buddhists to promote a "movement for plain living" that involved simplicity in dress and life style. It referred to Mahatma Gandhi's *khaddar* campaign to persuade people to abandon Western styles in clothing in favor of national dress. "For everyday wear, a simple dress common to all people (preferably based on the cloth and long-sleeved banian) is to be preferred to a Western outfit, which serves to split that nation."[56] On a related issue, the report said that Buddhists should not imitate "the Colonial overlords" by maintaining servants. The followers of the Buddha should adopt a "Buddhist mode of life," the chief features of which were "early rising, invoking the Triple Gem and practicing mental concentration, diligent and speedy execution of one's duties, and retiring to rest early."[57] The authors of the report believed that a national movement for plain living such as this would bring not only spiritual benefits but also economic benefits "as did the Puritan influence in England."[58]

The final four chapters of the report dealt very concisely with two other aspects of the problem: social services and the role and education of the *Sangha*. Compared to the previous chapter, which extended to over one hundred pages, these four only required fourteen pages. If the report were completely reformist in its approach, we might expect that these topics—social welfare and "The *Sangha* Today"—would lend themselves to innovative recommendations. But the recommendations and the analyses in these chapters had a decidedly traditional tone. In regard to social service or social welfare, the chief concern of the committee was to end the dominant role the Christian groups had played. The report recommended that the state take over and administer the hospitals and homes rather than aiding the Christian bodies who ran those institutions and sought to convert the Buddhists in them. The committee did not go on to develop any rationale or make any recommendations as to whether or how Buddhists should pursue social welfare, although we know that many Protestant Buddhists had long felt that this was a crucial issue.

In the chapter on "The *Sangha* Today" and the succeeding chapter, "*Pirivena* Education," the report sought to restore rather than reform the *Sangha*. Recalling once again the close relationship that existed historically between the *Sangha* and the laity, the report repeated its claim that this "close association was one of the direct causes of the amazing development of Sinhalese culture." Restoring this association represented a key to restoring the culture. The *bhikkhu* is described as "counsellor, teacher and spiritual head of the community."[59] This role "embraced all aspects of academic, education, moral guidance and participation in rite and ritual." Venerable Saraṇaṃkara, founder of the Siyam Nikāya, was praised as "the pioneer of the modern renaissance of the Sangha," and Vidyodaya and Vidyālaṅkāra *Pirivenas* were recognized as significant institutions. Thus, the report celebrated the orthodox *Sangha* and the traditional role of the *bhikkhus*, without making any proposals for reforming the *Sangha*. The *Sangha* was understood to have the responsibility "to minister to the needs of the laity," and the laity was responsible for serving as *dāyakas* or supporters of the *Sangha*.

The specific proposals made by the committee in these chapters pertained to increasing the number of *bhikkhus* and improving the *pirivena* education system. The report recommended the establishment of training colleges for *bhikkhus* where they "would be instructed in *Dhamma* and its exposition." Although the report did mention in passing that the training should include "*baṇa* preaching, social work, etc.," this single use of the phrase "social work, etc.," without any elaboration, represented the only hint at any new possibilities for the monastic role.

In the concluding chapter, "Tolerance," the report said simply that the Buddhists had tolerated enough. They did not ask for a favored position "at the expense of other religious groups," but they did expect the right to restore and practice their religion.

When it was published in 1956, the report of the Buddhist Committee of Enquiry received enthusiastic acclaim from the Sinhalese Buddhists. It brought together the interests of at least three major groups of Buddhists. The urban Protestant Buddhists had set up the committee, and the report reflected the evolution of their interpretation of Buddhism. Doctrinally they leaned toward traditionalism while still recognizing the need for development in the society. The committee also affirmed the views of the orthodox *Sangha*, the group whom Ames described as wishing "to restore or to retain certain privileges which were threatened."[60] The Protestant Buddhists accepted these *bhikkhus* in contrast to the political *bhikkhus*, and gave the orthodox

Siyam Nikāya high praise in the report. This gesture represented the beginning of the pendulum swing toward the reestablishment of the orthodox *Sangha*. To the views of these two groups the report added that of a third, the emerging Sinhala-educated elite, headed by the village leaders, the *āyurvedic* physicians, and the Sinhalese schoolteachers. These people, representing the nonurban Sinhalese Buddhist majority, had conveyed their views to the committee during its hearings throughout the island. Coming at a critical juncture of Sri Lankan history, the report expressed the hopes and desires of all these Buddhists for the rebirth of their religion and their nation. Each of these groups of Buddhists, in its own way, found its identity in the *Dhamma* of traditional Theravada. The report's introduction stated that "with the abandonment of the *Dhamma* the people of this country shall wither, fade away and perish."[61]

The Jayanti programs and the recommendations of the Committee of Enquiry's report charted a course for the future of the Buddhist revival and particularly for Protestant Buddhism. All of the governments in Sri Lanka since the Jayanti have sought in various ways to carry out this mandate to restore both Buddhism and the Buddhists to their rightful place. Given our vantage point over three decades later, what can we say about the outcome of the Jayanti and its programs for reviving Buddhism? The remainder of this chapter examines the impact of the Jayanti period on the Buddhist revival from 1956 to 1986. Without attempting to recount fully the political history of this period—a subject that has been capably studied by others[62]—we shall examine the development of the Buddhist revival and the evolution of Protestant Buddhism since the Jayanti.

Post-Jayanti Developments

To understand the evolution of Buddhism after the Jayanti we must, however, take note of at least one political event, the election of S. W. R. D. Bandaranaike as Prime Minister in 1956. His election had significance for Buddhism in several different ways. (1) It established a link between the government and the Buddhist religion that has been essential to the political and religious history of Sri Lanka since that time. (2) He implemented some key proposals both from the Buddhist Commission's report and from the Jayanti period generally. (3)

The assassination of Bandaranaike by a *bhikkhu* in September, 1959, ultimately led to an increase in the authority and prestige of the orthodox *Sangha,* as opposed to the politically involved *bhikkhus.*

The Jayanti year became an election year when the United National Party, which had ruled since independence, decided to move the elections up from 1957 to April, 1956. The report of the Buddhist Commission, presented to the public in February, 1956, mobilized the Buddhists and served as a campaign platform for Bandaranaike, who won because he espoused the two issues that most fired the emotions of the Sinhalese majority: religion and language. Leach has noted the irony of Bandaranaike, a member of the highest eschelons of the Anglophile, Christian elite, running for office "as the devoutly chauvinistic leader of Sinhalese Buddhists under the slogan: Sinhalese is the national language of Ceylon; Buddhism is our national religion."[63] Although Bandaranaike's family had been Christian for at least a century and counted among their number a great-uncle who was a Canon of the Church of England, Bandaranaike like many other elite Sinhalese had converted to Buddhism some years earlier. Now he recognized that the time was right for the Sinhalese Buddhist majority to assert their power in the newly independent democracy.

Bandaranaike pledged to implement the report of the Buddhist Committee of Enquiry and to make Sinhala the official language. His campaign was promoted by a new organization of political *bhikkhus,* the Eksath Bhikkhu Peramuna, led by the monk Māpiṭigama Buddharakkhita. The *bhikkhus* of the EBP campaigned actively for Bandaranaike, arguing that on his election hinged the salvation of both the nation and the religion. His overwhelming victory served to reestablish the notion that the government was the chief protector of Buddhism. As Leach remarks, "It is not the case that all good Buddhists are politicians, but it is nearly true that all effective politicians in Buddhist countries have, for centuries past, found it expedient to claim to be good Buddhists."[64] Although this political truth had not held in Sri Lanka since before the British period, it was to apply from the Jayanti to the present. The Buddhist populace believed that government action was needed to restore Buddhism to its "rightful place."

After his election, Bandaranaike passed three measures designed to aid this restoration. First, his government established a Ministry of

Cultural Affairs to carry out the report's recommendation for a ministry "to rehabilitate the religions which have suffered under colonial rule." The ministry served as the government's official agency for matters pertaining to Buddhism, although Hinduism and Islam also received token attention. This agency administered the projects begun by the Jayanti Bauddha Mandalaya, including the translation of the *Tipiṭaka* into Sinhala, the Buddhist Encyclopedia, and the various renovations of Buddhist shrines. To address the problem of the lack of organization among Buddhists, the ministry instituted temple societies called Vihāra Sāsanārakṣhaka Societies, which were intended to strengthen the relations between the *bhikkhus* and laity in local temples. Other objectives were "to promote knowledge and the observance of *sil*, to establish and improve Sunday *Dhamma* schools, to promote temperance activities and to work for the prevention of crime."[65]

A second measure aimed at restoring Buddhism and carrying out the Buddhist Commission's recommendations was the establishment of a Buddha Sāsana Commission in 1957. The report had called for the creation of "an incorporated Buddha Sāsana Council to which may be entrusted all the prerogatives of the Buddhist kings as regards the Buddhist religion."[66] The Sāsana Commission was charged to investigate the feasibility of such a council to deal with such matters as monastic courts, Buddhist temporalities, and other matters pertaining to the regulation of the *Sangha*. Although the membership of the Sāsana Commission included ten monks and five laymen, the orthodox Siyam Nikāya opposed the commission's establishment from the outset, regarding it as an attempt by the laity to regulate the *Sangha*.

Bandaranaike's third program in support of Buddhism involved granting university status in 1958 to two important *piriveṇas*, Vidyodaya and Vidyālaṇkāra. Although at first the universities began on the sites of the old *piriveṇas*, after a few years two new universities were built on new campuses, but organizationally they still represented upgradings of the *piriveṇas* to university status. Vidyodaya University and Vidyālaṇkāra University reflected the central issues of the time: they employed Sinhala as their language of instruction and offered courses in Buddhism and the Buddhist scriptures in addition to secular subjects. The creation of these universities had not been an explicit recommendation of the Buddhist Commission's report, but had been considered for some time by leading Buddhists, including some of the Commission's members. The report had praised these two historic *pirivenas* at Maligakanka and Peliyagoda for their roles in the renaissance of the *Sangha*. The two institutions had had a long and distinguished history of educating monks and even some Westerners such as T. W. Rhys Davids, the founder of the Pali Text Society. DeSilva maintains that the decision to implement this idea came in the wake of the Buddhist monks' opposition to the government's language policy (see below). He describes this decision as "a quick if not desperate, remedy for an impossible situation. It was a classic instance of how not to establish Universities."[67]

The new Buddhist universities with *bhikkhus* as vice-chancellors were created "for the advancement and dissemination of knowledge and for the promotion of Sinhala and Buddhist culture."[68] The student bodies of these schools included monks as well as lay students. The monks followed the same curriculum as the lay students for the bachelor's or master's degrees, although the monks were required to take certain special courses in Buddhist subjects. From the outset this arrangement met opposition from Buddhist laypersons who thought it inappropriate for monks to be studying secular subjects and possibly associating with female students who at first were only admitted to pursue external degrees but later were allowed to attend classes as regular students. An editorial in *The Buddhist* catches the flavor of this opposition: "The Pirivena University Scheme is a Machiavellian device, a subtle contrivance to destroy gradually the *Dhamma* preserved for us through the ages by a simple people."[69] Despite this opposition, however, the two universities were created, and contributed to the development of the country by making higher education available to many more students than before. The move also enabled *bhikkhus* to widen their share of influence in the country. Some distinguished scholars from the *Sangha* served in the faculties and administrations of these universities. Venerable Dr. Walpola Rahula served for a term as vice-chancellor of Vidyodaya University.

In addition to these actions of Bandaranaike's government, some other events prior to his assassination had significant effects on the Buddhist resurgence. One central question that Bandaranaike failed to resolve was whether Buddhism should be the state religion of Sri Lanka. Before he had been elected he had said, "The adoption of Buddhism as the state religion will usher in an era of religio-democratic socialism."[70] Although the Buddhist Commission had argued that Buddhism should not be made the state religion of a secular democracy, many Buddhist groups continued to favor the proposal. Bandaranaike could not accommodate them, however, because he found that his coalition government lacked the votes to override the Constitution, which stated that the government could not confer any advantages on any one religious group to the exclusion of the others.

On the other burning issue of the day—the demand for Sinhala only—Bandaranaike was also unable to deliver what he had promised in his campaign. Although his government passed a bill making Sinhala the sole official language, it faced the political necessity of allowing the Tamils somehow to regard their language as a parallel national language for their people. When Bandaranaike negotiated this matter with the Tamils, however, the Sinhalese *bhikkhus* conducted massive protest marches. As Smith describes his predicament *vis-à-vis* the monks, "Bandaranaike found their unyielding stand on this issue helpful in the 1956 election but thereafter embarrassing and destructive."[71] When Bandaranaike finally acceded to the monks' demands and rescinded his agreement with the Tamils, the Tamils were outraged and communal riots broke out in the country.

Because Bandaranaike proved unable to fulfill his commitments to the *Sangha* in general and to certain members of the *Sangha* in particular, one political *bhikkhu* who had helped to elect him arranged for his assassination.[72] He dispatched another *bhikkhu* to Bandaranaike's residence to shoot him. This event profoundly altered the course of the Buddhist revival. The majority of the laymen, taking a fairly traditional view of the roles of monks and laity, already opposed monastic involvement in politics. The assassination of a popular Buddhist Prime Minister by a *bhikkhu* reinforced this opposition immensely. DeSilva observes that "in retrospect the cause of the *bhikkhu* involvement in politics never really recovered from this."[73] Any progress that the *Sangha* had made in the liberalization of their role in society evaporated in the wake of Bandaranaike's murder. The Buddhist public called for the monks to return to the temples and to follow the traditional monastic code of discipline, the *Vinaya*. As a result, the nonpolitical and traditional leadership of the *Sangha*, particularly the *Mahānāyakas* of the Malvatta and Asgiriya chapters of the Siyam

Nikāya, gained increased esteem and authority. The political *bhikkhus'* actions ultimately had the effect of making it possible for the orthodox Kandyan *bhikkhus* to recapture what they had sought since the outset of the revival: their traditional position as spokesmen for the *Sangha*. From this time on, the ruling governments increasingly honored these two *Mahānāyakas*. They were given official residences in Colombo as well as in Kandy, and elected officials made it a point to visit them soon after taking office as a sign of deference to their authority. Because of this increase in the prestige of the Kandyan hierarchy, deSilva has described the period from 1960 to 1984 as the "Triumph of Orthodoxy,"[74] The overall result of Bandaranaike's assassination was to make traditionalism or neotraditionalism more attractive to the laity.

The Influence of the Jayanti Programs

After the assassination of Bandaranaike, successive governments enacted most of the other major programs proposed during the Jayanti in an attempt to bring about the twofold aim of restoring the Buddhist heritage and ushering in an era of peace and prosperity for the nation. In tracing the outcomes of these programs we can see how the Jayanti influenced the Buddhist revival. Time has shown that many of the Jayanti programs, especially the recommenations of the Buddhist Commission, did not produce the intended results; nevertheless, the orientation established by the report and the programs endured, reinforcing the outlook described above as neotraditional.

To account for the programs that did not prove successful, we should recall the inherent contradiction or ambiguity in the neotraditional position. The authors of the proposals sought both to restore the traditional forms of Theravada and to have them prove relevant to modern contexts and problems. The ambiguities involved were similar to those Leach described as the "complexities of the underlying contradictions of cultural identity, part 'tradition,' part 'modern.' "[75] Buddhists became disillusioned with some programs because they failed to meet either the criterion of restoring the past or that of resolving the present, or both. As Ames comments, there is always "a limit on how much can be restored from the past." Because the context has changed, "restoration thus becomes as well a new creation."[76] In some cases, as we shall see below, this new creation was acceptable to the Buddhists, but in a number of other cases it clearly was not.

The Committee of Enquiry's recommendations for changing the contemporary social conditions exemplified this problem. The committee had desired to restore a Buddhist civilization modeled on that of Asoka, "under the beneficent influence of which his empire grew to greatness at an astonishing pace."[77] What was needed, the committee had reported, was to displace the Western, materialistic values of colonialism and to reinstate authentic Buddhist values. To accomplish this the report had recommended a series of prohibitions and a number of positive changes in the life style of the Buddhists. Some of the prohibitions were not too difficult to enact. The government banned horse racing and the importation or publication of obscene books and magazines. Others, however, proved more difficult. The government has not been able to prohibit the production and sale of liquor, although temperance continues to be a widely accepted Buddhist ideal.

The recommendations for other changes in the modern life style have also proved difficult to accomplish. The government tried to legislate one of the central recommendations in this area when, in the mid sixties, it enacted a bill making *poya* days, rather than Sundays, the legal weekly holidays for the nation. The proponents of this plan argued that since *poya* days were not official holidays, many Buddhists were unable to "take the precepts" at the temple and thereby lost the "vital contact between Buddhist laymen and the *Sangha*."[78] The government tried to foster Buddhism by passing legislation making all four *poya* days, and half of the workday preceeding each *poya* day, public holidays. The result was chaos. Since the *poya* days, following the lunar cycle, seldom fell on the same day of the week, the work weeks varied in length. One might be a four-day week; the next might be a six-day week. People had trouble keeping track of the *poyas*. The situation created special problems for business and government. Productivity was irregular, and foreign trade was hampered by the uncertainty of the work weeks.

Even though the intent had been to cast off Western influences, ironically the system of *poyas* that was adopted represented another instance of Protestant Buddhism. Although technically all four lunar days were *poya* days, most lay Buddhists had traditionally observed only the full-moon *poya* day. Gombrich, writing about conditions before this law was adopted, noted that few temples had preaching services on any *poya* but the full-moon day, although some held services also on the no-moon *poya*. Most Buddhists went to the temple to take the precepts on the full-moon *poya* only.[79] The Buddhist reformers, however, had made all four *poyas* holidays in imitation of the Western pattern.

Ultimately, in July, 1971, the government abandoned the *poya* holiday scheme and returned to the standard calendar, retaining the full-moon *poya* each month as a public holiday. The *Sangha* protested this move, as did laymen's groups such as the ACBC. A leader of the Buddhist Congress told me that this reversal of policy proved that Sri Lanka was still dominated by foreign influences and that the government lacked the strength to stand up to them. However, at that time, following the 1971 insurgency, when the government was seeking normalcy and stability, returning to a standard calendar seemed advantageous. In addition, it was not clear that having the *poyas* as public holidays had resulted in any great change in the traditional pattern of temple attendance; most Buddhists still attended the temple only on the full-moon *poya*.

The other recommendations for reinstituting a "Buddhist mode of living" were even more difficult to bring about. Dress codes and daily routines could not be legislated. For a time many men, especially politicians and government officials, did adopt the white cloth and banian as the national dress instead of trousers and suits. This trend seems to be passing, however, as not many of the younger generation have adopted this style of dress. Similarly, the report's recommendation that people adopt a "Puritan life style" by having no servants, rising early, and generally following an ideal of "plain living," does not seem to have brought great changes. To be sure, simplicity of life continues to be a much-admired virtue among the Buddhists, and Buddhists praise those who are able to lead a simple life with few material possessions. But this attitude was not created by the report's recommendations. It was a traditional value that has had continuity in Sri Lanka. Nevertheless, despite this admiration for plain living, most urban and even semiurban Buddhists today have found it difficult to adopt that life style. These Sinhalese Buddhists have continued to employ servants, to own automobiles, and to acquire other modern amenities such as television sets, which now are producing other kinds of changes in their life styles.

The recommendations by the Buddhist committee for changing social conditions had represented the most direct attempt to reform the lives of lay Buddhists and restore the golden age of Buddhist civilization. Actually, however, the changes that were recommended had less to do with classical Buddhist civilization than with the customs of Sinhalese village life, for that was what the reformers recalled as the premodern or precolonial civilization. These ideas represented a nostalgia for simpler times, for the idyllic life of the Buddhist village. Buddhists found, however, that such a life style, although admirable, was neither practical nor completely desirable in the modern urban context. The traditional village customs could not be adopted wholesale to constitute a modern Buddhist social ethic.

Another example of a Jayanti program that was abandoned because of underlying contradictions inherent in the neotraditionalist reforms was the Buddhist university scheme. Enacted by Bandaranaike, this experiment with monastic universities was discontinued in 1966-67 when the two *piriveṇa* universities, Vidyodaya and Vidyālaṇkāra, were converted to secular universities with no ties to the *Sangha*. Lay Buddhists inside and outside of the government found that these universities were not fulfilling the purposes for which they were established. In actuality, the purposes and the means employed to fulfill them had been inconsistent. The Buddhists conceived the *piriveṇa* universities with traditional aims in mind. They wanted to educate lay students in a university that taught the *Dhamma* as well as secular subjects. It seemed desirable for lay students to learn both from *bhikkhus* as well as along with *bhikkhus* in order to increase their appreciation for the *Sangha*. As one proponent of the system wrote, "It is only learning . . . higher learning by *bhikkhus* and laity jointly that can arrest a 'deterioration' of Sinhalese Buddhist culture."[80] Leach remarked that with regard to the purposes of these universities the Sinhalese were engaging in "a kind of voluntary self-deception." "When Sinhalese parents seek higher education for their children, they mean Western style higher education; but at the same time they want their children to grow up as Sinhalese and not as second class Europeans—and on this point there is ambiguity."[81] The *bhikkhus*, it was argued, needed higher education to equip them to exist in the modern world and to be able to relate to the educated lay Buddhist populace. A basic assumption of the entire plan was that *bhikkhus* and laymen would emerge from the university better able to follow traditional monastic and lay roles in society.

The Buddhist universities, however, did not serve as the best means to attain these goals. When the *bhikkhus* and the laity were educated together, the *bhikkhus* tended to become more like laymen. Many of the *bhikkhus* chose to follow secular courses of study rather than Buddhist subjects, and upon graduation applied for the secular positions that they were qualified to fill. A large number of these *bhikkhus* left the *Sangha* altogether after they graduated. Thus, instead of strengthening the traditional roles, these universities did almost exactly the opposite. Rather than improving the communication between monks and laymen on the *Dhamma*, these universities made such communication more difficult. The lay students either lost respect for the *bhikkhus* or regarded them as peers rather than mediators of the *Dhamma*.

As early as 1962, only three years after they had been established, the government set up a Universities Commission to enquire into the success of the two Buddhist universities. This commission's report reveals the traditional assumptions laymen held about the proper roles for *bhikkhus* and laypersons. Regarding *bhikkhus* it said, "The educational needs of a person who has expressly renounced the household life in order that he may work out his release from *Samsara* . . . are fundamentally different from the disciplines that are associated with modern universities." The commission concluded that monastic and lay education should not be combined. When *bhikkhus* study secular subjects, they are led "away from the serene calmness of *bhikkhus* life." And when *bhikkhus* become more worldly, the laity "are deprived of their moral leadership" and left "like a rudderless boat in a tempestuous sea."[82] Many Buddhist laymen today still agree with the government commission on this issue. One prominent lay leader whom I interviewed explained that the Buddhist universities had been discontinued because having *bhikkhus* studying secular subjects and sitting in classes with women caused problems (although women were not in the actual classes with monks until after 1966). Also he felt, as many Buddhists do, that there have been too many *bhikkhus* who used their position to gain entrance to the university and then left the monastic order upon graduation.

Progressive *bhikkhus* complained that these laymen wanted them to sit in the temple as motionless and inactive as the Buddha statues. In some ways that perception was correct. The traditionalist laity expected the *bhikkhus* to change or affect society not by acting in it in the same ways that laymen did, but by living and breathing the *Dhamma* and more or less transmitting its effective truth into the society around them by preaching, advising, and meditating. Of this traditional ideal King has written, "The Good Society is a society in which *the Buddhist holy man or saint living in the midst of a holy community radiates virtue and social health into the surrounding society of lay-believers."*[83]

Malalgoda explains that the conversion of Vidyodaya and Vidyālaṅkāra to ordinary universities was another result of "the ascendency of traditionalist Buddhism."[84] Ultimately the government changed the names of these universities, thereby removing even that connection with the monastic *pirivena* tradition. The reason given was that all universities were to have names indicating their locations, such as Peradeniya University and Colombo University. Thus, Vidyālaṅkāra became Kelaniya University and Vidyodaya became Sri Jayawardenepura University. This decision was taken after the 1971 insurgency during which Vidyodaya and Vidyālaṅkāra students, some *bhikkhus* included, had been actively involved on the side of the insurgents who sought to topple the government. That politics played a role in the choice of the new name for Vidyodaya was roundly denied by the officials.

Other educational reforms that were enacted also failed to advance the cause of Buddhism in the way that their authors had envisioned. The *bhikkhu* training colleges proposed in the report were established in several locations in the island. Their aim was to educate young *bhikkhus* in the *Dhamma*. Some of them had even more specialized courses preparing *bhikkhus* for *Dhammadūta*, or missionary work.[85] A senior *bhikkhu* in the Asgiriya chapter confirmed in an interview the opinion of most observers, however, that these Bhikkhu training colleges have not been successful.

The Buddhist Commission's report anticipated that the nationalization of the school system in Sri Lanka would result in Buddhism being given a prominent place in both education and the culture at large. It was thought that if Buddhism could replace Christianity in the school curriculum, Buddhist values could be inculcated and established. The government nationalized the majority of the state-assisted schools in 1960. The schools of all religious groups were nationalized, including those of the Buddhist Theosophical Society. Only a few of the larger and more prominent Christian schools remained independent by refusing government aid.

Has this transfer of the schools to state management led to an increased understanding of Buddhism? Certainly it has helped. Buddhist thought and Pali are taught to thousands of students by competent teachers, usually laypersons. Some Buddhists today, however, feel that the plan has not worked to the advantage of the Buddhists. Malalgoda commented that the nationalization of the schools not only put the oldest Buddhist educational organization, the Buddhist Theosophical Society, virtually out of business, but the Buddhist leadership in general "thereby lost a good deal of their independent power, influence and patronage in the field of education."[86] An official of the Buddhist Congress complained in 1983 that the Buddhists who went along with the nationalization plan "lost their schools." Whereas those Christians who refused to join the system and were allowed to keep their schools on the condition that they would be self-supporting, not only retained their schools but have begun receiving state aid once more.

The basic contradiction with regard to the schools seems to be that while the Buddhist leaders wanted traditional *Dhamma* instruction given a major role in the curriculum, the teachers and the parents desired the best modern curriculum for the students. Even if the *Dhamma* is given emphasis in such a curriculum, it takes on a different meaning. The neotraditionalist *bhikkhus* and lay leaders who made the recommendations about Buddhist education believed the *Dhamma* needed only to be "restored to its rightful place" in its "pristine purity," not to be reinterpreted. But when the *Dhamma* is placed in the context of a modern curriculum, it is inevitably reinterpreted by the students who are learning both. Although this may not be a bad result, it was not what the neotraditionalists intended.

Another important recommendation from the first and major section of the Buddhist Committee of Enquiry's report—that a Buddha Sāsana Council be established—was never implemented. The commission that Bandaranaike appointed to make recommendations on this matter presented their report to him in 1959. Before the report could be published, however, Bandaranaike was assassinated. When the report finally came out later that year, the attitude of the public toward the *Sangha* had changed because of the assassination, which meant that this report was inevitably viewed as an instrument for "purifying" the *Sangha*, although that was not its original intent. It recommended creating a Buddha Sāsana Council comprising monks and laymen that would serve as the administrative and legislative body for Buddhism in the country.[87] This body was intended to serve as the modern government's arm for carrying out all the duties of the Buddhist kings toward the religion as "assumed by the British Crown in 1815."[88] In addition the report proposed a system of courts or tribunals for the *Sangha*, a government commissioner of temple lands, and a system for registering *bhikkhus* and ensuring discipline. When Mrs. Bandaranaike came to power in 1960, she sought unsuccessfully to enact this plan. The Siyam Nikāya, which had opposed the idea from the outset, mounted a campaign in opposition and, in the face of it, neither Mrs. Bandaranaike nor her successors were able to gain enough support for the measure.

Numerous accounts have been given of why the Sāsana Council was never established;[89] without repeating these, we would point to one central issue in this conflict: the interpretation of the monastic vocation. In the aftermath of the assassination, with the revelations about *bhikkhus* involved in political intrigue and corruption, the Protestant Buddhist laity, who already held a fairly conservative view of the role of a *bhikkhu*, desired more than ever to restore the traditional vocation of the *Sangha*. Although still believing the expressions of the Committee of Enquiry about "the wholesome influence of the *Sangha*" and the importance of "contact between Buddhist laymen and the *Sangha*,"[90] the laity now had doubts about whether the existing *Sangha* came up to this standard. What was needed was to purify the *Sangha* "by removing from the noble Order of *bhikkhus* those undisciplined individuals who lead corrupt lives and bring discredit to the *Sangha*."[91] Purifying or cleansing the *Sangha* meant restoring, in a quite fundamentalist sense, the scriptural code of conduct of the *Vinaya*.

The laity thus came to regard the Sāsana Council and the system of courts as the ideal means for accomplishing this reform. "One of the surest means of cleansing the Sāsana for all time," a layman's group declared, was "to implement the report of the Sāsana Commission."[92] The problem with this approach was that they were using a newly created, democratic institution—the proposed Sāsana Council—to accomplish traditional reform or restoration. As Bardwell Smith explains, "To create jurisdictional bodies of this sort, however, without giving serious attention to Vinaya reform and the vocation of the *bhikkhu* in the light of present needs, is to miss central opportunities, even to betray Buddhism."[93] Activist *bhikkhus*, such as the Venerable Dr. Walpola Rahula, had long maintained that the vocation of the *bhikkhu* should be reinterpreted for the modern age. Rahula had even argued that the *Vinaya*, the second section of the *Tipiṭaka*, "was not ultimate truth but only a convention agreed upon for the smooth conduct of a particular community."[94] Rahula also observed that "the political, economic and social conditions of today are different from those of the time of the Buddha, and that consequently the life of *bhikkhus* today is also different from that of the *bhikkhus* at that time."[95] The underlying intent of the Sāsana Commission's recommendations seems to have been compatible with this desire to adapt the life of the *Sangha* to the modern age. The laity, however, after witnessing what one group of political *bhikkhus* had done to Bandaranaike, whom the public regarded as a leader dedicated to restoring Theravada, were in no mood to consider a modern reinterpretation of the monastic vocation. As neotraditionalists, they believed that the *Sangha* should revert to its fundamental discipline, and they read the Sāsana Commission report in that light.

The *Sangha*, for its part, opposed this proposal on several grounds. It felt that the proposed Sāsana Council represented an attempt by the laity to control the *Sangha* and limit its freedom. They did not find reassuring the replies by laymen that "there is in our view not the slightest impediment in the proposal to a *bhikkhu* conducting himself in accordance with the Vinaya though some have tried to show that it is an impediment to the freedom of the *Sangha*."[96] Most opposed to the measure was the hierarchy of the Siyam Nikāya, which had the greatest landholdings and thus stood to lose the most financially. They predicted dire consequences if the proposal were to be adopted: "If the Sāsana Commission Report is implemented, without doubt the few remaining members of the *Sangha* will give up their robes and disappear from the Order."[97]

In the end the government gave in to *Mahānayākas* of the Malvatta and Asgiriya chapters of the Siyam Nikāya and abandoned the proposal, thus demonstrating once more the power and prestige that these orthodox *bhikkhus* had come to have. The Prime Minister in 1959, W. Dahanayake, expressed his unwillingness to oppose them, saying, "I do not want to implement any proposal if the Malvatta and Asgiriya Chapters say no."[98] The Sāsana Commission's recommendations had raised many fears on the part of the *Sangha* about their freedom, their financial support, and about the potential for "a totally new ecclesiastical polity."[99] Ironically, the chief opponent of the proposal, the Siyam Nikāya's orthodox leaders, were probably closest to the laity in their conservative interpretation of the role of the *bhikkhu*. Even if the measure had passed, they could have maintained their traditional role. They did not wish, however, to concede any power to the laity in the matter of *Sangha* reform. If reform were necessary, they argued, it must come from within the *Sangha* itself. In the end, therefore, they forced the government to concede this right and to say, in effect, that the *Sangha* was orthodox already. As Donald Smith observed, "The forces of reform, even with the leadership of the government, were no match for the defenders of the status quo."[100] The losers in this struggle were those *bhikkhus* and laity who favored a meaningful reinterpretation of the monastic role.

Although many of the Jayanti period's recommendations and programs failed to accomplish the restoration of Buddhism that their authors had envisioned, other Jayanti programs had more success and, moreover, the spirit of momentum of the Jayanti fueled the revival of Buddhism. To ascertain their views on the question of whether Buddhism had been restored, I met with three of the four surviving members of the Buddhist Committee of Enquiry. While they conceded that the Buddha Sāsana Council had never been established and that other programs had not succeeded, they all believed that Buddhism has been restored in Sri Lanka and that the Jayanti as well as the Report had been major factors in this restoration. Venerable M. Paññāsīha explained that the "appreciable change of heart" among the Sinhalese Buddhists that came with the Jayanti led to a renewal of Buddhism. To be sure, this represents a subjective opinion held by men who served on the committee and therefore have a vested interest in believing that it succeeded. In some ways, however, they are correct. Despite the failure of many Jayanti programs, Buddhism has been revived since the Jayanti. We can identify three ways that the Jayanti and especially the Buddhist Commission's report contributed to this revival: (1) it reawakened the Sinhalese Buddhists' consciousness of their identity; (2) it established the government in the role of the protector of Buddhism; and (3) it kindled the development among the lay Buddhists of the neotraditional interpretation of Theravada.

The Sinhalese Buddhist Identity

First, with regard to the Buddhists' sense of identity, the Jayanti represented the mythology of the integral relation between the Sinhalese race and Buddhism more powerfully than anyone had since Dharmapala. The millennial expectations surrounding the Jayanti gave this mystique of "the land, the race and the faith"[101] a new relevance for the Sinhalese. As Bardwell Smith discerned, "Large sections of the population were caught up in a renewed search for their Sinhalese self-consciousness."[102] Accepting this mythological credo based on the Buddhist Chronicles, the Sinhalese affirmed its basic tenets. They believed that they were destined to be the protectors of the *Dhamma* and that their ancestors had carried out this charge in the past by preserving Buddhism in "its prestine purity." Furthermore, they felt sure that the pristine *Dhamma* had brought prosperity to Lanka during its golden age before the intrusion of foreign powers. Following this logic, the report had argued and the Sinhalese had come to believe that they had a sacred duty or a "manifest destiny" to restore the *Dhamma* and thereby restore their own prosperity.

This cycle of myths, or salvation history, has motivated the Sinhalese to revive their culture and their religion. After centuries of foreign domination the Buddhists have found a new pride in their heritage and have sought to establish the new nation on Buddhist principles rather than Western ones. They have also poured enormous wealth and energy into reviving the institutions of Buddhism. Temples, *stupas*, Buddha statues, and monasteries have been built, indicating the resurgence of Buddhism. If one compares the state of Buddhism today with the low ebb it reached during the British period, one cannot doubt that Buddhism has been revived. Much of this activity, especially the building and restoring of Buddhist institutions, has occurred since the Jayanti. Ames correctly observed that with regard to the Sinhalese restoration of Buddhism, "Surely history will judge that they have done well in their intentions, given the circumstances. Buddhism thrives in Ceylon today perhaps as much as it ever has; with the printing press, radio, film and mass education, the Buddhist teachings are being spread among the masses more effectively than they ever could before."[103]

An interesting aspect of this revival of the Sinhalese identity and of Buddhism has been that it has fostered a certain logic that has made it a continuing process. The Buddhists believed that restoring the *Dhamma* would bring prosperity. Therefore, whatever prosperity has been achieved so far must be the result of the restoration of the *Dhamma*; and if full prosperity has not yet been achieved, it is because further restoration of the *Dhamma* is needed. This logic manifests itself in a rhetoric of ongoing revival. This rhetoric, popularized by the Jayanti and the Buddhist Commission's report, can be found in present-day political speeches, in newspaper editorials, and in other statements by Sinhalese Buddhists. The rhetoric proclaims, much as the report did thirty years ago, that Buddhism and Sinhalese culture still must be restored. Monastic leaders, politicians, and Buddhist lay leaders regularly declare that Buddhism or the *Dhamma* must be restored and Sinhalese Buddhists must take their rightful place in the land to ensure this restoration. It was this rhetoric that inspired *bhikkhus* to lead the campaign for the Sinhala language during S. W. R. D. Bandaranaike's time and to campaign for Sinhalese rights on other occasions since then.

Just as the report blamed the decline of Buddhism on the Christians and the colonial powers who conspired to subvert it, so contemporary Sinhalese using the rhetoric of revival continue to charge that other foreign opponents are thwarting the restoration of Theravada. Bechert points out what we noted in chapter two, that Dharmapāla was among the first to perceive "the decay of Buddhism as a result of foreign influence."[104] The Buddhist Commission's report, although "not a balanced account of the facts" in this regard,[105] fired the emotions of the Sinhalese. Their sense of being united against a common enemy contributed much to the consciousness of a Sinhalese Buddhist identity. Today this rhetoric of persecution continues to be used to unite the Buddhists and to explain why Buddhism has not been fully "restored."

Examples of this rhetoric abound in publications as well as in ordinary discourse among Buddhists. For example, a letter to the editor published in a 1981 issue of *The Buddhist* renewed the traditional warning by saying that Rome had ordered the conversion of non-Catholics "by any means, be they legal or illegal, moral or immoral."[106]

Other modern versions of this warning say that Buddhism is threatened today not by military but economic might, and not from its traditional enemy, the West, but from the East. A leading *bhikkhu* explained to me that as Sri Lanka has increased its contacts with other Asian countries, Mahayana Buddhist influences have begun to come in and have weakened Theravada. A Buddhist lay leader charged that the revival of Buddhism today is threatened by influences from Sri Lanka's trading partners such as Singapore and the Middle Eastern nations. Another frequent theme today charges that tourism poses a major threat to Buddhism. An editor writes, "The very people who exploited the country as colonial masters are once again doing the same thing in a different guise."[107] Tourism has brought in a new wave of secularism and materialism, not to mention drugs, prostitution, and nudity on the beaches. Another Buddhist adds to the threat from tourism that of television, which transmits alien values into the home. While there can be no doubt that secularism, tourism, and television do pose serious problems for modern society, the Buddhists see them as particularly threatening to Buddhist culture and the restoration of Buddhism. Even more recently Buddhists have proclaimed the Tamil separatists as threatening the *Dhamma* by threatening the nation.

A final interesting aspect of this rhetoric of an ongoing revival can be seen in the Buddhists' continuing calls for a return to simpler living. Even though the report's recommendations that attempted to restore such conditions were tried unsuccessfully, the Sinhalese continue to associate a simplified life style with a restoration of Buddhist values. Buddhists continue also to advocate other standard themes, including purifying the *Sangha*, and preventing the missionaries from using social welfare organizations as a pretense for converting Buddhists.[108]

Government Protection

Second, in addition to restoring the Sinhalese identity and generating an outlook of continuing revival, the Jayanti and the report advanced the revival by fostering closer relations between the government and Buddhism. The mythology of the report emphasized the symmetry and equivalence of "the land, the race and the faith." During the Jayanti the traditional association of the nation and the religion was a dominant theme. Donald Smith pointed out that the tradition of the religious neutrality of the state, which the liberals had preserved, was largely forgotten: "The identification of Buddhism with the state on this occasion was all but complete, and a precedent was established for massive intervention by the government in religious affairs."[109]

In an influential article reviewing the Buddhist Commission's report, the Sri Lankan historian G. C. Mendis argued that the report had broken with tradition and employed reformist reasoning: "Instead of emphasizing the vanity of life and suggesting a withdrawal from the world and its misery to put an end to birth and rebirth, they suggest the transformation of the political and social system of Ceylon in such a way as to enable Buddhism to thrive."[110] Mendis makes some incorrect assumptions in his review. First, he assumes that the report was written to purify the *Sangha*, whereas more than anything it represented a manifesto for lay Buddhism. Second, he writes as if renunciation to achieve *Nibbāna* were the only aim of the tradition. But, as we saw in chapter one, traditional Theravada held that while renunciation and *Nibbāna* represented goals for virtuosos among the *Sangha*, most *bhikkhus* as well as lay persons were on the mundane path, seeking only a more favorable rebirth. Finally, he implies that the world-affirming approach of transforming the political and social system has no place in a Buddhism that teaches renunciation. He is partially correct, of course. If his previous assumption were true, this one would follow. The ideal of renunciation is world-denying, but the mundane path was in a limited way, within the logic of *saṃsāra*, world-affirming or at least world-accommodating. Lay Buddhism had traditionally given high priority to shaping the political and social systems so that they supported Buddhism. One of the great continuities running through Theravada Buddhist societies, Tambiah has demonstrated, is the "Asokan mythology . . . that the king is the patron and protector of the religion."[111] Theravadins have held that the government's support is essential for providing a social context in which the *Dhamma* can be both heard and observed.

The Buddhist Commission's report had sounded this theme throughout. The initial chapter, "Religion and State in Ceylon," based its recommendations on the belief that Asoka had left his heritage of *dhammic* government to the Sinhalese, "the sons and daughters of Asoka." Following Asoka's example, the Sinhalese kings had protected Buddhism. "The Sinhalese monarch 'protected' the Sāsana and maintained its purity. The word 'protected' is the nearest equivalent to the word signifying the functions of a Sinhalese king as regards the religion."[112] Thus, the report made several recommendations pertaining to the restoration of this essential relation between *Sangha* and state. Mendis was correct in observing that the central recommendation in this area, that a Buddha Sāsana Council be established, represented an innovation. "The Buddhist Commissioners also do not suggest that Buddhism have the same relation to the government as in ancient times."[113] The Sāsana Council was to be a semiautonomous body, financed by the state but leaving the administration and support of Buddhism in the hands of the council of *bhikkus* and laymen. It is significant that this departure from tradition was never implemented. Other recommendations from this section of the report, however, were implemented and served to establish more traditional forms of government support and protection of Buddhism.

The report had recommended that the government cease aiding Christianity and begin compensating and rehabilitating Buddhism after centuries of neglect. This recommendation, as we have seen, was carried out in a variety of ways, by nationalizing the schools, by passing laws that prevented welfare agencies from aiding people of other faiths, and by revoking other forms of preferential treatment. Since the Jayanti the government has tilted completely in the direction of Buddhism, and its policies have aided Buddhism at every turn.

One of the specific ways that it has protected Buddhism has been through the creation of a governmental department to attend to Buddhist interests. This represented a specific recommendation of the report. The Ministry of Cultural Affairs, established by Bandaranaike in 1956, has since been supplemented by a Department of Buddhist

Affairs, set up in 1981. The basic intent of these agencies is to promote the Buddhist *Dhamma* as the basis of the culture.

Some of the other original Jayanti projects have been administered by the Ministry of Cultural Affairs. The ministry administrators point out that the translation of the *Tipiṭaka* into Sinhala has been completed and is now sold through their bookshop. This project, however, has had an interesting outcome that illustrates the nature of the Buddhism they have "restored." As originally conceived, the translation had a reformist intent: putting the scriptures into the language of the laity so that all would have access to the original sacred texts. This intention became obscured by two factors. First, the *bhikkhus* on the translation committee, apparently unable to envision the project as a popular translation, rendered the scriptures into what has been described as a high, literary form of Sinhala, employing many Sanskrit terms. Second, partly because of this literary style of the translation but partly also because of their understanding of their own role, the laity have not purchased the volumes for their own reading. A scholar-monk explained that when laypersons purchase the *Tipiṭaka* volumes, it is usually for the purpose of presenting them to a *bhikkhu* as a gift. This result is interesting, for here is a Jayanti program that was enacted and completed, yet its outcome has had the same effect as innovative programs that were not completed: it strengthens traditionalist Theravada. The roles of monks and laity remain fixed even when a possibility exists for the laity to expand their role, as in this case by studying the translated *Tipiṭaka*.

Another project inherited by the Ministry has been the Encyclopedia of Buddhism. This project has not been completed, and prospects look dim. Some fascicles have been issued, and in 1983 the editor, Professor J. Dhirasekere, explained that they had progressed as far as the letter "e." Problems such as a shortage of scholars to work on the project and printing delays have caused the *Encyclopedia* to fall far behind schedule. The editor has now discovered that some of the early, completed but not yet published, articles are already out of date. Nevertheless, he expressed hope that the task could be accomplished because it would benefit humanity by showing that the Buddhist texts and doctrines offer solutions for modern problems.

The current projects of the Ministry of Cultural Affairs and its Department of Buddhist Affairs reflect some of the ways that the government supports traditional Theravada. *Dhamma* schools operated by the Sāsanarakshaka Societies in the temples receive high priority from the Department of Buddhist Affairs. The department also administers the registration of *bhikkhus* and has plans to register the nuns, or *sil mātāvas*. It also gives financial aid to individual temples for repairs and new construction. The department prides itself on its role in sending *bhikkhus* as *dhammadūtas*. In 1983 the director reported that "a large slice" of their budget was committed to promoting the *Dhamma* in this way. *Bhikkhus* had been sent to India, Malaysia, Africa, England, and America, and more requests for these missionaries were pending. For laypeople the department has sponsored pilgrimages to Buddhist shrines in India.

One of the major new endeavors under the Ministry of Cultural Affairs is the Cultural Triangle Project, a joint project with UNESCO to restore the ancient cities of Anuradhapura, Sigiriya, Polonnaruwa, and Kandy. Promising significant archaeological discoveries and the restoration of important monuments, this project has obvious significance for the revival of Sinhalese Buddhism. "The Cultural Triangle has to be preserved . . . since it forms part of the country's historical core and gives expression to its religious values, national identity and artistic creativity."[114] The government, somewhat paradoxically, has backed this project because it also will benefit tourism.

Although the government has become the protector of Buddhism, it has not established Buddhism as the state religion, a question that has been debated since before the Jayanti. The Buddhist Commission's report argued that this step should not be taken because "a state religion is incompatible with the Government representing such a [pluralistic] Nation and it is anomalous for a secular state like ours to have a Government exercising the powers of a Buddhist monarch."[115] The commission's reluctance led them to advocate the Buddha Sāsana Council. Later Buddhists and later governments have been less reluctant to argue for declaring Buddhism the state religion of Sri Lanka. S. W. R. D. Bandaranaike had advocated such a move in his campaign. After the Jayanti, as the government came increasingly under the control of Buddhists, the Sinhalese began to regard declaring Buddhism the official religion as appropriate to their Buddhist heritage even if it was inappropriate for the pluralistic religious and ethnic composition of the country. The Constitution of Ceylon, however, which required that all religious groups be treated equally and that individuals have the freedom to choose any religion prevented the installation of Buddhism as the state religion. In 1971 Mrs. Sirimavo Bandaranaike announced that "the government is taking steps to declare Buddhism as a state religion of the country under the new Republican constitution."[116] Although Malalasekera, speaking for the ACBC at that time, said that the new constitution should be based on Buddhist principles, he still did not favor making Buddhism the state religion. All that was needed, he said, was for "the religion of the majority of the people to be given its rightful place" and for "the state to protect and foster Buddhism."[117] Other Buddhist groups, however, backed Mrs. Bandaranaike. The Sangha Sabhā or council of the three *Nikāyas* expressed a desire for Buddhism as the state religion. Later, aftr Malalasekera's time, the ACBC also urged that this step be taken.

Despite these demands, Buddhism was not officially declared the state religion of Sri Lanka. The new republican constitutions of 1972 and 1978 defined the close relationship between the government and the religion but did not make Buddhism the official religion of the nation: "The Republic of Sri Lanka shall give to Buddhism the foremost place and accordingly it shall be the duty of the state to protect and foster Buddhism while assuring to all religions the rights guaranteed by section 18(1)(d)."[118] The new constitutions recognized the de facto situation that had come to exist between Buddhism and the government.

The Neotraditional Viewpoint

Finally, the third legacy of the report and the Jayanti to the Buddhist revival during the post-Jayanti period has been the very viewpoint and spirit of neotraditionalism that inspired the report. If the recommendations of the report have not been accepted, the viewpoint of traditional Theravada that it advocated has. During the past three decades the Buddhism of the laity has evolved along the lines begun by the lay organizations, whose basic viewpoint came to fruition in the Jayanti. This emerging neotraditionalism has not involved all Buddhists for, as we shall see in the following chapters, important reformist interpretations have also emerged; but the mainstream of urban and semiurban Buddhist laity seems to be following this interpretation. Malalgoda, noting the emergence of traditionalism after independence, explained that "traditionalist Buddhism—into which Protestant Buddhism easily merged—in fact involved a reversal of the conditions under which the latter had thrived. Instead of the separation of politics and religion, there was now a convergence of the two, and monks who had been pushed into the background reappeared in the limelight."[119] The Buddhist laity subscribing to the beliefs about Sinhala-Buddhist nationalism and advocating close relations between Buddhism and government developed this path of neotraditionalism.

What characterizes this neotraditional path for the laity? Its chief characteristics conform to the description of "practical Buddhism" given by Jayatilaka. It was no coincidence that Jayatilaka's account of the layman's path, originally written in 1901, was republished in the YMBA journal in 1981.[120] If modernism or reformism is distinguished by what Bechert termed the elimination of "the old separation of the supramundane and mundane spheres,"[121] then this neotraditionalism is distinguished by a restoration of that separation. *Nibbāna* does not represent a plausible goal. The goal becomes what Jayatilaka termed "the gradual development of man" over many rebirths.[122]

Comparing the neotraditionalists' viewpoint with the motifs of reformism outlined in chapter one, we find that neotraditionalism is not optimistic about the individual's potential for enlightenment, at least not in this life. In the place of universalism and the egalitarian view of the spiritual quest, the neotraditionalists restore a hierarchical path. Laypersons have roles distinct from *bhikkhus*; some beings are more advanced than others. Thus, the neotraditionalists follow the gradual path. As we have seen, they advocate restoring to the *bhikkhus* the traditional task of mediating the *Dhamma* to the laity. The *bhikkhus* also serve as mediators for the laity in the Buddhist rituals of merit-making which constitute the primary means to their goal.

In this post-Jayanti period both Buddhist rituals and the rituals of magical animism seem to have become increasingly important in Sri Lanka. This increase parallels the growth of neotraditionalism. Although pure reformism scorns ritualism and devotion, the neo-traditionalists have embraced it. Temples compete to have the largest and best-attended ritual ceremonies. Whereas previously the Äsala Perahära in Kandy represented the largest procession, in recent years, with the support of the laity, temples in the Colombo area such as Bellanwila Rāja Mahā Vihāra, Gangaramaya Vihāra, and Kelaniya Rājā Mahā Vihāra have staged almost equally elaborate *perahäras*. A *mahānāyaka* of a temple in Colombo proudly told me that his temple held each year the "biggest *Kaṭhina* procession in the city." Almsgiving and *pirit* ceremonies represent other important traditional rituals observed by lay Buddhists today. Some traditional rituals such as the *Bodhipūjā*, worship of the Bo tree, have had dramatic increases in popularity in the post-Jayanti period. *Bodhipūjā*, like *pirit*, serves as a means of employing Buddhist ritual for both merit and, most importantly, this-worldly benefits. Seneviratne and Wickremeratne have shown how individual *bhikkhus*, such as Venerable Pānadurā Ariyadhamma, have popularized the *Bodhipūjā* among middle-class youth.[123]

The ritual worship of the *devas* associated with Buddhism has also increased in popularity during this period. The early Protestant Buddhists, following the examples of Dharmapala and Olcott, rejected this side of Sinhalese religion. Olcott's *Catechism* declared that the Buddha condemned "the worship of gods, demons, trees, etc.[124] English-educated lay Buddhists followed this example even though they had a more traditional view of Buddhism than Olcott and Dharmapala. Educated urban lay Buddhists of Jayatilaka's and even Malalasekera's generation were somewhat embarrassed by the *deva*-worshiping aspects of traditional religion. Even as recently as twenty-five years ago, Ames could write that "magical-animism is not becoming more rationalized or systematized like Buddhism, nor synthesized with it."[125]

At some point during this period, however, the worship of the *devas* did begin to become both more important and more acceptable to urban lay Buddhists. Obeyesekere has explained that "contemporary elite Buddhists involved in the family and the larger society" could not discard the *devas* as easily as Dharmapala had because they needed some resource to whom they could appeal to grant favors and fulfill immediate needs. "Today's elite Buddhists therefore still depend on *devas*."[126] Obeyesekere contends that the frustrations involved in urban life led to "a cognitive reordering of these beliefs so as to make them fit the urban ethos."[127] Indeed, the worship of *devas* in modern times often appears to threaten to eclipse the purely Buddhist practices. The worship of the god Kataragama, for instance, has become extremely popular among both urban and rural laity. To quote Obeyesekere again, Kataragama, or Skanda, "is preeminently the deity of the upwardly mobile man—the businessman and the politician, the student studying for his examinations, the bureaucrat waiting for his promotion."[128] Thousands of Buddhists make the annual pilgrimage to the central shrine of Kataragama to attend the annual festival. Secondary shrines to Kataragama located in prominent Buddhist temples often appear to have become almost more popular than the Buddha shrines in the same temple.[129]

The final characteristic to note about this neotraditional Buddhism is one that has often been misunderstood by interpreters: its social concern and social activism. This element does not seem consistent with its otherwise traditional, world-denying approach. Mendis referred to this motif as a break with tradition in his critique of the Buddhist Commission's report. We can understand it as a partial carry-over from Protestant Buddhism's imitation of Protestant social service programs. Traditional Buddhism itself, however, provided for a certain kind of accommodation or affirmation of the world. Since *Nibbāna* was understood to be a remote goal, and renunciation of the world to reach it was not believed to represent a viable option for most people, then those on the mundane path had to cope with this world. Bardwell Smith noted that while the traditional gradual path tends "toward a purist ethic at one end of the scale, it resembles an accommodationist ethic at the other. . . . Thus Buddhism has within it not only a world-negating element that offers men release from the suffering of samsara but a world-affirming element that acknowledges the necessity of dealing with the world in worldly ways."[130]

Both in its attempts to gain governmental support for Buddhism and in its activities in the area of social welfare, the neotraditional elements of the contemporary lay movement seek to accommodate Buddhism to the modern situation. The activism of modern lay Buddhists can be seen as an attempt to work out an updated version of the traditional Buddhist ethic for householders. Contemporary Buddhists often refer to Asoka's formulation of the *Dhamma* as a model for the householder's ethic. To be sure, the ethic and the activities of today's Theravadins differ from those of the past because conditions differ. But just as the scriptures of Buddhism have sufficient ambiguity to allow interpreters to ground a variety of positions in them, so the Buddhist ethic of accommodation, which is scriptural, can be interpreted variously for varying situations. These lay Buddhists have interpreted the traditional Buddhist lay ethic in new ways but have attempted to remain true to the traditional understanding. Faced with the necessity of finding ways to apply the traditional ethic in the modern context, they seek in their own way precisely what modern interpreters of Buddhism have pointed to as a pressing need: "a social ethic commensurate with modern institutional life."[131] The lay Buddhists have developed this ethic more through practice than through theoretical reflection. If they have been too eclectic and not very philosophical in their search, they have at least understood the importance of the ethic and its centrality for Buddhism. One prominent Buddhist lay leader summarized his view of the importance of acting in the world when he observed to me that "Buddhism is just doing good and helping people. We must simply do good for so many lifetimes and then we can worry about the other details."

This neotraditional Buddhism represents the common practice of a large percentage of the educated lay Buddhists today, but we can take the lay organizations, the YMBA and the ACBC, as particular examples of it. The members of these societies are sincere in their practice of this path for householders and in their pragmatic adaptations of traditional Theravada to the modern world. An officer of the YMBA made an interesting comment that reveals the neotraditionalist outlook on these matters when he said, "Since we cannot stop modern ideas, we must tolerate them and go on being Buddhists." These lay organizations have more or less followed this maxim by continuing to have the same kinds of Buddhist activities they have always had, yet also addressing contemporary issues.

Their activities can be divided into four areas: (1) religious activities for the members; (2) social service activities; (3) taking positions on contemporary issues and problems; and (4) missionary activities. First (1.), the religious activities clearly reflect their traditional understanding of the layperson's role. On full-moon *poya* days both the ACBC and the YMBA sponsor Buddhist services for their members. They invite monks to preach, have Buddha *pūjā* ceremonies, and organize "*sil* campaigns" which encourage people to observe the eight or ten precepts during *poya*. On other occasions they hold almsgiving services, *pinkamas* or merit-making services, and *pirit* services. The scene at the headquarters of the ACBC and the YMBA on a *poya* day resembles that at the larger temples: hundreds of lay Buddhists, many of them elderly, dressed in white, spending the day following the precepts and joining in the rituals. Neither organization emphasizes meditation for the laity, although the YMBA has occasionally held classes in meditation on Sundays.

The YMBA continues to sponsor *Dhamma* schools and to conduct *Dhamma* exams for children. Although for a time the Ministry of Cultural Affairs took charge of these exams, the YMBA happily regained control of them in 1982.

(2.) Social service has continued to represent a significant activity for these groups. The Buddhist Congress's National Council of Social Services administers some twenty-seven institutions, and the YMBA administers a number of institutions of its own. These charities include orphanages, homes for the handicapped, retirement homes for *bhikkhus* and laity, as well as some newer ventures such as a hostel in the Free Trade Zone for young women employed there.

(3.) The third area of activity by the ACBC and the YMBA has involved taking positions on contemporary problems and safeguarding the interests of Buddhists. The Buddhist Congress has always constituted a Buddhist lobby or pressure group. Their first objective as stated in their charter is "to promote, foster and protect the interests of Buddhism and of the Buddhists and to safeguard the rights and privileges of the Buddhists."[132] That was the reason they initiated the Buddhist Committee of Enquiry. Today, both groups actively represent the cause of Buddhism to the government. The issues they have taken up in recent years shed light on the interests of lay Buddhists. Monastic reform has continued to constitute an important issue. Both laymen's groups defer to the *Sangha* and hold it in high regard, but they have also passed resolutions urging reforms.[133] In 1983 the ACBC was still advocating a Sāsana Council and a judiciary for monks, provisions from the never-enacted Sāsana Commission Report. They also sought to help the Buddhist nuns, the *sil mātāvas*, by gathering information and persuading the Department of Buddhist Affairs to assist them. Buddhist education has been another priority. They recommended the establishment of a Buddhist university for *bhikkhus* and the reform of the state school system to give Buddhism its proper place in the schools.

Contemporary moral issues continue to represent a major concern of the lay Buddhist groups and they have lobbied for these also. At the annual meeting of the ACBC in 1985 the members adopted a resolution urging all Buddhists to refrain from eating beef. They adduced an interesting combination of traditional and modern logic in support of this resolution. On the one hand they argued that on grounds of nonharming, Buddhists should not eat the animals that help the rice farmer, and on the other hand they contended that a vegetarian diet is to be preferred because it is healthier. Similar moral objections have been raised against liquor and tobacco. They have protested the government's support of these practices through taxation and other means. In a Buddhist country the government should seek to achieve a *dhammic* society. Similarly, on moral grounds they object to the government's support of commercial fishing through its Ministry of Fisheries.

In 1985 the ACBC adopted a resolution calling for Buddhists to cease engaging in birth control. Their argument against this issue, however, did not involve moral reasons but demographic and *dhammic* ones. They held that if present trends continue, the Sinhalese will be a minority in the country within fifteen years. Thus, they should avoid birth control so the Sinhalese will be able to fulfill their responsibility of protecting and propagating the Buddha *Sāsana*.

Another issue that has concerned these organizations recently has been the welfare of Buddhists in the northern and eastern provinces. They have petitioned the government to protect the *bhikkhus* and the temples in those areas. The conflict with the Tamils has been a major concern, and these lay organizations have sought to bring peace. Both the ACBC and the YMBA have passed resolutions calling for the government to revoke the party system because "political parties, while being perhaps the most competent to suggest solutions to political problems . . . may overlook if not ignore the preferences of the members of the community they claim to represent which includes the large mass of Tamil people as well as the Sinhala people." In short, these laymen said that the politicians looking for popular courses of action had created this conflict and disturbed the harmony between the Sinhalese and Tamils "which was rooted in a religious and cultural affinity, between the two major communities."[134]

In response to all of these contemporary issues, the ACBC in 1985 was planning to initiate another Buddhist Committee of Enquiry. The leaders felt that a large part of the first committee's report had not been implemented, and that new problems today needed addressing. The leaders of the YMBA, however, disagreed saying that since Buddhism has been given the "foremost place" by the Constitution, it has been restored to its proper place.

(4.) The lay Buddhists today continue to believe that missionaries of the *Dhamma*, *dhammadūtas*, should be sent to other lands. The World Fellowship of Buddhists, through its *Dhammadūta* Activities Committee headed by Mr. Albert Edirisinghe, has moved on this front. Using a terminology reminiscent of Protestant missions, they seek the "propagation of the *Dhamma*" so that "its benign spirit of service and sacrifice may pervade the entire world."[135] In addition to sending *bhikkhus* to various parts of the world, they have distributed Buddhist tracts and placed anthologies of the Buddha's teachings in hotels in Sri Lanka. "Now every tourist who visits the country is given the opportunity of reading . . . the teaching of the compassionate Buddha that is the panacea for all of the world's afflictions."[136]

Conclusion

To summarize the outcome of the Jayanti from our perspective three decades later, we can say that the Buddhists who took as their principal duty the restoration of Buddhism to its "rightful place" have achieved one but not both of the results they believed would follow from this restoration. They have rediscovered their heritage and identity, but they have not simultaneously established the kingdom of peace and prosperity that they anticipated. As they have reinterpreted the Buddhist tradition, they have attended to the need to recover their identity, but they have not adequately addressed the corollary task of responsiveness. To be sure, to a people emerging from centuries of colonial rule, rediscovering their identity constituted a necessary first response to their contemporary context. The Sinhalese sought to reestablish their identity and their culture in order to become truly independent of Western influences. The reassertion of the Sinhala-Buddhist mythology and the revival of neotraditional Buddhism during this period have been central to their quest. But although the restoration of Buddhism and the Buddhist mythology has brought numerous benefits, including increased self-respect and cultural pride, it does not seem to have constituted the most adequate response to several dimensions of the modern context. In particular, neotraditional Sinhalese Buddhism has not offered the most promising responses to either the social context or the individual context.

The social context has represented a particularly difficult problem. The Sinhalese have wrestled with launching a new nation with all the domestic and international difficulties entailed, while at the same time coping with waves of scientific and technological modernization and also establishing their cultural identity. Although, as Ames noted, they have wanted to become modern without becoming Western,[137] the traditional or neotraditional Buddhist identity has not always facilitated social change and progress. The Buddhists have put forward social service schemes and have compassionately aided the needy in society. But beyond a few basic social welfare institutions, the neotraditional interpretation of the Buddhist heritage has not supplied an adequate social ethic for modern problems. The social reform recommendations of the Buddhist Commission's report failed to restore the ideal Buddhist society they envisioned. These traditional proposals failed largely because they were not appropriate to the modern context. As we observed, many of the recommendations for social change seem to have arisen out of a nostalgia for the traditional Sinhalese Buddhist village life style. They represented what one commentator on social change has referred to as "attitudes and values that were integral parts of the value system of the closed agricultural society" from which the Buddhists were emerging.[138] In the face of rapid change and Westernization, the new urban elite longed for the simpler life and mores of the village. Yet, even though reform proposals based on this nostalgia for the past failed, the lay Buddhists have continued to seek moralistic reforms.

Similarly, the neotraditional interpretation of Buddhist values has not constituted an adequate basis for national progress. Although the government of Sri Lanka has cast itself in the role of the protector of Buddhism, it has had difficulty formulating a progressive policy consistent with Buddhist values. Two examples will illustrate the Sri Lankan dilemma at this point. When the government has sought to be true to its Sinhala–Buddhist heritage, it has followed policies that may not have been the most progressive. Leach has observed that Sinhalese politicans since D. S. Senanayake "have preferred to build grandiose irrigation works rather than factories," even though factories were needed more, because in building the dams and tanks they were following the model of the ancient Sinhalese kings.[139] On the other hand, when the government has committed itself to measures designed to bring economic development, it has found little support in the Buddhist tradition, for, as Obeyesekere has noted, "Economic development and technological advances are perceived as aspects of Western scientific materialism and therefore devalued."[140] Although accommodation to the world is necessary, traditional Theravada values advocate greater simplicity, not greater wealth, in the world.

The most serious failure of neotraditional Buddhists to respond adequately to the modern context has been in the area of Sinhala-Tamil relations. Using as a charter the mythology of the "divine right" of the Sinhalese to protect Buddhism, contemporary Buddhists have exploited their majority position and alienated the Tamil minority. To be sure, there is no doubt that the Buddhists had both the right and the necessity to regain the power that had been denied them by the colonial governments. It was both natural and traditional for them to seek to use governmental means to restore their Buddhist heritage. However, there can also be no doubt that politicians and other Sinhalese went too far in restoring not only Buddhism but also the Sinhalese Buddhists to their "rightful place." As Bardwell Smith commented, "Political capital has been made of indigenous religion, of folk-Buddhism and of orthodox Theravada, with the assistance of elements within the *Sangha*, by candidates seeking to ingratiate themselves with the rural masses and the more sophisticated."[141]

This politicization of the religion reinforced the neotraditionalist interpretation. Not only the politicians but, at times, elements of the *Sangha* and other Buddhists also have been both too literal and too zealous about their responsibility to protect the *sāsana*. When the *bhikkhus* marched on the Prime Minister's residence in 1958 in support of the "Sinhala Only" legislation, and again when they demonstrated in 1986 and 1987 in opposition to the President's offer of provincial autonomy to the Tamils, they claimed that they were defending both Sinhala nationalism and Buddhism. In these cases, however, traditional Buddhism has become too closely bound up with Sinhala nationalism; the mythology has been taken too literally. It cannot be that the *Dhamma* demands this kind of intolerance toward a people with whom the Sinhalese have deep cultural ties. But a traditionalist interpretation of the religion and of the Buddhist Chronicles and the encouragement of the politicians has fostered these views.

One clear outcome of the Jayanti and of the traditionalist interpretation of Buddhism that links lanaguage, race, and religion, then, has been this further separation of the Sinhalese and the Tamils. Over twenty years ago Donald Smith wrote prophetically about this "Sinhalese Buddhist Revolution" and the victories that the Sinhalese claimed: "Certain injustices have been rectified, valid communal grievances have been redressed. But the cost has been high, paid in the coin of national integration. The communalization of politics during this period has set in motion forces which will not be easy to reverse."[142]

After the riots of July, 1983, there were signs that the Buddhists had begun to recognize the necessity of a reversal of these forces. In the wake of the violence by the Sinhalese toward the Tamils, many Buddhists with whom I spoke denied that the attackers had been Sinhalese Buddhists, declaring that they may have been Sinhalese but they could not have been Buddhists. This response represented one of the first moves since the Jayanti toward disavowing the necessary combination of the Sinhalese and Buddhist identities. Explaining the tragic events, Buddhists said, "Do not say that this was done by Sinhalese Buddhists, for Buddhism had nothing to do with it." A leading *bhikkhu*, who had served on the Buddhist Committee of Enquiry, commented that the violence indicated that Buddhism had not been restored in the lives and intentions of many Sinhalese. Whether Buddhists can profit from this recognition of the shortcomings in their interpretation and application of Buddhism remains to be seen. Let us hope that the situation has not progressed too far on both sides for wisdom and peace to prevail.

Finally, with regard to the individual context as well as the social, the neotraditional interpretation has appeared to many not to represent the most appropriate response. As we have seen, this interpretation has dictated definite, inflexible roles for laity and monks. The true goal of human liberation and fulfillment, *Nibbāna*, it has declared out of reach for most laity and monks who must follow the "preliminary course" of merit-making and rebirth. Two basic assumptions of Buddhism, however, prevent one from saying that this interpretation has no relevance today. Buddhism has held (1) that *karma* stratifies beings on a spiritual continuum and (2) that because of this stratification individuals have differing spiritual needs and potentials. Thus, theoretically, for many Buddhists today a neotraditional interpretation that defines the householder's life in the modern world should be entirely appropriate. And in practice this interpretation does seem to have sufficed for a large percentage of the Sinhalese. Offering moral guidelines, rituals, and deities to rely on here, it has held out the hope of a better life to come en route to eventual liberation.

By this same logic of the gradual path, however, other Buddhists have found this traditional householder's level insufficient and stifling. They have argued,

The goals of Buddhism are not the temple rites and ceremonies; these may at best be elementary exercises for training the individual for his march toward the goals. The goals are the outcome of a development within himself. This development is nothing but a complete grasp of the reality of one's own living-experience.[143]

Thus, rejecting the neotraditional formulation, these Buddhists have developed more truly reformist interpretations of Theravada with a better balance of identity and responsiveness. These interpretations have been more optimistic about the individual's spiritual potential and more relevant to the individual's practice of Buddhism in the modern social context.

The following chapters examine two kinds of reformist interpretations that have developed in the revival of Buddhism in Sri Lanka: the meditation movement and the social action movement as exemplified by the Sarvodaya Movement. If the neotraditional viewpoint of lay Buddhism could be described by Swearer as "oriented more towards a reiteration of pasts values than a dynamic reassessment of Buddhism" and as "more of a resurgence than a reformation,"[144] the movements that we shall consider in the following chapters seem to move beyond neotraditionalism on all of these points. Significantly, however, they do not break entirely with the interpretations we have studied thus far, for they also represent developments of Protestant Buddhism and the Jayanti period.

Notes

1. The figure 5,000 came from Buddhaghosa's commentary, Samantapāsādikā VI, although the theme of renewal is not found there. See also Richard Gombrich, *Precept and Practice: Traditional Buddhism in the Rural Highlands of Ceylon* (Oxford: Oxford University Press, 1971), 284 n. 28.
2. *Mahāvṃsa*, ed. Wilhelem Geiger (London: Pali Text Society, 1958), ch. 7, 62f.
3. D. C. Vijayavardhana, *Dharma Vijaya (Triumph of Righteousness)* or *The Revolt in the Temple* (Colombo: Sinha Publications, 1953), 3.
4. Donald E. Smith, ed., *South Asian Politics and Religion* (Princeton: Princeton University Press, 1966), 458.
5. Michael Ames, "Ideological and Social Change in Ceylon," *Human Organization*, 22 (1963): 48; W. Howard Wriggins, *Ceylon: Dilemmas of a New Nation* (Princeton: Princeton University Press, 1960), 173.
6. G. P. Malalasekera, "Fifty Years of Service," *Golden Jubilee Souvenir* (All Ceylon Buddhist Congress, 1969), 20f.
7. See *Vinaya Piṭaka*, II, 256 f. *Anguttara Nikāya*, IV, 274ff.
8. Gombrich, *Precept and Practice*, 284n.28, notes that Buddhaghosa "equates *Dhamma* with *paṭivedha* (realization) which will disappear in five stages of 1000 years each, and *pariyatti* (learning) which will disappear with it." He shows that a version of this pessimistic form of the tradition is known in Sinhalese popular traditions. This understanding of a five-thousand-year life for the *Dhamma* was also expressed in the *katikavata* of Parakramabahu I (1153-1186 C.E.). Mendis says, "This shows that the Buddhists of those times accepted the Hindu ideas of cosmogony; that the world was gradually deteriorating" (G. C. Mendis, *Ceylon Today and Yesterday* [Colombo: Lake House Press, 1963], 147). Chapter four below will discuss the people's knowledge of this prediction and their use of it today.
9. Vijayavardhana, *Dharma Vijaya*, 3. The author explains that this myth derived from a verse in a work written during the reign of King Parākramabāhu VI of Kotte. Gananath Obeyesekere notes that the Diyasena myth became popular among Sinhala peasants during the British period. Demoralized, the Buddhists grasped at this hope. Diyasena was to be a hero who would "kill all the Christians and non-believers and reestablish the glory of the Buddha *Sāsana*." See Obeyesekere, "Personal Identity and Cultural Crisis: The Case of Anagārika Dharmapala of Sri Lanka," in *The Biographical Process: Studies in the History and Psychology of Religion*, ed. Frank E. Reynolds and Donald Capps (The Hague: Mouton, 1976), 224.
10. Rachaka, "A Short History of the Y.M.B.A., 1898-1958," *The Buddhist* 29 (May 1958): 51.
11. The Buddhist Committee of Enquiry, *The Betrayal of Buddhism: An Abridged Version of the Report of the Buddhist Committee of Enquiry* (Balangoda: Dharmavijaya Press, 1956), iii.
12. J. P. Rathirana, "Hail! Jayanti," *The Buddhist*, 27 (May 1956): 67.

13. H. R. Perera, *Buddhism in Ceylon, Its Past and Present* (Kandy: Buddhist Publication Society, 1966), 78.
14. G. P. Malalasekera, "2500" (editorial), *The Buddhist*, 27 (May 1956): 1.
15. G. P. Malalasekera, "Presidential Address" to the All Ceylon Buddhist Congress, 1953, cited in Heinz Bechert, *Buddhismus, Staat und Gesellschaft in den Ländern des Theravāda-Buddhismus* (Wiesbaden: Otto Harrassowitz, 1973), 3: 472.
16. Venerable Mirisse Gunasiri Mahāthera, "The Teaching That Revolutionised Human Thought," *The Buddhist*, 27 (May 1956): 33.
17. G. P. Malalasekera, *2500 Years of Buddhism* (Colombo: World Fellowship of Buddhists, 1982), 11.
18. Perera, *Buddhism in Ceylon*, 78.
19. Malalasekera, cited in Bechert, *Buddhismus*, 3: 469.
20. "Bauddha Mandalaya Programme For Buddha Jayanti," *The Buddhist* 27 (May 1956), 99–100.
21. *Dictionary of Pali Proper Names* (London: Luzac, 1960).
22. G. P. Malalasekera, "Encyclopedia of Buddhism—Its Plan and Scope," *The Buddhist* 29 (May 1958): 58f.
23. Smith, *South Asian Politics*, 461.
24. See N. A. Jayawickrama and W. G. Weeraratne, *The World Fellowship of Buddhists and Its Founder President G. P. Malalasekera* (Colombo: World Fellowship of Buddhists, 1982).
25. K. Malalgoda, "Buddhism in Sri Lanka: Continuity and Change," in *Sri Lanka: A Survey*, ed. K. M. deSilva (London: C. Hurst, 1976), 388.
26. G. P. Malalasekera, "Buddhism in the Modern World," in *Vesak Sirisara*, ed. K. Jināananda Thera and H. P. Jayawardena (Panadura: Sri Saddharmadāna Samitiya Saranapālāramaya, Wālana, 1971), 4.
27. Cited in Bechert, *Buddhismus*, 3: 467.
28. The Committee of Inquiry's members as listed in the foreword to the Report, were Ven. Ambanwelle Siddharta Dhammānanda, presently Anunāyake of the Malvatta Chapter; Ven. Haliyale Sumanatissa of the Asgiriya Chapter; Ven. Paṇḍita Palannoruwe Vimaladhamma, Vice-Principal of Vidyodaya *Piriveṇa*, Colombo; Ven. Balangoḍa Ānanda Maitreya, Principal of Sri Dhammānanda *Piriveṇa*, Balangoḍa; Ven. Paṇḍita Sri Gnanaloka, Vice-Principal of Sārasvati *Piriveṇa*, Balagalla; Ven. Koṭahēnē Paññākitti, Vice-Principal of Vidyalankara *Piriveṇa*, Kelaniya; Ven. Maḍihē Paññāsīha; Dr. G. P. Malasekera; Dr. T. Vimalānanda; P. de S. Kularatne; D. C. Wijayawardena; L. H. Mettananda; T. B. Ellepola (who resigned later); C. D. S. Siriwardene.
29. Wriggins, *Ceylon*, 195.
30. G. C. Mendis, *Ceylon Today and Yesterday: Main Currents of Ceylon History* (Colombo: Associated Newspapers, 1963), 148.
31. Smith, *South Asian Politics*, 463.
32. Wriggins, *Ceylon*, 196f.
33. Smith, *South Asian Politics*, 463.
34. *Betrayal of Buddhism*, 99.
35. *Betrayal of Buddhism*, 101.

36. *Betrayal of Buddhism*, 84.
37. Donald K. Swearer, "Lay Buddhism and the Buddhist Revival in Ceylon," *Journal of the American Academy of Religion*, 38 (1970): 263.
38. Bellah, *Religion and Progress in Modern Asia*, (New York: Free Press, 1965), 212–13.
39. Michael Ames, "Westernization or Modernization: The Case of Sinhalese Buddhism," *Social Compass*, 20 (1973): 162.
40. The eight chapters of the report were: I. Religion and State in Ceylon; II. Education; III. Contemporary Social Conditions; IV. Economic Conditions; V. Social Services; VI. The *Sangha* Today; VII. *Pirivena* Education; VIII. Tolerance. Since the report has been analyzed in detail elsewhere (see Smith, *South Asian Politics*. and Bechert, *Buddhismus*) this chapter summarizes and analyzes those elements most relevant to the Buddhist revival.
41. *Betrayal of Buddhism*, 37.
42. Wriggins, *Ceylon*, 197.
43. Cited in Bechert, *Buddhismus*, 3: 461.
44. *Betrayal of Buddhism*, 41.
45. Smith, *South Asian Politics*, 465.
46. *Betrayal of Buddhism*, 32.
47. Cited in Bechert, *Buddhismus*, 3: 459.
48. Smith, *South Asian Politics*, 480.
49. Wriggins, *Ceylon*, 202.
50. *Betrayal of Buddhism*, 94.
51. Smith, *South Asian Politics*, 482.
52. Wriggins, *Ceylon*, 204.
53. Smith, *South Asian Politics*, 463.
54. The introduction to chapter 3 of the report points out that when the Sinhalese originally adopted the Buddhist values from Mahinda, they were able to develop an advanced civilization in 150 years, which was less time than it took the United States, "a country with vast natural resources," to develop.
55. *Poya* days are the four days each month marking the phases of the lunar cycle, with the full-moon day *(pasaḷosvaka poya)* being the major *poya* day when most Buddhists traditionally visited the temples. The term derives from the Pali *uposatha*. In Theravada the monks are required to recite the *Pāṭimokkha*, the disciplinary code, on the full-moon and no-moon *(māsa-poya)* days.
56. *Betrayal of Buddhism*, 102.
57. *Betrayal of Buddhism*, 105.
58. *Betrayal of Buddhism*, 103.
59. *Betrayal of Buddhism*, 115–16.
60. Ames, "Ideological and Social Change," 47.
61. *Betrayal of Buddhism*, iii.
62. See, for example: K. M. deSilva, *A History of Sri Lanka* (Berkeley: University of California, 1981); K. M. deSilva, ed., *Sri Lanka: A Survey* (London: Hurst, 1976); T. Fernando and R. N. Kearney, *Modern Sri Lanka: A Society in Transition* (Syracuse: Syracuse University Press, 1978); R. N. Kearney, *The Politics of Ceylon (Sri Lanka)* (Ithaca, NY: Cornell University Press, 1973); Urdmila Phadnis, *Religion and Politics*

in Sri Lanka (New Delhi: 1976); Marshall R. Singer, *The Emerging Elite: A Study of Political Leadership in Ceylon* (Cambridge, MA: M.I.T. Press, 1964); D. E. Smith, *South Asian Politics and Religion;* A. J. Wilson, *Politics in Sri Lanka 1947-1979* (London: Macmillan, 1979); and W. Howard Wriggins, *Ceylon: Dilemmas of a New Nation.*

63. Edmund Leach, "Buddhism in the Post-Colonial Political Order in Burma and Ceylon," *Daedalus* 102 (1973): 45.

64. Leach, "Buddhism in the Post-Colonial Political Order," 48.

65. Smith, *South Asian Politics*, 474.

66. *Betrayal of Buddhism*, 41.

67. deSilva, "Buddhism, Nationalism and Politics," 37.

68. Vidyodaya University and Vidyālaṇkāra University Act, No. 45 of 1958, section 5(a). Cited in Smith, *South Asian Politics*, 475.

69. *The Buddhist* 31 (June 1960): 98.

70. Smith, *South Asian Politics*, 456.

71. Smith, *South Asian Politics*, 477.

72. For the details see Leach, "Buddhism in the Post-Colonial Order," 45f; Smith, *South Asian Politics*, 489–99.

73. deSilva, "Buddhism, Nationalism and Politics," 39.

74. deSilva, "Buddhism, Nationalism and Politics," 41.

75. Leach, "Buddhism in the Post-Colonial Political Order," 44.

76. Ames, "*Westernization or Modernization*," 162.

77. *Betrayal of Buddhism*, 99.

78. *Betrayal of Buddhism*, 104.

79. Gombrich, *Precept and Practice*, 273f.

80. Cited in Michael Ames, "The Impact of Western Education on Religion and Society in Ceylon," *Pacific Affairs*, 40 (1967): 36.

81. Leach, "Buddhism in the Post-Colonial Political Order," 39.

82. D. C. R. Gunawardena, P. H. Wickremasinghe, and D. E. Wijewardena, *Report of the Universities Commission 1962* (Sessional Paper 16 of 1963; Colombo: Government Press), 22, 40. Cited in Ames, "The Impact of Western Education," 35.

83. Winston King, *In the Hope of Nibbāna: An Essay on Theravada Buddhist Ethics* (LaSalle, IL: Open Court, 1964), 185 (Italics in original.).

84. Malalgoda, "Buddhism in Sri Lanka," 389.

85. See "Bhikkhu Training Colleges," *The Buddhist*, 25 (Sept. 1954): 139.

86. Malalgoda, "Buddhism in Sri Lanka," 388.

87. Smith, *South Asian Politics*, 501. Also see Bardwell Smith, "Sinhalese Buddhism and the Dilemmas of Reinterpretation," *The Two Wheels of Dhamma*, ed. B. L. Smith (Chambersburg, Pa: American Academy of Religion, 1972), 93f.

88. *Betrayal of Buddhism*, 41.

89. See Bardwell Smith, "Sinhalese Buddhism and the Dilemmas of Reinterpretation," 92; Bechert, *Buddhismus*, 1: 267ff; deSilva, "Buddhism, Nationalism and Politics," 43f.; Donald E. Smith, *South Asian Politics*. 504f.

90. *Betrayal of Buddhism*, 84, 115f.

91. "Divergent Views on the Sāsana Report," *World Buddhism* 8 (1960): 10f.

92. "Divergent Views on the Sāsana Report," 11.

93. Bardwell Smith, "Sinhalese Buddhism and the Dilemmas of Reinterpretation," 93.
94. Cited in Smith, "Sinhalese Buddhism and the Dilemmas of Reinterpretation," 93.
95. Walpola Rahula, *The Heritage of the Bhikkhu*, trans., K. P. G. Wijayasurendra (New York: Grove Press, 1974), 131.
96. "Giving Buddhism Its Rightful Place," *World Buddhism* 13 (1965): 12.
97. "Divergent Views on the Sāsana Report," 11.
98. "Divergent Views on the Sāsana Report," 11.
99. Bardwell Smith, "Sinhalese Buddhism and the Dilemmas of Reinterpretation," 92.
100. Donald Smith, *South Asian Politics*, 506.
101. Donald Smith, *South Asian Politics*, 458.
102. Bardwell Smith, "Sinhalese Buddhism and the Dilemmas of Reinterpretation," 89.
103. Ames, "Westernization or Modernization," 161f.
104. Heinz Bechert, "Theravada Buddhist *Sangha:* Some General observations on Historical and Political Factors in its Development," *Journal of the Association of Asian Studies* 29 (1970): 776.
105. Mendis, *Ceylon*, 146.
106. *The Buddhist,* 52 (Aug. 1981): 131.
107. Editorial, *The Buddhist* 51 (Mar.–Apr. 1981): 1.
108. Amazingly this latter charge was made by a prominent Buddhist layman when the Christian groups sought to aid refugees after the 1983 riots. He said that the refugee camps were only a pretext for making converts. Its use illustrates the enduring power of the report's rhetoric.
109. Donald Smith, *South Asian Politics*, 460.
110. Mendis, *Ceylon*, 148.
111. S. J. Tambiah, "The Persistence and Transformation of Tradition in Southeast Asia, with Special Reference to Thailand," *Daedalus* 102 (1973), 58.
112. *Betrayal of Buddhism*, 148.
113. Mendis, *Ceylon*, 148.
114. "UNESCO–Sri Lanka Project of the Cultural Triangle," brochure, n.d., p. 5.
115. Betrayal of Buddhism. 4. Even in 1983 the surviving members of the committee still opposed granting state religion status to Buddhism.
116. "Buddhism Will Be State Religion, Says Premier," *World Buddhism* 19 (1971): 192f.
117. "Buddhism Will Be State Religion," 193.
118. deSilva, "Buddhism, Nationalism and Politics," 45.
119. Malalgoda, "Buddhism in Sri Lanka," 388.
120. D. B. Jayatilaka, "Practical Buddhism," *The Buddhist* (July 1901); repr. *The Buddhist* 51 (Jan. 1981); 2–17.
121. Heinz Bechert, "*Sangha,* State, Society, 'Nation': Persistence of Traditions in 'Post-Traditional' Buddhist Societies," *Daedalus* 102 (1973): 91.
122. Jayatilaka, "Practical Buddhism," 2.
123. H. L. Seneviratne and S. Wickremeratne, "Bodhipūjā: Collective Representations of Sri Lanka Youth," *American Ethnologist* 4 (1980): 734–43.
124. Henry Steel Olcott, *The Buddhist Catechism* (Madras: Theosophical Publishing House, 1970), 55f.
125. Ames, "Ideological and Social Change," 46.

126. Obeyesekere, "Personal Identity and Cultural Crisis," 249.

127. Gananath Obeyesekere, "Religious Symbolism and Political Change in Ceylon," in *The Two Wheels of Dhamma*, 76.

128. Obeyesekere, "Religious Symbolism and Political Change," 74.

129. To be sure, the Buddhists who visit Kataragama's shrine in a temple are presumed to have visited the Buddha's shrine first. But it would be an interesting project to investigate the primary reasons that these people visit the temple.

130. Bardwell Smith, "Toward a Buddhist Anthropology: The Problem of the Secular, *Journal of the American Academy of Religion*, 36.3 (1968), 2.

131. Bardwell Smith, "Toward a Buddhist Anthropology," 203.

132. Parliament of Ceylon, Act No. 24 of 1955, Third Session 54-55, Government Publishing Bureau. Cited also in Swearer, "Lay Buddhism and the Buddhist Revival in Ceylon," 271 n. 51. He lists also the other aims and objectives given in the charter of the Buddhist Congress.

133. Even the organizational structure of the Buddhist Congress reflects its view of the proper roles for *bhikkhus* and laypersons. Its board of directors comprises fifteen leading *bhikkhus* and no laymen. The *Mahānāyakas* of the Malvatta and Asgiriya chapters of the Siyam Nikāya head the list of board members.

134. Noel Wijenaike, Honarary General Secretary, Young Men's Buddhist Association-Colombo, Summary of the Report for 1983/84, p. 5.

135. "The Dhammadūta Activities Committee in Action," *Bauddha Marga Vesak Annual* (1983), 69.

136. "Dhammadūta Activities Committee," 73.

137. Ames, "Westernization or Modernization," 163.

138. Soedjatmoko, "Cultural Motivation to Progress: The 'Exterior' and the 'Interior' Views," in Robert Bellah, ed., *Religion and Progress in Modern Asia* (New York: Free Press, 1965), 5.

139. Leach, "Buddhism in the Post-Colonial Political Order," 39.

140. Obeyesekere, "Religious Symbolism and Political Change," 66.

141. Bardwell Smith, "Sinhalese Buddhism and the Dilemmas of Reinterpretation," 97.

142. Donald Smith, *South Asian Politics*, 488.

143. Bogoda Premaratne, "The Social Welfare Objectives of the Buddhist Congress," *Golden Jubilee Souvenir* (All Ceylon Buddhist Congress, 1969), 122.

144. Swearer, "Lay Buddhism and the Buddhist Revival," 273.

4

The Insight Meditation
(*Vipassanā Bhāvanā*) Movement

The preceding chapters have examined two patterns of response that set the course for the early stages of the Sinhalese Buddhist revival. In the midst of the preparations for the Buddha Jayanti and the development of the neotraditionalist interpretation, another pattern of response was emerging. The insight meditation, or *vipassanā bhāvanā*, movement began in the 1950s but received little attention during the Jayanti celebrations. It did not figure in the traditionalistic reforms proposed by the Buddhist Committee of Inquiry in 1956, proposals that set the agenda for Jayanti Buddhism. Nevertheless, the insight meditation movement grew and developed to the point that it became one of the dominant movements of the revival, while many of the reforms proposed during the Buddha Jayanti faded and declined, as we have seen. Although the insight meditation movement can be said to have grown out of the earlier pattern of response of Protestant Buddhism as did the neotraditionalism of the Jayanti, it differed in that it represented a true reformist movement. The insight meditation movement found a reinterpreted identity for Theravada by employing two of the approaches Bellah describes as typical of reformism: a return to the early texts and a rejection of much of the intervening tradition.[1] Because of these approaches the insight meditation movement developed an interpretation that differed sharply from the neotraditionalist viewpoint of Jayanti Buddhism. The interpretation of

Buddhism by *vipassanā* meditation advocates expressed most of the motifs of reformism that we noted in chapter one. Like the neotraditionalists the meditation reformers also based their interpretation on the Buddhist scriptures and sought to re-present the true ideas and practices of Buddhism. Instead of espousing the commentarial viewpoint, however, these interpreters went directly back to the "early Buddhism" of the Canon for their charter. Their vision of Buddhism highlighted not the gradual path to *Nibbāna* but the ethic of self-cultivation by both monks and laypersons alike.[2] They sought to revitalize Buddhism much more radically, advocating a universalism that opened the tradition to all people in new ways and encouraged all Buddhists to become spiritual virtuosos.

This chapter examines the insight meditation movement by contrasting its interpretation of the tradition and its response to modernity with that of the traditionalists. The reform of meditation, more than any other single issue, brought the two groups, the neotraditionalists and the reformists, into direct conflict on questions of ideology and practice. This conflict has continued down to the present time, although the popularity of the *vipassanā* movement seems to be gradually eroding the opposition of the traditionalists and neotraditionalists. After a brief history of the insight meditation, or *vipassanā bhāvanā*, movement, we shall consider five points of belief and practice that distinguish this response pattern and contrast these with the views of the traditionalists. The five points considered may be seen, on the one hand, as factors that have contributed to the popularity of the meditation movement, putting it in the forefront of the modern reformation, and, on the other hand, as factors that brought the movement into opposition with the traditionalist and neotraditionalist elements of the Theravada *Sangha* and laity. The five points are (1) beliefs about the plausibility of arahantship and *Nibbāna*; (2) beliefs concerning the necessity of renunciation; (3) beliefs about the study of the *Tipiṭaka*, (4) the ritual system of *bhāvanā* or meditation and its usefulness; and (5) the methods of practicing *vipassanā bhāvanā*.

History of the Vipassanā Bhāvanā Movement

During the early 50s a group of the leading Buddhist laymen among the English-educated elite in Ceylon society began to discuss the prospect of developing *vipassanā bhāvanā* centers in Sri Lanka. Some of these laymen, such as H. Sri Nissanka, had traveled to Burma and had become aware of the popularity that meditation enjoyed among the laity there.[3] Sri Nissanka had actually taken temporary ordination as a monk in a Burmese-related Amarupura Nikāya temple in Colombo and then studied meditation in Burma.[4] Burma had exerted an important influence on Sri Lanka since the nineteenth century, when it was the source of Sinhalese *Sanqha* reform, and the twentieth century saw continued significant interchange between Sri Lanka and Burma, with many monks going there for study and training in meditation.

Aware of and excited by this religious ferment in Burma, and anticipating the great event of the Buddha Jayanti only a few years in the future, these Protestant Buddhist laity formed the *Lanka Vipassanā Bhāvanā Samitiya* (Lanka Insight Meditation Society). With the encouragement and assistance of the Prime Minister, Sir John Kotelawala, and the Burmese ambassador in Ceylon, U Ba Lwin, the society made a formal request to the Burmese government and to Mahasi Sayadaw to send teachers to Sri Lanka to begin meditation courses for laypersons and monks. A Sinhalese elder, the Venerable Kahatapitiya Sumathipala, who was in Burma when the request came, had practiced meditation at Thathana Yeiktha, Mahasi Sayadaw's temple and the center of the *vipassanā* movement in Rangoon. Therefore, he was consulted by the Burmese about plans to send a delegation to Ceylon. Soon after this Ven. Sumathipala returned to Ceylon and organized the arrangements there. With his help the lay society acquired land for the first meditation center and laid other plans for promoting *vipassanā*.

A Burmese delegation of four theras, led by U Sujata, a close assistant to Mahasi Sayadaw, arrived in Ceylon on July 29, 1955.[5] Sir John Kotelawala and J. R. Jayawardene were among the leading Sinhalese laity who received the Burmese monks. The Burmese delegation did not include Mahasi Sayadaw, who was involved in the Sixth Buddhist Council then in session in Burma, but he, as the main figure responsible for dispatching his monastic associates, sent a message of goodwill.

Although H. Sri Nissanka had died during the previous year, his wife and family, having become closely involved in the budding meditation movement, invited the Burmese monks to reside at their house on Maya Avenue.[6] The Burmese monks offered meditation classes first at Sri Nissanka's house and later at meditation centers established in Colombo. Hundreds of laypeople received training during the first few months. The people who participated in these meditation classes represented the English-educated elite. A meditator who attended the classes told me that the Burmese monks conducted the classes through an interpreter who translated their lectures into English.

After several months the new meditation movement encountered two major problems. On one hand, the Burmese monks were dissatisfied that more Sri Lankan monks had not attended their classes; on the other hand, some Sri Lankan monks began to voice opposition to the entire movement as a false and foreign intrusion into the Sri Lankan Theravada tradition. To settle these problems a group of Buddhist laymen organized another society for meditation, the *Siyane Vipassanā Bhāvanā Samitiya,* and founded a meditation center outside of Colombo near Delgoda and Kelaniya on a former estate called Kanduboda Watte. Subsequently called simply Kanduboda, this center became the hub of the *vipassanā* movement in Sri Lanka, although other meditation centers such as the important one on McCarthy Road (now Wijerama Mawata) played major parts. The senior Burmese monk in the delegation, Venerable U Sujata, served as the first "principal" of Kanduboda, although his seems to have been largely an honorary title since he had by then—or soon afterward—returned to Burma. The first resident director of the center was Venerable Kahatapitiya Sumathipala.

Venerable Sumathipala was a member of the Svejin Sabha of the Amarapura Nikāya, a group within the Ceylon *Sanqha* that had maintained close contacts with Burma over the years. Born in 1896, Venerable Sumathipala obtained his lower ordination as a monk in Ceylon in 1907; after his *pirivena* education he traveled to Burma, where he received higher ordination. Spending six years in Burma (1913–19), he became proficient in *vipassanā bhāvanā* at the Thathana Yeiktha center in Rangoon.[7] He was to return to Burma several times in his career and, as noted above, he was there when the Burmese arranged to send the meditation emissaries to Ceylon.

Venerable Sumathipala was a good choice to direct the new *vipassanā bhāvanā* center in Ceylon, for he was both an able administrator and an accomplished meditator, qualities not found together in too many modern monks. Under his guidance Kanduboda became an internationally known center for meditation training for laity and monks. With strong support from the *vipassanā* society and other lay devotees, the head monk oversaw the building of excellent facilities for meditation. The center came to include separate quarters for monks, for female ascetics (*dasa sil mātāvas*), for laymen, and for laywomen. Eventually the complex also included separate facilities for foreigners. These buildings were designed to provide each meditator with a private or semiprivate *kuṭi,* or cell. Walkways for walking meditation as well as dining halls, shrine rooms, bath facilities, and all things necessary for serious meditation were provided.[8]

Unlike the situation in ordinary Theravada temples, *vipassanā bhāvanā,* insight meditation, occupied the central place at Kanduboda. The schedule, like the facilities, was arranged to provide maximum emphasis on meditation. The progress of the lay meditators, or yogis, as they were called, was carefully monitored by monks experienced in meditation. In 1962 Venerable K. Seevali was ordained at Kanduboda and became the guru for the foreign yogis. Laity as well as monks could come to Kanduboda and stay for as long as they liked pursuing *vipassanā* and all their needs would be provided without charge. The center represented a serious attempt to provide opportunities for laity to pursue the path of meditation.

Because of the great interest among the laity in meditation, other centers also sprang up soon after Kanduboda. The Gotama Tapovanaya at Rajagiriya was established by Venerable Kuduwelle Vangisa Thera in 1960. Venerable Vangisa, also a member of the Amarapura Nikāya, learned *vipassanā* from Ven. U Sujata, and had resided for a time at Kanduboda. With the encouragement of another society of laity he built a very attractive *vipassanā bhāvanā* center on an estate near Kotte. This center, Gotama Tapovanaya, like Kanduboda, also provided kuṭis for laymen, for laywomen, for monks, and for female ascetics.

Both Kanduboda and Gotama Tapovanaya have enjoyed a popularity that has increased right down to the present. Since its founding Kanduboda has taught *vipassanā bhāvanā* to more than twenty thousand persons, Sinhalese laypersons and monks as well as foreigners.[9] At present it houses approximately fifty to seventy-five meditators at a time. Most laity go to Kanduboda for periods of two weeks to a month, although it is not uncommon for people to stay longer, and many people who go for short stays return from time to time to refresh themselves and their meditation skills. Although its primary role has been to popularize and facilitate meditation by laypersons, Gombrich correctly observes that it has had an impact upon the monks as well: "Most of the teachers and some of the pupils are in robes, and Kanduboda has thus had a direct influence on the *Sangha*."[10]

Because of their popularity with the Buddhist laity, the original centers—Kanduboda, the International Vipassanā Meditation Center on McCarthy Road, and Gotama Tapovanaya—have started branch centers. Kanduboda has spawned offshoots in such places as Homagama, Mavatagama, and Polonnaruva, while branch Tapovanaya centers have been established in Mihintale, Padaviya, Kegalle, and Kandy. Most of the newer centers, begun in the sixties and seventies, follow the same pattern as the original centers, offering meditation instruction to laity as well as providing facilities for laypersons to reside at the center.[11] In addition, these centers, like the original centers, furnish meditation opportunities to laity on *poya* days when thousands of people visit the centers. On these sacred Buddhist holidays laypersons stream into the centers before dawn to spend the full-moon day participating in programs of meditation instruction and practice. Dressed in white, the people crowd shoulder to shoulder into the preaching hall with laymen on one side and laywomen on the other to hear the instructions about meditation. Those who cannot find room in the preaching hall find places on the grounds in order to follow the teachings and to meditate for hours. In the evenings some laypersons return home, but many remain overnight to continue meditating in the hall.

When the founders of both Kanduboda and Gotama Tapovanaya died in 1982, they left behind a strong *vipassanā bhāvanā* movement. The importance of this movement and the central part it plays in the modern Buddhist reformation can be seen from the enormous popularity of the *bhāvanā* centers. These centers and the monks who reside in them are generously supported by the gifts of the laity. Like the forest hermitages for monks, the meditation centers are supported by laity from distant parts of the island who sign up a year or more in advance for the opportunity to bring *dāna*, or one-day's food, to the centers. But unlike the forest hermitages, laity also come from all over the island to participate in meditation at these centers. Although all Theravada temples provide programs for laity on *poya* days, the *bhāvanā* centers are absolutely deluged with laity on these days, with hundreds of people preferring to travel great distances on bone-jarring buses in order to meditate at a *vipassanā bhāvanā* center rather than simply visiting their local temple. Many of the branch centers, such as the one at Homagama or the Kandy Tapovanaya, seem almost as popular as their parent centers. This indicates that the *bhāvanā* movement has not only grown in popularity with its original audience, the English-speaking elite or middle class, but also has expanded its participant base within the society. The branch centers have carried the movement out from Colombo into the village areas, and the village laity who visit the centers to meditate now probably outnumber the urban laity.

If the *vipassanā bhāvanā* movement met opposition from traditionalist Sinhalese monks almost from the outset, the growing popularity and expansion of the movement have led to continued opposition and criticism by some traditionalist or neotraditionalist Buddhists, both monks and laypersons. To be sure, not all neotraditionalists have openly opposed the *vipassanā* movement; many have adopted an attitude of Buddhist tolerance and forbearance toward the movement, neither condemning it nor endorsing it. And in recent years the *vipassanā* movement's popularity has begun to overcome these Buddhists' reservations about it. But a fundamental conflict existed from the first between the orthodox, neotraditionalist Theravadins and the Theravadin reformers who promoted *vipassanā*. This conflict has its source in the different interpretations and cosmologies of these two groups. Thus, by contrasting the *vipassanā bhāvanā* reformers with the traditionalists and neotraditionalists on the following five aspects of ideology and practice, we can see the nature and significance of the *vipassanā* movement's reinterpretation of Theravada.

Five Points of Contrast

1. Arahantship

The central idea or belief that distinguishes the lay meditation movement in general, and the *vipassanā bhāvanā* centers in particular, from traditionalist Theravada is a belief in the plausibility of arahantship today. The Buddhists who founded the *vipassanā* movement and the leaders of the centers at present have maintained that arahantship and *Nibbāna* represent realistic, attainable goals for all people, for monks as well as for laypersons. According to these Buddhists the heart of Buddhism is the spiritual quest for the fruition of the noble path (*ariya magga phāla*): the attainment of the goal of arahantship. Gombrich regards this as "the biggest change which Buddhism in Sri Lanka has undergone in the twentieth century: the belief that every Buddhist should seek his own salvation in this life, which means that he should practice meditation (*bhāvanā*)."[12]

Westerners familiar with the Buddhist scriptures that describe the attaiment of *Nibbāna* by the Buddha's disciples might have difficulty seeing how belief in the plausibility of *Nibbāna* could represent a radical or reforming idea in Buddhism. The radicalness of the idea, however, results because Theravada traditionally has emphasized the remoteness of *Nibbāna* and the long, gradual nature of the path to it. Ames observed, "Traditionally, and in rural areas today, salvation (*Nirvāna, Nibbāna*) was considered hundreds of births away; it was a long path to travel even for the virtuous."[13]

Gombrich notes that the Theravada monks whom he interviewed believed that the Buddha's *sāsana*, the period during which his teachings had meaning for people and the goals were attainable, had declined. The Theravada tradition has held that the *sāsana* would endure for five thousand years, but during that period it would gradually decline. Gombrich found that monks invoked the decline of the *sāsana* to explain the absence of *arahants* in Sri Lanka. According to Gombrich's informants the last known *arahant* was Maliyadeva, who lived during the time of King Duṭugämuṇu, around 101–77 BCE.[14]

In my interviews with monks who can be said to represent the traditionalist or and neotraditionalist viewpoint, I found the same skepticism about the existence of *arahants* today and a general pessimism about the plausibility of arahantship as a viable goal. To investigate this question I went first to the leaders of the two main branches of the Siyam Nikāya, the Asgiriya and Malvatta fraternities in Kandy.

Since the time of King Kirti Sri Rājasiṃha (1747–98 CE), the Asgiriya and Malvatta monasteries have been at the head of the *Sangha* and have set the standards for othodoxy for the majority of Sinhalese Theravadins. In addition to commanding the two major branches of the Siyam Nikāya, the leaders of these two monasteries share the control of the Daḷadā Māligāva, the Temple of the Tooth Relic, in Kandy, and regard themselves as the direct spiritual descendants of the *arahant* Mahinda. Thus, the monastic leaders of both Asgiriya and Malvatta speak for and represent the Kandyan establishment, the traditionalist forces that Ames described. In addition, the Asgiriya monastery originally represented the forest-dwelling sect of monks (*araññavāsin*). By virtue of their ancestry, one might expect these two monasteries to advocate the plausibility of arahantship; however, interviews with their leaders indicated that this is not the case.

A member of the ruling council (*sangha sabhā*) of the Asgiriya monastery and chapter of the Siyam Nikāya explained that it is impossible for anyone to attain arahantship in this time; indeed, he said that no one today achieves even the state of stream-enterer (*sotāpanna*). His reason for denying the possibility of arahantship today was that he believed the *sāsana* has declined. He explained his view by giving the analogy of a farmer's field. The field cannot produce a crop unless everything is right: the conditions, the soil, and the seed. Similarly, for attaining the goal of Buddhism one must have the right social conditions, good teachers, and good pupils. All of these elements, he felt, are lacking at the present time.

The head of the Malvatta chapter of the Siyam Nikāya, Venerable Wimalakirithi Sri Sumana Paṇḍiṭha Sirimalvatte Ānanda Mahānāyaka Thera, expressed very much the same view. No one today, he said, can achieve either the higher stages of the path (*magga phālas*) or arahantship. These goals are impossible because people's minds are not developed enough, not pure enough. Another senior Kandyan monk associated with the Malvatta monastery expanded on this explanation by comparing the present age with the time in which the Buddha lived. In the Buddha's time the life span of human beings was 80 to 120 years, he said, but now people live only 60 to 80 years. This actuarial calculation seemed to reflect the legend about the Buddha's choosing to be born when human beings' lives were one hundred years long. That people today do not live as long as they used to was taken by this Thera to be a sign of the decline of the *sāsana*. Continuing, he said that people who were fortunate enough to be born during the Buddha's time must have had very great merit, and therefore they could easily attain arahantship. People born today, on the other hand, do not possess very much merit and cannot expect the same attainments.

This same comparison was made by several other monks, and seems to be commonly accepted by the traditionalist *Sangha:* the people born during the Buddha's time were advanced beings with very good *karma*, which is the reason they were born into such an auspicious context. Thus, they could attain things we cannot, both because of the power of the Buddha's teaching and because of their own perfection. This reasoning reflects the Theravada commentarial legends about the Buddha's disciples who became *arahants.* All of these individuals, according to the legends (as discussed in chapter one) had been perfecting their *karma* for countless lifetimes by great works of generosity and virtue. Ironically, these legends, probably intended originally to encourage Buddhists to strive, now seen in this way have the effect of discouraging striving by making the goal appear impossible.

To complete his analysis of the present human predicament, the Kandyan monk said that people in the Buddha's time were *tihetuka*, or born with positive "root conditions" and without the three defilements of greed, hatred, and delusion. Today, however, people are *ahetuka*, or devoid of any meritorious qualities. Not only are people today unsuited to becoming *arahants*, but society is also unsuitable for *arahants.* "Everything is artificial and people's bodies are weak," he said.

These representatives of the monastic hierarchy held out no hope that beings today could become *arahants* or even fulfill the lower stages of the path. When asked whether anyone in recent history had achieved arahantship, the senior monk from the Asgiriya chapter reflected for a few moments before replying that possibly some monks during the Anurādhapura period had become *arahants.* He inferred this from the texts, he said. Another leading monk believed that there had been no *arahants* for at least one hundred years. A well-known scholar-monk told me, as Gombrich's informants had told him, that Maliyadeva was the last *arahant.*

Other traditionalist monks responded somewhat more cautiously to the questions, "Are there any *arahants* today?" "Is arahantship possible today?" A senior monk, the *Anunāyaka Thera* or second in command of the Asgiriya fraternity, answered that according to the scriptures arahantship is possible as long as the *Dhamma* exists. He went on to say, however, that while arahantship may be theoretically or doctrinally possible, it is realistically impossible because of the absence today of both suitable teachers and people with pure, clear minds. In fact, he said, no one today attains even the lower stages of the path (*magga phāla*). Numerous other Siyam Nikāya monks gave similar answers, maintaining that we can never be certain whether *arahants* still exist or not because spirtually developed beings would not proclaim their attainments. This cautious, agnostic opinion probably represents the majority view among the traditionalist monks, a view based on the scriptural injunction that persons should not boast about their spiritual development. One scholar-monk said that the teachings tell us that as long as the *Vinaya* is observed, arahantship is possible. None of the monks whom we met, however, despite their caution about ruling out the possibility of arahantship, thought that arahantship was probable today. One monk suggested that there might be *arahants* in Burma, and another nominated the Brahmaloka, the heavenly realm, as a possible location for *arahants* today. Most monks seemed to agree with the Kandyan monk who declared that while we cannot be certain that there are no *arahants* today, he had neither met any nor heard reports of any. Not even the forest-dwelling monks, he thought, could attain arahantship today.

To the specific question of whether a layperson might attain arahantship today, the traditionalist monks gave an even more negative answer. If the *sāsana* has declined to the point that even monks find it impossible to attain arahantship, then it will surely be even more impossible for laity. Although these monks were well aware of the canonical texts describing laypeople attaining arahantship, they weighed the theoretical possibility of this happening today against the actual probability of it. Laypeople, they said, lead lives that are too entangled in the world; they are too busy and distracted to pursue the path that leads to arahantship. One monk observed that since monks who have to administer temple affairs are too involved in the world to have the purity of mind necessary for arahantship, then householders stand even further from the goal. Five or six monks dealt with the question by giving an interesting interpretation to the canonical texts that tell of laypersons becoming *arahants*. They said we cannot deny that in the Buddha's time some laypersons achieved *Nibbāna* and ara-hantship. Nevertheless, the important thing to note about these stories, the monks said, is that even the Buddha had only limited success in bringing laypeople to arahantship. If the laypeople who lived in the Buddha's time—i.e., the best people, who had the Buddha as their teacher—had difficulty attaining arahantship, how much more difficult is it going to be today? One monk observed that even the Buddha's father, Suddhodana, attained arahantship only very slowly, by stages.

If arahantship today is not probable, maybe not even possible, then what do the orthodox monks think the objective of Buddhists should be? This represents an important question, for what is at stake here is the matter of what the traditionalist Buddhist leaders regard as the viable or operative goal of the religion. The prevailing answer to this question was given definitively by the *Mahānāyaka* of the Malvatta monastery, who responded that the goal for Buddhists today, whether monks or laypersons, should be to "lay a foundation for future births." Since no one today can achieve arahantship, he said, people should prepare for the future by acquiring merit and purifying their minds. Thus, preparation constitutes the religious task, and a more favorable rebirth the religious goal of Theravadins. Another neo-traditionalist monk explained this objective of rebirth by saying that the goal of women should be to be reborn as men, the goal of men should be to be reborn as monks, and the goal of monks should be to be reborn at a time when arahantship is attainable. On another occasion a Kandyan monk, an educator, said that the task for Buddhists today is set out in the "Karaniyametta-Sutta."[15] This sutta represents a course of discipline and meditation that the Buddha is said to have given to a group of forest-dwelling monks. Although it was not clear whether our informant meant that this sutta applies to laity as well as monks today, he said that people should follow the initial stages of development it prescribed. According to the sutta these initial stages consist of perfection of morality, restraint of the senses, contentment with a simplified life, and conquest of desire.

In advocating these views, the *Mahānāyaka* and the other traditionalist or neotraditionalist monks were adhering to the traditional Theravada understanding of the goal and the path as set out by Buddhaghosa in the *Visuddhimagga* and the Pali Commentaries. On this understanding *Nibbāna* remains the ultimate goal; but as Ames has shown, when attainment of *Nibbāna* becomes such a distant goal, immediate and subordinant goals gain importance and give the tradition a distinctive character.[16] These interviews with orthodox leaders also confirmed Maquet's findings that the Sinhalese Buddhists, despite believing *Nibbāna* to be "the ultimate aim of life for monks as well as for laymen," hold that *Nibbāna* is "inaccessible in the near future" for both groups. Noting that the prevailing belief among the Sinhalese is that liberation cannot be attained before countless rebirths, Maquet observes that this postponement "tends to make the serious pursuit of liberation psychologically meaningless."[17] As we shall see, however, the pursuit of liberation through meditation takes on a different value and meaning when the goal is considered at hand rather than remote.

The leaders of the *vipassanā bhāvanā* centers disagree with the Kandyan traditionalist monks about the possibility of arahantship. The Sinhalese monks who head these meditation centers believe that arahantship and *Nibbāna* represent attainable goals for Buddhists today. During interviews they said that merely seeking a more favorable rebirth is not enough, since the ultimate goal can be attained. One monk described the path to arahantship as readily accessible. "Anyone," he said, "can become a stream-enterer and go on to arahantship." Another monk, who heads a large meditation center and is an ordination-descendant of the Burmese monks who began the movement, said that some people could attain the goal in one week. As his source for this claim, he cited the "Satipaṭṭhāna Sutta," which states that if a person follows its course of training for as little as seven days, he can achieve liberation. This statement, although textual, was obviously made to emphasize the point that *Nibbāna* is attainable. The meditation leaders do not mean that *vipassanā* is simple or that everyone can reach *Nibbāna* in as little as seven days. Two other meditation center leaders said that to attain the noble path, a person does not even have to be a Buddhist; however, they also said that once a person becomes a stream-enterer, he will definitely return to this world as a Buddhist in his next life.

Not only do these monks who head the *bhāvanā* centers believe arahantship is attainable, they also feel that the goal has been attained, or almost attained, by some people in recent times. The director of the

Homagama center said that many people believed that Mahasi Sayadaw was an *arahant*. He said, however, that he personally believed that Mahasi Sayadaw was an *anāgāmin*, a non-returner, the penultimate stage. His belief was based on his own meetings with Mahasi Sayadaw and on the reports by Mahasi Sayadaw's associates that he manifested all the outward signs of an *arahant*. For example, Mahasi Sayadaw was reported to have always been relaxed, never angry, never fearful, and to have had boundless generosity.

Other meditation center monks also made reference to recent figures who were believed to have been *arahants*. The founder of Kanduboda, for example, was frequently mentioned as a person who had reached "an advanced state." Some thought he must have been an *arahant*, while others felt that he was "at least an *anāgāmin*." In this regard, it is interesting that the new statue of Venerable Sumathipala, erected at Kanduboda after his death in 1982, resembles a Buddha image and evokes great reverence from Buddhists who visit the center. Another interesting reference to living *arahants* was made by the current director of Kanduboda. In guiding me around his center, he explained that a new group of residences in a remote area of the grounds had been built especially for meditators who wish to live there until they become *arahants*.

2. Renunciation

When asked whether people must renounce the lay life and become monks or nuns in order to attain arahantship, the meditation center leaders again disagreed with the Kandyan monks and with the traditional Theravada interpretation that renunciation of the lay life represents a prerequisite for progress. As Jayatilaka expressed it, "Renunciation is the price which everyone must pay for emancipation. It is the golden key which alone can open the gates of Immortality."[18] The *bhāvanā* center Buddhists, however, reject this interpretation. Renunciation of the lay life is not necessary for attainment of the goal, they believe. To support this position they also cite the canonical texts about laypersons who attained the goal. The scripturalism of these reformers allows them to argue that if the *Tipiṭaka* texts say that in the Buddha's time both laity and monks attained arahantship, then people can and should do the same today. They do not agree with the traditionalist monks that the best people lived only in the Buddha's day, nor do they interpret the texts to say how few laypersons attained the goal under the Buddha's guidance; rather, they emphasize how many did so. One *bhāvanā* center leader cited a canonical story that during the Buddha's time there were seven crores (seventy million) of stream-enterers in Savatthi and five crores of them were laymen. Similarly, other meditation leaders bolstered their position by referring to other canonical stories about lay persons who became *arahants*.

Just as renunciation of the household life represented a cornerstone of traditional Theravada's gradual path, so the elimination of it by these reformers signals a significant difference in their interpretation of the path. They understand the path in pragmatic, this-worldly terms. The basis for this optimistic interpretation of the path lies, they believe, in the proper understanding of the doctrines of *karma* and rebirth (*saṃsāra*). As we have seen, the Kandyan monks stress the need to perfect one's *karma* in order to attain a more favorable rebirth in the future. The meditation center monks, however, emphasize the extent to which people have already perfected their *karma* in order to be reborn favorably in this life. For the traditionalists *karma* and rebirth are interpreted in a way that limits the possibility of arahantship in this life; but for the reformists *karma* and rebirth explain why the goal is attainable now.

The head of the Homagama *vipassanā bhāvanā* center commented on this point by saying that while arahantship is possible for all people, a person's *karma* and progress during previous lives determine whether he can attain the goal in this life. We can never be sure about how much progress people have attained during their previous lives, but those who realize arahantship quickly do so because of previous positive *karma*. He went on to say that people become interested in meditation and decide to visit *bhāvanā* centers because of the impulses from their previous lives. Almost all the meditation center monks interviewed mentioned that the general interest that laity show in *vipassanā* meditation today indicates that the interested people are individuals who had advanced significantly toward the goal in previous lives. A being who is born now as a human being, able to hear and understand the *Dhamma*, with both the inclination and the opportunity to visit a *vipassanā bhāvanā* center where teachers can guide him on the path, can be sure that his progress in previous lives has brought him to this fortunate birth. In this life such people now have the opportunity to complete the path, or, if not, they will at least be reborn much closer to the goal next time.

The meditation center spokesmen, then, do not subscribe to the view that the *sāsana* has declined. Being born in this age represents not a hindrance to the attainment of *Nibbāna* but a great advantage in attaining it. These monks, as we have seen, regard the present age as an auspicious time for the attainment of arahantship. One monk said, "Man makes the epoch, not vice versa."

By advocating that laity spend an extended period of time (usually three weeks or a month) at a meditation center where they can get an intensive grounding in *vipassanā bhāvanā*, the meditation center leaders actually could be said to be opting for a limited or temporary form of renunciation. One monk thought that during a one-month stay at a meditation center a layperson could make rapid progress on the path, perhaps even attaining arahantship during that period. With this foundation of meditation experience the layperson can continue to meditate at home while living the householder's life. After returning from this intensive period of meditation, laypeople may find it difficult to practice meditation at home, with all the distractions of a household, the monks said, but it can be done. If a layperson is skillful enough, he can turn the distractions and problems of household life into aids to meditation; the distractions can help one practice one-pointedness of mind and can be seen as challenges to one's detachment and equanimity.

The head of the Kotte Tapovanaya expressed a belief shared by many others also: that laity who practiced meditation might be able to attain *Nibbāna* "at the last moment before death." Perhaps the basis for this idea lies in the traditional belief, expressed in the Milindapañha, that if a person becomes an *arahant* he must become a monk within one day or he will die.[19] But by waiting until the last moment to attain *Nibbāna*, a layperson can avoid this rule and live all his life as a householder.

The acceptance of a "this-worldly asceticism" and the rejection of the necessity of renunciation, of going forth as a monk or a nun (*pabbajjā*), represent a clear break with traditional Theravada Buddhism and manifest further the reformist views of this movement. The *bhāvanā* center leaders, however, are not the first group of Theravada reformers to teach this. Anagārika Dharmapāla advocated this-worldly asceticism for laity, and other Sinhalese Buddhist reformers also have sought to apply meditation to daily life in the world, saying that a person can meditate anywhere—for example, in a restaurant or in a bus queue. As Venerable Walpola Sri Rahula Thera has written, "If you understand the spirit of Buddhism correctly (and not only its letter), you can surely follow and practice it while living the life of an ordinary man."[20]

3. Study of the Dhamma

Traditional Sinhalese Theravada has held not only that renunciation is necessary before one can make progress toward arahantship but also that study of the *Tipiṭaka* constitutes an additional prerequisite. On this question the Kandyan monks and the meditation center leaders again differ sharply. This issue represents a central concern for the Theravada school of Buddhism because Theravada traditionally has regarded the *Tipiṭaka* as "the word of the Buddha" (*Buddha Vacana*) and has held that the scriptures occupy the place of the Buddha for present-day Buddhists.[21] In accord with the Buddha's proclamation that "my *Dhamma* and *Vinaya* shall be your teacher when I am gone,"[22] the Theravadins have venerated the *Tipiṭaka* as the only guide to the truth. As indicated, both groups of reformers accept the centrality of the scriptures; but does being scripturalists mean that the reformers endorse the traditional beliefs about the relevance of study of the *Tipiṭaka* to the path?

The monastic leaders of the Siyam Nikāya today reflect the traditional Theravada view concerning the study of the *Tipiṭaka*. When asked whether study of the *Tipiṭaka* is necessary before meditation and possible attainment, these monks unanimously answered in the affirmative. The *Mahānāyaka* of Malvatta said that study is necessary because the more knowledge one has, the better prepared he is for meditation. An *Anunayaka* of the Asgiriya fraternity explained that unless one first studies the *Dhamma*, he cannot possibly find the way in meditation. Other orthodox monastic leaders agreed with this necessity for studying the *Dhamma*. To meditate, they said, one needs to know what the Buddha taught concerning the path, for it is highly unlikely that a person who had no knowledge of the *Dhamma* could attain the goal. One monk said the analogy here would be that of a person without an education in science trying to duplicate all of Einstein's scientific discoveries; a very extraordinary person might happen to do it, although the chances are extremely slim. Similarly, although a very extraordinary person, without any knowledge of the *Dhamma*, might happen to have success in meditation, it is not likely that even an extraordinary person could do this, much less an ordinary one. Only Buddhas and *Paccekabuddhas* find the truth on their own; ordinary people must follow—and therefore study—the Buddha's teachings.

Another way of underscoring the importance of study for meditation was given by several monks who apealed to the three-stage process of study (*pariyatti*), practice (*paṭipatti*), and realization (*paṭivedha*). In this three-stage formulation study constitutes the essential basis on which all higher progress rests. This traditional idea, still maintained by orthodox monks today, was stated by Buddhaghosa: "Even if there be a hundred or a thousand monks practicing (*paṭipatti*) *vipassanā*, there will be no realization (*paṭivedha*) of the Noble Path if there is no learning (*pariyatti*)" (A.A. 52f).

Although the Kandyan hierarchy and probably most Sinhalese monks today still adhere to this traditional formulation set down by Buddhaghosa, the *vipassanā* center monks reject it. These leaders say that study of the *Dhamma* is not essential for practice or realization. Study cannot be considered essential, one monk explained, since the Buddha and others mentioned in the texts had not studied prior to their realization. Other *bhāvanā* leaders explained the matter in practical terms, saying that it is better for a person not to study before taking up *vipassanā bhāvanā* because then he will have no expectations and will not be confused by his initial experiences. They said that after one meditates for a time and reaches some of the lower stages of the path, then he develops an interest in studying the *Dhamma*, and when that occurs, it is the proper time for study.

The positions that the two groups take on this issue reveal again their traditionalist and reformist interpretations of Theravada respectively. The reformers have by no means rejected the *Tipiṭaka*; both groups remain scripturalists and appeal to the texts for support. While the Kandyan monks can appeal to Buddhaghosa's commentaries, the authoritative formulation of traditional Theravada, the meditation center reformers can appeal to the Canon itself for support of their views, even for their belief that study of the texts is not a prerequisite. For example, the reformers refer to texts such as this passage:

> If a man recites and preaches many scriptural texts, but does not act accordingly, that heedless man is like a cowherd who counts another's cows, he has no share in the life of a holy man. If a man recites and preaches few scriptural texts, but his conduct is in accord with the *Dhamma* . . . he shares in the life of a holy man (*Dhammapada* 1. 19–20).

Another aspect of the conflict between these two groups becomes evident in this issue: it is a conflict between scholar-monks and meditator-monks. This conflict represents an ancient debate in Theravada Buddhism. The commentaries relate that as far back as the first century B.C.E., Theravadins in Sri Lanka squared off on this issue. At that time one group of monks, the *Paṃsukūlikas*, proclaimed practice or meditation (*paṭipatti*) to be the basis of the *sāsana*, while another group of monks, the *Dhammakathikas*, proclaimed study (*pariyatti*).[23] Since the country was facing a famine that threatened to decimate the *Sangha*, the *Dhammakathikas* won the dispute, for they argued that if the *Dhamma* was not widely studied and transmitted, it would disappear should famine strike down the key scholar-monks. According to the commentaries, this confirmation of learning as a more important task than practice led to the division of the *Sangha*, as some monks chose to become scholars and others meditators. Those who accepted the study of the *Tipiṭaka* as their duty belonged to the group known as *gantha-dhuras*, and those who devoted themselves to meditation were called *vipassanā-dhuras*. Studying and teaching, as well as meditating, the *gantha-dhura* monks lived among the people as *grāmavāsīs*, village dwellers, and developed what can be called "parish Buddhism." The *vipassanā-dhuras* withdrew from society and lived as Āraṇyavāsī, forest-dwellers, placing total emphasis on meditation. As the Theravada tradition developed over time, the scholar-monks came to dominate. As Walpola Rahula writes, "Out of the two vocations, *gantha-dhura* was regarded as more important than *vipassanā-dhura*."[24]

Down to the present, therefore, the traditionalist and neotraditionalist Theravada monks have understood their primary task to be study of the *Dhamma*. The leaders of the *Sangha* have been the scholar-monks who could teach and preach effectively. Study of the *Dhamma* did not, in theory, preclude meditation, but in fact the scholar-monks frequently had little time for *vipassanā*. As Gombrich reports, contemporary monks explained to him that "*granthadhura* monks could not be expected to meditate" and that "as a *granthadhura* monk his knowledge of meditation was purely theoretical."[25]

It is not surprising, therefore, that the Kandyan hierarchy along with most Sinhalese Theravada monks today hold study of the *Dhamma* to be a duty that must be fulfilled before one can progress to meditation and realization. In challenging this ancient tradition that has shaped Theravada for almost two thousand years, the *vipassanā* center leaders are put in a difficult position. They take the part of the *vipassanā-dhuras* of old, stressing experience over scholasticism. Bypassing the *Visuddhimagga* with its elaborate, gradual path, the reformers ground their claim in the canonical texts which speak of the availability of insight. In so doing, these modern-day *vipassanā-dhuras* again opt for a pragmatic interpretation rather than the traditional one.

4. *The Practice of* Bhāvanā *by Laypersons*

The meditation centers put these reformist beliefs about arahant-ship and its plausibility for laypersons into practice by teaching and guiding laity in meditation in a much more extensive way than traditional Sinhalese Theravada has done. This emphasis on the practice of *bhāvanā* has generated a revitalization of Theravada that has caused the laity to throng to the meditation centers.

Since the traditionalist Sinhalese Theravada *Sangha* has not regarded arahantship as a plausible goal in this life, it has not promoted *bhāvanā* as a practice for laity. Even *gantha-dhura* monks, as Gombrich points out, do not pursue meditation extensively; thus we would not expect that they would encourage the laity to meditate. The *Mahānāyaka* of Malvatta explained the orthodox monastic view of meditation in this way: Having declared that he did not believe arahant-ship could be attained in this age, he said that he nevertheless did advise the monks under his charge to meditate in order to clear their minds and to prepare themselves for future births. If even the monks do not have much incentive to practice meditation, the laity in traditional Theravada have even less. As Maquet found, traditional Sinhalese Theravada affirms two paradoxical statements: "Liberation is the ultimate goal of life, but inaccessible in the near future," and "Meditation is essential and little practiced."[26] These two paradoxes of traditional Theravada are related in that the former accounts for the latter.

To understand the significance of meditation or *bhāvanā* for traditional Theravada laity, it is useful to recall Ames's analysis of the four vocations in Buddhism.[27] These four vocations can be grouped according to whether they follow the ritual system of meditating or that of merit-making. "The *bhāvanaya* meditating ritual system is the preoccupation of the religious virtuosos who are more concerned about striving for salvation than about earning a happy rebirth."[28] The hermit monks and the lay devotees are virtuosos in their religious practice, but they are far outnumbered by the village monks and householders who accept the lower goal of rebirth.

The advantage of Ames's model is that it accurately shows that in traditional Sinhalese Theravada most monks and most laity have not regarded meditation as the primary ritual task of their vocation. To be sure, some laity as well as some monks have taken up meditation as their primary task, but they have been a minority, perhaps even more of a minority than Ames's model suggests. The traditional Sinhalese layperson's view of meditation is represented in the following explanation by a layman who had recently begun meditating actively under the guidance of a *vipassanā bhāvanā* center. When I asked whether his concern with practicing meditation had been shared by his parents and grandparents, he said that they did not do meditation very extensively. Although they had high respect for meditation, and for anyone who practiced it, their own practice of it was limited to a few minutes of *mettā bhāvanā*, or meditation on lovingkindness, done on *poya* days at the temple. They believed that intensive meditation was too difficult for householders, and that if they were ever to do serious meditation at all, it should be in their old age after retirement. This explanation verifies Ames's model of the two vocations for laity and indicates how the two are related. These people regarded the vocation of a lay devotee to be an option for one's later years, almost on the model of the forest-dweller in the Hindu tradition.

To be sure, though, the vocation of the lay devotee, seriously pursuing meditation and the goal, seems never to have entirely disappeared from traditional Theravada, even if lay devotees may never have been present in large numbers. Venerable Nyanaponika, for example, said that in the past in Sri Lanka, he had never encountered too many people actively striving for *Nibbāna*, but occasionally in his visits to villages he met extraordinary individuals who had taken up the life of a lay devotee or an *anaqārika* in order to seek the goal through meditation.[29] Other people confirmed this kind of report. One man said that his father in his later years used to arise at 3:00 A.M. every day in order to do meditation.

Not all lay devotees undertake this vocation only in old age, although that represents the paradigm. A counter-example is a person such as the *sil mäniyō* whom I met in the southeastern part of the island. She had lived in a village near Kegalle and had begun doing *vipassanā bhāvanā* in earnest in her village when she was in middle age. After she had some success in meditation, she left the village, eventually taking the ten precepts (*dasa sil*) that today represent renunciation for a woman.

If, however, the lay devotee who concerns himself or herself with meditation has not been unknown in traditional Theravada, the vocation of the householder, not practicing meditation as a primary ritual task, has been the norm. The examples given above indicate that it is not entirely accurate to say that traditional householders did not practice meditation at all; some did practice meditation at least on *poya* days at the temple. If we want to contrast traditional Theravada with the *vipassanā bhāvanā* movement, therefore, the question to ask is not whether traditional Theravada householders practiced meditation at all, but rather what was their understanding of *bhāvanā* and its place in their ritual system, and how extensive and intensive was their pursuit of *bhāvanā*.

Traditionalist Sinhalese householders' practice of *bhāvanā* has been governed by their goals, and as Ames's model indicates and my interviews with monks would lead us to expect, these householders have not regarded *Nibbāna* as a plausible goal in this life, aiming instead for a happy rebirth. As a senior monk in Colombo explained, the ordinary layman's objective is to be reborn in heaven. They see the hierarchy of Buddhist goals to be heaven, the *Brahmaloka*, and then *Nibbāna*. With what appeared to be nervous laughter, he continued that ordinary people neither desire nor expect to attain *Nibbāna* in this life. It does appear, as Jayatilaka wrote, that "Buddhism . . . has by no means lost sight of the importance of the preliminary course, absolutely necessary to prepare a being for the final battle against the foes of *saṃsāra.*"[30]

Householders pursuing this preliminary course follow what we have seen to be the traditional ritual system of merit-making. In "resuscitating" Buddhism, the traditionalists have promoted these practices that have continuity with the traditional Theravada of the Commentary and the village. Rahula writes that in ancient Ceylon, "acquiring merit of various kinds as security for the next world was the motive underlying the religion of the laity, from the king down to the poor peasant."[31]

Ames defines this merit-making system as having three components: *dāna*, giving; *sīla*, following the moral precepts; and *bhāvanā*, meditating.[32] Several of my informants independently suggested these same three elements as the content of their parents' practice of Buddhism in their village, and most Theravadins would concur. The inclusion of *bhāvanā* as an element in this merit-making ritual system signifies two things. First, it indicates the connection between this ritual system and the higher *bhāvanā* ritual system followed by virtuosos. The *bhāvanā* ritual system also comprised three parts in traditional Theravada: morality (*sīla*); concentration (*samādhi*); and wisdom (*paññā*). These two ritual systems should not be understood to constitute two distinct religions or subreligions. The two are inextricably linked. The merit-making ritual system leads on to the meditation ritual system and derives its meaning from the ultimate goal of *Nibbāna*. *Bhāvanā* serves as the link between these two systems, indicating that both lead to *Nibbāna*, even if *Nibbāna* is seen as a distant goal for householders. Second, the presence of *bhāvanā* in both systems indicates that *bhāvanā* has a somewhat different meaning or function in the two systems. In the merit-making ritual system it functions as another form of meritorious activity to prepare one for rebirth and the higher path; whereas, in the meditating ritual system *bhāvanā* constitutes the path itself and is done in order to realize the goal.

Since *bhāvanā* represents only one part of the ritual system for householders in traditionalist Theravada, it does not consume a great deal of the householder's time or energy. Most householders have understood it to be one of the rituals to be done on *poya* days or other holy days under the direction of the monks. A typical *poya* day schedule from a traditionalist temple indicates the relation of meditation or *bhāvanā* to other ritual elements of the service.[33]

A.M.	6:00-6:30	Administering precepts (*sīla*)
	6:30-6:40	*Bhāvanā*
	6:40-7:00	*Buddha pūjā* and chanting *gāthās*
	7:00-8:00	*Dāna* for monks: breakfast
	8:00-9:00	Listening to radio sermon (*baṇa*)
	9:00-9:20	*Bhāvanā* (*mettā bhāvanā*)
	9:30-10:30	*Dhamma* lecture
	10:30-11:00	*Buddha pūjā*
	11:00-11:30	*Dāna* for monks: dinner
	11:30-1:00	Rest
P.M.	1:00-2:00	Satipaṭṭhāna Sutta chanting
	2:00-3:00	Buddhism lecture by a layman
	3:00-4:00	Buddhist sermon by a monk
	4:00-4:30	*Bhāvanā*
	5:00-6:00	Evening preaching (*baṇa*)
	6:00	Most householders depart but a few stay for evening
	7:00	*Buddha pūjā*
		Bodhi pūjā
	8:00	Radio sermon
	10:30	Radio *pirit* chanting

From this schedule *bhāvanā* appears to be one small part of a cycle of rituals performed for and by the laity on *poya* days. At this temple only one hour of a seventeen-hour program is devoted to *bhāvanā*, and this one hour of meditation is split into three short periods. During these periods various forms of *samātha bhāvanā*, or concentration meditation, might be practiced. The laity would be led in practices of meditation such as breathing meditation (*ānāpānasati*), the recollection of the Buddha (*Buddhānussati*), the development of lovingkindness (*mettā bhāvanā*), or mindfulness of the body (*kāyagatāsati bhāvanā*). Neither the monks nor the householders, however, expect significant results from these short periods of meditation. When asked about the nature of *bhāvanā* taught at his temple on *poyas*, one monk said that it did not matter what kind of meditation was taught because the laity could not achieve *Nibbāna*. Corroborating this, a layman, who has now become an ardent meditator through a meditation center, explained that all his life he had gone to the temples, done *bhāvanā* in brief sessions on *poya* days, and then forgotten about it for the rest of the week. The beliefs of the monks about the plausibility of arahantship clearly translate into the expectations of the laity.

In traditional Sinhalese Theravada temples, as the above schedule indicates, meditation was not thought to be the most, or even one of the most, important rituals for householders. *Dhamma* talks and sermons occupy the major place in the schedule, followed by offerings to the *Sangha*, *pūjās*, offerings to the Buddha image and the Bo tree, and the chanting of *gāthās*, verses. All of these activities are accorded more time than *bhāvanā*. Preaching, *baṇa*, is regarded by the traditionalist monks as one of the most important aspects of a *poya* program for laity. The head of the temple whose schedule is given here was extremely proud that his temple had recently had its 847th *baṇa* service. He also mentioned that his temple had offered *Dhamma* lectures on *poya* days for forty years. Until recent times and the rise of the *vipassanā* movement, the laity were always much more interested in these sermons, he said, than in practicing meditation.

That meditation has traditionally been assigned a subordinate place in this ritual system became clear also from the comments of the head monk of a Colombo temple. Explaining the *poya* day schedule at his temple, he said that the half hour for meditation followed the afternoon sermon hour, but whenever the sermon ran long they would simply omit the meditation period in order to put the program back on schedule. The highlight of this temple's year was its *perahera*, procession, held in conjunction with the *Kaṭhina* ceremony, which the monk described as "the biggest in the country." At other temples where very little emphasis was put on *bhāvanā* other merit-making rituals such as *dāna* or *pūjā* received great emphasis. Temples vie with each other to have the grandest *peraheras* or the lengthiest *pirit* chantings.[34] These rituals hold more appeal for the neotraditionalist householders than does meditation.

In the *poya* day schedule given above the event scheduled for 1:00 p.m. requires explanation. Although we expected that this would be a period of meditation based on the Satipaṭṭhāna Sutta—the "Foundation of Mindfulness" discourse, an important text on the practice of insight meditation—it turned out to be a lengthy recitation or chanting of that sutta in Pali. No meditation as such was done during this period. According to several informants this chanting exemplifies a common phenomenon. One man, an *anagārika* who teaches insight meditation, explained that many village Buddhists equate chanting *gāthās* or suttas with meditation. Gombrich comments that we "must not be misled by the fact that there is a traditional lay practice which is sometimes called meditation. Pious laity may . . . recite Pali verses or other formulae (*gāthā*). Their recitation may be referred to as *bhāvanā*; but in cross-cultural terms it is what one would call a devotional exercise."[35] Another of our informants, who grew up in a village, said she never heard the temple monks teach the methods of meditation given in the Satipaṭṭhāna Sutta. Instead, that sutta was always chanted in Pali, although none of the laity knew what it meant. The children memorized portions of the Pali sutta and chanted it all night to earn merit (*pin*). Her parents told her that if she fell asleep while chanting, the demons would come and steal her merit. Although her parents owned an ola-leaf manuscript of the sutta, they never read it or practiced its meditation. Instead, they kept the manuscript in their "treasure chest," taking it out on special occasions to venerate the book but not to practice *satipaṭṭhāna*, the "foundation of mindfulness."

Clearly, then, householders in traditional and neotraditional Theravada do not practice *bhāvanā* extensively. The temples provide for a few brief periods of meditation on *poya* days, but an hour of meditation at a superficial level once a month, or once a week at most, is insufficient to enable a person to attain mental purity or the development of insight. Developing the mind and attaining wisdom, however, are not the goals of traditionalist householders, and brief periods of meditation are consistent with their objectives of earning merit and attaining a happy rebirth.

To see the differences in the practice of meditation by the *vipassanā bhāvanā* centers and their leaders, we can ask of them the questions we asked of the traditionalist Theravadins: What is their understanding of *bhāvanā*? What is its place in their ritual system? How extensive and intensive is their practice of meditation?

In answer to the question about their understanding of meditation, it may be useful at this point to explain briefly the nature and practice of *vipassanā* by these reformists. *Vipassanā* represents the distinctive Theravada form of meditation. The term *vipassanā* derives from the Pali root meaning "to see"; *vipassanā* is understood to be a way of seeing or gaining an insight into reality. Closely related to *vipassanā* is another Theravada concept, *sati*, mindfulness or awareness. *Vipassanā*, insight meditation, is developed through the practice of *sati*, mindfulness. The two most important texts on meditation in Theravada and the two texts on which the *vipassanā* reformers base their teachings are the Satipaṭṭhāna Sutta (discourse on the Foundations of Mindfulness) and the *Visuddhimagga* (*Path of Purification*).[36] Indicating the centrality of *sati* in the classical Theravada path, the introduction to the Mahāsatipaṭṭhāna Sutta describes the method it teaches as "the one and only way for the purification of beings, . . . for the destruction of suffering, . . . for the realization of Nibbana."[37] A modern *vipassanā* teacher points to the connection between *sati* and *vipassanā* when he says, "Insight meditation is also called the way of mindfulness."[38]

To generate *vipassanā* or insight, the meditator develops mindfulness of each of the four foundations of mindfulness: the body, sensations (*vedanā*), states of mind (*citta*), and the mental objects (*dhamma*) which represent the verification of the teachings of the *Dhamma* in his own experience. The sutta prescribes specific ways to meditate on each of these four foundations or topics, and the path of *vipassanā* taught by reformers today follows these ways fairly closely. *Vipassanā* teachers point out that the four foundations can be subsumed under the two categories of mind (*nāma*) and body (*rūpa*). The essence of *vipassanā* is the developing of awareness (*sati*) of the factors of mind and body as they arise and disappear in the present moment.

Although the teachings of contemporary *vipassanā* teachers vary, they all represent modern interpretations of this path from the Satipaṭṭhāna Sutta and the *Visuddhimagga*. For example, when one reads the writings of Mahasi Sayadaw, the teacher who has had the greatest influence on the movement in Sri Lanka, one is impressed by the extent to which he based his method squarely on these texts.[39] According to Mahasi Sayadaw's method, to begin the practice of *vipassanā* a person goes to a teacher at a meditation center. The teacher instructs the new meditator on how to develop mindfulness of the body by focusing attention on the process of breathing. Although the tradition says that the meditator should observe the breath by focusing on the inhalation and the exhalation at the tip of the nose, Mahasi Sayadaw taught that one should observe the rise and fall of the abdomen with each breath: "For the beginner it is a very effective method of developing the facilities of attention, concentration of mind and insight in contemplation."[40] This new technique represents one of several ways that Mahasi Sayadaw reinterpreted the tradition for contemporary Buddhists. If distracting thoughts arise while the meditator is observing the process of breathing, he is instructed to make mental notes of them. If a memory arises, he notes "remembering"; if a physical pain arises, he notes "pain." As his meditation progresses, the meditator learns to be mindful of every thought and action without identifying with them. When he walks, he notes each aspect of the movement, such as "intending to move," "lifting," moving," "placing." In a meditation retreat center the entire day is devoted to developing in silence this kind of dispassionate awareness of all aspects of one's being. Mindfulness must be cultivated during every activity, even while eating, washing, or resting.

The effect of *vipassanā* is to make the meditator aware of the conditioned and empty process of existence. In the arising and disappearing of breath, thoughts, feelings, and other objects, the meditator experiences directly the truth of impermanence (*anicca*). He perceives also the truth of no-soul (*anattā*) in the impersonal rise and fall of the aggregates. As Mahasi Sayadaw notes about the mindfulness of breathing, "The meditator understands thus, 'At the moment of breathing-in, there is just the rising movement of the abdomen and the knowing of the movement, but there is no self besides; at the moment of breathing out, there is just the falling movement of the abdomen and the knowing of the movement, but there is no self besides."[41] Observing this process of rise and fall, the meditator comprehends also the third characteristic of being, suffering (*dukkha*). He sees that, "it is through ignorance that we enjoy life. But in truth, there is nothing to enjoy. There is a continuous arising and disappearing by which we are harassed ever and anon. This is dreadful indeed."[42]

Focusing on the rise and fall of phenomena in the present moment, the meditator proceeds through the seven stages of the purification of the mind.[43] He comes to understand the conditioned nature of all things. He develops all of the qualities of mental purity mentioned in the traditional texts on meditation, such as the five spiritual faculties (*indriya*): faith, energy, mindfulness, concentration, and wisdom. King observes that *vipassanā* amounts to an "existentializing of the Theravada worldview."[44] Venerable Nyanaponika describes the result of *vipassanā* through mindfulness as threefold: knowing, shaping, and liberating the mind. The meditator comes to know reality as it is, his mind is shaped and trained to live only in the present moment, and these experiences of insight forge liberation and nonattachment. "Bare attention schools us in the art of letting go, weans us from busyness and from habitual interfering."[45] Mahasi Sayadaw had no hesitation about saying that one who can follow this path of *vipassanā* to its end can attain the goal of Buddhism. He said, "As soon as the five faculties (*indriya*) of faith, energy, mindfulness, concentration and wisdom are developed in an even manner, he will realize nibbāna."[46]

This universalizing of both the practice and the goal of Buddhism indicates the *vipassanā* reformers' rejection of the traditional model of Theravada with its four vocations, as outlined by Ames. The model of Buddhism advocated by the reformists allows no place for a division of labor between virtuosos who seek the true goal and other Buddhists who aim only for a better rebirth. Believing that arahantship represents a plausible goal for all monks and laypersons, the reformists maintain that all Buddhists have the same vocation: to seek *Nibbāna* in this life. The lay life should not be regarded as a preliminary course, they argue, for the layperson has great possibilities.

A senior monk at one meditation center maintained with Mahasi Sayadaw that the proper goal for the layperson is not to be reborn happier or wealthier, but to develop a pure mind, free of defilements, and to become spiritually advanced. If one does not attain arahantship in this process, he will at least be reborn closer to the goal next time. Another monk similarly pointed to the mundane as well as supramundane benefits of striving for arahantship. In the process of attaining ultimate liberation, a layperson, this monk said, can also cure his mental and physical problems. The goal of arahantship and *Nibbāna* thus is not only plausible but also extremely relevant to the life of the layperson.

Just as the insight meditation movement reinterprets the notion of vocations, so it also reinterprets the conception of the related ritual systems. For the *vipassanā* movement there cannot be two ritual systems, but only one, since all people seek the same objective. Although the essence of this unified ritual system is *bhāvanā*, the meditation center leaders do not discard all the other elements of Buddhist practice. However, they clearly give *vipassanā bhāvanā* the central place, with everything else subordinated to it.[47]

To answer the other questions posed above, we can see the place of *bhāvanā* in this ritual system and the extensiveness of its practice by noting the activities at the meditation centers. The schedule below from the Kandy Tapovanaya indicates the daily routine followed by monks and laity in a typical center.

A.M.	4:30	Awaken	
	5:00	Tea	
	5:30	*Pirit* and *Buddha pūjā*	
	6:00	*Bhāvanā*	
	6:30	Work around the center	
	7:00	*Dāna*: breakfast	
	7:30	*Bhāvanā*	
	10:00	*Dhamma* talk	
	11:00	*Dāna*: lunch	
P.M.	12:00	Rest or *bhāvanā*	
	2:30	*Buddha pūjā*	
	3:00	*Bhāvanā*	
	5:00	Work around the center	
	6:00	*Pirit*	
	6:30	Tea	
	7:00	*Bhāvanā*	
	10:30	Retire	

Anyone familiar with the daily routine in a traditional temple and the traditional schedule of a Buddhist monk's or layperson's life will be struck by the emphasis on *bhāvanā* in the above schedule. Although it resembles the schedule of a forest hermitage, this schedule is employed by meditation centers to regulate the lives of laypersons, *bhikkhus*, and female ascetics (*dasa sil mātāvas*). Meditation constitutes the primary activity; other ritual services such as *pirit* and *pūjā* also have a place, however. The presence of these other services signifies that the meditation movement has not severed all its ties with traditional Theravada, but has reordered its priorities. Meditation receives the most emphasis because developing one's mind requires time. One center leader compared *vipassanā* meditation to the process of starting a fire by friction. Just as a fire can be started only if one rubs the two sticks together continuously for a long time, so wisdom arises only if one continuously practices meditation. No results can be attained if a person's practice is occasional or sporadic.

The above daily schedule for the Kandy center would be modified somewhat on *poya* days when hundreds of laypersons visit the center for the day. On *poyas*, the 5:30 A.M. *pirit* and *Buddha pūjā* would be followed by the recitation of the Threefold Refuge (*Tisarana*) and the administering of the eight or ten precepts (*sīla*) to the laity. The work periods are usually eliminated on *poyas* because the center becomes too crowded, and one or two additional *Dhamma* talks or sermons would be included in the afternoon's schedule—one after lunch and another in the late afternoon.

Although the meditation center's *poya* service schedule comprises most of the same elements as the *poya* services at traditional temples, the arrangement of the elements is quite different, again signifying the restructured ritual system. Everything revolves around *vipassanā bhāvanā*, even for the laity who have come for one day. Although there are sermons for the laity, the sermons teach *vipassanā bhāvanā*. On a typical *poya* day the head of the Kandy Tapovanaya delivered a sermon in which he directly addressed the need for persons to reorder their ritual priorities. The goal of *Nibbāna*, he declared, is available to those who strive. One can attain liberation from *samsāra* as well as freedom from the hindrances (*nīvaranas*) and defilements (*kilesas*) of life. To do this, however, a Buddhist must go beyond giving (*dāna*) and morality (*sīla*)—the elements of the merit-making ritual system—to *bhāvanā*. Giving and morality have utility, he said, but they do not bring *Nibbāna*. For that, one must do insight meditation in earnest.

The monk's sermon puts the ritual system of the meditation movement in its proper perspective. Clearly, the traditional practices such as *dāna, sīla*, and *pūjā* have a place. Laity still bring food (*dāna*) to the meditation centers daily, but this *dāna* is offered to the resident lay meditators, called yogis, as well as to the *bhikkhus*. *Sīla*, ethical conduct, has by no means been abandoned, either. The moral life, the virtue of restraint, constitutes a key to success in meditation. Although one may be surprised to find the *pūjās* or ritual offerings still observed—and some centers seem to give these a very minor role—a high-ranking center leader explained that the Buddha *pūjā* and the *Bodhi pūjā*, or offerings to the Bo tree, are useful in the development of the mind. All of these ritual practices, however, become reinterpreted and made to serve the practice of meditation itself.

The daily schedule from Kanduboda, the oldest meditation center, contrasts even more sharply with the daily schedule—or even with the *poya* schedule of a traditional temple (see above). The schedule below indicates that *vipassanā* is indeed the central, and almost the only, activity at Kanduboda.

A.M.	3:00	Awaken; wash and take tea
	3:10	Walking meditation or seated meditation
	3:30	Recollection of the Buddha (*Buddhānussati*)
	4:30	Seated *bhāvanā*
	5:30	Tea and *bhāvanā*
	6:30	*Dāna*: breakfast
	7:15	Group meditation and guru conferences
	8:15	Tea
	8:30	Satipaṭṭhāna: mindfulness of sitting, standing, lying, or walking
	11:00	*Dāna*: lunch (eaten with mindfulness)
	11:30	Free
P.M.	12:30	*Bhāvanā*
	1:15	Tea
	2:00	*Bhāvanā* and conferences
	6:00	*Buddha pūjā*
	6:30	Tea
	6:35	Bathing
	7:15	*Bhāvanā*
	8:15	Further *bhāvanā*
	10:00	Retire

Following this schedule, laypersons as well as *bhikkhus* who retreat to Kanduboda pursue meditation for almost fourteen hours per day. Actually, Kanduboda teaches that every act should be done with mindfulness or awareness. Thus, even eating and bathing become meditations as Mahasi Sayadaw instructed. At Kanduboda this schedule for the yogis does not change for *poya* or any other day. The only devotional element in the schedule is the 6:00 p.m. *Buddha pūjā*. Those who go to Kanduboda discover both the difficulty and the necessity of doing *vipassanā* continuously in this way. They perceive that it would be virtually impossible to make progress in mental development without intensive practice of meditation and the development of the ability to be mindful of all activities.

With the reinterpretion of the vocation of Buddhists and the reinterpretation of the ritual system, the *vipassanā bhāvanā* movement leaders feel that they have restored the true meaning to Buddhism. The rituals traditionally employed by householders for making merit acquire their proper meaning only when they are related to the central ritual, *bhāvanā*. The meditation centers promote meditation for laity in a way that traditional Buddhist laity of the past could scarcely have imagined. Unlike the traditional temples where the Satipaṭṭhāna Sutta has functioned primarily as a chant on *poya* days, these centers teach the laity to practice the techniques of mindfulness (*sati*) given in that sutta. A foreign meditation teacher, Sister Khema, summed up the changes in practice that the meditation centers have brought about when she told me "*Vipassanā bhāvanā* is something new in Sri Lanka."

(5) The Vipassanā Method and the Orthodox Critics

This *vipassanā bhāvanā* has not gone unchallenged by the traditionalist Sinhalese *Sangha*. Although some, or even many, traditionalist monks have seen no harm in the *vipassanā* centers, other monks have strongly opposed them. To some extent their opposition can be seen as a reaction to the tremendous success and popularity of the meditation centers. The laypeople's thronging the centers on *poya* days undoubtedly threatened many monks who maintained traditionalist temples. On a deeper level, however, traditionalist monks opposed the *vipassanā* movement because it presented innovations that did not cohere to traditional Sinhalese Theravada doctrine and practice. The teachings of the meditation centers about the availability of the goal and about *vipassanā* and *satipaṭṭhāna* as practical methods for reaching the goal in this life, and their opening of these methods to the laity, all represented innovations that shocked traditional Theravadins. The dispute that arose because of these innovations and the charges that the conservative critics made reveal some important differences between the *vipassanā* movement and traditional Sinhalese Theravada.

The most outspoken criticism of the meditation movement came from three elders of the Vajirārāma temple in Colombo: the Venerables Soma Thera, Kassapa Thera, and Kheminda Thera. All three belonged to the Amarapura Nikāya of the *Sangha*, a Nikāya that maintained strong relations with Burma. Venerable Soma Thera and Venerable Kheminda Thera had received their higher ordination in Burma. Venerable Kassapa Thera had entered the *Sangha* at the age of sixty-five after a long career as a physician. Since all three belonged to the English-educated elite and had ties to Burma, they might have been expected to side with the Burmese monks and the Sinhalese laity who began the meditation centers. Instead, however, they castigated the meditation centers for teaching unorthodox methods that threatened the true *Dhamma* and endangered both the institution of Buddhism and the Buddhists themselves.[48]

Venerable Kassapa Thera set the tone of this criticism in a book entitled *Protection of the Sambuddha Sāsana*. In the book he charged that "wrong beliefs, confusion and disorder have reached a new peak with the new Burmese Government sponsored belly meditation emanating from Sāsana Yeiktha in Rangoon."[49] This statement reflects the resentment that Kassapa Thera and others felt toward the Burmese intrusion into Ceylon, an intrusion that was enjoying great popularity when Kassapa wrote. Sāsana (or Thathana) Yeiktha was Mahasi Sayadaw's temple in Burma, and as sponsor of the mission to establish the meditation centers in Ceylon, Mahasi Sayadaw became the focus of the criticism by Kassapa and others. Kassapa Thera accused Mahasi Sayadaw of teaching a "counterfeit *Dhamma*" that threatened the true *Dhamma*. "There is real danger to the continued life of the Pure *Dhamma* in Sri Lanka right now in this Jayanti year," he wrote.[50] This perception of imminent danger seems to have been the motivating factor behind the traditionalist opposition to Mahasi Sayadaw and the *vipassanā bhāvanā* movement, a perception of danger to the *Dhamma* as well as to the guardians of *Dhamma* in Sri Lanka.

Charging that the new meditation centers were "misleading the gullible and the neurotic, most of whom, here as in Burma, are women," Kassapa declared that his intention was to help Buddhists "avoid the false methods parading as genuine teachings of the Buddha."[51] The "false method" that Kassapa found most threatening was Mahasi Sayadaw's teaching that breathing meditation (ānānāpana-sati) could be practiced by concentrating on the rise and fall of the abdomen, rather than by observing the breath at the tip of the nose, as it had traditionally been taught. Mahasi Sayadaw had sanctioned this method of developing mindfulness of breathing because many people found it easier to observe the breath in this way. Although he said that this method also had a sound basis in the texts, his primary reason for teaching it seems to have been that so many of his students had success using this method to develop "one-pointedness" of mind.[52] Burmese vipassanā methods have always had a practical side. Kassapa Thera, however, lashed out at this practice as "an ancient tantric stunt belly meditation that has been reborn."[53] He also called it a "Vetulya road," implying that it might have connections with some Mahāyāna beliefs. If this were not enough, he continued, "the forces of Māra are attempting to foist ancient evil practices" on the Sinhalese people. Kassapa elaborated on the connection between this method and tantra by explaining that the "umbilical area" represents the "Nabhi mandala of Tantrayana." Mahasi Sayadaw's teaching people to meditate on breathing in this way went against the path set forth in the suttas. Instead of being meditation on breathing, the practice becomes, Kassapa charged, "bowel displacement" meditation, and he labeled Mahasi Sayadaw "the bowel displacement teacher."[54]

These emotional criticisms reflect the intensity of the threat perceived in the bhāvanā movement by traditionalist monks. Kassapa Thera and others opposed and resented the movement with its "new" methods and its foreign teachers, whom they regarded as upstarts. Kassapa compared this breathing meditation technique to Hindu prāṇāyāma, which he had learned in India when "Mahasi Sayadaw was perhaps not yet born."[55]

While affirming Venerable Kassapa's fiery criticism of the vipassanā movement, Venerable Kheminda offered a more substantive and scholarly critique of this movement and the meditation methods taught by Mahasi Sayadaw and his followers.[56] Calling these bhāvanā practices the "new Burmese methods," he objected to them on two grounds: they (1) lacked authority and (2) violated the paradigm of the gradual path. Venerable Kheminda summed up his objections to these *bhāvanā* methods when he labeled them "*vipassanā* two-step shortcuts."[57]

Clearly a traditionalist in the Theravada mold, Venerable Kheminda argued that the suttas alone have the "ultimate authority on matters of *Dhamma*," and any system of meditation must follow the suttas to have validity. In an interview Kheminda said that when the meditation movement was beginning in Sri Lanka, Mahasi Sayadaw asked him to help propagate the *vipassanā* teachings, since the two of them had been friends in Burma. Kheminda refused. He said friendship is one thing, but loyalty to the *Dhamma* must be paramount. He would not help Mahasi Sayadaw spread teachings that were not in accord with the *Dhamma*. The *vipassanā* techniques of the meditation movement, Kheminda believed, were Mahasi Sayadaw's own ideas—and should have been proclaimed as such. "I do not think that anybody questions the good intentions of the Venerable Mahasi Sayadaw," he wrote. "Yet one has to bear in mind that they are not substitutes for the correct presentation of the *Dhamma*."[58] Pointing to the Mahāpadesa Sutta, which sets forth criteria for determining the authority of teachings by comparing them with the suttas and the rules of discipline, Kheminda charged that Mahasi Sayadaw's teachings were not in accord with *Buddha Vacana*, the word of the Buddha.[59]

The aspect of Mahasi Sayadaw's *vipassanā* method that Kheminda found most heretical was that it did not conform to the three-stage gradual path set forth clearly in the suttas; instead, the new method proclaimed that all people—whether or not they were even Buddhists—could proceed directly to the practice of *vipassanā*. Kheminda maintained that the gradual path with its "three aggregates"—virtue (*sīla*), concentration (*samādhi*), and insight (*paññā*)—and its seven purifications as laid out in the "Rathavinīta Sutta" and in the handbook of Theravada, the *Visuddhimagga*, constituted the "invariable sequence" for meditation. "This order has been established by the Buddha," wrote Kheminda, and cannot be changed "by altering the sequence prescribed by the Master or by skipping any item."[60] The Buddha taught that everything arises because of causes and conditions, thus the elements of the path must be accomplished in their proper order where "each aggregate is the necessary condition for the one that follows it."[61]

The Buddhist Revival in Sri Lanka

Since the stages of the path follow in a set order, Kheminda argued that it is not possible for meditators to skip over concentration (samādhi) and the trance states (jhāna) in order to go directly to the practice of insight (vipassanā) because concentration represents the necessary condition for insight. Insight depends upon concentration, because unless the trance states are developed, the five hindrances (pañcanīvarana) cannot be eliminated, and as long as the five hindrances are present one cannot attain wisdom and insight.[62]

Kheminda's book is a tour de force, citing numerous suttas and commentaries in an attempt to support this view that vipassanā always has trance (jhāna) and concentration (samādhi) as prerequisites. Although, to be sure, many sutta passages do proclaim the "invariable sequence" of the gradual path, many others seem ambiguous. When suttas suggest that concentration might not be necessary for insight, however, Kheminda resorts to Buddhaghosa's commentaries, where the suttas were almost always interpreted in ways that agreed with the gradual path of the Visuddhimagga. Throughout his book, in his endeavor to reconcile all the teachings regarding meditation, Kheminda's method resembles the method of interpretation prescribed in the Netti Pakarana. The Netti, a late canonical or early postcanonical text, presents an interpretative method for discerning the one true meaning of the Dhamma that is implicit in any sutta. The Netti's method consists of interpreting all teachings in light of what orthodoxy held to be the central core of the Dhamma.[63] Interestingly, the Netti seems to have devised this method of interpretation to protect the Dhamma against heretical interpretations and new schools of Buddhism. For his part Kheminda employs this method to find the view that concentration (samādhi) and the trance states (jhānas) are integral to the gradual path implicit in all suttas about meditation. The following statement by Venerable Kheminda, referring to the three main aggregates of the path, could almost be a quote from the Netti: "And when one or two of these three (sīla, samādhi, paññā) are given, those versed in the Dhamma and with no theories to uphold, are not confused or misled thereby, but are able to fill in any unstated factor or factors, as the cause may be."[64] Both the Netti and Venerable Kheminda were concerned with combating "heretics" and protecting the true Dhamma.

Venerable Kheminda's criticisms of the *vipassanā* movement were first published in the Sri Lankan journal *World Buddhism* in 1966. His articles elicited responses from Mahasi Sayadaw and the Burmese teachers of *vipassanā* and spawned a series of debates on this topic that appeared in *World Buddhism* from July, 1966, to December, 1970.[65] These debates brought out the major points of differences between the traditionalist or neotraditionalist Sinhalese view of meditation and the reformist view of the meditation leaders. The chief spokesman for the *vipassanā* movement was Venerable Sayadaw U Nyanuttara, who was appointed to this task by Mahasi Sayadaw himself. In these debates the Burmese meditation leaders, speaking for the entire *vipassanā* movement, took their scripturalist stance to dispute Venerable Kheminda's view that the gradual path constituted the only textually authoritative path to the goal.

The *vipassanā* leaders agreed with Venerable Kheminda in upholding the authority of the suttas. Their reading of the suttas, however, differed from Kheminda's reading, and they criticized him for saying that the Buddha set out only one path for all people, when most interpreters have said that the Buddha adjusted his teachings to the abilities of his hearers. Specifically, the meditators argued that Buddha presented the option for some people to practice *vipassanā* only, without prior development of concentration (*samādhi*) or trance (*jhāna*). This type of meditator was called in the Theravada texts a *vipassanā-yānika*, one who has insight as his vehicle, and was contrasted with the *samātha-yānika*, one who has concentration as his vehicle. The distinction between these two paths occurs first in the commentaries, but is said to be implicit in the suttas. The *samātha-yānika* develops insight preceded by concentration, whereas the *vipassanā-yānika* develops concentration preceded by insight.[66] The Burmese meditation teachers concluded, "Thus the *Aṇguttara* Text, Commentary and Sub-Commentary clearly show that a *Vipassanā-yānika* can proceed directly with insight exercises without previous development of access concentration and absorption concentration, and thereby can develop not only *Vipassanā-ñāṇa* (insight wisdom) but also *Magga-phala ñāṇa* (path fruition wisdom)."[67]

In his attempt to force all the texts into agreement with his view of the gradual path, Kheminda argued that the *vipassanā-yānika* does not proceed directly to insight meditation. His argument turns on the

Visuddhimagga passage describing the third purification, purification of view, which says that at the third purification the *samātha-yānika* develops concentration and then insight, while the *vipassanā-yānika* bypasses concentration. All that the passage says, argued Kheminda, is that the *vipassanā-yānika* does not have to enter into the *jhānic* concentration state *again* before developing wisdom. The fact that the two types of meditators are not differentiated until the third purification, that is, after the purification of concentration (*samādhi*), implies that both had already followed the same gradual path of virtue and concentration up to that point.[68]

The meditation leaders howled in protest at Kheminda's interpretation of this passage, charging that Kheminda was the one who was teaching non-*Dhamma* as *Dhamma*. On balance, we would have to say that Kheminda's interpretation, while not impossible, is fairly improbable. The straightforward meaning of the text seems to be that the *vipassanā-yānika* follows a path that does not reach full concentration until after insight has been attained. That this path exists in the Theravada texts cannot be disputed very cogently. As a Western scholar of Theravada has written; "The 'bare insight worker,' [the *vipassanā-yānika*], the one without jhanic powers, [is] perhaps atypical, but clearly existent and orthodox."[69] The Burmese said the same. Although most meditators probably passed through the concentration stages en route to insight, "the fact of some reaching *vipassanā* and the final state of Bodhi directly has but to be accepted."[70] One form of proof cited by the meditators for this "fact" was the stories in the suttas about people attaining *vipassanā* and the fruitions of the path when they were listening to the Buddha preach the *Dhamma*.

Having demonstrated that the *vipassanā* method has authoritative status in the Pali Canon as well as in the commentaries and subcommentaries compiled in Sri Lanka, the meditators observed that instead of labeling *vipassanā bhāvanā* the "new Burmese method," it should be called "the old Ceylon method."[71] The Burmese teachers conceded nothing to Venerable Kheminda in textual scholarship in attempting to prove their point about *vipassanā*.

If the meditators based the authority and validity of *vipassanā bhāvanā* on textual grounds, the same source of authority that Kheminda and the traditionalists relied upon, they also introduced an additional basis for its authority: the actual experiences of modern-day meditators. Sayadaw U Nyanuttara wrote that Mahasi Sayadaw had developed his *vipassanā* teaching "on the strength not only of Ceylon Commentaries, but also of the practical experiences of the yogis."[72] Mahasi Sayadaw is described as a "māhāthera, well-versed both in *pariyatti* [study] and in *paṭipatti* [practice]."[73] For the Burmese who began the *bhāvanā* movement the goal was believed to be both plausible and realized by monks such as Mahasi Sayadaw. Because Venerable Kheminda challenged Mahasi Sayadaw's views, he was compared by the Burmese teachers to Sati Thera, a *bhikkhu* who contradicted the Buddha and suffered because of it. On a somewhat more charitable note—yet still recognizing the difference between Kheminda's scholastic acquaintance with the path and Mahasi Sayadaw's practical experience—the Burmese said, "A fervent wish may be expressed that the Venerable Kheminda Thera and persons of his ilk do not rest content with the mere knowledge of the *samātha-yānika* method but instead practise it diligently."[74]

As a final point in support of *vipassanā bhāvanā* the Burmese defenders asked: Which method is easier and faster, *vipassanā*-only or the complete gradual path? Their answer, of course, was that *vipassanā*-only was quicker and therefore more viable for "this woeful time when the life span is very short."[75] If a person sought to perfect *jhānic* concentration before practicing *vipassanā*, he might die before reaching insight. Therefore, from purely pragmatic considerations the Burmese argued that *vipassanā* has authority and validity today. Winston King confirms that in Burma "a kind of consensus exists that the modern age and modern people are best suited to *vipassanā* as independent spiritual technique for achieving enlightenment, largely bypassing jhanic-style practice."[76]

The traditionalist Sinhalese Theravadins, however, were moved neither by the meditation leaders' arguments from expediency nor by their arguments from experience. Since the Sinhalese have generally believed the goal to be unattainable in this lifetime, the meditation teachers' warning that if the traditionalists insisted that *jhāna* be perfected first, they might cause a person to "lose his life's opportunity to develop insight" had little effect on the traditionalists. Venerable Kheminda's response to such reasoning was to say that these views are "so typical of this age of speed and restlessness," but do not alter the necessity of following Theravada's gradual path.[77] In the same way, the argument from the personal experiences of the meditators also lacked cogency for the traditionalists. The Vajirārāma critics did not accept the validity of the *vipassanā* leaders' experiences. Neither Mahasi Sayadaw nor his generals, whom the meditation movement regarded as *arahants* or at least path-attainers, elicited any particular veneration from the conservative critics. From the traditionalists' viewpoint the *bhāvanā* leaders could not have attained what the traditionalists considered to be unattainable. Likewise, the claims of attainment by lay meditators who went to the new meditation centers were discounted. Venerable Kassapa wrote that the people who practice this meditation "do not exhibit the calm, concentrated, happy look mentioned in the texts."[78]

Since the method was wrong, the Vajirārāma *bhikkhus* argued, the results would be wrong as well. To document this point they cited a number of cases where people had experienced terrible results from pursuing *vipassanā bhāvanā*. Kassapa wrote of two women who learned meditation at Kanduboda and "went melancholic, dejected and crazed. But happily under skilled attention both have now recovered."[79] Other traditionalist Sinhalese cited similar stories to prove that meditation is a dangerous business; if one does not learn and practice it properly—that is, according to the gradual path of *sīla*, *samādhi*, and *paññā*—terrible mental disturbances could result. This idea that bypassing concentration (*samādhi*) could cause insanity seems to have been widely believed by traditionalist Sinhalese monks and laity.

Although the heat of these debates between the traditionalists and the Burmese and Sinhalese *vipassanā* leaders has cooled in recent years, the basic objections of the traditionalists still remain. The traditionalists are committed to the threefold-training system of the gradual path and have difficulty abandoning that. Those traditionalist monks who have begun to recognize the validity of the views of the *vipassanā* leaders often qualify the *vipassanā*-only path by adding that at least a small amount of concentration should be done first. Venerable Kheminda's opposition to the *vipassanā* movement has not changed, however. In 1980 he published *The Way of Buddhist Meditation*, restating his views; the book was reviewed favorably in the press and widely cited throughout the country. So the debate has not ended; but at present it might be described as more of a dialogue, with most traditionalist monks willing to hear, albeit cautiously, what the *vipassanā* leaders have to say.

Conclusion

The traditionalists' and the insight meditation leaders' differences on these questions surrounding the issue of meditation amount to contrasting solutions to the practical hermeneutical dilemma of identity and responsiveness. Compared to traditional Theravada, the insight meditation leaders have a reformist interpretation of the identity of the religion. They offer a rational interpretation of both the goal and the path of Buddhism. Perceiving the goal of arahantship and *Nibbāna* to be plausible, these reformers regard the path as immediate rather than mediate or gradual. Their optimistic, world-affirming interpretation of the goal makes possible a path of this-worldly asceticism. Insight meditation leads to *Nibbāna* here and now, they believe.

Ames observed that, in general, the modern reformation in Theravada has been characterized by four themes: universalism, pragmatism, achievement, and antiritualism.[80] The insight meditation movement's interpretation manifests all four of these themes, and in all four ways diverges from traditionalism. Allowing everyone to practice meditation in earnest, it is universalistic and antihierarchical. Believing that meditation will not only accomplish the goal but also generate mundane benefits such as mental and physical health, the reformers are pragmatic. An achievement orientation characterizes the reformers' religious quest, just as it did the secular lives of the new elite who initiated this movement. And since the goal can be achieved, rituals of merit-making lose much of their importance as ways of relating to the ultimate reality. The meditation movement offers more direct means of actualizing one's human potential.

The contrast between the insight meditation reformers' interpretation and that of traditional Theravada is illustrated also by their understandings of the concepts of *karma* and *saṃsāra*. Both groups use these concepts to explain the availability of the goal and the nature of the path. *Karma* and *saṃsāra* point to how and where meaning can be found. For the neotraditionalists the emphasis falls on the past, where *karma* was once perfected by the great *arahants*, and on the future, where Buddhists today must follow the gradual path through endless rounds of *saṃsāra* in order to purify their *karma* and achieve wisdom. The reformists, however, emphasize the present and believe that people today have the potential to perfect their *karma*. It has been done; others can do it. The *sāsana* has not declined; the golden age does not lie exclusively in either the past or the future, but can exist in the present.

This change from a neotraditionalist Theravada of merit-making and scholarship to a reformist Theravada of meditation and experience has constituted one of the major forces in the Sinhalese Buddhist reformation, especially in the past two decades. As we have seen, some traditionalist monks have regarded these changes as heretical and dangerous, and even some Westerners have questioned the validity of a Buddhist emphasis on *Nibbāna* here and now. But although the *vipassanā bhāvanā* reformers' interpretation may seem new, it is not novel. Solid scripturalists, these reformists find their charter in the Pali Canon, in an early stage of Buddhism believed to predate commentarial Theravada with its gradual path. Just as the modern-day forest monks, whom Carrithers describes,[81] have adopted a self-cultivation ideal based on the early texts, so the *vipassanā* reformers follow the self-cultivation model of the early period of Buddhism when the path was considered open to all and the *Sangha* was in fact a fourfold *Sangha* of monks, nuns, laymen, and laywomen. The *vipassanā* reformers have good grounds for their views; the richness of the canonical teachings certainly permits such an interpretation.

This understanding of the identity of Theravada has enabled the reformists to deal meaningfully with the other aspect of the hermeneutical dilemma: responsiveness. It may be that the growing success of the *vipassanā bhāvānā* movement and its emergence as a central factor in the reformation has resulted from the adequacy of this response to the modern context. By contrast, the simultaneous decline of many of the reforms and movements proposed under Jayanti Buddhism by the traditionalists may be explained by their waning appropriateness to the changing social context. The meditation reformers found the identity for Theravada in a Buddhism that stressed the individual, and this may have been more appropriate for a society moving rapidly away from the strong group restraints of the village. In this context the ideal of arahantship here and now seemed more practical and plausible than did the highly structured gradual path with its gradations of rebirth. With the increasing urbanization of Sri Lankan society, this cosmology has appealed to increasing numbers of people, and the meditation movement has grown dramatically. Even among the traditionalists change is occurring, for many traditional temples have begun to offer meditation classes for the laity, following the lead of the *vipassanā bhāvanā* reformers.

Notes

1. Robert N. Bellah ed., *Religion and Progress in Modern Asia* (New York: Free Press, 1965), 210.
2. See Michael Carrithers, *The Forest Monks of Sri Lanka: An Anthropological and Historical Study* (New Delhi: Oxford University Press, 1983), 141f.
3. See P. G. Gunatillika, *A Biography of H. Sri Nissanka* (Colombo: Helavira Press, 1947).
4. Richard Gombrich, "From Monastery to Meditation Centre: Lay Meditation in Modern Sri Lanka," in *Buddhist Studies: Ancient and Modern*, ed. P. Denwood and A. Piatigorsky (London: Curzon Press, 1983), 28.
5. *Ceylon Daily News*, July 30, 1955, p. 1.
6. Gombrich, "From Monastery to Meditation Centre," 28.
7. A brief biography and obituary notice of Ven. Sumathipala was given in the *Buddhist Forum* (London, 1982), 40f.
8. See Jacques Maquet, "Expressive Space and Theravada Values: A Meditation Monastery in Sri Lanka," *Ethos* 3 (1975): p. 1-21.
9. Bogoda Premaratne, "The International Centre for Training in Buddhist Meditation at Kanduboda, Sri Lanka" (pamphlet published in 1984 on the occasion of the fourteenth General Conference of the World Fellowhship of Buddhists).
10. Gombrich, "Monastery to Meditation Center," 29.
11. Some branch centers, however, do not as yet have facilities for laity to reside for long periods.
12. Gombrich, "Monastery to Meditation Center," 21.
13. Michael Ames, "Ideological and Social Change in Ceylon," *Human Organization*, 22 (1963): 49.
14. Richard Gombrich, *Precept and Practice: Traditional Buddhism in the Rural Highlands of Sri Lanka* (Oxford: Oxford Univ. Press, 1971), 284f.
15. This sutta is found in the *Suttanipāta*, ed. D. Anderson and H. Smith (London: Pali Text Society, 1913), 25-26.
16. Michael Ames, "Magical Animism and Buddhism: A Structural Analysis of the Sinhalese Religious System," *Journal of Asian Studies* 23 (1964): 27, 32.
17. Jacques Maquet, "Meditation in Contemporary Sri Lanka: Idea and Practice," *Journal of Transpersonal Psychology* 7, (1975): 184.
18. D. B. Jayatilaka, "Practical Buddhism," *The Buddhist* 51 (Jan. 1981; repr. from *The Buddhist*, July 1901) 2.
19. *The Milinda Pañha*, ed. V. Trenckner (London: Pali Text Society, 1962), 264f.
20. Walpola Rahula, *What the Buddha Taught* (New York: Grove Press, 1974), 76.

21. See George D. Bond, 'The Word of the Buddha': The Tipiṭaka and Its Interpretation in the Theravada Buddhist Tradition (Colombo: Gunasena and Co., 1983).
22. The Dīgha Nikāya, ed. T. W. Rhys Davids and J. Carpenter (London: Pali Text Society, 1889), 2: 154.
23. Walpola Rahula, History of Buddhism in Ceylon: The Anurādhapura Period, 3rd Century BC-10th Century BC (Colombo: Gunasena and Co., 1959), 158ff.
24. Rahula, History of Buddhism, 160.
25. Gombrich, Precept and Practice, 281.
26. Maquet, "Meditation in Contemporary Sri Lanka," 184.
27. Ames, "Magical Animism and Buddhism," 28-33.
28. Ames, "Magical Animism and Buddhism," 30.
29. This was related to me by Venerable Nyanaponika in a conversation at his hermitage in the Udawatakele forest preserve.
30. Jayatilaka, "Practical Buddhism," 2.
31. Rahula, History, 254.
32. Ames, "Magical Animism and Buddhism," 30.
33. This temple schedule comes from a temple on the outskirts of Colombo and is representative of many others I observed.
34. Pirit is a ritual in which the bhikkhus chant certain Buddhist texts for the purpose of producing good effects or warding off evil. It represents an interesting example of the Indian notion of the power of truth. See Gombrich, Precept and Practice, 201-06; and Lily de Silva., Paritta: The Buddhist Ceremony for Peace and Prosperity in Spolia Zeylanica, Vol. 36, Part I (Colombo: National Museum, 1981).
35. Gombrich, "Monastery to Meditation Centre," 22.
36. The Satipaṭṭhāna Sutta is found in the Majjhima Nikāya, Vol. 1 (sutta 10), and the Mahāsatipaṭṭhāna Sutta in the Dīgha Nikāya, Vol. 2, (sutta 22).
37. Dīgha Nikāya, 2: 290.
38. Achan Sobin Namto, A Short Introduction to Insight Meditation (Chicago: The Chicago Meditation Center, n.d.), 3.
39. Among his writings on this topic are The Progress of Insight: A Treatise on Buddhist Satipaṭṭhāna Meditation, trans. Nyanaponika Thera (Kandy: The Buddhist Publication Society, 1978), a treatise written in both Burmese and Pali, with the Pali version serving as a kind of modern sutta or scripture for meditation; Practical Insight Meditation, trans. U Pe Thin and U Tin (Kandy: Buddhist Publication Society, 1980); and "Insight Meditation: Basic and Progressive Stages," in Living Buddhist Masters, ed. Jack Kornfield (Santa Cruz, CA: Unity Press, 1977).
40. Mahasi Sayadaw, "Insight Meditation," 57.
41. Mahasi Sayadaw, The Progress of Insight, 8.
42. Mahasi Sayadaw, "Insight Meditation," 71.
43. The seven stages of purification occur in the Pali Canon in the Majjhima Nikāya, sutta 24, the Rathavinīta Sutta. They are purifications (visuddhi) of morality (sīla), of mind (citta), of view (diṭṭhi), by overcoming doubt (kankhā-vitarana), by knowledge and vision of what is and is not the path (maggāmaggañāṇādassana), by knowledge and vision of the path progress (paṭipadā-ñāṇādassana), and of knowledge and vision (ñāṇadassana). These seven stages formed the outline for the Visuddhimagga.

44. Winston King, *Theravada Meditation: The Transformation of Yoga* (University Park: Pennsylvania State University Press, 1980), 94.
45. Nyanaponika Thera, *The Heart of Buddhist Meditation* (New York: Samuel Weiser, 1973), 43.
46. Mahasi Sayadaw, "Insight Meditation," 80.
47. At some meditation centers, such as Kanduboda, the devotional rituals have been eliminated for the meditating yogis. Their only activity is meditation. See Maquet, "Expressive Space and Theravada Values," 16.
48. The opposition to the meditation movement by these members of the Amarapura Nikāya indicates that neotraditionalism is not restricted to the Siyam Nikāya and the Kandyan monks. The temple at which these monks resided, Vajirārāma, has been a bastion of conservatism and neotraditionalism.
49. Kassapa Thera, *Protection of the Sambuddha Sāsana: A Collection of Articles on Meditation* (Colombo: Henry Prelis, 1957), iii.
50. Kassapa, *Protection*, 66.
51. Kassapa, *Protection*, v.
52. Mahasi Sayadaw, *Practical Insight Meditation*, iii, 4.
53. Kassapa, *Protection*, v.
54. Kassapa, *Protection*, 2.
55. Kassapa, *Protection*, 5.
56. Kheminda Thera, *The Way of Buddhist Meditation* (Colombo: Lake House Publishers, 1980).
57. This explanation was given to me by Ven. Kheminda in an interview in 1983.
58. Cited in *Satipaṭṭhāna Vipassanā Meditation: Criticisms and Replies* (Rangoon: Buddha Sāsana Nuggaha Organization, 1977), 68.
59. The Mahāpadesa Sutta can be found in the *Dīgha Nikāya*, 2: 124-26.
60. Kheminda, *Way of Buddhist Meditation*, 11.
61. Kheminda, *Way of Buddhist Meditation*, 11.
62. Kheminda, *Way of Buddhist Meditation*, 13.
63. Bond, *Word of the Buddha*, ch. 2.
64. Kheminda, *Way of Buddhist Meditation*, 64.
65. These debates were later collected and published as a book; *Satipaṭṭhāna Vipassonā Meditation: Criticisms and Replies* (cited above).
66. *Satipaṭṭhāna Vipassanā Meditation*, 17-18.
67. *Sattipaṭṭhāna Vipassanā Meditation*, 19.
68. Kheminda, *Way of Buddhist Meditation*, 39.
69. Winston King, *Theravada Meditation*, 94.
70. *Satipaṭṭhāna Vipassanā Meditation*, 25.
71. *Satipaṭṭhāna Vipassanā Meditation*, 17.
72. *Satipaṭṭhāna Vipassanā Meditation*, 29.
73. *Satipaṭṭhāna Vipassanā Meditation*, 313.
74. *Satipaṭṭhāna Vipassanā Meditation*, 35.
75. *Satipaṭṭhāna Vipassanā Meditation*, 310.
76. King, *Theravada Meditation*, 116.
77. Kheminda, *Way of Buddhist Meditation*, 3.

78. Kassapa, *Protection*, 12.
79. Kassapa, *Protection*, 12.
80. Ames, "Ideological and Social Change in Ceylon," 50.
81. Carrithers, *The Forest Monks of Sri Lanka*, 142.

5

Individual Lay Meditators: Unity and Diversity in the Practice of *Vipassanā*

Having examined the outlines of the *vipassanā* movement and the opinions of its leaders, we turn in this chapter to a further assessment of this movement based on the views and experiences of individual lay meditators.[1] The case histories and beliefs of a variety of lay meditators are examined according to the categories and motifs discussed in chapter 1 to see how they have interpreted *vipassanā* in their lives. What insights and benefits does *vipassanā* hold for these contemporary Buddhists? To what extent has *vipassanā* led them to break with traditional or neotraditional Theravada? Gombrich described the meditation movement as "the biggest change which Buddhism in Sri Lanka has undergone in the twentieth century: the belief that every Buddhist should seek his own salvation in this life."[2] Under the umbrella of the meditation movement both the seeking and the salvation have assumed a variety of forms as the lay meditators have found rational and pragmatic interpretations of both the path and the goal of the tradition. In the case histories and viewpoints of a variety of lay meditators we can see both the depth of meaning that meditation has for its practitioners and the diversity of the movement.

Case Histories and an Analysis

The meditator who perhaps best exemplifies the origins of the *vipassanā* movement is Miss Abeyasekere, an elderly woman who studied

177

meditation under the Burmese monks who came to Sri Lanka in 1955. The leader of the Burmese delegation, U Sujata, served as her guru, and she remembers vividly the halcyon days when the meditation movement began. Now in her seventies, Miss Abeyasekere teaches the Burmese methods of *vipassanā* to others at a small meditation center at her home. U Sujata told her to build a center and teach lay people because having a proper teacher is crucial to the spread of *vipassanā*. Her center is small, with only four or five rooms for resident meditators and a meditation hall. She has instructed numerous people in the decade and a half that she has been teaching, and many of them often return for short retreats or refresher courses. In her view there are no longer many qualified teachers who can guide students to the *Dhamma* they have seen firsthand. She follows the "full Mahasi Sayadaw method" without deviation, adapting her instruction to students' needs and personalities.

Her views about meditation and its relevance to the lay life affirm those of the *vipassanā* leaders discussed in the previous chapter. She has "no doubts" that arahantship is possible today. However, U Sujata told her that only a Buddha can determine whether a person actually has attained arahantship. Nevertheless, she believes that U Sujata himself has surely achieved an "advanced state, much higher than Venerable Sumathipala." As befits one who has started a center, Miss Abeyasekere has great optimism about the spiritual potential of the laity. If laypeople have the "right qualities" and determination, there are no barriers to their achieving the goals. She admits, however, that the true *vipassanā* path is difficult; it should be practiced for twenty hours per day when one is learning at a center.

Although the layperson who is learning meditation can benefit from a quiet environment and a proper teacher, he does not need to renounce the world in order to succeed at meditation. "*Vipassanā* itself is renunciation," Miss Abeyasekere explained. For example, if a meditator experiences pain, he can practice mindfulness to renounce anxiety and attachment concerning it. The meditator has to renounce greed, hatred, and delusion through *bhāvanā*. In general, one who pursues *vipassanā* can live in the world yet withdraw from the ordinary ways of being in the world. Although Miss Abeysekere does not claim that *vipassanā* is easy, she clearly teaches a path of this-worldly asceticism for the laity.

Study, the other traditional requirement for meditation, can also be discarded. Miss Abeyasekere believes that study of the *Dhamma* is not necessary, and can possibly be harmful to a lay meditator. Meditators fare better if they go to the teacher with a fresh mind. If they have studied *Dhamma* in the past, they should forget what they have learned and not be attached to it. After one has practiced meditation for awhile, the *Dhamma* becomes clear and one can understand what it means. This advice corresponds to that given by the teachers at Kanduboda and the other successors to the Burmese.

With regard to why people pursue meditation, she holds that the primary goal is to escape *saṃsāra* and to reach *Nibbāna* in this life: "Buddhism is for this life." Before reaching the ultimate goal, however, the meditator also attains some immediate benefits from *vipassanā*. Overcoming anger, impatience, anxiety, and other "character defects," the lay meditator is better able to cope with life. These short-term benefits represent necessary steps on the way to the chief benefit of *vipassanā*: the control and liberation of mind and body (*nāma-rūpa*) and liberation.

In her life style and in her views on these matters, Miss Abeyasekere continues the Burmese lineage in Sri Lanka, although she has little contact with centers such as Kanduboda. Profoundly influenced by the Burmese teachers who reintroduced *vipassanā* to Sri Lanka, she has spread that influence to others who regard her as an extraordinary guru. Committed to the value of *vipassanā* and sensitive to the needs of other people, she was reluctant to begin teaching for fear that people might go mad during the difficult initial stages. Once she began, with the direct encouragement of Mahasi Sayadaw and U Sujata, she had success in teaching both the method and the gospel of *vipassanā*. Perhaps the only way she seems to have amended the strict approach to *vipassanā* is in conceding that rituals such as the *Buddha pūjā* might be useful. Rituals do not have central importance she believes, but might help some people develop faith (*saddhā*). Indeed, Miss Abeyasekere excused herself from one of our interviews to go perform *Buddha pūjā* before the clock struck twelve noon.

Another meditator, Mrs. Visākhā, exemplifies the ideals of Kanduboda; she began meditating at that center about a decade ago. Coming from a traditional Buddhist family, she grew up as a "pious Buddhist" who went regularly to the temple, observed the precepts, and performed the rituals. She received an English education, attended the university, and after graduation began a career. She married a prominent Buddhist layman and had several children. Despite all these outward signs of success, she experienced problems at home and frustrations in her work. When a friend heard her describe her problems, she suggested that Mrs. Visākhā go to Kanduboda to try *vipassanā*. She went but found the regimen very difficult. After five days she became ill and left. Determined to try it again, she returned to Kanduboda after some time but again lasted only five days and was unable "to complete the course." Finally she went back a third time accompanied by her teen-aged daughter. Staying eight days, they both completed the course.

The path of meditation she learned at Kanduboda differed from the traditional Buddhism that she had known before. In her village temple the monks never taught meditation (*satipaṭṭhāna*) to the laypeople, but stressed only the standard means and goals of merit-making: giving, observing the precepts, and the hope of rebirth. People in the village knew what *bhāvanā* was, but they did not see it as a possibility for householders. Although they often did five minutes of *mettā bhāvanā*, the lovingkindness meditation, on *poya* days at the temple, this practice had little effect on their daily life.

Mrs. Visākhā found that her village Buddhist heritage did not relate to her life in an urban setting. She turned to *vipassanā* as a way to find Buddhist solutions to new problems. Mrs. Visākhā had the same motivation for beginning *vipassanā* as many other lay Buddhists in this movement: a search for rational answers to the questions "What is the meaning of my existence?" and "How can I solve these problems?"

At Kanduboda she joined others who were looking for answers. When she went with her daughter, the center had in residence fifteen Sri Lankan householders, four foreigners, and two *dasa sil mātāvas* or nuns. The course was difficult. Arising at 3 a.m. they meditated with few breaks until 10 p.m. The meditation teacher dealt with the novice meditators sternly, destroying their confidence and ridiculing their learning. All that mattered, he said, was the practice of *vipassanā*. He had the meditators begin with the meditation on the mindfulness of breathing (*ānāpānasati*) and then directed them to other forms of mindfulness meditation. By the end of her stay Mrs. Visākhā had completed the course, which meant that the teacher saw she had achieved a level of mindfulness sufficient to enable her to practice *vipassanā* on her own. She described this experience as a flash of insight in which the meditator understands the true meaning of the *Dhamma*. She saw the depths of Buddhist doctrines such as impermanence (*anicca*), no soul (*anattā*) and unsatisfactoriness (*dukkha*). She became certain of the truth, the truth about the *Dhamma* as well as about how to live and face her life.

As a result of this experience of *vipassanā* and of the continued practice of meditation for ten years, she has come to some conclusions about the goal of Buddhism and how to attain it. *Nibbāna* represents the true goal and can be reached in this life. She does not refer to what she has experienced as *Nibbāna* but as a temporary *nirodha*, or cessation of ignorance and unprofitable states. This state of cessation can be attained when one is doing *vipassanā*, but it does not last and has to be renewed repeatedly. Householders have a better opportunity than monks to achieve success in *vipassanā* because by living in the world they experience more desire, anger, and frustration—that is, more *dukkha*. Mrs. Visākhā, just as Miss Abeyasekere, also said that true renunciation does not mean leaving the world to become a monk but giving up pride, greed, hatred, and other defilements. To reach this goal study of the *Dhamma* is not necessary. Even though Mrs. Visākhā had studied Buddhist philosophy extensively, she felt that it was not helpful in the pursuit of meditation. Her guru had ridiculed her book-knowledge of *Dhamma*. She thinks that study has been stressed by monks who have little experience in meditation, whereas in the Buddha's time monks did not study or learn the entire *Tipiṭaka*. Instead they learned only one meditation topic. Through the penetration of that topic the early monks were able to understand the entire *Dhamma* intuitively.[3]

Since Mrs. Visākhā began the practice of meditation in order to find answers to practical and existential questions, it is important to see how she felt that *vipassanā* addressed those questions. What benefits does she derive from *vipassanā*? This question has implications for the entire *vipassanā* movement, for when meditators discuss the benefits of meditation, it often seems that they have rationalized or ethicized the results of meditation to the point that these results scarcely resemble the traditional or textual goals of *vipassanā*. We shall return to this question again after considering a wider range of lay meditators.

Mrs. Visākhā describes a variety of benefits that she has experienced since beginning *vipassanā*. She says that meditators can solve domestic problems or problems in personal relationships. *Vipassanā* gives one the self-confidence to meet people without anxiety. It provides peace of mind. The meditator who dwells in lovingkindness toward all beings does not get upset or irritable. The actual practice of meditation provides time for the body and mind to rest, relax, and recover from the turmoil of the world.

On a somewhat deeper level meditation enables the meditator to understand and observe the mind. One gains *saddhā*, confidence. By observing the mind one is able to deal with the roots of one's problems. For example, if a person is unhappy, looking at the mind can reveal the source of his unhappiness and then he can deal with that directly. Through mindfulness a meditator becomes aware of thoughts and feelings, and can either eliminate them or choose how to respond to them. A meditator who sees reality according to impermanence, no soul, and unsatisfactoriness (*anicca, anattā, dukkha*) overcomes all attachment to life.

To illustrate this last point Mrs. Visākhā told of the death of her daughter. The daughter, who had accompanied Mrs. Visākhā to Kanduboda and became an accomplished meditator, developed a chronic illness. Althugh Mrs. Visākhā was understandably grief-stricken, her daughter regarded the illness as an obvious example of *anicca, anattā,* and *dukkha*. During her last days she told her mother, "See how the body lets you down." She did not lament or complain about her condition, but simply meditated and observed it. From her daughter's insight and the instruction of her guru, Mrs. Visākhā also was able to meditate in the face of this tragedy. Through the loving-kindness meditation she cut off her anxiety and anger, eventually reaching a state of equanimity and nonattachment equivalent to that of her daughter. The practice of meditation enabled the family to have peace in the midst of death. Although her condition grew steadily worse, the daughter continued to meditate, never shedding a tear, maintaining a good attitude. The meditation worked. It provided a textual benefit, nonattachment, that had a practical application for both the daughter and the family in this crisis.

Mrs. Visākhā continues to pursue the rituals of traditional Theravada such as *Buddha pūjā*, but says she now finds a new depth in them. She meditates while doing *pūjā*, thereby achieving a form of *samādhi*, calm concentration, through the ritual. She could never go back to being a traditional Buddhist, however, for *vipassanā* has revealed much more of the religion to her. She says that if you have resided at a *vipassanā* center and heard the teachings of the gurus, you are no longer interested in or challenged by the preaching (*baṇa*) of traditional monks at traditional temples.

We see another aspect of the *vipassanā* movement in a third meditator, Mrs. Fernando. Now in her middle fifties, she had been raised in a Catholic family, a part of the emerging elite class in colonial Ceylon. She had received an English education in good Catholic schools and married a tea planter. Living most of her married life on a tea estate in the mountains, she raised a large family. They lived in luxury, driving fine automobiles and belonging to the planters' clubs. Gradually, though, her marriage disintegrated, and she finally divorced her husband. After the divorce she moved to the Colombo area.

During this difficult period of her life Mrs. Fernando began reading books about meditation. She had converted from Catholicism to Buddhism many years before but had never practiced it very actively. She eagerly studied the books and pamphlets of the Buddhist Publication Society concerning meditation. From these writings she was able to begin meditating on her own without any contact with a teacher or a meditation center. Later she sought instruction from various *bhikkhus*, but never visited a meditation center and always considered books her main source of information about meditation.

Perhaps because she stands somewhat outside the mainstream of the *vipassanā* movement and has read a wide variety of books on meditation, Mrs. Fernando has some interesting views about it. She regards the lovingkindness meditation, *mettā bhāvanā*, as the most important path. The development of *mettā* enables one to overcome anger and hatred toward others. She seems to have a slightly Christian interpretation of *mettā bhāvanā*—which is not surprising, given her background. To do *mettā* meditation, she explained, you must regard all people as children and learn to love them in that way. When lovingkindness develops, anger subsides, and one can have the peace of mind to progress toward enlightenment. Certain prerequisites must be observed, however, in order to succeed in meditation. A meditator must follow a vegetarian diet. One cannot eat flesh and do the meditation on lovingkindness toward all beings. The time of day also has an effect on one's meditation. The best time to meditate is at three a.m., when a "ray" from the heavens comes down, and it is best if one sits on the kind of grass that the ancient yogis sat on, for it has herbal qualities that aid in meditation.

Clearly, the *mettā* meditation had enabled Mrs. Fernando to cope with the break-up of her family, but she regards it as much more than a cure for psychological problems. She has no doubt that she can become at least a stream-enterer, if not an *arahant*. A highly respected senior *bhikkhu*, she says, told her that she would definitely become a stream-enterer. Her progress in this path was due in part to progress in her previous life. In that life she perfected the ability to achieve mindfulness, so that achieving perfect mindfulness is easy for her now. Since she has known of "several ladies" who have attained higher stages of the path, Mrs. Fernando has confidence that she also can.

Self-educated in meditation, Mrs. Fernando regards study as an important part of the meditation process. Although this opinion differs from that of other *vipassanā* meditators, in many other ways Mrs. Fernando agrees with them. The rituals at the temple have little importance for her. The Buddha did not prescribe the rituals and *pūjās*; they resulted from the corruption of the religion by the monks in later times. Mrs. Fernando seldom visits the temple near her house. The laypeople there just gossip, and the monks there cannot help a layperson who is striving to attain the goals of meditation. Most *bhikkhus* waste the tremendous opportunity they have to pursue meditation, she believes.

Mrs. Fernando feels that laypeople have an advantage over the bhikkhus because the laypeople experience more suffering, *dukkha*, and thus can see life truly. Women have an even greater advantage than laymen, for women experience much more *dukkha* than men. Speaking no doubt from her own experience, she said that women are weaker and feel more suffering. This same idea was expressed by many other women meditators, as well as by meditation teachers who instruct women. This observation serves as their explanation for why more women than men take up meditation. The chief monk at Kanduboda said that more women seek out meditation because they have greater suffering. One woman meditator explained that women have to suffer both in bearing children and in raising them. Men, on the other hand, do not feel these pains. Men have only the pleasure of sex without the pain of childbearing, and they do not become attached to children in the same way that women do. Children provide fathers with happiness, not worries, according to one woman meditator. Another meditator added that women suffer more because they are bound to the home and do not have the conveniences to simplify housekeeping.

The opinion that women suffer more than men seemed to be shared fairly widely in Sri Lanka, and doubtless predates the *vipassanā* movement. In traditional Sinhalese society, where women had a subservient role, the notion that this *dukkha* is part of a woman's lot in life would have arisen naturally. The idea has traditionally been used to explain why more women than men seem to be interested in the ritual aspects of Buddhism. Now, however, this idea has been taken over by women meditators who say that *dukkha* gives women a definite advantage. The logic here seems somewhat paradoxical: increased *dukkha* leads to increased optimism about the spiritual potential of women. As a corollary to this idea, one woman observed that because *dukkha* is increasing for everyone who lives in modern society, meditation and its benefits are becoming more viable and possible for everyone.

In contrast to Mrs. Fernando, Mrs. Kulatunga has been to almost all of the *vipassanā* centers and was a student of Miss Abeyasekere. Aged sixty-five, this woman has close ties to the All Ceylon Buddhist Congress, in which her husband was a leader before his death. She has great confidence that meditation offers a viable path to liberation for householders. Laypersons can definitely attain the state of streamenterer, although most people find it "too great a bother" to try for it. She thought that there might be *arahants* in Sri Lanka, possibly at some of the forest hermitages, and that some of the Burmese monks definitely became *arahants*. To reach these goals, study is not necessary; meditation proceeds better if you do not know the scriptures. Renunciation is not necessary either; however, she seemed to think that a person needs the seclusion of a meditation center from time to time in order to progress.

Although she believes that she has received many benefits from meditation, her goal is to get closer to *Nibbāna* and to conquer *dukkha*. In her meditation she has had some extraordinary experiences, which give her confidence that she is making progress on the path. Another meditator told me that she thought because of these experiences Mrs. Kulatunga had reached one of the higher stages already. One such experience occurred when she had visions in meditation of her body aging rapidly and becoming a skeleton. After that she felt that she had neither a body nor senses; she interpreted this state as the cessation of mind and body. Another time she had seen a white light in meditation and then had all consciousness vanish. She felt she had no body. Because she had achieved this state in meditation, she was able to use her ability to meditate when she was hospitalized. She remained conscious through an entire operation without feeling any pain. These experiences have enabled her to understand the Buddha's teachings much more clearly than she ever had by studying them. She hoped to get the "results of the *Dhamma* now without waiting for another birth."

In general, the male meditators I met shared the same outlook on meditation as the women, but the men emphasized some aspects more than the women did. For example, the men agreed with the women in regarding renunciation as unnecessary for meditation. They also said that study of the *Dhamma* is not necessary; however, many of the men clearly had studied the theories behind meditation and made frequent references to the Pali terms for the various aspects of meditation. The laymen shared the optimism of the women about the plausibility of arahantship and the path today, but seemed more willing both to discuss their own experiences on the path and to suggest that they had reached advanced stages. This tendency among male meditators might be explained as a manifestation of the cultural expectations of the emerging elite class. Men in that class have been expected to achieve success in their endeavors.

One male meditator, a retired government official, spoke at length about his experiences and alluded to his progress. He had been to most of the major *vipassanā* centers and had taken meditation courses with foreign teachers. Other meditators recommended him to me as an advanced and proficient meditator. In our conversations he expressed the standard view that learning the *Dhamma* is unnecessary. The Buddha did not expect his monks to learn the entire *Dhamma*, but rather to emulate his attainment. Nevertheless, this gentleman, Mr. Gunasekere, went on to expound his experiences in meditation with as much philosophical detail as possible. As a result of his experiences, he felt "one hundred percent sure" that the Buddha's teaching about the path was correct. Some of his descriptions of the experiences, however, seemed to add little-known features to the Buddha's path.

Mr. Gunasekere explained that he followed the textual path of *sīla*, *samādhi*, and *vipassanā* because pure *vipassanā* as advocated by some Burmese teachers is not practical. He claimed to have passed through all the *jhānas*, or culminating stages of *samādhi*, and to have gone from the mundane, *lokiya*, to the supramundane, *lokuttara*, path. In the course of his meditative journeying he had had encounters with Māra, a demon who sought to destroy him. He came to see, however, that Māra represented only one's inner struggle and could be conquered. Other visions of demonic or angelic *devas* also plagued him from time to time. Proficient in *samādhi*, he developed what he called in English "the third eye" but explained in Pali terms as the *dibba cakkhu*, which was one of the Buddha's attainments upon reaching *Nibbāna*. This third eye reportedly enabled Mr. Gunasekere not only to see visions of the *devas* but also to cast a ray of light from his forehead that could light up a wall ten feet away.

While meditating Mr. Gunasekere had an experience in which he felt that his head and body were burning. He interpreted this sensation as the burning up of *karma*, an event necessary for a stream-enterer, *sotāpanna*, who must burn up his *karma* if he is to reduce the number of his rebirths to seven. Although he implied that he had reached this stage and even higher stages, he did not make explicit claims. Since explicit claims to spiritual attainment are taboo in the Theravada tradition, however, Mr. Gunasekere's implicit claims were clear enough.

Other laymen meditators described other experiences in meditation. A schoolteacher in his late fifties who had been meditating for about three years said that while meditating he frequently felt a "floating feeling." When this feeling came, he always had his eyes closed; but one day when he felt this way, he decided to open his eyes and found that he was suspended in the air about three feet off the floor. Since that time he says he has perfected the ability to levitate. He had not been to a *vipassanā* center to learn these techniques but considered an Australian monk his guru, although the Australian monk assured me that he had not taught the man to levitate.

More important than the unusual experiences that the laymen meditators related to me were their implicit, and sometimes not so implicit, assertions that they had achieved lofty stages on the path. These statements expressed the living optimism of the laity about the viability of the Theravada path. A retired police inspector, who pursues meditation now while living a kind of forest-dweller's existence, explained that all people should aim for becoming at least *sotāpannas*. The goal is not too difficult, he said, because it requires overcoming only three hindrances, the main one being the belief that one has a permanent self (*sakkāyadiṭṭhi*). Another layman, active in the ACBC and other Buddhist affairs, told of achieving the stage of "purification of knowledge and vision," *ñāna-dassana visuddhi*. This stage represents the last of the seven purifications of the traditional path as outlined in the *Visuddhimagga*, and is equivalent to completion of the path. He said that he had experienced the meaning of the *Dhamma* in his own life. To be sure, not all of the male meditators spoke about their attainments; one man, for example, said that his teacher at Kanduboda had told him not to tell anything about his accomplishments.

Two other related themes emerged frequently in my conversations with laymen who meditated. First, they were somewhat more open in their criticism of the *Sangha* than were the women; and second, many of them followed foreign meditation teachers. To find Theravada laymen critical of the *Sangha* is not unusual, since even traditional laymen have criticized the monks. The meditators, however, critiqued the neotraditionalist *Sangha* for neither practicing nor offering leadership in meditation. Many of their criticisms were like that of Mrs. Fernando, who said that most *bhikkhus* had become too worldly, building temples and raising funds instead of exploiting the opportunity that monastic life offered to practice meditation. One lay meditator gave the nonmeditating monks some credit, saying that those who officiate at the temples still serve the people; not meditating, he added, is their own problem. Other laymen, however, were not this generous. Monks who neglect meditation in this life will have to pay for it in their next life, one layman said. People tolerate the monks today only as a social necessity, but they resemble the blind leading the blind. Other meditators observed that the *Sangha* had reached a low point today where the monks attend the university but do not know the path to *Nibbāna*.

Individual Lay Meditators: Unity and Diversity in the Practice of *Vipassanā*

The lay meditators' criticism of the monks for not meditating repeats a fundamental theme in the Buddhist revival. From an early period the reformist laity have found themselves pitted against the orthodox *Sangha* in the quest for spiritual liberation. Although, as noted, the neotraditionalists have accepted both the traditional role for the laity and the authority of the orthodox *Sangha*, the lay meditators have accepted neither. Advocating universalism and a new role for the laity, the meditators have often been critical of the traditionalist *bhikkhus*. However, they have readily followed the *bhikkhus* who practice *vipassanā*. The lay meditators, who perceive meditation as both the true essence of Buddhism and its most important contribution to the present situation, naturally find themselves at odds with those *bhikkhus* who have regarded scholarship and service rather than meditation as their true duty.[4]

The shortage of skilled meditation teachers within the *Sangha* created a vacuum that lay meditators filled by turning to foreign gurus. The first foreign gurus in the development of *vipassanā*, of course, were the Burmese monks to whom the early Protestant Buddhist meditation seekers turned for help. They had some success in evoking an interest in meditation among the Sri Lankan *Sangha*, and a few Sri Lankan monks became meditation teachers. To be sure, the knowledge of meditation had never entirely disappeared among the Sri Lankan *Sangha*, where some monks became accomplished meditators long before the intrusion of the Burmese.[5] These monks, however, were clearly in the minority. This situation persisted even after the Burmese had established the *vipassanā* centers and returned home. Indeed, one reason the Burmese had threatened to return to Burma even sooner was that so few Sinhalese monks had come forward for the classes.

After the Burmese returned, the few Sinhalese monks who were either competent or interested in instructing the laity in meditation could not meet the demand that laypeople made to learn *vipassanā*. Although most monks were content with the traditional practices and rituals of the temples, the laypeople increasingly were not.

Thus, lay persons who sought a knowledge of meditation seem to have been influenced by a number of foreign teachers in addition to the Burmese. One layman gave a very interesting reason for both the acceptance of foreign teachers and the rejection of the local monks. A well-educated lawyer, he thought that most monks could not teach the educated, urban layman who wanted to know about meditation because the monks were predominantly from rural backgrounds and often poorly educated. This statement has many implications. It points to a class distinction between the reformist laity and large parts of the *Sangha*. This distinction has potential significance for our understanding of the whole revival, which, as we have seen, began among the emerging elite. Here the most important point to note is that the lawyer used this rationale to explain why he had turned to a variety of foreign teachers.

The lawyer's case is not unique. Many of the lay meditators, especially but not exclusively the men, named Indian, European, Australian, or American meditation teachers as the figures who had influenced them most. A large number of people mentioned S. N. Goenka, an Indian layman who conducted meditation classes in Sri Lanka. Goenka had been a disciple of the Burmese meditation teacher U Ba Khin. Some Sinhalese expressed confidence that Goenka has attained the *ariya magga*, reaching the stage of one of the Four Noble Persons. Many other meditators follow Sister Khema, an American woman now residing in Australia, who follows the life style of a Buddhist nun. She had come to Sri Lanka for a course of meditation at Kanduboda and by 1983 had become a regular visitor to Sri Lanka. She leads meditation retreats in various parts of the island and works to establish the rights of women who live as *dasa sil mātāvas*. Her reputation has spread rapidly because of her appearances on Sri Lankan television. Many people told me that she had attained the "advanced state" of a stream-enterer or something greater.

Lay meditators also mentioned other foreign teachers. There has been a long tradition of foreign monks in Sri Lanka: for example, the Venerable Nyāṇatiloka, who founded the Island Hermitage; the scholar, Venerable Ñāṇamoli; and the Venerable Nyanaponika, who resides today at the Forest Hermitage near Kandy and oversees the Buddhist Publication Society. These foreign monks have all been highly esteemed by the Sinhalese Buddhists generally and have been especially influential with the lay meditators.[6] Other foreigners have taken ordination in Sri Lanka in more recent times and have found favor among the lay meditators. Among these foreign monks we would mention three, although there have been many. Venerable

Dhammika, an Australian who received ordination in Sri Lanka, resided in the Kandy area for some time and taught meditation with sensitivity and compassion at the Kandy Meditation Centre. An American who took the name Yogavacara Rahula Bhikkhu and lived on the south coast at Seaside Kuti was recommended by a number of laymen as an exceptional meditation teacher.[7] Another American monk, Bhikkhu Bodhi, has earned the respect of meditators for his work as an assistant to Venerable Nyanaponika and the Buddhist Publication Society.[8]

Several lay meditators mentioned as their guru an Indian teacher of meditation, Anagārika Munindraji. That he was mentioned by several people as their primary source for instruction in meditation is interesting, for he teaches in India at a center in Bodh Gaya. Thus only those laymen wealthy enough to travel there could study with him. One man who proclaimed himself a disciple of Munindraji was indeed a wealthy businessman. Educated at Cambridge, this layman had first become interested in Indian philosophy and Vedanta. Later he rediscovered his own Buddhist tradition, and while on a pilgrimage to the Buddhist sacred sites met Munindraji, who taught him to meditate. Now he travels to Bodh Gaya annually to meditate under his guru's direction. Other laymen whom I met had also studied meditation with Munindraji at Bodh Gaya. These laymen serve as extreme examples of the way in which factors such as income and social class have figured in the emergence of the lay meditation movement and its break with the traditionalist *Sangha*.

Another explanation for the popularity of these non–Sri Lankan meditation teachers has been referred to as the "Olcott complex." That is, the Sinhalese Buddhists accept these foreign teachers and their ideas in the same way and for the same reason that earlier Buddhists accepted Colonel Olcott: because foreigners who espouse one's own tradition enhance its credibility and increase one's appreciation of it. Sister Khema acknowledged this phenomenon in our conversation, saying that she knew it was a partial explanation for her popularity. I do not think, however, that this is the whole explanation. A woman meditator told me that she had first heard of Sister Khema from a notice in the paper announcing one of her courses on *vipassanā*. She attended the course, and has followed Sister Khema ever since because Sister Khema knows how to explain meditation to laypeople.

She does not talk down to people the way the monks do, and a layperson can ask her about problems concerning household life that they cannot ask monks. This woman, along with the businessman who travels to Bodh Gaya to receive instruction in meditation and the lawyer who follows foreign teachers because he cannot relate to local monks, represent examples of lay Buddhists who have been alienated from traditional Theravada Buddhism and the *Sangha* and have sought new sources for understanding their identity. The lay meditation movement came about and the foreign teachers became necessary because lay Buddhists found themselves in new contexts where the old cosmology no longer made sense. The foreign meditation teachers who understand the modern context have provided reinterpretations of the Buddhist cosmology and practical methods for addressing one's situation through meditation.

If these lay Buddhists are wrestling with the problem of constructing a new cosmology, of finding new ways of understanding themselves and their tradition, why have they turned to meditation? To return to the question raised above, what do the meditators in general say both about their motives for beginning meditating and about the benefits they have received? The question of the motives, goals, and benefits involved in meditation by laypersons is complex. From my sample of lay meditators, however, I can offer some observations. I agree with Richard Gombrich, who wrote, "I am certainly not claiming that meditation is so badly taught in modern Sri Lanka that pupils are left unaware that the goal of Buddhist meditation is soteriological; but conversation with lay Buddhists has provided me with ample evidence that other motives often play a part."[9]

Lay meditators' motives for beginning to practice *vipassanā* are frequently very practical. In the examples cited above and in other cases I encountered, people took up meditation in response to crises in their lives: the breaking up of a marriage, the loss of a job, or entry into a new phase of life such as retirement. To be sure, some meditators simply said they began to do *vipassanā* because "We are Buddhists" and they now understood this to be a viable means of achieving Buddhist goals. All of the meditators I met, however, entered upon the path of meditation with a new optimism about both their own spiritual potential and the efficacy of *vipassanā* for reaching the benefits and goals of Theravada. Although the practical motives expressed appear at first to be very modern and utilitarian, they also resemble the motives for beginning meditation related in the Theravada texts. The Canon does not contain too much information about why people in the past took up meditation, but certain texts such as the *Therīgāthā* and its commentary shed light on this topic. The *Therīgāthā* relates that many women, such as Paṭācārā who grieved over the death of her family and Candā who suffered as a poor widow, took up the practice of meditation in response to existential crises not unlike those that meditators cite today.[10] Regarding these motives C. A. F. Rhys Davids wrote, "Escape, deliverance, freedom from suffering mental, moral, domestic, social—from some situation that has become intolerable—is hymned in the verses and explained in the Commentaries."[11] Of course, one significant difference is that the women in the *Therīgāthā* also renounced the world and became nuns, whereas lay Buddhists today argue that this step is not essential for the practice of meditation.

If many people said that they had very practical motives for beginning *vipassanā*, others stated that their goal was either to achieve or to get closer to *Nibbāna*, and, as we have seen, some implied or suggested that they had reached advanced stages of this path. Even if we make allowance here for a certain amount of pious conformity with expectations—that is, for people saying that their goal is *Nibbāna* only because that is the acceptable answer—we still find that many laypeople today take up the practice of meditation because they believe it to be a viable means of attaining the soteriological goal of Buddhism.

Closely related to this question of what motives or goals prompt lay Buddhists to begin to meditate is the question of whether the lay meditators have properly understood the benefits to be derived from *vipassanā*. Have modern meditators gone too far in rationalizing the benefits of meditation, taking it not only as the short path to *Nibbāna* but also as a panacea for all sorts of this-worldly problems? Or, even worse, have they considered the attaining of certain immediate benefits to be *Nibbāna* itself? From my contacts with the contemporary *vipassanā* meditators I would say that they seem to understand the distinction between the ultimate soteriological goals and what might be called the ancillary benefits of meditation. Some meditators, to be sure, make what can only be described as instrumentalist claims for *vipassanā*. One layman, for example, told of a man and a woman who had an insatiable desire for sex. It was all they thought about. They took up meditation—and also got married—and after two years they no longer had any sexual desire for each other. The same person also cited the example of an alcoholic who attended a *vipassanā* retreat and afterward no longer had a taste for liquor. The majority of the meditators whom I met, however, seemed to be operating with an interpretation of meditation that is consistent with the intent of the Theravada texts. Meditators cited many practical benefits that they derived from meditation but saw these as steps on the way to the goal rather than the goal itself. Meditation is understood by these Buddhists to be more than just a handy method for curing alcoholism.

Among the benefits that meditators said they derived from *vipassanā* were the attainment of peace of mind, less anxiety, and more self-confidence. Many meditators said that since they had been practicing *vipassanā* they had overcome anger and irritability. Relationships, they said, became much less complicated. Other benefits mentioned by meditators included improved memory, conquest of pain, and less attachment to possessions or persons. One woman said that before meditating she constantly wanted to socialize with people or attend movies or seek other forms of entertainment. Now, however, she does not feel driven to find entertainment. She is content.

The relation between these practical benefits and the soteriological goal of the whole meditation process was explained by one meditator who cited an interpretation given by S. N. Goenka. When you make sugar from cane, you also get molasses. This by-product of the refining process is nice and useful, but it is not the true object. So, in a similar way, these immediate benefits are useful now and possibly in the next life, but they do not replace the true goal of *vipassanā*. Other meditators gave similar explanations of the relation between benefits and the goal, indicating that lay Buddhists are aware of this distinction. Miss Abeyasekere, the meditation teacher, said that the practical benefits represent necessary ways that meditation improves one's life. Only by improving in these practical ways can one progress toward higher purifications of the mind. Any practice, she said, even if only for a moment, can lead to a better life now and in the future. Her summation of this point was, "Buddhism is for this life," by which she meant that both the benefits and *Nibbāna* can be attained here.

Although the meditators' testimonies about the practical benefits of meditation might appear to represent the essence of pragmatism or modernism, their viewpoint has a textual basis. Their interpretation of meditation seems consistent with Buddhaghosa's description of the immediate benefits that a meditator attains while en route to the ultimate goal. The *Visuddhimagga* says, for example, that the meditation on breathing, *ānāpānasati*, one of the forms of meditation commonly practiced by laypersons today, produces peace of mind, a blissful state of mind, and stills evil thoughts.[12] The exposition of the meditation on lovingkingness (*mettā*) sets out eleven traditional benefits of this meditation which is commonly practiced by laypersons today. Among these benefits are sleeping comfortably without evil dreams, being "dear to human beings"—or having good relationships—and being serene.[13] Those who develop mindfulness of the body, *kāyagatāsati*, are said to conquer boredom as well as fear and dread.[14] And one who meditates on the Buddha's qualities, *Buddhānusati*, attains happiness and gladness, is able to endure pain, is aware of his own transgressions, and "if he penetrates no higher is at least headed for a happy rebirth."[15] These passages and others in the *Visuddhimagga's* description of the path clearly posit mundane as well as supramundane results from meditation. Many of the immediate benefits mentioned by Buddhaghosa are very similar to the practical benefits that lay meditators describe today. Present-day lay meditators may have reinterpreted some of these benefits and found new ways of explaining how meditation improves one's life, but they seem to be describing the same phenomenon as Buddhaghosa.

In contemporary meditation as well as in the textual descriptions, the line between immediate benefits and the soteriological goal becomes very fine at some points because in many ways the path is not separate from the goal. Texts such as the *Aṭṭhakavagga* of the *Suttanipāta* indicate that the attainment of purified states of mind constitutes the goal; there is no other goal for which this attainment is only the preparation.[16] Contemporary meditators also seem to understand this idea when they speak of achieving certain kinds of benefits in meditation such as overcoming greed, hatred, and confusion (*lobha, dosa, moha*), or developing nonattachment. When meditators speak of being able to understand their own minds or to perceive their emotions and understand what has caused those emotions to arise, they are describing gains on the path to enlightenment that have been cited in traditional textual expositions. A meditator who can achieve these stages would receive the additional benefits of calmness and peace of mind. The example cited above of Mrs. Visakha's daughter indicates how understanding one's life in terms of *anattā* and *anicca* through meditation can have practical effects while also moving one closer to the goal. Meditators speak today about being able to see the flux of reality and, because of this vision, being able to live without attachment. The meditators, optimistic about achieving the ultimate goal, feel that these dhammic benefits from meditation indicate that they have made significant progress toward it. These experiences of benefits or achievements resonate with the texts to support their claims.

On the whole, lay meditators seem to operate with a viable and defensible reinterpretation of *vipassanā* and its effects on one's life. Although they have adapted meditation to the world in which they live, the meditators whom I met seemed to maintain the distinction between its immediate benefits and its ultimate goals. They have not eliminated the supramundane dimension, but feel that they can attain it in this life. They have not reduced the supramundane to the mundane but have shortened the distance between the two, believing that the laity have the potential to progress further along the mundane path. Although these views represent new interpretations for traditional Theravada, they have a sound textual basis, a point not lost on these scripturalist reformers.

The Spread of Vipassanā

The *vipassanā* movement continues to grow today. Although no objective statistics are available to document its growth, many indicators point to it. Some of my informants said that as *dukkha* increases in society—as a result of modernization processes—the interest in *vipassanā* naturally increases also. Another example of this burgeoning interest was cited by a monk at a traditional temple. He said that in the past at his temple the laypeople wanted only sermons on the *Jātaka* stories. Now, however, more young people come to him for instruction in meditation; they do not want to hear about the *Jātakas*. He attributed this change to the growth of education and the increase in the number of educated people for whom the old ways of understanding Buddhism no longer suffice. Some lay meditators with whom I spoke shared this monk's opinion. An official at a branch center of the YMBA expressed a similar view, saying that four years ago few people there knew about *vipassanā* but now many people expressed a desire to learn meditation. That center had arranged to have meditation classes once a week for its members. *Vipassanā* appears to be spreading in nonurban areas as well. Since the reformation has taken place primarily in urban areas and among urban Buddhists, the extension of the *vipassanā* movement to nonurban areas represents an important development. Mrs. Visākhā thought that many of the people she had met at Kanduboda came from what she called "back villages" rather than from the cities. Another meditator said that *vipassanā* is spreading today in Sri Lanka in "quiet ways" in both cities and village areas. Various local teachers, centers, and small groups propagate it all over the island. *Vipassanā* is not about to become the dominant or only practice of Theravada, however, he said, because of human nature and the difficulty of serious meditation.

These observations seem to present an accurate picture of the spread of *vipassanā*. It has not become the major focus of Theravada, for many people continue to be attracted to the ritual aspects of the tradition, as witnessed by the popularity of the *Bodhi pūjā*.[17] Indeed it may be that the ritualistic and *deva*-worshiping aspects of neotraditional Theravada have increased in popularity faster than *vipassanā*.[18] Nevertheless, *vipassanā* has spread and continues to spread from the urban areas where it was introduced by the Burmese to the rural areas where an understanding of the importance of meditation may have remained alive during even the darkest days of the colonial period. We see this growth in the expansion of the *vipassanā* centers. Not only have the original centers grown, but they have established branch centers across the island. In addition to these branch centers, in 1985 Kanduboda began a kind of outreach ministry by sending *vipassanā* teachers every Saturday to an otherwise traditional temple in the Maradana section of Colombo. There a group of about one hundred laypeople meet weekly to receive instruction in the practice of *vipassanā*.[19] In addition to these programs developed by the original *vipassanā* centers, other centers not directly related to the original centers have sprung up, started by both laypeople and monks. A good example would be the Kandy Meditation Center, where laymen meet on

Saturday afternoons to learn about *vipassanā* from teachers such as Venerable Dhammika, an Australian bhikkhu who follows the Burmese methods. The many other centers in and around Kandy, such as Nilambe and Rock Hill, also testify to the growth of the phenomenon. In addition to centers, laypeople have formed associations and groups for the purpose of teaching and practicing *vipassanā*, two of which we shall examine in the next chapter.

Further Dimensions of the Meditation Movement: Lay Virtuosos

Beyond the *vipassanā* centers and the lay groups the meditation movement finds expression in a variety of individuals who might be considered lay virtuosos. Since these people live by meditation and often serve as teachers of it, they represent further evidence for the growth and popularity of meditation. Although they clearly stand within the contemporary revival of Theravada, their exact relationship to the *vipassanā* resurgence is somewhat problematic, for some of these meditators seem to represent both continuities with an indigenous Sinhalese Buddhist meditation tradition as well as influences from the recent *vipassanā* movement. They differ from the typical lay meditators of recent times also in that these people have accepted renunciation in one form or another as necessary for meditation. Although they oppose the established *Sangha*, these virtuosos favor the life of renunciation. Several particularly interesting lay virtuosos illustrate other dimensions of both the meditation movement and the Buddhist revival.

The title *anagārika* lives on in Sri Lanka, where some men today still adopt this role begun by Dharmapāla. I heard of several contemporary *anagārikas* and met two of them. Anagārika Nārada and Anagārika Tibbotuvāvē were laymen who assumed this title in order to live lives of renunciation and meditation. Although these two *anagārikas* did not know each other, they both had been obviously influenced by the early Buddhist revival as well as by the meditation movement. These two contemporary *anagārikas*, however, not only hold some significantly different views from the *vipassanā* movement, but they also seem to have reinterpreted the *anagārika* ideal. Obeyesekere has characterized this ideal by saying that the *anagārika* wears a white robe, symbolizing that he has renounced the world while living in it. "His unique status permits him to engage in certain types of this-worldly activity difficult in theory for the monk to perform: political, social service and missionary activity."[20] While this description certainly summarizes the role of an *anagārika* as Dharmapāla established it, these two contemporary *anagārikas*, although claiming to follow Dharmapāla, neither wear white robes nor engage in these kinds of activities.

I first heard about Anagārika Nārada from a young man in Kandy who claimed to be his disciple. After relating at length the wonders of his guru, the young man gave me directions for finding him. Arriving at his ashram in the low country, I saw a cluster of buildings constructed from rough timber. The Anagārika Nārada lived in a small log cabin, or *kuṭi*, and met his followers in two open preaching halls nearby. In front of the buildings stood a small Bo tree and a flagpole displaying the Buddhist flag. Anagārika Nārada turned out to be a pleasant little hermit-looking figure in his mid sixties, wearing brown robes, not white, and a full beard. He had grown up in a village near Colombo and served in the army during the British period. In 1954 he became an *anagārika* by taking the ten precepts and going to the mountains around Sri Pada to meditate. Living in a cave, he practiced *mettā bhāvanā*, the meditation of lovingkindness, and found that nothing would harm him as long as he did that meditation. Even the leopards who inhabited the same cave lived with him in peace, although he saw the bones of other humans they had killed. After meditating in the cave for twelve years, he returned to society and began to teach lay followers.

Anagārika Nārada explains that the title *anagārika* designates a role falling between that of an *upāsaka*, an ordinary layman, and a *bhikkhu*. The *anagārika* takes ten precepts while the layman follows only five. He refers to an *anagārika* as a "higher layman," even though he lives a celibate life apart from society. Today it is better to be an *anagārika*, or a "higher layman," than either an ordinary layman or a monk. An *anagārika* escapes the entanglements of household life and, by accepting this form of renunciation, he gets rid of the defilements (*kilesas*). In contrast to monks, an *anagārika* has freedom to pursue his own path. Monks have difficulty fulfilling all of the rules surrounding the monastic life, but *anagārikas* have only the ten precepts to follow.

In addition to living a life of renunciation, Anagārika Nārada teaches a path of meditation that differs in several ways from that of *vipassanā bhāvanā*. *Mettā bhāvanā* represents his central practice and teaching, and he claims that this meditation is higher than *vipassanā* and leads to *Nibbāna* more quickly. Anagārika Nārada believes that arahantship can be attained today, but he himself does not seek it because his goal is to become a *bodhisattva* in order to return many times to assist beings.

Certain prerequisites to meditation also receive emphasis in Anagārika Nārada's teachings. These include following the precepts (*sīla*), offering *pūjā*) to the Buddha, and observing strict vegetarianism. He especially emphasizes morality and vegetarianiam. Nārada teaches that a person who eats meat will require much more time to attain the goal in meditation than will a vegetarian. That the practice of *Buddha pūjā* forms an important part of Nārada's path, indicates the basic lay nature of his teachings. His doctrines also include the *devas*; he teaches that if one does *bhakti* to the gods, they will show him the path.

Anagārika Nārada has formed a society for his followers, who number, he claims, in the thousands and who refer to him as *Sādhu*. Traveling around the island, Nārada lectures to these followers and to other people. He also welcomes devotees to his ashram, where he spends the rest of the time writing poetry and meditating. Living with him at the ashram when I visited was a former hotel chef who served as his chief disciple and cook.

Anagārika Nārada represents an interesting permutation of the lay meditation movement. Although a renunciate by his own design, he dislikes bhikkhus and feels that he follows a purer path than they do. Although a meditator, he advocates a heavy dose of ritualism and moralism. His goal of becoming a *bodhisattva*, while not unknown in Sinhalese Buddhism, plays no part in the *vipassanā* movement; however, several other lay meditators whom I met also expressed admiration for the ideal.[21] Nārada apparently has had little contact with the *vipassanā* centers, although he was shaped by the same forces of reformation in the mid-fifties. He represents, both in appearance and in his teachings, a sort of prophetic figure who has evolved out of both popular or village Theravada and the lay reformation, following and calling others to follow the path of lovingkindness meditation.

Individual Lay Meditators: Unity and Diversity in the Practice of *Vipassanā*

The second *anagārika* I met was Anagārika Tibbotuvāvē, an elderly gentleman who lives in a small Buddhist monastery in an isolated valley near Kandy. His interpretation of the *anagārika* role differs from that of Anagārika Narada. Anagārika Tibbotuvāvē came from the English-educated class and worked as a journalist and auctioneer before becoming an *anagārika* in 1965. He also was inspired by Dharmapāla, whom he had seen as a boy. Later he read Dharmapāla's writings and conceived a desire to emulate him. Anagŕika Tibbotuvāvē sees *anagārika* as a monastic role rather than a "higher layman." He explained that an *anagārika* "is really a monk," although he does not belong to an official order. His dress indicated his identification with the monastic life, since he wore a saffron sarong and upper robe. When I asked why he had not simply become a monk rather than an *anagārika*, he said he felt he was too old at that point to go through the required training. So he had gone to Venerable Nyanaponika, the highly respected German monk in Kandy, and taken the ten precepts to become an *anagārika*.

He believes that renunciation is essential if one wishes to become a stream-enterer, which he regards as the highest stage attainable in this time. He doubts that there are any *arahants* in the world today. His renunciation has not cut him off from the world, for he teaches and advises laypeople on meditation and other topics. An ardent student of the *Dhamma*, he maintains that the theory must be known before practice can succeed.

As a meditator and teacher Anagārika Tibbotuvāvē follows the textual approach of the Vajirārāma line instead of the new *vipassanā* teachings of the Burmese-inspired *vipassanā* centers, although he does not oppose the centers, as have Venerable Kheminda and his Vajirārāma associates. He thinks the centers help those who go there, but he has never visited a *vipassanā* center. According to this *anagārika*, the Burmese were not wrong in their methods, but they were not canonical—the same point made by the Vajirārāma monks.

Most of the Anagārika's students for meditation are elderly people from the surrrounding villages. He tries to help them progress to a higher practice of Buddhism than the rituals and *gāthā* chanting that they have traditionally known. These lay people have a great interest in meditation, he finds. He teaches them *samādhi* meditation techniques as well as *sati,* or mindfulness. At least one of his pupils has taken up the life of an *anagārika* also.

Anagārika Tibbotuvāvē stands more in the mainstream of the Buddhist revival than does Anagārika Nārada. Tibbotuvāvē represents a meditation missionary from the elite class of Sinhalese society who had assumed both the ascetic life and the task of extending the good news about meditation to the villagers. Although he does not follow the Burmese *vipassanā* line, he belongs to the meditation resurgence.

Just beyond these *anagārikas* on the spectrum of lay meditators we might place the *tāpasas,* or ascetic *bhikkhus,* and the *dasa sil mātāvas,* or nuns. Both of these groups accept renunciation but reject or do not belong to the orthodox *Sangha.* Since the nature of both the *tāpasas* and the *sil mātāvas* constitute major topics that have been well examined by others.[22] I shall not explore these in depth but wish to mention only two nuns whom I met. They are relevant to this chapter because they display another strand of the revitalization of meditation, but we should make clear that these women are not representative of the entire *sil mātāva* movement. We do not cite them to illustrate that movement, as a whole, but rather, to illustrate other aspects of the meditation movement.

The two women, a mother and her daughter, live as nuns in a village near Avissawela. They explained that their teacher had been a *tāpasa* monk, self-ordained and ascetic. Like Anagārika Nārada, he had discovered the correct methods of meditation while living in isolation in the jungle for sixteen years. This *tāpasa* monk actually was an incarnation of the *bodhisattva* Maitreya, they believed. He taught the *Dhamma* and the path of meditation to Kashyapa, the husband of one of the women and the father of the other. In 1956 all three members of the family—father, mother, and daughter—received "ordination" from the *tāpasa* monk. He soon left, but they have continued to communicate with him through visions. They have had no other teachers. They reject monks as teachers just as they reject orthodox ordination because they believe that the *Sangha* is impure today.

The mother went into great detail explaining the elements of their meditation path, noting that Kashyapa, who had died recently, could not get anyone to accept this form of meditation. Vegetarianism and moral purity constitute two essential preconditions for meditation. She believed that eating meat invited evil spirits that disturb your mind, whereas if you abstain from meat, the *devas* protect you. The moral code they follow consists of the eight *ājīvaṭṭhanga sīla* rather than the ten precepts. Study of the *Dhamma* is not necessary because one learns the *Dhamma* through meditation. They explained that the Buddha's teachings permeate the atmosphere just as radio waves do, and proper meditation allows one to "tune in" these teachings. Through this practice they believed that arahantship and *iddhi*, or miraculous powers, are definitely possible. Their method of meditation involves breathing meditation and meditation on the aggregates and the parts of the body. The mother said that meditation reveals the meaning of *anicca*, *anattā*, and *dukkha* and enables one to develop nonattachment. They were very serious about their meditation, arising at four every morning to begin sitting.

Some obvious differences separate these two meditators from the mainstream of the *vipassanā* movement. Their practice contains many of the elements that we find in the teachings of Anagārika Nārada and others who emerged from the village tradition rather than the literate textual tradition of meditation. The belief in spirits, the emphasis on vegetarianism, and the adaptation of the eightfold code of *sīla* all represent interesting elements of that tradition that we shall have occasion to examine further in chapter six. That the notion of the *bodhisattva* should emerge again in their beliefs indicates that the idea probably has deep roots in the popular tradition. Although some of these ideas distinguish these women from the Burmese lineage of *vipassanā* meditators, they too are part of the resurgence of meditation. They represent continuities with very old village Buddhist traditions of *upāsika*, laywomen virtuoso meditators, but have also been influenced by the reformation going on around them; for example, Kashyapa was ordained by the *tāpasa*, the ascetic monk, in 1956, the year of the Buddha Jayanti.

Completing this brief overview of the spectrum of meditators is a man who has attained some prominence—or notoriety—in contemporary Sri Lanka: Uttama Sādhu. He is a self-ordained *tāpasa* monk who has a center in Rattanapitiya and another in Battaramula, both near Colombo. Uttama Sādhu, who has scores of devoted followers, lives at his centers with a number of young male and female disciples. He represents the fringe of the meditation movement.[23]

Although Uttama Sādhu believes that renunciation is necessary to make progress on the path, he despises the orthodox *Sangha*. He says that the *bhikkhus* are not real Buddhists but only charlatans seeking an easy living. However, paradoxically, he also teaches that laypeople can only achieve success in meditation if they renounce the world, at least temporarily. He too stresses vegetarianism as an important precondition for meditation and progress on the path. That progress is possible he has no doubts. Indeed, he introduced me to a twelve-year-old boy, clad in brown monastic robes, who he said would not be reborn again—who, in other words, was either a living *arahant* or nonreturner. Other meditators might have confidence that *arahants* exist today, but Uttama Sāddhu has one—or several—residing at his ashram. Gombrich found that many of Uttama Sādhu's "monks" and "nuns" and Uttama Sādhu himself were believed by their followers to have reached higher stages of the path.[24]

The study of the *Dhamma* is not necessary for a meditator, Uttama Sādhu explained, because in meditation one can ascertain the true texts. The young *arahant* at his center was said to have acquired a knowledge of both Pāli and the Buddha's original Magadhi through *iddhi*, miraculous powers, based on meditating. Uttama Sādhu said that his nuns and some disciples were working on transcribing the "true *Tipiṭaka*" or the "cream of *Dhamma*" in the original Magadhi.

In addition to vegetarianism, another prerequisite for meditation, according to Uttama Sādhu, is *pūjā*. He went into detail about the various sorts of *pūjās* and their uses. With his emphasis on all these other practices, his teaching about meditation becomes somewhat obscured. Nevertheless, meditation does seem to represent a central pillar of both his practice and his teaching. Although he appeared conversant with the forms of meditation popular in traditional Sinhalese Theravada, *mettā bhāvanā*, the meditation on breathing and *Kāyagatā Sati*, meditation on the component parts of the body, Uttama Sādhu gave no evidence of being influenced by the Burmese *vipassanā* teachings.

Although Uttama Sādhu is a rather strange and extreme figure, he represents an interesting example of how the themes of the lay reformation and the meditation movement can appear in different ways. The individualism central to the reformation finds no better exponent than Uttama Sādhu. While rebelling against the established hierarchy, however, he also espouses renunciation, which separates him from the universalism of the lay reformation. He affirms in the strongest terms possible the immediacy of the path and the possibility of spiritual accomplishment in the present; indeed, he claims to have resident *arahants*. Along with these reformist tendencies, however, Uttama Sādhu displays ideas that probably derive from the popular tradition we have noted above. His lectures or sermons frequently concern the evils of meat eating and the advantages of *pūjā* to the gods. Unlike most lay reformers, Uttama Sādhu seems to believe more in the magical and supranormal than the rational. His center has a mystical atmosphere; his "nuns" and "*arahants*" move around slowly as if in trances. Meditation seems to be valued not so much for its rational benefits as for its supernatural empowerments. Uttama Sādhu and his disciples are scripturalists, but with a twist, since they have access to the true words of the Buddha in Māgadhī. Finally, Uttama Sādhu, like Anagārika Nārada, and others we have discussed takes the *bodhisattva* ideal as his goal, a goal that he claims to have realized.

Conclusion

This chapter has surveyed a variety of contemporary meditators who share, in varying ways, the outlook of the meditation revitalization movement. These meditators illustrate the range and diversity within the movement. Some of their differences in belief undoubtedly stem from social differences among the meditators, e.g., village versus urban or Sinhala educated versus English educated. Other differences have to do with the related matter of historical continuities versus transformations or reinterpretations: continuities with traditional village Buddhist meditation ideals or reinterpretations introduced with the *vipassanā* movement. One common denominator among all of these meditators, however, is their confident appropriation of meditation as a path for people who do not follow the orthodox, monastic life. The lay meditators have claimed meditation as their solution the dilemma of identity and responsiveness. Living in a new and complex social context, they employ meditation as perhaps the only viable means for coping with and understanding life as Buddhists.

Notes

1. This chapter is based on interviews and discussions with lay meditators in Sri Lanka during the period of my research, 1983–85. I interviewed over one hundred and fifty meditators who represented various aspects of the resurgence of meditation. All of their views could not be included in this chapter, of course. I have attempted to select representative meditators as case histories and to characterize the main lines of the practice of meditation today. I have not used the actual names of these lay meditators.

2. Richard Gombrich, "From Monastery to Meditation Center: Lay Meditation in Modern Sri Lanka," in *Buddhist Studies: Ancient and Modern*, ed. P. Denwood and A. Piatigorsky (London: Curzon Press, 1983), 21.

3. This explanation recalls the *Netti Pakaraṇa*'s logic of interpreting the *Dhamma*. The *Netti* teaches that if the interpreter penetrates one text well, he will know the entire *Dhamma*. The similarity here is probably not coincidental, since the *Netti's* system of interpretation of the *Dhamma* may have been closely bound up with experience of the *Dhamma* through meditation.

4. For details on the historic debate over whether scholarship (*gantha-dhura*) or meditation (*vipassanā-dhura*) should be the primary task of the *Sangha*, see Walpola Rahula, *History of Buddhism in Ceylon: The Anurādhapura Period* (Colombo: M.D. Gunasena, 1966), 159–62. The ideal solution, of course, was for the monks to do both scholarship and meditation. In recent history, the monks in Sri Lanka have been primarily scholars and advisers. They never lost sight of the meditation ideal, however, even if they did not pursue it. To verify this one can note the portraits and photographs hanging in Sri Lankan temples. These portraits, which depict the patriarchs of that particular temple, usually show these senior *bhikkhus* seated in a meditation pose— whether or not the man ever did a significant amount of meditation.

5. For information on the revival of the *Sangha* and meditation in the late eighteenth and early nineteenth centuries see Michael Carrithers, *The Forest Monks of Sri Lanka: An Anthropological and Historical Study* (Delhi: Oxford University Press, 1983), ch. 4.

6. Indeed, the foreign monks have contributed greatly to the resurgence of meditation through the Buddhist Publication Society works and other writings—e.g., Venerable Nyanaponika Thera's *The Heart of Buddhist Meditation* (London: Rider and Company, 1962).

7. See Yogavacara Rahula Bhikkhu, *The Way to Peace and Happiness* (Colombo: Mrs. H. M. Gunasekera Trust, n.d.).

8. One of his works is *The All-Embracing Net of Views: The Brahmajāla Sutta and Its Commentaries* (Kandy: Buddhist Publication Society, 1978).

9. Gombrich, "Monastery to Meditation Center," 28.

10. *Theragāthā*, ed. H. Oldenberg, and *Therīgāthā*, ed. R. Pischel, 1883, 2nd ed., e. K. R. Norman and L. Alsdorf. (London: Pali Text Society, 1966). *Therīgāthā Commentary*, ed. E. Müller (London: Pali Text Society, 1893).

11. C. A. F. Rhys Davids, *Psalms of the Sisters*, Vol. 1 of *Psalms of the Early Buddhists* (London: Pali Text Society, 1909), xxiv.

12. Buddhaghosa, *Visuddhimagga*, ed. C. A. F. Rhys Davids (London: Pali Text Society, 1975), 266ff.
13. *Visuddhimagga*, 305ff.
14. *Visuddhimagga*, 266.
15. *Visuddhimagga*, 212–13.
16. See *Sutta Nipāta*, ed. D. Andersen and H. Smith (London: Pali Text Society, 1913), 151-89. On this topic see Grace Burford, *"The Ideal Goal According to the Atthakavagga and Its Major Pali Commentaries"* (PhD. dissertation, Northwestern University, 1983).
17. See H. L. Seneviratne and Swarna Wickremeratne, "Bodhipuja: Collective Representations of Sri Lanka Youth," *American Ethnologist* 4 (1980): 734–43.
18. The following chapter discusses one particular example of the increased importance of the *devas*. Gananath Obeyesekere has commented on this phenomenon in his article "Religious Symbolism and Political Change in Ceylon," in *The Two Wheels of Dhamma: Essays on the Theravada Tradition in India and Ceylon*, ed. Bardwell L. Smith (Chambersburg, PA: American Academy of Religion, 1972), 58–78.
19. When I asked an experienced meditator from this group whether he thought that most of these poeple were serious about the practice of meditation, he said that they must be because the teacher had explained clearly that meditation should not be done only to attain merit. He told them that there was no reason to attend the class unless they wanted to progress in meditation.
20. Obeyesekere, "Religious Symbolism and Political Change" 68.
21. One of these laymen was A. T. Ariyaratne, who referred to the lay workers in the Sarvodaya Movement as having this ideal. His case will be treated in ch. 7.
22. On the *tāpasas* see Nur Yalman, "The Ascetic Buddhist Monks of Ceylon," *Ethnology* 1 (1962): 315–28; and Carrithers, *Forest Monks of Sri Lanka*, chs. 5–7. Accounts of the *sil mātāvas* include, Lowell Bloss, "Female Renunciants of Sri Lanka: The Dasasilmattawa," *Journal of the International Assoc. of Buddhist Studies* 10.1 (1987): 7–32. N. Salgado, *Female Religiosity: Case Studies of Buddhist Nuns in Sri Lanka*. (forthcoming) Also see C. Thamel, "The Religious Woman in a Buddhist Society: The Case of the Dasa-Sil Manio in Sri Lanka," *Dialogue* (Sri Lanka) n.s. 11 (1984), 53–68.
23. Articles about Uttama Sādhu have appeared in the newspapers in Sri Lanka; see *Weekend*, Sunday, Jan. 15, 1978, p. 10. For an excellent detailed analysis of him and his sect see R. Gombrich and G. Obeyesekere's book on Protestant Buddhism (Princeton: Princeton University Press, forthcoming).
24. Gombrich and Obeyesekere, "Three Buddhist Leaders," Chapter Ten of forthcoming book manuscript.

6

Lay Buddhist Meditation Societies

From the outset lay societies and associations have been in the fore-front of this spiritual revolution called the Buddhist revival. In chapters two and three we noted that the "mainline" lay associations, such as the All Ceylon Buddhist Congress and the Young Men's Buddhist Association, became exponents of the neotraditional interpretation of Buddhism. These groups have been active in promoting neotraditional forms of Buddhism and in trying to restore this kind of Buddhism to its "rightful place." Other, less "mainline" lay societies, however, have also been important in the Buddhist revival. Lay groups have arisen in various parts of the country, usually to advance reformist aspects of the Buddhist revival in a variety of ways. These associations, ordinarily small, have organized around issues such as monastic reform and study of the *Dhamma*. The group known as the Vinayavardhana Society, for example, broke completely with the *Sangha* and holds its own services and *Dhamma* classes for laity.[1] Other organizations of laity such as the Servants of the Buddha Society meet regularly to study and discuss the *Dhamma*, an activity not part of the traditional layman's role but integral to the new role that lay Buddhists have assumed in the revival.[2] A number of other associations have emerged to promote *vipassanā* for lay persons, another nontraditional lay activity. It was a lay society that invited the Burmese monks to come to Sri Lanka and teach *vipassanā* in the 1950s. Since that time a variety of lay societies have arisen to enable people to learn *vipassanā*. The continued growth of these groups testifies to the vitality and expansion of the *vipassanā* movement. This chapter examines two of these recent lay meditation societies as larger case studies illustrating other aspects of the *vipassanā* movement and its reinterpretation of the Theravada tradition.

A Lay Meditation Society at Getambe

In 1983 one of these lay *vipassanā* groups met at the Buddhist temple at Getambe, a historic site near Peradeniya on the Kandy-Colombo road.[3] In ancient times a ferry at Getambe enabled people to cross the Mahaweli River, and a sacred Bo tree at this spot continues to be revered by all travelers. At this temple about eighty to ninety lay-people gathered on Sunday afternoons to learn *vipassanā*. The majority of these meditators were women who came from a wide area, some traveling one or two hours to attend the sessions. This group exemplifies the spread of *vipassanā* to rural areas, since most of the people were from villages outside of the Kandy urban area. In contrast to the English-educated, urban elite meditators considered in the previous chapter, these people were largely Sinhala speakers; they were, for the most part, neither highly educated nor professional people. The spread of *vipassanā* to this group signifies a definite broadening of the base of the *vipassanā* movement.

Unlike most lay meditation groups, the Getambe group was founded by a Sinhalese monk. Venerable P. Sorata, who resided at the Getambe temple, had been trained in meditation at Kanduboda, had meditated at the Nilambe center near Peradeniya, and had participated in meditation courses taught by foreign teachers such as Goenka. Thus, although the founder of the group was a monk, he was a reformist monk who had been influenced by the lay and monastic reformers of the *vipassanā* movement. He began the group around 1980 when he decided that meditation could help the people who came to him with various problems, including illnesses, anxieties, and domestic problems. Traditionally monks might have performed rituals such as *pirit* to solve problems for householders, but Sorata taught the laypeople to meditate in order both to solve and to transcend their own problems. Sorata shared the views of the *vipassanā* reformers. He believed that *Nibbāna* can be attained in this life and that it does not require renunciation of the household life.

Venerable Sorata led this group with much insight and sensitivity to the needs of the people. A good counselor, he helped them reflect on their problems and difficulties. He used meditation as an extension of his counseling. Meditation, he said, helps people achieve both mental and physical health. He introduced people to the practice of meditation gradually, suggesting that they begin with five minutes of meditation twice a day. The meditation that he taught emphasized both the present and the pragmatic, which he felt was necessary for these laypeople who were neither as advanced nor as dedicated as the lay meditators at Kanduboda. But he did not exclude from his teaching the higher values and goals of meditation that the people could realize after they began practicing.

Interviews with the participants of the group at Getambe indicated that, on one hand, these meditators were somewhat more traditional than lay meditators I encountered in the urban areas, yet, on the other hand, they held similar views about the effectiveness of *vipassanā*. These people had fairly traditional views—for example, about the rituals of Buddhism. *Buddha pūjā* often constituted an important premeditation ritual at their Sunday afternoon sessions. They seemed to have little of the opposition to ritual in general that I found among many urban meditators. These village Buddhists lacked also the general dissatisfaction with the *Sangha* that other meditators had expressed. Perhaps they were satisfied with the *Sangha* because they had found a temple where an able monk taught them meditation. Another significant departure from the attitudes of other lay meditators was their attitude toward renunciation. When asked whether they felt that giving up the lay life would improve their meditation, the majority of the Getambe people whom I contacted responded positively. They did not think that it was absolutely necessary, but did feel it would be desirable.

This response runs counter to the dominant tendencies of the lay reformation. One explanation for it could be that many of the people in this group were women over the age of fifty, which in Sri Lankan culture is considered elderly. They seemed to have been influenced by and to have considered becoming *dasa sil mātāvas*, or nuns, in order to pursue meditation more fully. One woman said that she often thought about becoming a *dasa sil mātāva* but felt that she was too old. Another said she had had enormous arguments with her husband over this issue of renunciation and that he "felt neglected and died as a result." Other, younger women said they would like to renounce the household life but could not because of their responsibilities to their children.

Although their views on these topics mark them as fairly traditional, the Getambe meditators' opinions about the goals and the results of meditation indicate the extent to which they have absorbed the spirit of the *vipassanā* reformation. I asked all of the meditators whom I interviewed the open-ended question: Why do you meditate? Their responses fell into two general groups, but probably represent one viewpoint. About half said they meditated either "to shorten *saṃsāra*" or "to achieve *Nibbāna*." The other half gave answers that can be summarized as "to improve my mind" or "to overcome problems in life." With regard to the first response, some people said only "to shorten *saṃsāra*"; some said both "to shorten *saṃsāra* and to attain *Nibbāna*"; and a few said only "to attain *Nibbāna*." These responses seem to mean that they were seeking to reach *Nibbāna* either in this life or in their very next life. To clarify this question, I asked whether meditation was an activity for which one gains merit that will make the next life better. Everyone answered affirmatively, and some said that attaining a better rebirth was their aim. Others, however, said explicitly that although one attained merit from meditating, that was not the reason they were practicing meditation.

All of these somewhat traditional, fairly recent meditators expressed great optimism about the possibility of attaining *Nibbāna*. When asked whether a person can reach *Nibbāna* in this life, all said yes. Two people said attainment depended on whether one had accrued enough merit in previous lives. Everyone else, however, spoke about human effort now as the deciding factor. One woman said, "Yes, a person can attain *Nibbāna*, but we don't try hard enough." Her friend responded, "Yes, if one makes up one's mind to do it." Another said, "If we cannot attain it in this life, then maybe in our next life. It is all a matter of how much effort we exert." These village Buddhists who had now become meditators were expressing clearly two of the central motifs of the reformation: spiritual optimism and trust in the individual's ability to set and achieve goals. It was no longer merit from previous lives but effort in this life that made the difference. Although they were either less sanguine or more honest about their own expectations of attaining *Nibbāna* than some urban meditators we met, they had come to believe that *Nibbāna* was at least possible if not probable in this life. In any case, they no longer regarded it as "a thousand lives away."

About half of the meditators indicated that they meditated "to improve their mind" and "to overcome problems in life." This response seems to be related closely to the idea of "shortening *saṃsāra*," for several meditators explained that one does that by purifying the mind, and as that happens problems are overcome. To pursue this question, I asked these people whether they meditated primarily for practical benefits or for *Nibbāna*. The unanimous answer was "both."

When speaking about the benefits they had received from *vipassanā*, they mentioned very practical things. One said she had gained much peace of mind. Another mentioned less illness as a benefit from her meditation. A woman from a remote village said she had become more patient and tolerant and also had gotten rid of a headache she had for thirteen years. Another woman, who was from a poor family, said one benefit was that she did not feel hunger when meditating. All of these pragmatic benefits indicate that Venerable Sorata has succeeded in teaching these people how to use meditation to solve their own problems. The benefits, however, are not the only reasons these people meditate. One man, who meditated at Getambe regularly, explained that he practiced meditation to have a happy life but he also believed that it might be possible for him to achieve *Nibbāna*. Meditation leads both to benefits and to the ultimate goal, which is definitely attainable.

The Saddhamma Friends Society

The Saddhamma Friends Society (*Sadaham Mithuru Samuluwa*), also organized to promote meditation for laypersons, contrasts with the Getambe group in several ways. Begun by laymen themselves and eschewing almost all contact with the *Sangha*, this society represents, on the one hand, a true reformist movement, exemplifying almost all of the motifs characteristic of reformism. The stated purpose of the society is to "follow the philosophy of the Buddhas while continuing the lay life and receiving all advice to eradicate *dukkha*."[4] Although these could be traditional Buddhist goals, the SFS interprets them in a very reformist fashion. On the other hand, the SFS illustrates something of the extremes of reformism because, as the last clause of the statement above hints, it incorporates in its teachings and practices elements reminiscent of such diverse sources as theosophy, yoga, the forest monks, mother goddess worship, and tantra.

Although he says that it was not his idea to found a meditation society for lay Buddhists, Mr. D. C. P. Ratnakara began the SFS in 1962 and serves as its chief organizer.[5] The approximately two hundred members of the society consider him not only the head of their organization but also their guru. Mr. Ratnakara, however, did not set out to become a lay guru. Raised in a village in the Gampaha district, he attended Ānanda College and went on to the University of Ceylon. In education and outlook he belongs to the English-educated elite, and he describes himself as having been Westernized. He considered himself a rational Buddhist who did not believe in "mythological beings." As a youth, however, he had been interested in hypnotism and parapsychology. In school he had once helped a fellow student find a lost fountain pen by hypnotizing him so that he remembered where it was. He also read books on theosophy and Indian teachers such as Vivekananda and Krishnamurti. These interests in psychic phenomena and religion were to become prominent again later in his life in the founding of the society.

The events that led to the founding of SFS began around 1955 when Ratnakara's brother became ill and was taken to the hospital. Although the doctors could not determine what was wrong, he was extremely ill. Finally he went into a trance and began calling for Ratnakara, who determined, after some time, that his brother was possessed by some kind of spirit. Eventually this spirit communicated with Ratnakara through the brother while he was in a trance, telling him how to heal the man. Following the spirit's prescription, Ratnakara cured his brother. After this illness Ratnakara's brother began to receive other communications or "teachings" from this unknown spiritual source. At times the messages would come when Ratnakara was with him. At other times the brother, who lived in another town, received the messages at night by automatic writing. Getting up in the dead of night, he would write through inspiration, not knowing what he wrote. The next morning he would send the writings to Ratnakara by post. Mr. Ratnakara had by this time concluded that something extraordinary was happening, for they were receiving teachings on such topics as the evolution of the world, the process of rebirth, the structure of the cosmos, and the place of the *devas* in it. After these teachings had been coming for six or seven years and Ratnakara, his wife, and his brother had become accustomed to receiving knowledge about the nature of all reality as well as help with personal problems from the *devas* through the medium of the brother, the *devas* commanded Ratnakara to establish a society of people who could benefit from the teachings. The *devas* said that they could not continue giving their messages to only two or three people. After the society was established, however, the teachings changed, and the deities began teaching Ratnakara and his associates the true *Dhamma*.

Thus, the SFS was organized to receive the teachings of the deities, or *devas*. As we shall see, one of the things that makes this society unique is that its practices of meditation and its understanding of the *Dhamma* derive from this source. Establishing the society around this source represents the ultimate kind of reformist resort to early and authoritative teachers. The teachers, or *upādhyāyas* as Ratnakara calls them, had either been disciples of the Buddha or known the Buddha in previous lives. They are able, therefore, to teach the pure *Dhamma*, which is no longer available in the world. Access to this authoritative source sets the SFS apart from traditional Buddhism and shapes the members' attitudes toward it. Ratnakara summarizes the importance of these authorities for SFS by saying, "We are not toeing the line of the strict Theravada tradition or keeping to the sacred texts at all, for we are getting truth from teachers who have direct contact with the *Dhamma* and the Buddha as well."

The teachers seem to comprise several types of beings, all of whom can be contacted through paranormal means. The most important teachers are *devas*, headed by Sarasvatī, who is described as the patron deity of the society, although Ratnakara explains that "their" Sarasvatī is a deity subordinate to the real Sarasvatī. Most of the *devas* with whom the society communicates abide in the Tusita heaven.[6] With the help of the *devas*, Ratnakara's group can also contact other liberated beings such as *arahants*. The society also has frequent contact via the spiritual realm with enlightened human beings similar to the masters or mahatmas of the Theosophical Society.

Ratnakara outlines an elaborate cosmology to explain the nature of these *devas* or teachers. Summarized, this cosmology arranges the deities into three classes. At the top are the creative powers, *śaktis*, which can be symbolized by the three great deities, Sarasvatī, Bhadra Kālī, and Īśhvara. Below these powers and directly related to them are karmically born deities, some of whom take the same names as the *śaktis*. For example, here one finds another Sarasvatī. Then at even lower levels there are less powerful deities who serve the higher deities. This hierarchy of *devas* is what Ratnakara meant when he said that the Sarasvatī who brings them the messages is not the real Sarasvatī, not the *śakti* itself.[7]

Ratnakara's brother has continued to serve as the primary means of contacting the *devas*. However, some problems have arisen in the past because of this medium's habitual drinking. Unreliable messages would be sent to Ratnakara which he knew did not represent the *devas*. Thus, from time to time they have had to suspend the medium. Mrs. Ratnakara developed the ability to contact the *devas*, and Mr. Ratnakara also has some ability to communicate with them. Mrs. Ratnakara does not go into a trance and become possessed as a true medium but meditates and either through telepathy or astral travel is able to speak to the higher beings and to convey messages from them. She says that the *devas* appear to her as beautiful beings looking more or less the way they do in temples.

On one occasion I witnessed a ceremony in which Mrs. Ratnakara communicated with a being she described as a yogi living in the Himalayas. For this communication Mr. and Mrs. Ratnakara went into a small shrine room created by partitioning off one corner of their house. There they had an altar with a Buddha image and a picture of Sarasvatī. To begin the ceremony they recited to themselves a secret verse or *gāthā* and then did *samādhi* meditation to concentrate their minds. Mrs. Ratnakara then began to speak very slowly in a monotone, describing what she could see and feel as she sat in deep concentration. She said she felt that she was being taken to the Himalayas, where she followed a path through a cold forest until she came to a cave. Inside the cave she met a yogi, who was a regular teacher of the society. Through Mrs. Ratnakara, the yogi answered questions put by

Mr. Ratnakara and others. The yogi said that the pure *Dhamma* can be attained today if one knows how to contact "suitable teachers" in "suitable places." He went on to give a summary of this *Dhamma* and of the way of meditation leading to a realization of it.

This conjunction of the Buddha and the *devas* was evident also in the meetings of the SFS, where the altar again contained both a statue of the Buddha and a picture of the goddess Sarasvatī. The picture was twice as large as the Buddha statue, and both had oil lamps before them. One member told me that when he first joined the society he disliked having a picture of Sarasvatī displayed next to the Buddha image. He doubted the existence of such *devas*. In time, however, he has come to believe that the *devas* do exist just as other beings. The *devas*, he said, are as real, for example, as white people in the West who, when one has not seen them, also might seem impossible.

The relation between the Buddha and the *devas* in the SFS's system represents one of the most unusual and interesting aspects of its reinterpretation of the tradition. Traditional Theravada has what has been called a "dual organization," with a clear separation of the Buddha and the *devas*.[8] Their spatial separation in the temples, with the *devas* in their own shrines or *dēvālayas* and the Buddha in the center of the temple, symbolizes their doctrinal and functional separation. The two parts, with their complementary functions, constitute the traditional Sinhalese Buddhist religious system: the Buddha represents the ultimate goals of existence and the *devas* address immediate needs in life.[9] As Ames has observed, "Two important religious sub-systems have combined to solve this dual problem of human life—happiness in it and salvation from it."[10] In the minds of traditional Sinhalese Buddhists the dual system forms a whole, yet the Buddhists clearly understand the differences between the *devas* and the Buddha. Magical animism or commerce with the *devas* and spirits is not considered on a par with Buddhism by devout Buddhists. This does not mean that they avoid it; rather, they believe the *devas* have a different role than the Buddha, and only commerce with the Buddha and the *Dhamma* has an ultimate focus. In an attempt to explain this difference Ames, using Durkheim's perspective, wrote, "Buddhist ritual is sacred; magic ritual is profane."[11]

This dual yet complementary system has continued during the Buddhist reformation. Ames observed in an early article on the reformation that although the Buddhist side was evolving, "Magical animism is not becoming more rationalized or systematized, nor synthesized with it."[12] The relation between the Buddha and the *devas* in the SFS system, however, seems to indicate that the situation of the *devas* has changed, in at least this case. Obeyesekere noted this same kind of shift when he perceived that among the elite Buddhists, who constitute the central figures in the revival, "there is a greater dependence on *devas*, contradicting the [traditional] doctrinal position which devaluates the power of these beings."[13] For most neotraditional Buddhists this increased dependence takes place without altering the balance or separation between the two sides of the Sinhalese religious system. Thus, for example, *deva* rituals increase in popularity; and at the same time purely Buddhist rituals also become larger and more widely celebrated. The SFS, however, has altered this traditional balance and separation. It has moved in the direction of the kind of synthesis of the two subsystems that Ames did not see occurring in the late fifties. The spatial conjunction of the Buddha and Sarasvatī on the altar clearly symbolizes a shift in the relation between these two religious dimensions.

In some ways the SFS downplays the extent to which it has reinterpreted the Sinhalese Buddhist pantheon and the place of the Buddha in it, for Ratnakara explains that the Buddha remains supreme. Many of the teachers are said to have been disciples of the Buddha in previous lives, a connection that justifies their authority. One teacher has told them that she had been the daughter of a Sinhalese king and had known the Buddha's disciples and *arahants*. Other teachers lived as direct disciples of the Buddha in India. In Ratnakara's system the Buddha still stands for ultimate concerns; he does not address immediate needs. The *devas*—at least some of them—retain this function, providing advice, healing, and other benefits. Perhaps one symbol of this continued superiority of the Buddha over the *devas* might be that the Buddha is represented by a statue while Sarasvatī is represented only in pictorial form—although her picture is larger than the statue of the Buddha.

Nevertheless, in many ways the SFS has changed the relation between the Buddha and the *devas*. Although the Buddha has not assumed the role of a *deva* ministering to worldly needs, the *devas* in this system now address ultimate concerns. Some of the *devas* help SFS members with worldly problems also, but that seems to have become a secondary, not a primary, function and represents a role carried out by the lower *devas*. No longer separate spatially, the *devas* and the Buddha are not separate functionally either. The *devas* teach *Dhamma*. The teachings that Ratnakara has received from the *devas* include certain suttas called *deva* suttas, or discourses. They represent discourses that the Buddha did not teach; frequently, however, they relate stories about the Buddha. Although some *devas*—perhaps all the karmically born *devas* who lived on earth in the past—had known the Buddha and heard the *Dhamma* from him, the highest *devas*, the personifications of the great powers, the *śáktis*, in the universe, are not the Buddha's disciples. Ratnakara explains that these forces cannot be construed as Buddha's followers. These highest *devas* know the *Dhamma* independently of the Buddha. Since they are more or less coterminous with the ground of being, they seem to represent essentially manifestations of the *Dhamma* itself. Thus, although the Buddha surpasses in both wisdom and liberation those *devas* who are karmically born in the heavens, he can never surpass the *devas* who represent personifications of the *śaktis* or cosmic forces: Sarasvatī, Bhadra Kālī, and Ishvara.

The common denominator of the Buddha and the *devas* is the *Dhamma*. The constitution of the SFS states that "there is a *Dhamma* expounded by all Buddhas and verified by all great beings who have attained a state of liberation." The Buddha and the *devas* both teach this *Dhamma*; both are represented on the altar together; and the SFS observes both *Buddha pūjā* and *deva pūjā*.

Ratnakara clarifies the role of the *devas* with a simile about a prison. The *saṃsāric* world is like a prison that entraps us, and the *devas* are beings who have liberated themselves from the prison and are now in a position to help us escape. One person cannot escape from the prison, nor can all persons escape from it. One person cannot escape because he requires outside instruction about how to go about it. All persons cannot because all are not capable and courageous enough. Liberation requires outside help, which is what the *devas* provide to the SFS. That help, Ratnakara says, constitutes the difference between this society and ordinary societies—or traditional Theravada.

If the *devas* have been elevated in this system, the Buddha has been reduced somewhat or at least humanized in standing. The Buddha is said by the teachers to have been only a human being, a highly evolved human being who had reached perfection. In terms of Theravada doctrine, this is not a new idea, but the emphasis that the SFS places on the humanity of the Buddha differs from the attitude toward the Buddha in traditional Theravada practice. This humanizing and rationalizing of the Buddha, however, represents a basic motif of Buddhist reformism. Mrs. Ratnakara carries the belief a step further; she claims to have proven its truth since she has traveled astrally into the past and seen the Buddha. She describes him as an "ordinary person" who lived, ate, and worked as a normal person. He was not enormous in size, as he is often depicted in the temples. He did not live a soft, luxurious life, such as monks today do, but worked hard for the benefit of others, talking with other ordinary people and walking miles to serve them. One of the points that Mrs. Ratnakara stresses about the Buddha is that he was accessible to the people. He was not on a pedestal or unapproachable as some monks have been. He gave practical, nontechnical teachings, useful to the people.

On one level the SFS has stated nothing new by affirming that the Buddha was not and is not the controller of the cosmos. Nor is it an innovation to say that the *Dhamma* was prior to the Buddha. The Buddha said that he rediscovered the *Dhamma* that other Buddhas before had disclosed. They do propose innovative interpretations, however, when they teach that the controlling forces in the universe which existed before and, in some sense, above the Buddha are *devas*. The Buddha and these supreme *devas* cannot quite be compared, for he is a perfected human being and they are cosmic forces. Both have power and ultimate standing in their own way. The Buddha can neither transcend nor become these *devas*, and the *devas* cannot do what the Buddha has done. They have respect for each other without one being subordinate to the other. The SFS has, by this move, reordered the pantheon as it has been understood in traditional Theravada. Gombrich has noted the importance that the SFS has given to the goddess in this pantheon. He participated in a ritual in which it became clear that Sarasvatī and Bhadra Kālī represented the benign and frightening aspects of the mother goddess.[14] The importation of the mother goddess into Theravada constitutes another novel interpretation. But Mr. Ratnakara and SFS members regard it not as a reinterpretation of the tradition but rather as a revelation from the *devas* intended to correct the tradition.

Reinterpretation of Key Aspects of the Theravada Tradition

The *devas*, after instructing Ratnakara to establish a society, also told him how to frame the constitution for this new association. The organization and practices of the SFS indicate further ways that this society reinterprets the traditional Theravada perspective. The society's chief and defining characteristic is that it accepts only laypersons as members. The *devas* were quite specific, Ratnakara explains, in saying that no monks should have membership in the group. This stipulation reflects the basic reformist optimism that the SFS has about the possibility of laypersons attaining liberation. The purpose of the society is to enable laypersons to seek wisdom and *Nibbāna*. In addition to requiring lay status, the criteria for membership set out by the *devas* also state that prospective members believe in "other beings" and have an interest in Buddha *Dhamma*. The present constitution of the SFS adds to these the proviso that prospective members not hold any racial, religious, or class prejudices.

This universalism, opening the path to laity, which we have seen in other reformers, takes a new turn in the SFS, however, which goes on to say that not all laypersons are suited for membership. At least not all people can be accepted into the Inner Group that receives the esoteric teachings revealed by the *devas*. I asked how Ratnakara reconciled this kind of exclusivism with the tradition that the Buddha did not have the "closed fist of the guru," that he kept no teachings in reserve for elite disciples. His answer was that while the Buddha may not have had a "closed fist," he did not teach everything to everyone. Just as farmers sow seeds only on fertile soil, so the Buddha bestowed the *Dhamma* only on individuals who could benefit from it. Since people today also differ in such qualities as intelligence, courage, and ability, the SFS screens the people that it admits to the Inner Group. This elitism was implied in the simile of the prison, which said that "all cannot be freed."

As with most new interpretations among the reformers, this idea of an Inner Group can be defended on Buddhist grounds. Since the SFS is a society dedicated to seeking liberation, and since by virtue of previous *karma* not all persons are now ready to do this, the SFS feels justified in limiting membership and restricting the teachings to those who are ready. It presupposes the traditional notion of graded stages of development. The SFS accepts the traditional belief that the perfection of *karma* in previous lives constitutes the basis for progress in this life. As we have noted, other contemporary meditators discount the importance of *karma* when compared with human effort in the present. The SFS disagrees on this point, although it also places emphasis on effort.

Members of the Inner Group of the SFS believe that *karma* and rebirth account for their present association with each other and with the *devas*. With the aid of the *devas* and other teachers, they have traced their previous births back to a time in the ancient past when many of them lived together in a city in India. There the present chief teacher or *deva* was the ruler of a kingdom, and Mr. Ratnakara served as the *purohita*, or chief minister, to the ruler.

A pro-laity stance among Buddhist reformists has usually entailed an antimonastic position. Whereas some reformist Buddhists criticize the *Sangha* and call for it to purify itself, the SFS more or less ignores the *Sangha*. The society is not openly critical of the monks and does not seek to reform them. It feels that what the monks do has no relevance to the work and progress of laymembers of the SFS. As one member put it, it makes no difference what color clothing a person wears—yellow or white; he still must strive to achieve the goal of liberation. If the SFS has a basic criticism of monks, it is the same one heard from other meditators: monks today are wasting their opportunity for progress on the path. One SFS member objected that many monks do not know the path, and because of this they discourage people from striving by making it sound too difficult. Some members shared with other meditators the belief that the monastic life today actually prevents a person from making progress because the monks have everything supplied to them. They do not have a chance to observe real life and experience *dukkha*.

As a result of this prolaity stance the SFS alters the traditional pattern of lay-monastic relations. They do not invite monks to chant *pirit*, but instead have *pirit* ceremonies in which laymen do the chanting: *gihi pirit*. Similarly, they do not usually give offerings or *dāna* to monks, counseling that offerings should be given instead to the poor. Ratnakara teaches that to develop their generosity the members should regularly entertain strangers from whom they expect nothing in return. This change in traditional practice clearly reflects their reformist and rational roots. One member explained that the advantage of the SFS is that it enables them to pursue liberation "free from the control of the monks." The primary exception to this policy of refraining from contact with the *Sangha* is their appointing a well-respected forest monk as their patron and adviser. This appointment, which seems to have significance for their understanding of meditation, indicates that the SFS should be described as more prolaity than anticlerical. But the SFS does exemplify this prolaity motif perhaps better than any other group in the Buddhist revival, with the possible exception of the Vinayavardhana Society.

Ratnakara and his followers agree with other contemporary meditators that study of the texts does not constitute a prerequisite for meditation. Like others, they adopt a pragmatic approach, saying that the "*Dhamma* is not an education." One needs only certain fundamentals and certain instructions in order to begin practicing. They point out that just as a doctor does not teach a patient the science of medicine but rather uses it to cure him, so meditators do not need to study the *Dhamma* but need only to use it to overcome *dukkha*. Ratnakara, however, has another reason for saying that the study of the *Tipiṭaka* is not essential: he believes that the present Canon does not represent the true or complete *Dhamma*. The teachers have revealed that the *Tipiṭaka* is unreliable because in the past Brahmins infiltrated the *Sangha* and corrupted the texts. The *Tipiṭaka* as it exists today is not entirely "the word of the Buddha." The true record of the Buddha's teachings included much more than what is in the present texts. We know, for example, that the Buddha's first sermon was said to have lasted all night, and yet the present record of it is very brief. The real *Dhamma* also was not obscure and phrased in technical language. The present tendency of the *Sangha* to insist that one must understand Pali and technical philosophical terms in order to understand *Dhamma* is wrong, Ratnakara feels. The teachers have provided the pure *Dhamma*, "remarkable teachings not in any books." When Ratnakara teaches the *Dhamma* and meditation to either the members of the SFS or outsiders, he relies on this pure *Dhamma*. Even this *Dhamma*, however, should not be studied for its own sake, but only in order to succeed in liberation.

Ratnakara's group has no doubts that liberation, arahantship, can be attained by laypersons in this age. Their interpretation of *Nibbāna* is among the most optimistic and world affirming of any contemporary Theravadins. One member, for example, said that the monks teach that *Nibbāna* cannot be attained until Maitrī Buddha appears many eons from now. This teaching is wrong, however, because the SFS has a teacher who has already taught them what Maitrī Buddha will teach when he comes.[15] Thus, there is no need to wait to achieve *Nibbāna*.

What is *Nibbāna*? The SFS explains it in very pragmatic terms. One man said, "Living happily is *Nibbāna*." Ratnakara does not stress attaining *Nibbāna*; rather, he speaks about eliminating *dukkha*, obtaining release from unsatisfactoriness in this life. This should be our proximate goal. To eliminate *dukkha* we must replace negative mental states with positive ones, and when we progress in this direction we begin to actualize *Nibbāna*. Ratnakara also avoids using the traditional terms for the four holy persons: stream-enterer, once-returner, nonreturner and *arahant*. Because he feels these terms have become overused and associated primarily with the great *arahants* of the past, he demythologizes them. The term "stream-enterer" itself, for example, need not be used, but we can refer to one who has recognized the efficacy of practice, who has a certainty of development, and who cannot be misled into a wrong path. These humanized and rationalized conceptions of the goal are congruent with Ratnakara's explanation of the Buddha as an ordinary human being. *Nibbāna*, then, in these demythologized terms, is perfectly possible in this life for laypeople, and the pure *Dhamma* received from the teachers explains the path of meditation leading to it.

Meditation and the Path

The path followed by Ratnakara and the SFS comprises the three stages of the traditional Theravada path: ethical conduct (*sīla*); concentration (*samādhi*), and insight (*vipassanā, paññā*). Unlike the *vipassanā* centers, Ratnakara includes concentration, *samādhi*, as an important component. The similarity with traditional Theravada, however, does not extend much beyond the external form of the path, for the contents of this *magga* have been given by the *devas*, who know the best way to liberation.

The first stage, moral conduct (*sīla*), includes all of the precepts and the general approach to life in the world followed by the group. The *devas* did not formulate a set of precepts for the society but said that people should internalize the Buddhist approach to living. Nevertheless since the members, and especially the beginners in the group, needed guidelines, the teachers left it to Ratnakara to develop some rules. The society follows eight precepts that it calls the *ājīva aṭṭha sīla*, the eight precepts of (right) livelihood, or *brahmacariyaka sīla*, the precepts for the holy life. These precepts include vows to abstain from (1) taking life, (2) taking what is not given, (3) desires of the flesh, (4) lying, (5) slander, (6) harsh speech, (7) frivolous talk, and (8) wrong livelihood.[16] This formulation of the precepts differs from the eight or ten precepts that traditional Theravadins affirm on *poya* days when they "take *sil*." Their list of ten precepts agrees with Ratnakara's on the first four abstentions, but from number 5 to the end stipulates abstention from (5) the use of intoxicants, (6) eating at the wrong hour, (7) seeing performances of singing, dancing, and amusement, (8) wearing perfumes or ornaments, (9) sleeping on high beds, (10) accepting gold or silver. Ratnakara explains that this traditional formulation of the precepts represents a pre-Buddhist idea probably developed under Brahmanic influence. He recommends the eight precepts that he recommends to his members because the eight accord with the texts and conform to the pattern of life recommended in the Noble Eightfold Path. The eightfold version, he argues, is more Buddhistic, more congruent with the *Dhamma*.

Ratnakara's choice of a code of precepts represents another example of a reformist reversion to the original texts and teachings. The second set of precepts, now called *dasa sīla* by Buddhists, actually is called in the texts the ten *sikkhāpadās*, or training precepts, for those entering the Buddhist community, especially as monks or nuns. The code of precepts that Ratnakara recommends is called by the early texts the *dasa sīla*, or ten items of good Buddhist character. At some point in the development of the Theravada tradition the ten *sikkhāpadās* began to be termed the ten *sīlas*.[17] This substitution of the *sikkhāpadās* for the *sīlas* is documented in texts such as the *Jātakas*. After this substitution took place, traditional Theravada seems to have more or less shelved the original eight precepts, recognizing the ten training precepts instead as the code to be followed and affirmed by laity and monks alike in Buddhist rituals.

Ratnakara has revived the previous list of precepts as more original and more Buddhistic. He is probably correct in saying that the ten training precepts constituted a pre-Buddhist formulation. That does not seem to be the only reason that he passes over this list, however. Since the ten training precepts that the Sinhalese Theravada tradition now calls *dasa sīla* have strong connections with monastic life and since Ratnakara is attempting to reinterpret Buddhism for the laity, he no doubt preferred the earlier version of eight precepts because they prescribed an ethos more suited for the lay life. Although this list of eight precepts could easily be pre-Buddhist also, Ratnakara seems to be on solid ground textually when he says that this formulation represents the earlier code of *sīla*, or precepts. This move represents another challenge to traditional Theravada controlled by the *Sangha*.[18]

Members of the SFS live by a number of other written and unwritten guidelines also. One member explained that they do not follow the rules slavishly but strive for a middle path for modern times. Nonattachment and simplicity—traditional Buddhist virtues—receive new attention here. Ratnakara encourages the members to live simply, wearing simple not ornate clothing and living in simple houses. Clothing, housing, and possessions should be used only to meet basic needs, not to attain status in the world. For the same reasons marriage ceremonies and funerals should be simple, not elaborate. These guidelines echo the recommendations of the Buddhist Commission report, which were themselves expressions of a basic Protestant Buddhist ideal. The SFS, however, has had more success in persuading its members to adopt these guidelines than the report did in getting general public acceptance for its recommendations. The SFS places a strong emphasis also on the family. A simplifed life with warm family relations is the best context for progress on the path.

In addition to general guidelines such as these, Ratnakara has formulated a set of specific rules for members—and especially beginners—in the society. This list of twenty rules specifies practices conducive to a life that accords with *Dhamma* and strengthens one's meditation. Members are advised in the first rule to arise at 4 a.m. as an aspect of both simple living and meditative practice. Several of the rules concern dietary practices having a bearing on meditation. Vegetarianism is strongly recommended, and the rules urge that members also avoid other kinds of food such as spicy, salty, sour, or oily foods. These recommendations are said to arise from *āyurvedic* notions about diet. Intoxicants, although not prohibited in the society's version of the precepts, are forbidden by these rules. The rules recommend also that members fast one day of each week.

Several of the rules pertain to the nature of the members' involvement with the world. One rule states, "Learn to do your work by yourself." Another admonishes members not to associate with people who engage in "wrong activities." It goes on to say that members should help such people find a better path, if possible. On a positive note the rules counsel members to act so as not to hurt or offend anyone. They should talk to others in ways that increase unity and friendliness within the society. These rules reflect a bent toward isolationism on the part of the SFS. The members seem to follow the general religious ideal of being in the world but not of it.[19]

About half of these twenty explicit rules for members pertain to meditation or preparation for meditation. Two rules command that members abstain from looking at pictures or listening to stories that "excite one's carnal sensations." Males are told to think of all females as their sisters or their mother. Females should regard all males as their brothers or father. One rather cryptic rule commands, "Guard your *dhātu śakti*." Ratnakara explained that this rule refers to a male's guarding or preserving his semen. The rule goes on to say that "by increasing your *dhātu śakti* you safeguard your mental and physical health." Obeyesekere has pointed out that in Sri Lanka the loss of semen is associated with physical weakness.[20] Since this rule precedes the rule about abstaining from looking at erotic pictures, it may signify also a means of reducing desire. On another interpretation, however, it could point to tantric influences on their understanding of the path. Factors such as the prevalence of female deities, of Mrs. Ratnakara as the contact with those deities, and now this reference to not emitting one's semen all suggest the possibility of tantric influences.

These and other rules and precepts govern both the outward conduct of the members and their preparation for meditation. Ratnakara says that the teachers were not concerned about the rules as such but wanted to drive home the basic ideas of Buddhist morality. To that end they have given—and Ratnakara has transcribed in notebooks—

suttas or discourses pertaining to ethics and the reasons for ethical action. One such sutta tells of the *arahant* Mahinda confronting King Devānampiya Tissa in ancient Anurādhapura. Since the king was pondering the need to impose the death penalty on criminals, Mahinda explained to him the importance of nonviolence. Humans who understand pain must not kill as do animals, who do not understand that all beings feel pain and fear. Human beings must live by not harming so that others will respond in the same manner. The king, said Mahinda, must set the example for this behavior. Buddhists, who understand the advantages of ethical conduct, should act appropriately. This idea of understanding the reasons for our behavior and being able to respond or not respond out of wisdom lies at the heart of the path of meditation as the *devas* have made it known. It is also at the heart of reformism and its rationalizing of the means to the goal of the tradition. This wisdom represents the ultimate form of *sīla*, restraint or moral conduct, and it is to this end that Ratnakara tells laypeople not to take or affirm the traditional *sīla* on *poya* and not to worry about following customs such as wearing white to the temple. Nevertheless, until people reach this stage, the SFS prescribes the kind of rules we have outlined here.

The second stage of the path, concentration (*samādhi*), denotes the beginning of meditation per se, prepared for and supported by the Buddhist approach to living, or *sīla*. For Ratnakara as for traditional Theravada, *samādhi* entails calming the mind. Ratnakara's teachings on how to calm the mind describe a number of nontraditional as well as traditional techniques. The rules of the society recommend that members arrange a meditation room or space of their own in order to get the mind attuned to meditating there. After arising at four, the meditator should sit facing the north or the east and chant various Theravada verses or mantras, such as *Namo tassa bhagavato arahato Sammā-sambuddhassa*.[21] Ratnakara asserts that mantra chanting cuts off unnecessary thoughts and trains the mind in one-pointed concentration. Ratnakara's teachers instructed him in various methods of *samādhi* meditation, such as listening to the sound of flowing water or rain and looking at a lamp. As an aid in the development of meditation Ratnakara recommends that beginners practice hatha yoga exercises at least twice each week.

Another rule pertaining to *samādhi* recommends that people try to practice silence for one-half hour daily and then increase this time to three hours. By silence Ratnakara means emptiness of mind, calming the mind by cutting off the chattering stream of consciousness. This form of meditation constitutes one topic of Ratnakara's frequent lectures on meditation to audiences outside of the SFS. In one of these lectures Ratnakara describes the method and importance of this calmness or silence.

> We do not know how to live in emptiness. Every moment of our waking hours is filled with ego-centered activities. I would suggest that a person interested in meditation spend some time every day in complete silence. One has to begin with abstention from physical and psychological action. In the beginning one should try to follow the rhythm of breathing. The support of this rhythm can be used to divert attention from "thought-memory-response-process."
> A calmness prevails when the attention is turned inward. A relaxation is experienced when the thought process comes to an end. The first impact of such experience of emptiness is bewildering. Every other second the mind wants to imagine that something is happening. It wants to feel that it is getting some experience. The mind feels strangled when silence starts operating on it.
> One has to watch the movements of the mind without trying to control or suppress it. One has to go through the phase of suffocation, embarrassment and void. It is an unavoidable experience of loneliness through which everyone has to go once in his life.[22]

Pointing to the signficance of *samādhi*, Ratnakara continues, "If one can go through the physical exercises [yoga] as well as the hour of silence in the morning, one begins the day in the right manner . . . in a calm, peaceful and serene way." The calm produced by *samādhi* prepares the mind both for the day and for insight meditation; one's day becomes a constant insight meditation as one learns to meditate in the midst of life.

Another reason *samādhi* occupies a significant place in the path Ratnakara teaches is that *samādhi* represents the state of mind that facilitates contact with the *devas*. In the same lecture Ratnakara explains that "with the growth of sanity, peace and poise, many latent

powers begin to unfold. Occult powers begin to manifest themselves." In the ceremony I witnessed, Mrs. Ratnakara entered *samādhi*
"emptiness" in order to contact the *devas* and the yogi.

Finally, however, Ratnakara advises that people not linger too long
in the stage of *samādhi* but go on to mindfulness (*sati*) and insight
(*vipassanā*). Using the technical language of the *Visuddhimagga*,
Ratnakara explains that meditators need not go beyond access *samādhi*
(*upacāra*) before switching over to the foundations of mindfulness,
satipaṭṭhāna. He bypasses the *jhānas*, the trance states, traditionally
understood in Theravada as the culmination of *samādhi*.

After the mind has settled down in *samādhi* and has reached the
state of silence, which Ratnakara compares to Krishnamurti's "choice-
less awareness," *vipassanā* begins. The teachers have described this
highest form of meditation as "watching the mind." It requires cultivating mindfulness, *sati*, to be aware of how the mind works and how
it reacts to sensations and situations that arise. Liberation occurs
when one sees how the mind works, how nature works, and understands *Dhamma*.

Ratnakara's explanation of *vipassanā*, in the end extremely practical,
is based on an elaborate Abhidharmic analysis of human existence.
Given by the teachers, this analysis shows that human beings are
composites of three major forces. As long as an individual lacks
knowledge and understanding of these forces, regarding himself as
an independent self, he cannot break free from these forces of nature.
The three components of a being are the life principle (*jīvitindriya*),
mind (*citta*), and body (*rūpa-kāya*). The life principle and mind represent universal forces, the former signifying the force that brings about
growth and change everywhere and the latter indicating the universal
mind or thought energy. In a person all three components coalesce so
that the life force combines with a form and the universal mind begins
flowing through this being. Life proceeds as the mind generates reactions (*cetasikas*) to what enters the sphere of the senses. These reactions take three forms: (1) mundane (*lokiya*) survival thoughts such as
hunger or fear; (2) mundane karmic reactions such as desire, hatred,
or greed; and (3) supramundane (*lokuttara*) reactions that produce wisdom and understanding of the entire process. Thus, these reactions
are either karmically unprofitable, *akusala*, or karmically profitable,
kusala.[23]

On this model, the whole structure of life is such that nature, in the form of *jīvitindriya,* can be described as seeking to elicit karmic reactions in order to keep human beings bound up in *saṃsāra,* the process of rebirth. The goal of meditators must be to recognize nature's scheme and not get caught in it any further. The meditator needs to develop detachment and understanding through viewing the life process and seeing in it the three characteristics of *anicca, anattā,* and *dukkha.*

The human predicament has several dimensions on this interpretation. Ignorance of the truth about existence keeps beings trapped in *saṃsāra* because of karmic reactions. *Saṃsāra* itself has great complexity, as we learn from the cosmology revealed by the teachers that shows there are thousands of levels and systems of beings. Every aspect of both this world and the universe comes under the control of these deities. The lesson taught by this cosmology is that no one is free to do as he pleases. People must recognize that they cannot be liberated or fulfilled within *saṃsāra;* thus, they must seek ultimate liberation. The deities who have spoken to the Ratnakaras have revealed the true path by which people can do this, by understanding *Dhamma* through meditation.

Ratnakara related a sutta given by these deities to illustrate the human predicament and its solution.[24] This sutta was given by the *devas* through the medium at one of the meetings of SFS. The *devas* introduced it by saying that this is a discourse about the Buddha not found in the ordinary tradition of Buddhism. The sutta describes an occasion when the Buddha summoned all the monks at Jetavana to assemble to discuss the discipline. Some newly accepted monks came to the hall first and improperly sat in the seats reserved for senior monks. One senior monk, Vanadassi, seeing that his place had been taken by a novice, became irritated and refused to enter the hall. The Buddha, knowing Vanadassi's state of mind, summoned him and ordered him to go on a mission to a forest in another district of India. Vanadassi asked if he was being sent as a punishment for his behavior. The Buddha answered that it was not a punishment but a mission for the purpose of spreading *Dhamma* (*dhammadūta*).

In the forest Vanadassi met a Brahmin who engaged him in philosophical debate. The Brahmin argued that since all people encounter irritation in life and generate karmic reactions, all are tied to *saṃsāra* without any possibility of escape. Vanadassi, however, explained the nature of reactions, noting that irritation arises whenever a person is confronted with something he dislikes or whenever something he expects does not take place. If these things happen, people become angry and generate unprofitable *karma*. But it is possible to live without anger if one understands that he cannot control the course of life and need not react to it with irritation. Human beings, alone among all the kinds of beings, have the possibility of attaining this nonreacting wisdom that will lead to liberation. With this argument Vanadassi defeated the Brahmin and in the course of the debate understood his own mind and became an *arahant*.

Ratnakara teaches that if a meditator, like Vanadassi, develops understanding of the process of the mind and the life faculty, then he can enter that mental state where insight or realization of the *Dhamma* occurs spontaneously. This enlightenment occurs as a flash of insight that both transcends and supersedes rational understanding. For some people one flash of insight may be sufficient to bring liberation; others, however, may fall back into attachment after some time. The *Dhamma*-eye usually opens gradually, through a series of "*satoris*," Ratnakara teaches. This kind of realization can be attained by a layperson living in the world. When the *Dhamma*-eye opens, he achieves "living *Nibbāna*" or *saupādisesa Nibbāna*. At the moment of death the layperson who has attained living *Nibbāna* has an excellent opportunity to attain complete *Nibbāna* by renouncing all attachments along with the body.

Although the philosophical or psychological system behind *vipassanā* is complex, Ratnakara teaches members of the SFS not to worry too much about it. The *devas* have taught that the *Dhamma* should not be treated as an academic education but as the basis for practicing meditation. The method of meditation taught by this society is very practical: thinking about existence and watching the mind. In part, their *vipassanā* involves the somewhat unusual practice of rational reflection on existence. Ratnakara outlines six steps in the process of meditation: (1) calming the body (*sīla*); (2) calming the mind (*samādhi*); (3) *vipassanā*, reflecting on the mind and the nature of life; (4) listening to teachers; (5) discussion of the *Dhamma*; and (6) contemplation of it. In the final stage the process of contemplation goes beyond the rational and opens the mind with an intuitive flash of wisdom.

Ratnakara's method of meditation has some important differences from traditional *vipassanā*, yet also coincides with traditional *vipassanā* in many ways.

To understand Ratnakara's method of meditation, we can examine the meetings of the SFS where he applies it. The SFS has several kinds of meetings, but all involve this idea of meditation as right thinking about *Dhamma*. In local group meetings that take place monthly the members stay up throughout the night hearing the teachings from the *devas* via the medium or from Ratnakara's notes and then discussing the meaning of those teachings. Several times each year the society has meditation camps lasting from a weekend to an entire week. The week-long meditation camps have often been held at Situlpavuva Rājamahāvihāra, a Buddhist site near Kataragama. In 1985 I attended a weekend meditation camp held in a local primary school.

The instructions for the meditation camps, sent to the participants in advance, establish the context for meditation. Members can only bring visitors if they have received prior permission from the chief organizer. Prospective visitors are asked several questions, including whether they believe in gods. During the retreat the meditators affirm and observe the eight precepts. Meals are served on a monastic pattern, morning and noon, with no evening meal. The members are asked to consider the whole period of the camp as an exercise in mindfulness, examining their minds and recognizing the causes and effects in them. Conversation is limited to this examination of *Dhamma;* there is no idle conversation or gossiping.

At the retreat I attended, the members, most of whom were fifty to sixty years of age, approached the task of meditation with both seriousness of purpose and optimism. Arising every morning at four, they first did some nonstrenuous yoga exercises. Then and at various points during the day they had *pūjā* to the deities and to the Buddha. The main business, however, was meditation. Ratnakara frequently began the meditation sessions with a discourse such as the sutta about Vanadassi. Everyone sat in a circle on the floor with Ratnakara seated on a cushion slightly higher than the rest. The members listened intently to his lecture. Some people took notes in small exercise books. At the end of the lecture, before he retired to his separate quarters, Ratnakara assigned the meditators a question for reflection drawn from the discourse. One evening the discourse pertained to mental suffering, and Ratnakara asked the members to recall an instance when they felt pain of mind. Conversely, they were also to recall instances when something happened to them and they did not feel upset mentally. The larger group divided into small groups to discuss this topic. The people eagerly joined in the discussion, examining their instances of mental pain and attempting to recognize the causes. This rational examination of one's mental states is intended to lead to greater mindfulness (satī) of these states and their causes as they occur in daily life. Ratnakara regards *Dhamma* discussion as an integral part of the process of *vipassanā*.

On other days the meditators contemplated and discussed questions such as "Who am I?" They were asked to recall their thoughts about self as far back as they could remember. Other times they considered how sorrow affects a person or what evil thoughts they had had during that day. This pattern of *Dhamma* discourse, personal contemplation on an idea from it, group discussion, and *vipassanā* meditation constitutes the basic method of *vipassanā* around which Ratnakara has built the society.

Ratnakara's meditation path with its emphasis on rational reflection and discussion can be considered reformist in many ways. Presupposing an educated, literate constituency, it rationalizes the path of meditation for those in the world. On the other hand, his methods can be considered orthodox, or at least textual, in that they bring to life the techniques described in the Satipaṭṭhāna Sutta (Foundations of Mindfulness Sutta).[25] The second, third, and fourth stages of the meditation process outlined in this sutta involve cultivating awareness of feelings, mental states, and the major aspects of the *Dhamma* as they arise in one's life. Ratnakara's method seems well designed to bring about these forms of mindfulness for people living in the world. The rational discussions prepare the way for solitary contemplation during which the intuitive breakthroughs can occur. Since one of the aims of this method is to recognize how the mind reacts with irritation to conflicts in the world, Ratnakara contends that laypersons can do this meditation better than monks. Built around the traditional ideas of right thinking, Ratnakara's method of meditation has similarities to the "psychological pragmatism" that Carrithers attributes to the forest monk Venerable Ānandasiri. Carrithers notes that Venerable Ānandasiri follows the early texts in teaching that "as opposed to the trance states in which thought is suppressed, profitable thinking is to be cultivated."[26]

What impact have Ratnakara's method and teachings made on members of the SFS? One member summarized the advantages of the society by saying that Ratnakara has shown them "a shortcut to the *Dhamma*." A woman member said that before she joined the SFS she has been a "good Buddhist," but although she observed the precepts, she was not progressing on the path. Ratnakara taught her a practical application of the *Dhamma* that "works" and brings peace of mind. Over and over the members stressed two points in explaining the benefits of the SFS and of Ratnakara's teachings. They said they have learned to live in the world without anxiety or attachment, and that this approach to life, if extended, constitutes *Nibbāna*. A woman who had converted from Catholicism to Buddhism said she had learned through meditation how to accept the world, rather than living anxiously, trying to impose her will on all the events of life. A man at the meditation retreat declared he had learned to reduce attachment and thereby to reduce frustrations in life. We can imagine, he said, being able to eliminate all attachment and all frustrations, so that no matter what happens we will remain at peace: that would be *Nibbāna* in life. Independently, other members voiced the same opinion, that they had learned to live the *Dhamma* and eliminate *dukkha* to a greater or lesser extent.

These members have become ardent meditators through Ratnakara's guidance. Many say that they meditate for an hour daily at home in addition to the meditation camps. Some of the members, however, seem to find the rational aspects of Ratnakara's meditation methods better suited for domestic life. They said they did not do sitting meditation regularly, but they were able to watch the mind throughout the day.

The society itself and the fellowship with others who appreciate the *Dhamma* also represent important benefits of the SFS to many members. The local groups, located in various towns and meeting monthly, clearly serve as support groups for the members. Members of one local branch described their group as "one big family." They meet often for fellowship and have a youth group for their children. The women appreciate being able to discuss personal problems with other women who understand *Dhamma*. These laypeople believe that they can help each other with problems and progress much further than the monks can.

The comments of members about the advantages of meeting with others who understand the *Dhamma* when society at large has become corrupt reveal again the SFS's inclination toward isolationism or elitism. At one time Ratnakara had envisioned founding a *Dhamma* village where members of the society would live together. He saw it as a revival of the time in their previous lives when they had lived together in a city in ancient India that operated according to the *Dhamma*. In the *Dhamma* village everyone would live by "right livelihood," and they could have a meeting house for meditation and rituals. By 1985, however, Ratnakara had largely abandoned the idea because many members felt it was not economically feasible to relocate their homes.

Conclusion

These two lay meditation societies—the Getambe group and the Saddhamma Friends Society—represent very different perspectives within the *vipassanā* movement. In them we can see some of the directions in which the popularization of meditation has carried the Theravada tradition. The Getambe group stands closer to the traditional end of the spectrum of reformist movements. Its members are still fairly traditional in many ways: they affirm the rituals such as *Buddha pūjā*, they meet at the temple under the leadership of a monk, and many of them see actual renunciation to be a higher calling than the household life. These features are not too surprising given that the group comprises primarily village women who have not been part of the new urban elite that has carried the revival. The Getambe group represents emerging reformism, and it serves to indicate that *vipassanā* is continuing to spread. The SFS, on the other hand, does represent the new urban elite; almost all its members are highly educated and come from urban or suburban areas. This society has pushed to the limits of reformism. They have radically humanized the Buddha, subordinating him in some ways to the ultimate powers in the cosmos; they have so universalized the practice of the path that they find no need for monks; and their doctrines and practices rationalize both the goal and the means of the tradition. Indeed, the SFS might be said to have moved beyond the bounds of reformism because, although their system does rationalize the tradition, they believe that this reinterpretation has not been the product of reason but of revelation. In some ways a group such as the SFS, with its combination of rationalism and syncretism, might be said to be moving in the direction not simply of reforming Buddhism, but of forming a new religion, although the members would never accept that they are anything but good Buddhists.

Despite these differences, when it comes to meditation these two lay societies have many similarities. The members of both groups have fully accepted *vipassanā* as a means to attain the goal of *Nibbāna*, which they believe is no longer many lifetimes away. The spiritual optimism of reformism is expressed clearly in the attitudes and practices of these meditators. Ratnakara urges his members to seek *Nibbāna* in this life. For the most part, however, he does not often use the term *Nibbāna*, preferring to speak about reducing *dukkha* in our lives. As one SFS member said, "We cannot visualize or even hope for *Nibbāna*. But if we can be peaceful, not in conflict and not reacting, then that must be *Nibbāna*, or at least a glimpse of it." Ratnakara teaches that this kind of practical *Nibbāna* can be attained, if only in momentary flashes. Critics may argue that he is oversimplifying the profound philosophical, existential *dukkha* and *Nibbāna* of the Buddhist texts. And, clearly, he—or his teachers—have given *Nibbāna* a very rational interpretation. As noted earlier, however, it is not clear from the texts that *Nibbāna* applies only to a transcendental reality or state. The elimination of negative states such as lust, hatred, and delusion often appears in the texts to be synonymous with liberation from *dukkha*. Ratnakara focuses both meditation and *Nibbāna* on our practical life in the world, saying, "Daily life is the only life we know. It has to be lived sanely, healthily and richly."

We could perhaps take Mr. Ratnakara himself as the symbol of the basic difference between these two lay societies. If universalism represents an important characteristic of reformism, then the emergence of a lay guru and the willingness of a group to follow him almost to the exclusion of the monks signifies an advanced kind of reformism. Mr. Ratnakara is certainly not the only lay guru to appear in Sri Lanka in recent times. Since the time of Dharmapāla the role of lay guru has been taken up by a number of charismatic teachers. These gurus have included scholarly teachers such as Professor E. W. Adikaram, who traveled the country writing and lecturing on the *Dhamma* and had a devoted group of followers, as well as simple ascetics such as the Anagārika Nārada.[27] Mr. Ratnakara represents a good and sincere example of a lay guru. As other meditation reformers and most lay gurus have done, he has reinterpreted both the path and the goal to help the laity who follow him. Unpretentious and modest, Ratnakara has an almost prophetic attitude toward the reinterpretation of the tradition for the people.

Ratnakara explains that when he advises laypeople, especially the old women who come to talk with him, he feels pity for them because he sees that the path they follow will not lead very far. The most they can achieve by all their observance of *sil* and chanting of verses is rebirth in the heavens. He disagrees with this traditional path of merit-making because the Buddha appeared in our world and taught the *Dhamma* for the realization of *Nibbāna*. People should not be content with rebirth but should exploit their opportunity for self-realization.

Ratnakara's reinterpretation of the path and the goal certainly breaks with traditional Theravada; it also differs in many ways from other versions of *vipassanā*. His reinterpretation, however, deals justly with both the textual ideals of *vipassanā* and the demands of the modern context. Ratnakara interprets *vipassanā* for folk in the world and seems to have succeeded in enabling the members of the SFS to recover their identities as Buddhists and to cope with the demands of life in the world. Above all, he believes that meditation on the *Dhamma* should affirm the present. "Meditation," he has written, "is meeting eternity in the present moment. . . . It is facing the challenge of life in a non-fearful way."[28]

Ratnakara resembles a prophet not only in his zeal for setting out the way but also in his insistence that he is not teaching the *Dhamma* on his own wisdom or at his own initiative. The teachers came to him; he never had the idea to seek teachings from the *devas*. It was they who decided to start this society, not he. In this regard Ratnakara resembles also some of the Hindu reformers in the nineteenth and twentieth centuries who received supernatural revelations that led to reformist movements in Hinduism. Ramakrishna exemplified this kind of Indian reformer. Although Ratnakara's experiences with the *devas* do not seem as extreme as those of Ramakrishna, the phenomena have definite similarities. Like Ramakrishna, Ratnakara received visions that led to somewhat eclectic but always pragmatic interpretations of the path for his followers. In Ratnakara's case, however, he has not been the primary medium of revelation. Intelligent and sincere, Ratnakara might be better compared to Swami Vivekananda, for both interpreted extraordinary revelations in practical ways to found societies and make plain the path. With his *Dhamma* discussion questions, Ratnakara might also be compared to the Zen masters who employed *koans* as subjects of meditation. Like the Zen master, Ratnakara believes that the *Dhamma* applies to life. Meditation, he writes, "implies a firsthand discovery of the meaning of life."[29]

Notes

1. The Vinayavardhana laity follow a strict interpretation of Buddhist morality and charge that the current *Sangha* has abandoned the true *Vinaya*. See Steven Kemper, "Buddhism Without Bhikkhus: The Sri Lanka Vinaya Vardena Society," in *Religion and Legitimation of Power in Sri Lanka*, ed. Bardwell L. Smith (Chambersburg, PA.: Anima Books, 1978), 212–35.

2. The Servants of the Buddha Society was founded during the first quarter of this century by Dr. Cassius Perera. It continues to meet once each week at Maitri Hall in Colombo. Its energetic current president is Alec Robertson.

3. My information about this group comes from being a participant observer in the meditation sessions at Getambe regularly during the summer of 1983. I interviewed, either alone or with a research assistant and translator, thirty-six members of this group. Since the membership fluctuated around eighty to ninety members, I interviewed between one-third to one-half of the group. The homogeneity of the group makes the number of interviews conducted even more significant.

4. Constitution of *Sadaham Mithuru Samuluwa*, Article 2.

5. The information in this chapter was kindly related to me by Mr. Ratnakara during 1983 and 1985. He generously met often with me over a period of several months, explaining the ideas and the path followed by his society. He also arranged for me to meet a number of the members of the society and to attend one of their meditation retreats. I use his real name rather than a pseudonym because he asked me to do so.

6. The Tusita heaven, the heaven of bliss, is the fourth of the six heavenly realms of the sensuous sphere (*kāma loka*). This heavenly realm has special significance in Theravada Buddhist cosmology because it was here that the *bodhisatta* lived before being born as Gotama Buddha.

7. This explanation represents a brief summary of the society's beliefs about an elaborately detailed pantheon of *devas*. On one occasion Ratnakara posited Mahā Brahmā as the highest deity governing the earth.

8. See Hans-Dieter Evers, "Buddha and the Seven Gods: The Dual Organization of a Temple in Central Ceylon," *Journal of Asian Studies* 27 (1968): 541–50; Nur Yalman, "Dual Organization in Central Ceylon," *Anthropological Studies in Theravada Buddhism*, ed. M. Nash. (New Haven: Yale University Press, 1966), 197–223.

9. Obeyesekere refers to it as a Sinhalese Buddhist pantheon; see Gananath Obeyesekere, "The Great Tradition and the Little in the Perspective of Sinhalese Buddhism," *Journal of Asian Studies* 22 (1963), 142. See also Michael Ames, "Magical Animism and Buddhism: A Structural Analaysis of the Sinhalese Religious Systems," *Journal of Asian Studies*, 23 (1964), pp. 21–52.

10. Ames, "Magical Animism," 41.

11. Ames, "Magical Animism," 36.

12. Michael Ames, "Ideological and Social Change in Ceylon," *Human Organization* 22 (S 1963): 46.

13. Gananath Obeyesekere, "Religious Symbolism and Political Change in Ceylon," in *The Two Wheels of Dhamma: Essays on the Theravada Tradition in India and Ceylon*, ed. Bardwell L. Smith (Chambersburg, PA: American Academy of Religion, 1972), 73.

14. Richard Gombrich and Gananath Obeyesekere, *Buddhism Revisioned* (tentative title), Chapter Ten. (Princeton: Princeton University Press, in press.) Professor Gombrich has kindly shared this information with me.

15. This statement was ambiguous because it was not clear whether he referred to the *devas* or to Mr. Ratnakara.

16. The Pāli terms for these precepts are (1) *pānātipātà*; (2) *adinnādānā*; (3) *kāmesu micchācārā*; (4) *musāvādā*; (5) *pisuna-vācāya*; (6) *pharusa-vācāya*; (7) *samphappalāpa*; and (8) *micchājīva*.

17. T. W. Rhys Davids, *Pali Text Society Dictionary* (London: Pali Text Society, 1966), 712.

18. These eight precepts may have wider currency in the Buddhist revival, for we find some similar precepts followed by the Sarvodaya Movement and mentioned by Dharmapāla. Although I have not been able to find a source for their revival prior to Ratnakara, they seem to be known by many Buddhists today. It could be that they represent a continuous tradition, always known in the villages, although one Sri Lankan Buddhist scholar said that he had not heard of them being practiced until about ten years ago.

19. The Indian version of this proverb, attributed to many teachers both ancient and modern including Tukaram and Satya Sai Baba, says, "The boat is meant to go in the water, but the water must not go in the boat."

20. Gananath Obeyesekere, "Personal Identity and Cultural Crisis: The Case of Anagārika Dharmapala of Sri Lanka," in *The Biographical Process: Studies in the History and Psychology of Religion*, ed. Frank E. Reynolds and Donald Capps (The Hague: Mouton, 1976), 236.

21. This phrase, which occurs in many Buddhist texts and is chanted by Buddhists today as a statement of veneration, is not technicially a mantra but could function almost as one. It means "Homage to the supreme Buddha, the exalted one, the worthy one."

22. D. C. P. Ratnakara, "Self Education," unpublished manuscript of a series of lectures on meditation.
23. This is the Abhidharmic explanation as Ratnakara said he received it. For the most part, this analysis of existence agrees with the Theravada *Abhidhamma* tradition. Some question might be raised, however, about understanding *citta* as "universal mind."
24. The *devas* apparently gave this sutta in Sinhala. Ratnakara has this version of it in his notes.
25. This sutta occurs in two versions in the Canon: Mahā Satipaṭṭhāna Suttia, Dīgha Nikāya, (sutta 22) and *Satipaṭṭhāna Sutta, Majjhima Nikāya* (sutta 10).
26. Michael Carrithers, *The Forest Monks of Sri Lanka: An Anthropological and Historical Study* (Delhi: Oxford University Press, 1983), 276–77. Since Ratnakara is acquainted with Venerable Ānandasiri, we may wonder whether this similarity of method is coincidental.
27. Prof. Adikaram was the author of *Early History of Buddhism in Ceylon* (Colombo: Gunasena 1953). He also wrote and circulated many pamphlets expresing his ideas.
28. Ratnakara, "Self Education," 2.
29. Ratnakara, "Self Education," 2.

7

The Reinterpretation of the *Dhamma* for Social Action: The Sarvodaya Shramadāna Movement

Within the spectrum of responses that Sinhalese Buddhists have made to modernity, the corollary to the reinterpretation of meditation is the derivation of a socially relevant expression of Buddhism. Just as the meditation movement comprises expressions of Buddhism that emphasize the individual, so the responses that we shall consider in this chapter focus on interpretations of Buddhism within society. These two responses, meditation and social reform, each complementing the other in many ways, have constituted major crystallizations of reformism in the post–Jayanti period.

Since, as we have seen, the Buddhist revival has had a somewhat cumulative nature, these responses stressing a social ethic and social development have close connections with other and earlier responses. The Protestant Buddhists, we noted, regarded social service as very important. From an early period the All Ceylon Buddhist Congress had a section dealing with social service which engaged in numerous welfare projects. The responses that we consider here undoubtedly had their roots in these early attempts at social service; however, there is a major difference between the earlier social responses and the ones that have emerged since the Jayanti period. The early social service movements were patterned after Christian missionary models and had little grounding in or rationale from the Buddhist teachings. The new social movements represent serious attempts to establish and put into practice a socially relevant interpretation of the *Dhamma*. Whereas the previous movements had a tendency toward conservatism or traditionalism in their ideas about how to change society, the new movements represent reformism in the senses that Bellah, Swearer, Tambiah, Bardwell Smith, and others have described it.[1]

The architects of these more recent social reform movements belonged to the same Anglicized elite that emerged from the colonial period—or, perhaps, the second generation. They seek, just as other reformers did, to rediscover their Buddhist heritage and to reinterpret it to provide answers to the questions of modernity. The questions they have asked include not only the questions of individual identity that the *vipassanā* reformers asked, but also the questions of how to build the best Buddhist society in postcolonial Ceylon. These reformers looked at a different aspect of the problem of tradition and change, and arrived at some different solutions; they harked back to an ancient charter and adapted it to apply to modern conditions.

The most prominent example of this social interpretation of the tradition is the Sarvodaya Shramadāna Movement, led by A. T. Ariyaratne. Like the groups discussed in the previous chapter, Sarvodaya is a lay society. It has also promoted meditation, but the primary focus of its reinterpretation has been on social reform. Other movements along the same lines have emerged somewhat in imitation of Sarvodaya, and we shall briefly examine two of these other movements in the conclusion of our discussion of Sarvodaya. All of these movements have developed since 1956, and along with the *vipassanā* reforms represent optimistic new directions for the Buddhist revival.

These socially oriented Buddhists carry out the three moves that characterize reformism according to Bellah: they appeal to the early texts; they reject much of the intervening tradition; and they interpret the tradition to say that true Buddhism demands "social reform and national regeneration."[2] Being scripturalists, they ground their interpretations in suttas and other texts that provide guidelines for society. Their task here, however, is not without controversy, for many scholars have felt that traditional Theravada Buddhism lacked a genuine social ethic.[3] Smith observes that the question "is whether an adequate social ethic can be derived from a path concerned primarily for the perfecting of individuals."[4] Traditional and conservative Buddhists also have questioned the validity and legitimacy of Buddhist social reform. This statement by a

Buddhist *bhikkhu* reflects the kind of opposition the reformers have faced: "To induce the earnest and genuine *Bhikkhu* to take an interest in sanitary, agricultural or industrial progress is like asking a research scientist to break stones or getting a surgeon to fell timber."[5] The social reformers reject this interpretation of traditional Theravada, however, and contend that the social ethic was central to all periods of Buddhism. If Buddhism is to have meaning today, they argue, the social dimensions must be reestablished. Their interpretations of Buddhism give the basic motifs of reformism a social focus.

The most thorough and comprehensive reinterpretation of the tradition along social lines has been the Sarvodaya Shramadāna Movement. This movement, begun in Sri Lanka in 1958 by a Buddhist layman, A. T. Ariyaratne, has reinterpreted the *Dhamma* to provide a blueprint for a new social order and a "nonviolent revolution." Macy, describing this movement, writes, "Sarvodaya in its relationship to religion can be viewed as generating an Asian Buddhist form of 'social gospel,' a parallel to 'liberation theology' in the West."[6] Another author claims that Sarvodaya "reinterprets the Middle Path for the technological age."[7] Ariyaratne himself has explained that "the Sarvodaya Shramadāna Movement drew abundantly from the wealth of Buddhist thought which we have attempted to apply to the realization of socio-economic ideals in harmony with moral and spiritual ends."[8] The subtitle of one of Ariyaratne's booklets on his movement points up the intent of Sarvodaya: *The Sarvodaya Shramadāna Movement's Effort to Harmonize Tradition with Change.*[9] Ariyaratne and Sarvodaya represent Buddhist reformism both in their approach to the Buddhist tradition and in their interpretation of it to provide goals and means for social change and development. Taking seriously both the value of Sri Lanka's Buddhist heritage and the demands of the modern context, Ariyaratne has sought to balance identity and responsiveness.

Sarvodaya's Growth

The term Sarvodaya has an interesting history, having been used first by Mahatma Gandhi as the title of his translation of Ruskin's work, *Unto This Last*. Gandhi said Sarvodaya meant the "welfare or uplift of all" in the sense that a righteous and just society could not come about until and unless persons worked for the "welfare of all." Gandhi later used the term to refer generally to his movement. Other Indian Sarvodaya leaders such as Vinoba Bhave and Jayaprakash Narayan also understood Sarvodaya in this way. Ariyaratne studied Gandhi's ideas and visited Vinoba Bhave to learn about the Indian Sarvodaya Movement. When it came time to select a name for Ariyaratne's own movement, he chose the name Sarvodaya, but gave the term a Buddhist meaning by translating it as the "awakening of all."

Ariyaratne's Sarvodaya Movement had its genesis in a series of work camps conducted by Nalanda College in Colombo for its students. In 1958 the Social Service League of Nalanda College organized the first of these work camps in the village of Kanatoluwa, a poor, low-caste village in the North Central Province. Ariyaratne was at that time on the faculty of Nalanda College, and he along with others at the school arranged this work camp experience among the poor as a way of broadening the horizons of the students. The college sent some forty students, twelve boy scouts, a dozen teachers from Nalanda, and a number of teachers and government workers from elsewhere. They worked in the village for eleven days digging latrines, planting home gardens, repairing and refurbishing the school, and building a place for "religious worship."[10] While in the village the students and teachers lived and worked with the villagers, who were considered outcastes by people in the neighboring area. This "holiday work camp in a backward village," as it was called, proved to be very successful and attracted considerable attention in the country. Mrs. Bandaranaike, then the Prime Minister's wife, visited the camp and praised the work. After this auspicious beginning the Social Service League went on to arrange other work camps, which came to be called shramadāna camps, in other depressed villages throughout the island.

Clearly these early work camps manifested the spirit and ideals of the Protestant Buddhists who dominated the reformation around the time of the Buddha Jayanti. The aims of the volunteers who began the movement were similar to those of the National Council of Social Services of the All Ceylon Buddhist Congress. Interviews with some of the original volunteers disclosed that "other than the idea of doing something good to the less privileged, there was no other crystallized motivation found in them."[11] The benefits of these original shramadāna camps, in the sense of education and what Sarvodaya later called "awakening," accrued primarily to the students. By eating, living, and working with low-caste people, the students acquired a new perspective on Sri Lankan society and their place in it. They also learned firsthand the importance of manual labor by engaging in various kinds of practical work in the village. The teachers who arranged the camps felt that both of these lessons were valuable for youth coming from elite backgrounds.

The work camps also had profound effects on the villagers, although this aspect of the experience was not very structured in the beginning. The villagers changed by associating as equals for the first time in their lives with "high-class gentlemen." Their neighbors saw that if the "gentlemen from Colombo" could sit and eat with these people on an equal basis, then they could no longer treat them as unequals. The experience inspired and uplifted the poor villagers. This benefit, however, seems to have been secondary to the education planned for the work team, the benefactors of the village. Only later did Sarvodaya transform the *shramadāna* concept so that the education or awakening of villagers themselves through working to change their own predicament became the primary aim.

During the next eight years, from 1958 to 1966, hundreds of *shramadāna* camps were organized, with more than 300,000 volunteers participating. The Sarvodaya movement expanded rapidly, soon outgrowing the bounds of the Nalanda group. It came to involve youth and adults from various parts of the country as other voluntary organizations and government departments joined in. During this period Ariyaratne and other early leaders such as M. W. Karunananda, the principal of Nalanda, began to develop the philosophy of the Sarvodaya Shramadāna Movement. Using their experience in the villages, the leaders reflected on the aims and purposes of what they were doing. Another important figure in the process seems to have been L. G. Hewage, a professor of English and an ardent Buddhist.

The concept of *shramadāna* evolved from the first work camps and became the primary vehicle of the Sarvodaya movement. Ariyaratne saw *shramadāna* as a reinterpretation or recapturing of the true meaning of *dāna*, the Buddhist virtue of giving or generosity. *Shramadāna* was understood to mean the gift or sharing of one's time and labor. A *shramadāna* campaign came to be not only a work camp but an opportunity to help both the villagers and the volunteer workers to see themselves and their lives in a new perspective. To begin a *shramadāna*, leaders from Sarvodaya would visit a village and discuss its problems with the villagers. The village residents would identify a major problem, and the Sarvodaya leaders would show them that it could be solved through self-effort if everyone was willing to work together. Sarvodaya found that a major barrier to village development was the apathy and hopelessness of the poor villagers. Ariyaratne has written, "A Sarvodaya Shramadāna work camp has proved to be the most effective means of destroying the inertia of any moribund village community and of evoking appreciation of its own inherent strength and directing it towards the objective of improving its own conditions."[12] After the villagers had identified a problem, such as the need for a well or latrines, or for a road to link their village to the main road, then arrangements would be made for volunteers to come to the village to help with the project. During the actual work camp villagers and volunteers live and work together in a context permeated by Sarvodaya/Buddhist values. The workers refer to each other as brother or sister, mother or father, son or daughter. Community meetings called family gatherings are held daily and used to teach and discuss Sarvodaya's ideas about village development and human awakening. Thus, in addition to accomplishing some needed improvements in a village, these *shramadāna* camps constitute intensive microcosms in which people can live out Sarvodaya's philosophy and values to come to a new understanding of how society can work.

Ariyaratne has said that Sarvodaya derived its philosophy from its experience in the village. Through work in these villages Sarvodaya's leaders discovered two sources for shaping a development plan appropriate for Sri Lanka. The first source was the traditional Sinhala culture of the village. The values and traditions of the village constituted an important guide to an alternative grass-roots development. The second source was even more basic than the first in that it also inspired traditional Sinhalese village culture: this was the Buddhist *Dhamma*. As Ariyaratne has said, "The philosophy that influenced us most in evolving our Sarvodaya concept in Sri Lanka was Lord Buddha's teachings."[13] These two sources were blended to form the Sarvodaya philosophy. The important point to note is that the Sarvodaya Movement grew out of the practice of social service. Social service became social development based on Buddhist values and ideals. Ariyaratne has said that he had less than 10 percent of the philosophy in mind prior to going to the villages and learning firsthand about particular situations. One thing he did have prior to the praxis in the villages, however, was the conviction that the Buddhist heritage both could and should be applied in this work.[14]

In 1961 the young movement held a *shramadāna* camp at Anurādhapura as part of a nationwide effort to restore the ancient city. During this camp the participants selected the name Sarvodaya for the movement, and in a meeting held beneath the sacred Bo tree adopted a resolution pledging to further "the cause of the movement in the service of the spiritual and economic regeneration of Sri Lanka according to Buddhist values and principles."[15] These two actions reveal both the influence that the Indian Sarvodaya Movement begun by Mahatma Gandhi had on Ariyaratne and others during this period as well as the importance of the Buddhist heritage for the Sri Lankan Sarvodaya.

In 1967 Sarvodaya launched its "Hundred Villages Development Scheme," an ambitious plan to carry out *gramodaya*, village reawakening, in one hundred selected communities. This plan can be said to mark the evolution of Sarvodaya from a work camp movement to a development movement that could now be described as "a non-governmental agency with 'Shramadāna' as its genuine technique to initiate 'Sarvodaya' development programs in backward villages."[16] Up until then Sarvodaya had worked fairly closely with the government's rural development departments; but when that support was withdrawn, Sarvodaya turned to private donors and funding agencies. In this way it became a true nongovernmental organization. Within a few years after the Hundred Villages Development Scheme began, Sarvodaya was receiving substantial aid from European funding agencies.

With outside funding the movement grew rapidly. Ariyaratne resigned from the faculty of Nalanda College in 1972 to direct Sarvodaya on a full-time basis. He worked tirelessly to spread the gospel of Sarvodaya through *shramadāna* camps and development programs. His innovative social work received international recognition, first in the form of the Ramon Magsaysay Award for community leadership from the Philippines in 1969 and later with the King Baudoin

Award from Belgium in 1982. The movement grew both in scope and in organizational complexity. By 1971 the *gramodaya* development scheme was active in over four hundred villages.[17] In 1978 the movement reported that its programs were under way in over two thousand villages, and six years later Sarvodaya claimed to have undertaken the development of five thousand villages.[18] Having operated initially out of Ariyaratne's house in Colombo, Sarvodaya later moved its headquarters to Moratuwa, a suburb twelve miles south of Colombo, where it established a large administrative and educational complex. In addition to the headquarters complex Sarvodaya set up district centers, development education centers, farms, vocational training centers, *gramodaya* centers, and village *shramadāna* societies. As president of Sarvodaya, Ariyaratne came to head a huge staff of professional and volunteer development workers. Since 1980 Sarvodaya has attempted to decentralize to some degree by shifting power and control to the districts and the villages.

The Sources of Sarvodaya's Philosophy

As we noted earlier, Sarvodaya bases its movement and its philosophy on two sources: the *Tipiṭaka*, the Buddhist scriptures, and Sinhalese village culture. Reformist movements typically claim that their philosophy represents a reinterpretation of the authoritative tradition. In order to challenge existing structures and teachings, a reformist movement must appeal to a higher authority. Scripturalism represents, as Tambiah has observed, the search for timeless truths that can be balanced with situational truths to provide a solution to the dilemma of identity and responsiveness.[19] Sarvodaya, as other segments of the Buddhist reformation, has employed scripturalism to support its position. Returning to the Canon, it finds textual support for its reinterpretation of the Buddhist tradition in terms of social action and development.

This kind of scripturalism might be seen as another example of Protestant Buddhism, since the reformers seem to be following the example of early Western Buddhologists in returning to the "early texts" and rejecting "later" accretions in the tradition. We shall find, however, that Sarvodaya, although following this pattern, disagrees radically with the early Buddhologists about the "true" teachings of the tradition. Defending the notion that scripturalism is not a modern idea that Buddhists learned from the West, Tambiah notes that "the attempt to purify religion with its attendant features of devaluing ritual and superstition and returning to the canon is a recurring phenomenon in Buddhist societies, not just a feature of the modern renaissance."[20]

Sarvodaya's publications cite suttas that support its understanding of Buddhism as a religion that has as much to say about how to exist in the world as it does about how to transcend the world. Sarvodaya's apologists claim that this interpretation of the scriptures "represents not so much a departure from tradition as a return to the early teachings of its founder and a reclamation of their original meaning."[21] To support its call for social and economic change and the relevance of such changes to individual awakening, Sarvodaya seizes on suttas dealing with social and economic teachings. Ariyaratne points out, for example, that the Buddha set out guidelines for economic activity in suttas such as the Kutadanta Sutta.[22] In other suttas the Buddha gave social-ethical teachings for Buddhists to follow. Sarvodaya publications remind followers of the importance of the social philosophy contained in the Sigālovāda Sutta, with its teachings about one's duties toward others; in the Mahāmaṅgala Sutta, with its thirty-eight keys to living happily in the world; and in the Parābhava Sutta, which explains those actions that lead to one's defeat or downfall.[23] The Sarvodaya Movement places suttas such as these beside the standard doctrinal teachings in order to indicate the close relation between spiritual teachings and socioeconomic teachings. Sarvodaya also regards other texts such as the Jātakas, the life story of the Buddha, and the stories of the *arahants* as scriptures that "emphasize nothing but the value of serving others as the surest means of eventually attaining the ultimate goal."[24]

Ariyaratne's reinterpretation of the scriptures stresses that the Buddhist tradition comprises many elements, some spiritual and moral, some social, economic, and political. All of these elements have to be taken together; they exist in balance. An interpretation should not limit Buddhism to only spiritual teachings; "otherwise," Ariyaratne told me, "we end up confining Buddha's teachings only to the other world." That idea represents a serious misinterpretation, in his view, because if that had been the Buddha's intention, he would not have given so many teachings about social responsibilities and social philosophy.

Sarvodaya has faced opposition on this point, for many Buddhists as well as scholars of Buddhism have portrayed the tradition as world-denying. Almost since the inception of Buddhist studies in the West, scholarly opinion has held that Theravada is a world-denying tradition. One modern scholar wrote, "Buddhism was (and largely is) a-historical in viewpoint. It deals not with man in society or among his fellows, but with the individual man facing his eternal destiny. And it turns man supremely toward seeking a Good (*Nibbāna*) above all time and space orders. To tell the truth the Buddha had little, either of concern for society as such or of firm conviction of its possible improvability."[25]

Ariyaratne replies to those who view Buddhism in this way and who criticize his movement as a misrepresentation of the *Dhamma* that such interpretations of Theravada came about primarily because of the colonial experience. He feels that Buddhism lost its social focus as part of a deliberate scheme by the colonial powers. The colonial governments undercut the authority of the *Sangha* and separated the people from their heritage.

We have seen in chapter one how the British deprived the *bhikkhus* of many of their traditional roles and contributed to Theravada's becoming less relevant to society. Ariyaratne charges, however, that Buddhist scholars assisted the colonial government in cutting Buddhism off from its social moorings: "In the Buddha's teachings as much emphasis is given to community awakening and community organizational factors as to the awakening of the individual. This fact was unfortunately lost from view during the long colonial period when Western powers attempted to weaken the influence of the *Sangha* and to separate the subjugated people from the inspiration to dignity, power, and freedom which they could find in their tradition."[26] The academics described the role of the monk as that of a recluse because of the "fear the western scholars had of the monks as conscientizers of the people, with capacity to inspire the people to rebel against the colonial rulers."[27]

Although one may disagree with Ariyaratne about whether social teachings received equal attention with individual teachings in the earliest Buddhism, he makes an interesting point about the contextual determinism of Buddhist scholarship during the colonial period. To be sure, scholars of Buddhism were not completely determined by, and in the service of, colonialism. But as Kantowski observes, "I do not think it is necessary to explain that the image of other-worldly asceticism was used as a self-justification for capitalist penetration and colonial rule, just as Marxists had approved Britain's role in India as that of an unconscious tool of history to bring about a fundamental revolution in the social state of Asia."[28] Similarly, Edward Said has shown the extent to which scholarship reflects the political realities of the scholar's society.[29] So without assuming that Buddhist scholars during the nineteenth century were involved in a conspiracy with the government to suppress the *Sangha* and distort the tradition, one can agree that the colonial situation altered the face of the tradition and influenced the way both adherents and scholars viewed it. Western scholars of Buddhism during the nineteenth and early twentieth centuries tended to concentrate on what they understood to be the earliest forms of the Buddhist tradition. For this they looked to the "early" texts and the supramundane ideal, and passed over any "later" texts or commentaries that depicted the world-affirming aspects of the tradition. To be sure, the scholars of this period did not create the ideals of renunciation and merit-making for rebirth, but the context in which they worked had thrown these aspects of the tradition into high relief so that it made sense to understand Buddhism as having only these world-denying foci. Only in recent times has Buddhist studies begun to correct this one-sided portrait of the Buddhist tradition. Although it seems difficult to dispute that the ultimate goal of a classic formulation of Theravada such as Buddhaghosa's *Visuddhimagga* is a supramundane *Nibbāna*, scholars increasingly have come to recognize that the gradual path spelled out in that text and other texts had also many lower stages and goals. The tradition was complex. Mundane aspects complemented the supramundane to comprise the whole tradition.

Ariyaratne's point has been that what is at issue here is not just a theoretical matter of how one understands early Theravada but a practical matter of how to reinterpret the tradition in order to restore a balance or a middle path between the goal of liberation, which he calls the "extreme end," and the social and political goals. Although this question of a balance can still be disputed, it forms the essence of Ariyaratne's reformist interpretation of the *Dhamma*. Other reform-minded Theravadins have similarly argued for a this-worldly interpretation of ancient Buddhism. The Venerable Dr. Walpola Rahula, for example, began his treatise on the true role of the *bhikkhu* with this statement: "Buddhism is based on service to others."[30] Ariyaratne is confident that such an interpretation not only does justice to the Theravada tradition but also provides the most appropriate and effective response to the modern context: "We believe that Buddhist teaching devoid of this revolutionary meaning and application is incapable of facing the realities of the modern materialistic society."[31]

Obeyesekere has made a more substantive criticism of Sarvodaya's scripturalism with its focus on social and ethical teachings. He argues that since one cardinal teaching of Buddhism is impermanence, *anicca*, society cannot be a permanent entity, and it would seem very odd if the Buddha laid down "a set of permanent principles" for an impermanent society.[32] The social ethics that the Buddha gave were appropriate for his society but should not be taken as eternal verities applicable to all societies.

This argument represents a Buddhist version of the hermeneutical dilemma of how or whether it is possible to interpret teachings given in an ancient context to be meaningful in the present context. How is it possible to move from what the text meant to what it means? Obeyesekere feels that the Buddhist view that "society itself lacks any ontic reality" makes this transfer of meaning especially difficult. Although I do not necessarily agree that Buddhism has a more difficult hermeneutical problem because of the doctrine of *anicca*, I do agree with Obeyesekere's proposed solution to the problem of the transfer of meaning: the interpreter must rely on the spirit of the Buddha's teachings to derive social or ethical teachings relevant to the present.[33]

Although its writings never state the problem in these terms, Sarvodaya also seems to concur in principle, with this solution to the problem of how to reinterpret the *Dhamma*. Ariyaratne and other leaders refer to the suttas on socioeconomic topics, but they seem to stress not so much the specific social or economic teachings in these suttas but the mere fact that the Buddha gave social and ethical teachings. To be sure, Ariyaratne in one of his books on Sarvodaya spells out all of the recommendations from the Sigālovāda Sutta and two other suttas.[34] The details are not unimportant, and many Sarvodayans undoubtedly take the injunctions in these suttas literally. In most instances, however, Sarvodaya's writings simply invoke the titles of one sutta or another to make the point that the Buddha gave teachings for this world. Sarvodaya's philosophy and the writings by Ariyaratne and others do not rely heavily on these specific social and economic suttas. Sarvodaya's philosophy depends more upon the reinterpretation of the central principles of *Dhamma* to show how they constitute a path for the world. For Sarvodaya, scripturalism is not restricted to this small group of suttas.

The other source that Sarvodaya appeals to as the basis for its philosophy, Sinhalese village culture, probably is less important in this regard than the *Dhamma*. Ariyaratne says that he learned Buddhist values and Sinhalese traditional ideals from the villagers with whom he worked. He maintains that he found in the villages vestiges of an ancient, pure, socially relevant Buddhist tradition which Sarvodaya has sought to revive. These village ideals and village culture came to shape the social and development goals that Sarvodaya set.

Critics have charged that Ariyaratne idealizes village culture and romanticizes ancient village life in order to promote village reform.[35] Although this charge seems to have validity, Ariyaratne has an interesting response. "My philosophy," he says, "is to combine all that is good or positive about medieval society" and not to dwell on the negative aspects.[36] Sarvodaya's approach here resembles that of other social reform movements that appeal, with more or less accuracy, to the past as a charter for reforms in the present. Singer refers to this method of justifying reforms as "archaization": "To deny the alleged novelty of an innovation by asserting its antiquity is to recognize and accept it as an integral part of the indigenous culture."[37] Obeyesekere observes that although Sarvodaya's vision of ancient village social patterns is "fictitious," it has been able to use this vision to inspire reforms such as *shramadāna*, selfless labor.[38]

Although it seems certain that Ariyaratne and other leaders of Sarvodaya did learn about social development from the villagers with whom they worked, many of the ideas in Sarvodaya's philosophy that are said to derive from the culture can more surely be traced back to the scriptures. Deciding between these two sources can be difficult, however, because the values found in Sinhalese village culture derived in large part from the *Dhamma*. In working out his reformulation of Buddhist values, Ariyaratne seems to have relied more upon the doctrinal forms of these values. For example, Sarvodaya promotes the four *sangaha vatthūni*, "grounds of kindness," as the social guidelines for its communities. The four are *dāna* (liberality), *peyyavajja* (kindly speech), *atthacariyā* (useful work), and *samānattatā* (equality). Ariyaratne teaches that these principles formed the basis for Sri Lanka's social life in ancient times, and can be revived to develop an ideal society today. In one of his works he recounts a very idealized version of Sri Lanka's cultural history in order to argue that these four principles were basic to ancient society. *Dāna*, liberality or sharing, can be seen to have applied in ancient Sri Lanka, he argues, for the people and the king shared both the labor and the fruits of their agricultural endeavors. The fourth principle, equality, was practiced when both the king and the peasant worked "knee deep in the mud in the paddy field."[39]

Although this idyllic view of ancient Sinhalese culture cannot be proven and seems rather unlikely, it serves to establish the charter for these principles which actually have their roots in the Buddhist scriptures. That this charter is either idealistic or fictitious is not too significant for Sarvodaya's programs, although it reinforces the observation that Ariyaratne depends more upon the texts than upon the Sinhalese tradition. The important point for Sarvodaya is not how these principles were observed in ancient times but how they can be reinterpreted for today. Understood now in pragmatic, world-affirming ways, the four principles constitute both the means and the ends of social change for Sarvodaya. They promote social awakening by enabling a group that follows them to begin to actualize the social ideals at the outset of the process of social change.

Sarvodaya's reinterpretation of these principles involves their rationalization. *Dāna*, for example, traditionally implied almsgiving to the Buddha or the *Sangha* and the practices of merit-making. Reinterpreted to apply to this world, *dāna* becomes the social ideal of sharing: sharing one's wealth and one's labor, as in *shramadāna*, for the welfare of all. The second principle, *peyyavajja*, kindly speech, Sarvodaya applies by encouraging all of its workers to address each other with familial terms. Women, depending on both their age and that of the speaker, would be addressed as mother, daughter, older sister, or younger sister; men as father, son, older brother, or younger brother.

This practice is intended to produce a sense of fellowship among people striving for a common goal and to break down negative social forces such as caste, rivalry, inequality, hatred, and desire. These principles thus constitute a pragmatic expression of the "healthier social environment" that leads to both social and individual awakening. Ariyaratne claims that these four form the basis for all of Sarvodaya's village development programs.[40]

Since he finds the charter for his movement in texts depicting a socially relevant Buddhism, Ariyaratne rejects those forms of traditional Theravada that lack a social focus. For Sarvodaya the true *Dhamma* is world-affirming, and for too long Sinhalese Theravada has emphasized the ideal of renunciation and the otherworldliness of the path. Sarvodaya rejects those aspects of traditional Theravada that have an otherworldly focus or that have primarily otherworldly goals. This category includes many forms of Sinhalese Theravada practiced in recent historical time. Sarvodaya rejects, for example, all interpretations of monasticism that expect the monks to live aloof from worldly affairs. Similarly rejected is the path of merit-making for the laity which has rebirth as its primary goal. The magical-animistic side of Sinhalese religion, the veneration of gods and demons, is rejected as "unnecessary decorations." The *bhikkhus*, Ariyaratne explained, have taught laypersons only ways of gathering merit in this life for rebirth, which leads him to object that the Buddhist temples only "look after the souls of people after death. . . . We are not getting full use out of them."[41]

Is Sarvodaya a Buddhist Movement?

Related to the issue of Sarvodaya's rejection of many of the prevailing forms of traditional Theravada is the question of whether Sarvodaya should be considered a Buddhist movement. To outsiders Sarvodaya seems clearly to constitute a Buddhist movement. Kantowski has noted that Sarvodaya began as a part of Buddhist revivalism.[42] Others, including Macy, have described Sarvodaya as a social gospel or liberation theology form of the Buddhist tradition.[43] Ariyaratne and the leaders of Sarvodaya, however, have refused in recent years to identify it as a Buddhist movement, although they are quite willing to admit that the philosophy and the primary influences shaping

Sarvodaya have come from Theravada. Ariyaratne has said, "Our message of awakening transcends any effort to categorize it as the teaching of a particular creed."[44] Sarvodaya, he argues, is based on Buddhism but is not a Buddhist movement.[45] Although its leaders give a variety of reasons for this view, their denial that Sarvodaya is a Buddhist movement can in itself be seen to represent a reformist stance. Reformist movements frequently rebel against traditional labels in order to differentiate themselves from traditional establishments.

One reason Sarvodaya's leaders cite to explain why it should not be considered a Buddhist movement is that it interprets and employs the teachings in a new way. A senior monk, or thera, who serves as the principal of Sarvodaya's Training Institute for *bhikkhus* at Pathakada told me, "You cannot brand Sarvodaya as Buddhist," for although *bhikkhus* are involved, it is based on "Buddhist ethical teachings not the higher philosophy."[46] Dr. Ratnapala, the head of Sarvodaya's research division, explained that we should not call Sarvodaya a Buddhist movement because it took the essence of Buddhist thought and "reinterpreted it as humanistic to a certain extent following a Buddhist line." A thera who heads a meditation center closely associated with Sarvodaya said that Sarvodaya is not a Buddhist organization because it is not based on the totality of Buddhist thought. It accomplishes "a practical application of Buddhist ways of living." Similarly, another thera, who serves as an adviser or patron to Sarvodaya, said that "Sarvodaya is primarily a social service organization." These informants expressed the idea that because Sarvodaya has reinterpreted and applied Buddhist thought differently from traditional Theravada, it is not a Buddhist movement in the official or usual sense.

Other informants reasoned that since Sarvodaya draws on or expresses the thought of all religions, not just Buddhism, it should not be labeled a Buddhist movement. In founding Sarvodaya, Ariyaratne studied the ideas of Gandhi and Vinoba Bhave. This point is frequently cited in Ariyaratne's writings in defense of the view that Sarvodaya should not be considered a Buddhist movement. However, he frequently seems to vitiate this argument by insisting that although these Gandhian influences were there at the outset of Sarvodaya, they were not as important as the influence of the Sinhala Buddhist culture of Sri Lanka. "We have our own indigenous character both in thought and action as far as the Ceylon Movement is concerned."[47] He has even expressed regret at adopting the name Sarvodaya because although his movement became totally different from the Indian movement, people continued to compare them.[48]

Nevertheless, Ariyaratne and the leaders of the movement believe that Sarvodaya should not be regarded as Buddhist because the goals it seeks and the means it employs are common to all religious traditions. "Through the philosophy of Sarvodaya—based on loving-kindness, compassionate action, altruistic joy and equanimity . . . people of different faiths and ethnic origins are motivated to carve out a way of life and a path of development founded on these ideals."[49] A district coordinator for Sarvodaya explained that the movement is nonsectarian because it uses religious ideas found in all traditions. There is nothing uniquely Buddhist, he argued, about love, compassion, and sharing. Sounding the same theme, another senior district leader explained that Sarvodaya takes a "comparative religions approach." Its philosophy does not employ Buddhist ideas that are not shared by all religions; for example, members generally avoid discussions of rebirth.

Another frequently cited reason for saying Sarvodaya is not a Buddhist movement is that it works with people from all religious groups, not just Buddhists. A senior *bhikkhu* argued vigorously that Sarvodaya is the only organization that serves all people without noticing religious differences. Sarvodaya had been instrumental, he felt, in breaking down the barriers between Christians and Buddhists. Another *bhikkhu* said that because Sarvodaya works in all the religious communities of the country, it is not a Buddhist organization. He went on to add, however, that because its philosophy and Ariyaratne's "behavior" are Buddhist, it is basically Buddhist. Demonstrating that this argument carries weight with participants, a Tamil man who works as a teacher at one of Sarvodaya's training centers explained that he did not regard it as a Buddhist organization: "There is no politics and no religion in Sarvodaya. The only thing is to do what is right and help people." Macy has cited similar examples from Christians who were involved with Sarvodaya and felt no discrimination, although they recognized that the Buddhist influences predominated.[50] A Muslim who worked with Sarvodaya said that he thought even Muhammed could accept Sarvodaya's basic teachings.

On the other side of this issue, in contrast to the replies of the Sarvodaya leaders, numerous factors as well as informants suggest that Sarvodaya does represent a Buddhist movement. The pervasive symbolism of the movement has been drawn totally from Buddhism. If, for example, one visits the headquarters of Sarvodaya in Moratuwa, one finds a complex of relatively new, whitewashed buildings with a signboard in front reading:

> This abode of young men and women trainees who strive to establish a Sarvodaya social order in Sri Lanka and the world in keeping with the noble eightfold path of the Buddhist philosophy is named the
> "Damsak Mandira"
> and it is built in the shape of the Dhamma Chakka [Wheel of doctrine].

Inside the octagonal dhamma-wheel complex there is a Buddha statue and a small lotus pond, in addition to a meeting hall, offices, classrooms, and dormitories. Another prominent symbol, the official seal of Sarvodaya, which appears on countless signboards and publications and in other places, is officially described as "a light red open lotus flower with the rising sun in the background." These and other outward symbols strengthen the impression of Sarvodaya's dependence on central ideas of the *Dhamma* which inform Sarvodaya's intention and meaning.

Although the leaders of Sarvodaya may be wary of designating it a Buddhist movement, at least two groups of Sarvodaya workers with whom I spoke had no such reservations. The first was a group of fifteen preschool teachers who were taking a training course at a district center. When asked whether they considered Sarvodaya a Buddhist movement, all of them said yes. In their schools they all taught *Dhamma*, the five precepts (*pañcā sīla*), the Jātakas, and other aspects of Buddhism, and they regarded these Buddhist subjects as a major part of their curriculum. Asked the same question, a group of twelve *bhikkhus* enrolled in Sarvodaya's Pathakada Training Institute for *bhikkhus* replied unanimously that Sarvodaya is a Buddhist movement. Some of the *bhikkhus* went on to say, however, that they could work with people from all religious communities.

In addition to the positive replies to this question, it might clarify the matter to note some other factors behind the Sarvodaya leaders' negative replies. One important factor has been the growth of the movement and its expansion into non-Buddhist villages and areas of Sri Lanka. At the outset Sarvodaya seems to have addressed an exclusively Sinhala Buddhist constituency. Having begun in a Buddhist college and being led by Buddhist laymen, it moved in Buddhist circles. As the movement grew and its reputation spread, it began to organize *shramadānas* in Hindu, Muslim, and Christian areas, and this seems to have necessitated giving more thought to the question of whether it was a Buddhist movement. Since one major aim was a total social revolution along the lines of their philosophy, Sarvodaya's leaders doubtless saw the necessity of stressing the ecumenical and universal nature of the teachings. This shift did not seem great to them because, as we have seen, Ariyaratne assumed that Buddhist ideals were shared by other religions.

A longtime Sarvodaya supporter who serves on its Executive Council said that in 1971 Sarvodaya made a conscious decision not to use exclusively Buddhist concepts. They would emphasize only those ideas that translated into all the other Sri Lankan religions. This 1971 decision to downplay the Buddhist nature of the philosophy was confirmed by a high-level Sarvodaya official at the Moratuwa headquarters, who explained that although the philosophy is Buddhist, it is also universal. Ratnapala also described this evolution of the movement's strategy: Sarvodaya "decided to interpret Buddhist principles on a wider basis so as to make them acceptable to all religions and different ethnic groups."[51]

Thus the answer to the question of whether Sarvodaya is a Buddhist movement is shaped by the context in which Sarvodaya operates. In work in non-Buddhist areas it deemphasizes its Buddhist origins. One leader who told me that Sarvodaya is not a Buddhist movement today added, however, that "in Buddhist areas it is a Buddhist movement." Ariyaratne confirmed this when he said he sometimes uses Buddhist ideas such as merit to explain to Buddhists the value of engaging in *shramadāna* work. He would not, however, use this explanation if he were working with Christians or Muslims.

The positive replies given by the *bhikkhus* and the preschool teachers also support this understanding of Sarvodaya. When the leaders say it is not a Buddhist movement, they do so knowing the scope of the movement today and knowing that in answering such questions put by Westerners, they are speaking to people who do not belong to the Sinhala Buddhist community. If, however, they were speaking to Buddhist villagers, it would not be as important for them to stress universality or ecumenicity.

Another, unstated reason that could lie behind the leaders' answers is what might be called an international public relations factor. Since Sarvodaya became dependent on foreign funding, it has had to be careful of its image. Describing itself as a nonsectarian movement may have made for a warmer reception from European donor agencies. But again, Sarvodaya could do this with a clear conscience, for in its own view its teachings were already universal and nonsectarian.

The solution to this question might be to say in good Buddhist fashion that Sarvodaya both is and is not a Buddhist movement. In its origins and as perceived by Sarvodaya workers in Buddhist villages, it clearly is a Buddhist movement. The school teachers and the *bhikkhus* would be surprised to hear that anyone thought that it was not. But as the leaders of Sarvodaya and the monks who advise the movement observe, it differs in significant ways from traditional Theravada. These leaders' denials that it is a Buddhist movement, however, amount to an affirmation that it represents a reformist Buddhist movement, for the leaders agree that Sarvodaya has given a new interpretation to Buddhism and has applied its philosophy in new ways.

On one hand, it could be seen as a matter of terminology or definition whether we describe Sarvodaya as a Buddhist movement or not, and we might do well to agree with Macy, who said, "Sarvodaya is predominantly Buddhist both in its membership (there is a higher proportion of Buddhists in Sarvodaya than in the country) and in public expressions of its philosophy."[52] On the other hand, however, there is a more significant issue implied in this question of whether Sarvodaya is a Buddhist movement, and this issue is reflected both in the responses of the leaders and in much of Sarvodaya's teachings. The issue or question is this: Is Sarvodaya simply a movement employing Buddhist ideas and symbols to promote and facilitate alternative means of social and economic development, or does it go beyond being a development movement by retaining, in some form, the central Buddhist ideals of liberation? The answers given by the leaders of the movement seem ambiguous on this point. Some leaders and advisers, we have noted, say that Sarvodaya is based only on the social ethics of Buddhism, not the higher philosophy. Others describe it as a "humanistic" application of Buddhist ideas. Ariyaratne, however, who insists that Sarvodaya should not be described as a Buddhist movement, has also said, "The ultimate goal of Sarvodaya is *Nibbāna*."[53]

To put it another way: the question about which the replies of Sarvodaya's leaders and the official writings seem somewhat ambiguous is, Are Buddhist philosophy and values merely auxiliary to its social development aims, or are they central and essential to what Sarvodaya is about? To be sure, Sarvodaya's leaders have found it necessary to stress the ecumenical and secular aspects of its Buddhist philosophy in order to serve all segments of Sri Lanka's pluralistic society. When one examines Sarvodaya's overall intent, however, it becomes clear that these concessions to ecumenicity do not change the essential Buddhist nature of the movement. The aims of Sarvodaya as expressed in its philosophy and its social programs place Buddhist ideals at the center of the movement. It has reinterpreted the Buddhist ideals. That is one reason its leaders seem so ambiguous about calling it a Buddhist movement. Reformist though it may be, however, Sarvodaya is nevertheless Buddhist at heart. In its central intention it is more than just a social or economic development movement; it represents a carefully planned attempt to apply the Buddhist ideals to the modern world to solve the problems of meaning and modernization.

Sarvodaya's Philosophy

The reformist Buddhist nature of Sarvodaya is seen in the philosophy of the movement, expressed in numerous publications and taught in detail to its members and volunteers. As we have observed, Ariyaratne has based this philosophy on the Buddhist scriptures, and says that he also drew upon the Sinhalese Buddhist cultural heritage surviving among the villagers—although the primary source for the philosophy seems to have been the Buddhist *Dhamma*. Although not a philosopher or Buddhist scholar by training, Ariyaratne has skillfully and pragmatically reshaped Buddhist ideals to address the challenges of modernity. Early in his career he aligned himself with the rationalist elements in the Buddhist revival by saying that he believed that Buddhism alone offers a way to withstand the destructive power of science and to "channel it along the path of general progress and well-being of all in society."[54]

Although he gave a Sri Lankan translation to the term Sarvodaya, calling it the "awakening of all," it seems clear that Ariyaratne imbibed a great deal from the Indian Sarvodaya movement. In addition to the name, at least two important presuppositions of the Indian movement appear in the Sri Lankan version. The first is the belief of Gandhi and Vinoba Bhave that to work for the welfare of others, to seek to realize the goal of Sarvodaya, is at the same time to follow a path to self-realization. Strongly influenced by the *Bhagavad Gītā*, Gandhi chose the path of *karma yoga*, understood as this-worldly asceticism. This idea has great significance in Ariyaratne's Sarvodaya philosophy, where it is more reformist and radical than it was in Gandhi's thought, since Gandhi stood within the tradition of the *Gītā*. Kantowski notes a basic philosophical difference between Gandhi's Hindu Sarvodaya and Ariyaratne's Buddhist Sarvodaya. "Gandhi tried to realize his true Self through dedication to the Service of All; Sarvodaya workers in Sri Lanka express their Non-Self by Sharing with All. Starting from different assumptions both concepts lead Sarvodaya in India and Sri Lanka into society and not out of it."[55] A second presupposition has to do with the background of Gandhi's thought and the influence of Tolstoy. Gandhi's Sarvodaya program reflected Tolstoy's idea that progress could only come through spiritual force. Sarvodaya's emphasis upon the spiritual aspect of development represents a reaffirmation of this idea.

Ariyaratne inherited these ideas but reshaped them in line with the Buddhist heritage of Sri Lanka. He said, "While the word 'Sarvodaya' with its literal meaning was adopted from India, the interpretation of its deep meaning as relevant to our own Sinhala Buddhist culture and national population is completely our own."[56] The Buddhist slant given to the Sarvodaya Movement by Ariyaratne shows up at once in his translating the name as the "Awakening of All." Awakening signifies the gaining of wisdom, enlightenment, and awareness of the true nature of reality. Ariyaratne explains this notion of awakening in a variety of ways, such as liberation, personality development, fulfillment of one's potential, and even self-realization. The image behind all of these forms of awakening is the supremely awakened one, the Buddha. Ariyaratne implies that the ultimate goal of Sarvodaya is the same as the goal of Theravada—liberating wisdom or salvific truth—when he explains that one must realize or awaken to the three characteristics of existence: impermanence (*anicca*), unsatisfactoriness (*dukkha*), and no-self (*anattā*). He writes that personality development "should take place in a direction to bring about the realization of the three foregoing principles leading to correct insight."[57] Ariyaratne further explains that the "awakening of all" is equivalent to the sum of "all these spiritual concepts found in Buddhism."[58] Although Sarvodaya places this ultimate Buddhist ideal at the center of the movement, it reinterprets both the ideal and the means of attaining it in social terms, providing a ground plan for a socially relevant Buddhism.

Since awakening constitutes the controlling ideal of the movement, Sarvodaya represents more than a development movement with Buddhist trappings. Ariyaratne describes Sarvodaya by saying, "The Movement undertakes community development projects but it is something more than a mere community development activity." It is, Ariyaratne prefers to say, a total, nonviolent revolution seeking "a total change in the outlook of man both towards himself and towards others in the community."[59] Kantowski views Sarvodaya in the same way, saying it is not "an extension agency" with programs "to improve the so-called 'quality of life' in certain rural areas. . . . All the practical programs started are only one of several means of achieving the ultimate end, namely the development in each individual of an insight into the true nature of things, thus relieving his suffering."[60]

Sarvodaya appears as a reformist movement, with a world-affirming interpretation of Buddhist teachings, when it advocates throughout its philosophy that this awakening must be a twofold process involving both the individual and the world. Ariyaratne has described the goal of Sarvodaya as a twofold liberation. Both forms of awakening are necessary and integrally linked, for an individual cannot awaken to his full potential if he is surrounded by an oppressive, corrupt society, and "it is useless developing the world unless there is development of the human in man."[61] The circular relationship of these two forms of awakening makes Gandhi's notion of *karma yoga*, self-realization through social involvement, both necessary and possible. Work in the world purifies individuals while it creates a better world, which in turn provides greater support for awakening. This logic carries over to Sarvodaya's practical social programs where, as Macy observes, "Community development is seen as the means for helping the people to realize goals that are essentially religious."[62]

Sarvodaya finds the charter for this dual awakening process in the Buddha's middle path. Sarvodaya represents a middle path that avoids the extremes of either a strictly spiritual religious movement or a materialistic social development movement. In his writings Ariyaratne frequently appeals to this analogy of the middle way with some justification, because Sarvodaya is trying to balance world-denying religious spiritual ideals with world-affirming social and economic ideals. Clearly, however, Sarvodaya represents a new middle path and not the traditional one. This new path offers, as Kantowski says, "a timely raft for crossing the stream of today's illusions—the trappings of modernization."[63]

The important point to note about this new path is that by advocating both the spiritual and the social it arrives at a new understanding of both. Macy has observed, "The very name Sarvodaya redefines development."[64] But it is also true that Sarvodaya reinterprets the *Dhamma* in an equally revolutionary way. The twofold liberation that Sarvodaya seeks is based upon this twofold reinterpretation.

The Reinterpretation of Development

Development for Sarvodaya becomes essentially a synonym for awakening. Sarvodaya calls into question all of the Western models of development that have been used in Sri Lanka from the colonial period to the present. These forms of development have often created rather than solved the nation's problems because they have imposed economic goals on the society without consideration for the values or culture of the people. Sarvodaya seeks an integrated development program that places human beings above everything else. Development must begin and end with people and should be based on the people's values, which for Sarvodaya are Buddhist values. It seeks grass-roots, village-based development, not development planning imposed from on high. Real development facilitates human awakening rather than increasing the GNP or the industrialization of the country. Goulet compares Sarvodaya's reinterpretation of development to the ideas of Lebret, who "stressed the essential difference between 'being' and 'having,' " or Ivan Illich, who criticized the "paradoxical counter-development nature of what is generally called development."[65] A Sarvodaya village leader who also happened to be a *bhikkhu* explained to me how Sarvodaya's idea of development, which he called "Buddhist development," differs from that of the government. The government's idea of development is to come into an area and construct hospitals, police stations, and such. Sarvodaya's idea, he said, is to bring about a form of development and awakening that eliminates the need for hospitals and police stations.

Ariyaratne has learned from his experience in building the Sarvodaya Movement that most government and international development planners regard awakening or spiritual goals as irrelevant to development. But the whole program of Sarvodaya testifies that awakening has the greatest relevance. Development must be an integrated operation, not just the attempt to create wealth and affluence. To cite Ariyaratne's vision of this, "Development as understood by the common man is an integrated process of total change that is taking place within individuals, families, groups, rural and urban communities, nations and the world bringing socio-economic and spiritual-cultural progress in one and all."[66]

Sarvodaya's teachings spell out the integrated nature of the development and awakening processes. Awakening is seen taking place in four spheres that constitute the goals of the Sarvodaya Movement: 1). *paurushodaya*, awakening of the individual; 2). *gramodaya*, awakening of the village; 3). *deshodaya*, awakening of the nation; 4). *vishvodaya*, awakening of the world.[67] These spheres are not separate but closely intertwined; they represent an extension of the idea of the dual revolution. Awakening takes place simultaneously in the individual and in the ever-widening circles of society in which he is involved. As the individual becomes liberated from ignorance, society becomes liberated from poverty, injustice, and other social evils. Ariyaratne describes the process: "The ideal of a just economic order and a righteous political system can only be built on the development of a sound personality and group awakening process."[68]

This idea of an integrated development is also expressed in Sarvodaya's teachings by the six elements that constitute development. These elements—frequently displayed on charts adorning the walls of Sarvodaya centers—show the interconnections between spiritual and social development as well as the logic behind Sarvodaya's development model. They are

(i) A moral element (*sīla*): where abstinence from killing, stealing, moral misconduct, lying and consuming intoxicants form the most important ingredients for the ordinary laymen.

(ii) A cultural element: where customs, beliefs, traditions, art, music, song, dance and drama, etc., help to keep together a community of people as a cohesive whole.

(iii) A spiritual element: where the awakening of one's mind through concentration to wisdom (*Samādhi* to *Paññā*) leading to a state where unconditioned happiness (*Nibbāna*) or final cessation of all suffering can be achieved.

(iv) A social element: where quality of life in a society is ensured.

(v) A political element: where all the members of a community enjoy fundamental and equal human rights before the law.

(vi) An economic element: where human needs are met progressively beginning with the most basic needs and all the time conforming to the five elements enumerated above.[69]

The first three elements represent the Sinhalese Buddhist elements and the last three the secular or social elements. By linking them all together in this way Sarvodaya indicates that the two kinds of development cannot be separated. Development is a "complex organic process" in which the Buddhist elements cannot be limited to the spiritual side only. Thus, in addition to teaching that development has a spiritual goal, Sarvodaya teaches that the means to that goal come from the Buddhist tradition; Buddhist values from the spiritual, cultural, and moral spheres provide the best guidelines for social, political, and economic development. This is the social gospel interpretation of the Buddha's teachings, which Ariyaratne contends is not only relevant to the modern context but represents an accurate rendering of the Buddha's intention.

Both Sarvodaya's ideal for society and its concrete programs in the villages draw upon specific Buddhist values. Rather than seeking economic growth, Sarvodaya seeks "right livelihood," one of the steps in the Buddha's Eightfold Path. Right livelihood implies other values that run counter to the standard model of Western development. For example, right livelihood stresses harmony and the quality of life rather than ambition and working for profit only. Similarly, Sarvodaya insists that society should be based on the ideal of nonviolence, *ahiṃsā*. Ariyaratne has said that this ideal underlies the whole Sarvodaya Movement and is another synonym for the name of the movement. A commentator on the movement has said of Sarvodaya's concept of *ahiṃsa*: "The Sarvodaya concept is more profound than the mere abstention from physical violence; it includes the deeper concern to avoid doing violence to a way of life, to avoid forms of change which disrupt communities and destroy or impair their capacity to organize the whole of their experience."[70]

Nonaggression, noncompetitiveness, and nonambition represent other traditional Buddhist values integral to Sarvodaya's ideal social order but foreign to both capitalism and materialism. These values have their basis in the Buddhist definition of desire as the primary evil leading people away from self-realization. Another expression of the aversion to desire in traditional Buddhism is the ideal of the simple life. As exemplified by the monastic ideal with its limited requisites, the best life according to Buddhism is a simplified life, without an abundance of possessions. Sarvodaya has incorporated this ideal in its development plan for formulating what it calls the "ten basic human needs."

Sarvodaya defines these basic human needs as 1) a clean and beautiful environment; 2) an adequate supply of safe water; 3) minimum requirements of clothing; 4) a balanced diet; 5) simple housing; 6) basic health care; 7) communication facilities; 8) energy; 9) total education related to life and living; 10) cultural and spiritual needs.[71] The movement arrived at this list of ten needs by conducting a survey among 660 villagers. Ratnapala told me that although employment and income ranked high in the survey, neither was included in the list because they were felt to represent means rather than ends. These basic human needs provide direction along the new middle path and demonstrate again the interrelation of the material and spiritual aspects of social change.

Other Buddhist values such as compassion, *karuṇā*, and lovingkindness, *mettā*, also shape Sarvodaya's understanding of development and the good life. They represent the values of the Buddhist people reinterpreted by Ariyaratne to provide a meaningful alternative development. This reinterpretation was necessary, one Sarvodaya leader explained, to provide a plausible alternative to Western development models whose proponents proclaimed "Do as the West has done and you too will achieve prosperity." Such claims were difficult to refute and carried great weight with people who had seen the power of the colonial governments. Sarvodaya, however, appeals to values even more deeply ingrained in the culture, ancient Buddhist values, and it points to the legends of Sri Lanka as a *Dhammadīpa* (island of righteousness) and a *Dhanyagara* (land of plenty) to establish alternative ideals. Ariyaratne says that *Dhammadīpa* and *Dhanyagara* mean "a society where economic prosperity and righteousness are harmoniously combined."[72] He further proclaims that these ideals are "always foremost in the minds of Sarvodaya workers."[73] These ancient images, enshrined in the Chronicles, demonstrate both the feasibility and the superiority of a Buddhist-based model for society. They evoke a combination of patriotism and Buddhist loyalty in support of this model. As Macy notes, Ariyaratne, as Dharmapāla before him, "summons the population to the noble task of building anew on its ancient strengths."[74] Sarvodaya's references to these images of Sri Lanka's golden age can be understood not as longing for the past but as affirmation of the present and optimism about the possibility for social change.

The exact nature of the interrelationship of the spiritual and social goals in Sarvodaya's vision of development is perhaps best illustrated by a saying used in the movement to describe *shramadāna* work: "We build the road and the road builds us." This saying catches the point that material development work done on behalf of society also serves spiritual purposes. As Ariyaratne explains, Sarvodaya really cannot fail; the road may fail by being washed out, but the personality awakening that occurred in the building of it will endure.

This saying demonstrates that although the social and spiritual factors in development depend on each other, the spiritual has primacy. Ariyaratne says, "All development efforts should be aimed at the achievement of the fullest awakening of the human personality."[75] Sounding somewhat like an evangelist, he declares that the "spiritual reawakening of mankind" represents "a crying need."[76] This is the new interpretation that Sarvodaya has given to development: the initial goal of social development becomes individual awakening, *paurushodaya*. Once awakened, the individual becomes the most effective change agent for the society in which he lives.

In one sense this plan for development represents a traditional Buddhist schema: the individual must be changed if society is to be changed. Employing this plan as the basis for a modern-day village development movement, however, has meant that Sarvodaya has radically redefined development ideology in light of the *Dhamma*. At the same time, Sarvodaya has also reinterpreted the *Dhamma* in reformist ways. The saying cited above illustrates this as well by implying that personality awakening comes about by means of *shramadāna* work in the world.

Reinterpretation of the Dhamma

Sarvodaya redefines the *Dhamma* in two major ways: first, in its understanding of the goal of awakening or liberation; and second, in its view of the means to that goal. When Sarvodaya stresses individual awakening as the beginning of any development, it seems close to traditional Buddhism, where *bhāvanā* or mental/spiritual development was the only development that mattered. But does Sarvodaya really re-present that ideal? As described in chapter four, traditional *bhāvanā* led to supramundane wisdom and required renunciation of the world. Has Sarvodaya retained these ideas? Or has it fulfilled instead Bechert's definition of Buddhist modernism, which "does away with the old separation of the supramundane and mundane spheres"?[77] How does Sarvodaya's view of the goal of individual awakening compare not only to that of traditional Theravada but also to that of the *vipassanā bhāvanā* movement? We can ask of Sarvodaya the same questions that we asked of the *vipassanā* reformers: Do they seek the goal of arahantship? Is renunciation necessary to attain that goal?

Sarvodaya shares with the *vipassanā* proponents an optimism about the human potential for spiritual attainment. Rather than invoking the decline of the *sāsana*, the leaders of Sarvodaya regard the present time as ripe with possibilities for actualizing both the spiritual and social ideals of the Buddhist tradition. Ariyaratne proclaims that "every human being has the potential to attain supreme enlightenment."[78] Personality awakening at its highest level can result in arahantship even in the present age. Ariyaratne does not hesitate to describe personality awakening as *paññā*, liberating wisdom, or "the final goal of attaining unconditioned supreme happiness or Nirvana."[79] The process of personality awakening "is consummated in the final attainment of Arahanthood."[80] *Nibbāna* represents the ultimate goal of every Sarvodaya worker, according to Ariyaratne.

Sarvodaya describes this supramundane *Nibbāna* which is the ultimate goal of personality awakening in more or less traditional terms. *Nibbāna* means attaining wisdom about the nature of reality, freedom from rebirth, and deathlessness. Also in traditional terms, Sarvodaya regards personality awakening to be a very gradual process spanning many lifetimes of an individual. Ariyaratne writes that personality development "not only embraces a total life process but a whole cycle of lives—births and deaths—finally aiming at a state of deathlessness or non-birth."[81] Because people find themselves at various places in this process, their development proceeds at different rates. Sarvodaya provides opportunities for each person "to realize his own stage of development in relation to his total personality, development potentialities and the exact place he occupies in this world of time and space, men and matter."[82] In the normal scheme of things, however, not many people have developed sufficiently to attain the "extreme end" of the process, supramundane *Nibbāna*, in the near future. Ariyaratne writes that the awakening process should enable persons "to awaken their personalities to the fullest—during their present existence in this world" without hampering their continued development, "culminating in the attainment of *Nibbāna* in a subsequent life."[83]

Thus far, Sarvodaya adheres fairly closely to traditional Theravada doctrine about *Nibbāna* and the gradual path, but it begins to reinterpret the *Dhamma* in reformist and innovative ways when it discusses the lower stages of the process of awakening. Here supramundane *Nibbāna* becomes more or less a backdrop or a theoretical goal against which Sarvodaya can develop its functional goal, mundane awakening. Although personality awakening theoretically means an enlightenment equivalent to the Buddha's, for Sarvodaya in practice it means something more mundane and pragmatic.

Sarvodaya eliminates the separation between the supramundane and mundane spheres by concentrating almost exclusively on the mundane forms of awakening. As a Thera involved with Sarvodaya explained, Sarvodaya cannot have a mass-movement based on supra-mundane enlightenment, so it stresses enlightenment primarily in a worldly way while leaving open the possibility of the supramundane. In some ways, then, Sarvodaya seems to be doing what Theravada always did in practice, especially on the level of the laity: removing *Nibbāna* to the remote future and focusing attention on this life. Sarvodaya's focus on this life, however, is more accommodationist than traditional Theravada for Sarvodaya concentrates not on seeking a better rebirth but on reaching awakening or enlightenment in ways that are relevant to the world; indeed, it objects strongly to the traditional accommodationist beliefs about merit-making and rebirth. Sarvodaya gives new meaning to enlightenment by orienting it to this world. As Macy writes, "Sarvodaya's goal and process of awakening pulls one headlong into the 'real' world."[84]

Mundane awakening appears to have both spiritual and rational aspects. As the slogan about building the road indicates, people can be awakened to higher spiritual qualities such as cooperation, selflessness, and goodwill. Ariyaratne commented that everywhere he travels he meets people who were involved in the early *shramadāna* camps and who say that their lives were changed by the experience. They were awakened; they did not attain full enlightenment but came away with "a more enlightened mind."[85] For the villagers these spiritual goals have a practical effect in raising the consciousness of both the individual and the community. This form of awakening resembles what Bellah refers to as "the increased capacity for rational goal-setting."[86] Using Buddhist ideals such as self-development and self-reliance, Sarvodaya seeks to teach villagers trapped in cycles of poverty to realize their potential for improving their lives. Ariyaratne says that "Sarvodaya does not believe that economic stagnation and poverty are inevitable—it is consistent with the Buddhist principle that salvation lies primarily in one's own hands, be it an individual or a group."[87] Taking charge of one's own life and recognizing one's basic human dignity are goals villagers can achieve now. These goals relate to the *Dhamma* because personal fetters such as greed, hatred, and ignorance must be conquered in order to reach them.

As part of its teachings about awakening Sarvodaya has reoriented the understanding of *karma* to this world. *Karma* has been misunderstood as fate and as a force related only to past or future lives, but

Ariyaratne stresses that *karma* is under our control and we can change it. Poor people in Sri Lankan society, Ariyaratne explained, have to be "reminded" of the true meaning of *karma*, for they have been told by the power structure—including the colonial government—that they are poor because of their *karma*. In keeping with reformist optimism Sarvodaya rejects this view of *karma* as "a pessimistic and unalterable law."[88] *Karma* constitutes only one of four factors that shape personality awakening: the environmental factor, the biological factor, the mental factor, and the karmic factor.[89] Similarly, the commentarial doctrine of the five *niyāmas* is referred to as proof that *karma* represents only one of many factors influencing a person's life. *Karma* should be understood as potential rather than as "some mysterious unknown power to which we must helplessly submit ourselves." The good news is that "it is possible for us to divert the course of our karma" by awakening the other aspects of our personality.[90]

Sarvodaya's reinterpretation of the Four Noble Truths provides a good example of the kind of mundane awakening it seeks. Summarizing the Buddha's central teaching, the Four Noble Truths were the subject of the Buddha's first discourse. These truths have traditionally been interpreted by Buddhists as indicators of the existential human predicament and its solution. Sarvodaya reinterprets them, however, in social terms. The first truth, *dukkha* (suffering or unsatisfactoriness), is translated as "There is a decadent village." This concrete form of suffering becomes the focus of mundane awakening. Villagers should recognize the problems in their environment such as poverty, disease, oppression, and disunity. The second truth, *samudaya* (the origin of suffering), now signifies that the decadent condition of the village has one or more causes. Charts on the walls of Sarvodaya centers teach that the causes lie in factors such as egoism, competition, greed, and hatred. Macy notes that "in the training of village organizers, these human failings are noted as having been exacerbated by the practices and attitudes of former colonial powers and especially by the acquisitiveness bred by capitalism."[91]

The third truth, *nirodha* (cessation), understood in traditional Buddhism as an indicator of *Nibbāna*, becomes hope that the villagers' suffering can cease. The means to solving the problem lies in the fourth truth, the Eightfold Path. Macy offers an excellent example of the mundane explication of the stages of the Eightfold Path when she cites a Sarvodaya teacher's explanation of right mindfulness or awareness, (*sati*): "Right Mindfulness—that means stay open and alert to the needs of the village. . . . Look to see what is needed—latrines, water, road."[92] Ariyaratne points out that by treading this path, one "becomes part of a mass social movement towards human progress and conscious social change."[93]

At first glance Sarvodaya's expression of the Four Noble Truths in this fashion seems to represent almost a parody of the Buddha's original lofty philosophical teachings. Macy reports that some scholars whom she consulted considered Sarvodaya's reinterpretation to be "a newfangled adulteration of Buddhism, lacking doctrinal respectability. To present release from suffering in terms of irrigation, literacy, and marketing cooperatives appeared to them to trivialize the *Dharma*."[94] She goes on to say, however, that when she asked a learned Buddhist monk about this interpretation of the truths, his answer was to say there is "no problem." "But it is the same teaching, don't you see? Whether you put it on the psycho-spiritual plane or the socio-economic plane, there is suffering and there is cessation of suffering."[95]

Perhaps the learned monk's comments referred to the commentarial teaching that *dukkha* can be understood as having several forms: *dukkha* as ordinary suffering, *dukkha* as the product of change, and *dukkha* as conditioned states.[96] Sarvodaya's use of the term falls in the first category, *dukkha* as ordinary suffering, but it is clearly bound up with the other forms of suffering according to the commentators. I asked Ariyaratne whether he thought that the Four Noble Truths had originally been applied to the social sphere, as Sarvodaya has interpreted them. He replied that their primary reference was of course to a higher philosophical suffering, but he uses them in this way to raise the consciousness of the ordinary villager by showing that this basic fourfold dynamic applies to society and to the concrete suffering that villagers experience.

Interpreting the Four Noble Truths in this fashion reveals again the integrated nature of the process of awakening and development. Mundane awakening, liberating individuals from poverty, ignorance, and inertia, takes place in society and leads to social awakening, which in turn provides a more dharmic environment that makes greater individual awakening possible. The gradual path has a social component, for as Macy observes, "One cannot listen to the *Dharma* on an empty stomach."[97] Ariyaratne described the circularity of development and awakening by saying, "All these things must be related to the central purpose of life: the ability to reach higher and higher states of mind." This is the dual development process mentioned earlier; individual liberation produces *jana shakti*, people's power, and vice versa. Macy sees the interconnectedness of the process to be grounded in the Buddhist doctrine of *paṭiccasamuppāda*, "dependent co-arising."[98] All things are interrelated, and people perceive this truth through concrete action.

The circularity of the awakening process points to the other aspect of Sarvodaya's reinterpretation of the *Dhamma*, the reinterpretation of the path. This-worldly asceticism becomes the means for reaching world-affirming enlightenment. Ariyaratne said that "to change society we must purify ourselves, and the purification process we need is brought about by working in society." This path constitutes the crucial link between the individual and society in Sarvodaya's whole scheme of awakening and development, for it provides a means to awaken both self and society together. At times Ariyaratne compares Sarvodaya's conception of the path to the *bodhisattva* ideal, the being who postpones his own enlightenment in order to remain in the world to work for the enlightenment of all.[99] The *Bhagavad Gītā*'s ideal of the *karma yogi*, especially as updated by Gandhi, however, constitutes a more relevant comparison. Pragmatic and rational, this path emphasizes the theme of achievement which has importance for reformist Buddhism.

When asked whether renunciation, the traditional means to enlightenment, is necessary to reach the goal of total enlightenment or awakening, Ariyaratne replied that it depends on the person. Some people are more inclined toward renunciation; others are more inclined toward activity. Each person should decide for himself how he can make the greatest contribution to society. Clearly, however, Sarvodaya's whole program presupposes that renunciation does not represent the only path—or even the most suitable path—for the majority of people. In one of his writings, after discussing the Eightfold Path, Ariyaratne adds this note: "One who renounces the household life completely and strives after spiritual enlightenment can tread this eightfold path to perfection. But any ordinary man too can apply these principles in his day-to-day worldly life if he has the will to do so."[100] In another work he says, "According to the extent of each person's mental development and determination this spiritual path can be followed while living in society."[101] Sarvodaya conceives of this path in universalist and immediate terms. All persons, laity as well as monks, can follow the way in the world to reach the goal without assistance. The path remains a gradual one, but work on the path occurs in the world and does not necessarily lead to a life where one renounces the world. Ariyaratne appears to be slightly ambiguous about whether renunciation still constitutes a higher path for a later life. He has implied this possibility by occasionally expressing the sentiment that he would like to retire from the world someday to pursue a more spiritual life; but again, this view could be understood as a matter of his particular individual preference. That work in the world is for Sarvodaya a valid path to mundane awakening, however, is beyond doubt. Testifying to the success of this approach, Ariyaratne proclaims that "a consistent effort on our part to liberate ourselves from greed, hatred and ignorance through a social action program whose usefulness goes beyond self-interest can generate a hopeful force in the right direction."[102]

Although this-worldly asceticism characterizes all of Sarvodaya's activities, the *shramadāna* campaign represents the epitome of this path to awakening. By working in the village, not by retreating to the forest, Sarvodaya members can generate a self-realization process. Macy refers to the *shramadāna* compaign as "a quasi religious event."[103]

The movement takes four traditional Buddhist concepts, the four *Brahma Vihāras*, Abodes of Brahma, to describe and prescribe how this-worldly asceticism proceeds in *shramadāna* camps and other projects. Ariyaratne claims that in Sri Lankan culture traditionally the awakening of the personality was based on these four principles.[104] Sarvodaya takes the first principle, *mettā*, lovingkindness, to mean respect for all life, cultivating love for all beings. This principle leads to the second, *karuṇā*, compassion, which Sarvodaya understands as compassionate action, putting one's love for humanity into practice. As Ariyaratne says, "There is so much suffering going on around us that those who are mindful of respect for life should go in search of those who are suffering and try to help remove the cause of their suffering."[105]

Muditā, sympathetic joy, results from acting on the first two principles because one sees how one's efforts have helped others. This joy
represents an important factor in Sarvodaya's mundane awakening,
for to be awake and liberated is to be joyful. Sarvodaya doesn't downplay the element of joy derived from losing oneself in the service of
society. Joy, after all, represents an important aspect of the enlightened state; *arahants* have traditionally been depicted as embodiments
of selfless joy and peace of mind. When asked why he began working
with Sarvodaya and what he hoped to gain, a Sarvodaya leader
replied that he began and continues because this work makes him
happy. The fourth principle, *upekkhā*, equanimity, becomes important
initially because people inevitably criticize Sarvodaya workers, even
for unselfish actions. In the long run, however, this criticism enables
the workers to develop a certain detachment and a personality structure unshaken by praise or blame, by gain or loss.

These four principles represent the four requisites for personality
awakening according to Sarvodaya. This interpretation of the *Brahma
Vihāras* demonstrates again how Sarvodaya has reoriented both the
means and the ends of the *Dhamma* to the world. In the texts of traditional Theravada the *Brahma Vihāras* represented fairly lofty practices
of *samādhi* meditation that resulted in the *jhānas*, or trance states. Traditionally they were to be cultivated not through action in the world
but by withdrawing from the world. As subjects of meditation these
topics produced peaceful mental states, not an ethic for social involvement. The meditator who perfected the mental states of lovingkindness or compassion infused these qualities into the world not by social
work but by a process that King has described as "individualized radi-
ation of virtue and health out into society by holy persons."[106] To be
sure, many *arahants* are said to have lived lives of compassionate service, but there was no requirement that meditation lead to service.
The *Brahma Vihāras* represented exercises in mental purification,
intended to calm the mind and produce both equanimity and the
world-recessive trance states called *jhānas*.

When I asked Ariyaratne about his reinterpretation of these concepts, he defended his view by appealing again to the premise that the
Dhamma has many levels of meaning. He had no doubt that employing these concepts as *samādhi* meditation subjects was a more
profound level, but he contended that they can also be used by ordi-

nary people to analyze their thoughts and deeds in order to achieve self-realization. This approach is more practical, for it can be done by householders in their day-to-day life. In Sarvodaya the concepts have come to represent the value base for development; they explain both why one should seek awakening and development and how it can be done. A *bhikkhu* who serves as an adviser to the movement supported Sarvodaya's use of the *Brahma Vihāras* by saying that on the mundane plane these ideas have ethical implications and can be employed in a social philosophy.

Sarvodaya and Meditation

Sarvodaya's attitude toward renunciation and the *Brahma Vihāras* raises the question of what place meditation has in the movement. Macy contends that Sarvodaya has brought another innovation to Sri Lankan Buddhism by "wedding meditation and social action."[107] She is correct in saying that they have combined these two practices, but the emphasis clearly falls on social action, with meditation constituting only a support system for it. To the extent that Sarvodaya employs meditation at all, it gives meditation a pragmatic, mundane interpretation. *Mettā* meditation, the meditation on lovingkindness, represents almost the only form of meditation practiced in the movement. In *shramadāna* camps the "family gatherings" at the beginning, middle, and end of each day often include a few minutes of *mettā* meditation. This meditation helps to purify one's mind and generate what Ariyaratne calls an energy of love that counteracts the negative thoughts in our "psychosphere."[108] But this purified thought must not end there, for the thought energy must be used to work for the welfare of all. In another explanation of the link between meditation and social action Ariyaratne writes that meditating on lovingkindness enables people to realize "the oneness of all lives."[109] Although this realization of oneness might not find very much explicit support in traditional Theravada philosophy, it provides an important basis for action in the world.

Apart from the *mettā bhāvanā*, meditation in either a traditional sense or in the sense that it is taught by the *vipassanā* centers—that is, as an activity for its own sake leading to higher consciousness—does not constitute a central pursuit in Sarvodaya. The path Sarvodaya has created or recreated differs from the path of meditation. This is not to say that meditation is not useful in Sarvodaya's path, but it seems clear that Sarvodaya's path to enlightenment follows a different course from that of the *vipassanā* tradition. When I asked Ariyaratne about the place of meditation in the movement, he confirmed its pragmatic role. The short periods of meditation at *shramadāna* camps are intended only as reminders to the people that, as Ariyaratne said, "this movement has a spiritual base and is not like just "any other rat race." It also reminds people of the value of seeking right awareness. Acknowledging that people are free to go on to cultivate the meditations on mindfulness or awareness, just as they are free to go beyond mundane awakening to seek supramundane, Ariyaratne said that meditation is not Sarvodaya's "exclusive job." It is the exclusive emphasis of meditation centers. Ariyaratne saw no conflict between the *vipassanā* movement and his movement, since they complement each other.

Other Sarvodaya leaders also said that meditation plays a secondary, but useful, role in the movement. The monk who heads the meditation center sponsored by Sarvodaya, which is located near the headquarters in Moratuwa, said that not too many Sarvodaya workers come to his center for instruction in meditation, although Ariyaratne was said to be a frequent participant in the center's meditation sessions. This monk, who has devoted himself to meditation for many years, did not seem worried about the low level of interest in pursuing serious meditation by Sarvodaya's workers because he felt that Sarvodaya's main task was to awaken people to the world.

The leader of one of Sarvodaya's large district centers gave a lengthy explanation of *mettā* meditation that supported this monk's observations. "*Mettā* meditation by itself will not work"; rather, one must do something constructive, what he called "real work," and then you could make a contribution to the people. He took a very rational and pragmatic view of *mettā* meditation: it is not enough just to sit around and think loving, compassionate thoughts; one must put them into action. His rationalism, however, was a uniquely Buddhist or Sarvodayan kind of rationalism, not quite as Western as it sounded at first, for he believed strongly that *mettā* meditation released what Ariyaratne has described as "spiritual energy."[110] This spiritual energy goes far beyond just creating goodwill among people; it has magical powers. He said that he had once employed *mettā* meditation to influence local politicians to assist Sarvodaya in some of its village projects. Another time, when his young volunteers' rice field was threatened by a drought, he organized a group *mettā* meditation that produced rain. Even the magical effects of *mettā* meditation have social relevance for this Sarvodaya leader.

Meditation, then, has much the same standing as renunciation in Sarvodaya's plan. It remains an option for those who incline toward it, but it no longer represents the only means of awakening to the truth. Meditation can be useful in many ways, but the main path for Sarvodaya involves attaining purification and liberation by acting in the world. Kantowski points out the significance of this reinterpretation of the path. "Sarvodaya's village workers do not run away from life but accept their social rules and obligations. They are convinced that it is not only through meditation that one can cast off the illusionary cobwebs of 'I' and 'Mine,' but also through 'sharing of one's time, thought and energy for the awakening of All.' "[111] We have seen in the examples of the *Brahma Vihāras* how this awakening process could enable a person who worked in society to penetrate the truth in practical ways. Sarvodaya teaches that "right understanding is the ability of a person to comprehend the true nature of living things," a wisdom that can be gained through action as well as through contemplation. Awakening takes place in the world, not in what Macy describes as "mystical . . . private quests."[112]

Sarvodaya's Apparent Traditionalism

Although Sarvodaya represents a reformist movement, some aspects of its philosophy and programs appear somewhat traditionalistic. Two points need to be made about this apparent traditionalism. First, since movements seldom represent pure types, Sarvodaya probably could be described as more traditionalist than reformist in some respects. Second, in most instances where Sarvodaya appears traditional, upon closer examination one sees that for the most part it is actually reforming the tradition in pragmatic ways. Two examples can be noted: the formulation of the ten basic human needs and Sarvodaya's attitude toward the *Sangha*.

The advice that Sarvodaya gives its members in the formulation of the ten basic human needs often seems both traditionalistic and moralistic. In a small handbook the movement spells out the ten basic needs in general and then offers 167 injunctions and recommendations relating to the practice of these standards.[113] It recommends, for example, that people follow a vegetarian diet, a recommendation that has a traditionalistic valence in South Asia generally. Although the Theravada Buddhist tradition does not require vegetarianism of its followers, and the texts say that the Buddha himself was not a vegetarian, vegetarianism is widely admired by Sinhalese Buddhists as a meritorious and virtuous practice. It has been recommended by many Protestant Buddhists including Dharmapāla. Most Sinhalese Theravadins regard vegetarianism as a moral issue related to the first precept prohibiting killing. Although meat is listed in the basic human needs handbook as a component of one of the basic food groups, Sarvodaya emphasizes vegetarianism both in the other recommendations of the handbook and in the meals that it serves to its workers and trainees at the headquarters and elsewhere.

Sarvodaya's teachings include other moralistic and traditionalistic themes such as abstinence, opposition to smoking and drugs, and conservative advice about dress and social conduct. Sarvodaya advises that people "avoid taking intoxicants totally." Although this ideal is one of the Buddhist precepts, or sīla, the handbook does not refer to the precepts but explains this injunction with rational evidence about the health and financial risks of alcoholism. The Buddhist tradition, however, represents the ultimate source of this ideal, unless one regards it as further imitation of Protestant Christianity. In a similar way Sarvodaya advises against smoking and all "stimulants" such as ganja and opium. A survey of Sarvodaya's leaders showed that 61 percent disagreed with the statement that "the movement will have to change some of its traditional attitudes to things like smoking and drinking if it hopes to attract young people today."[114]

Other forms of traditionalism also find support in Sarvodaya. The basic human needs handbook advises people to continue or revive various cultural and religious observances. Folksongs and folklore should be perpetuated. Traditional life-cycle rituals such as the celebration of a birth, the naming ceremony, the ceremony where a child is taken to a sage for instruction in the alphabet, and other rituals should be preserved. It urges also that people "celebrate the major religious festivals with due decorum."[115]

A somewhat different kind of traditionalism can be seen in injunctions that appear to recommend middle-class values to the people. These recommendations seem inappropriate if Sarvodaya's intended audience is, as it claims, the "poorest of the poor." Under rules related to dwellings, for example, Sarvodaya gives advice about how to arrange the "visitor's room." This might strike the "poorest of the poor" as particularly ironic. The recommendations for clothing which call for each person to own six sets of clothing, including one set for dress occasions, might also seem beyond the reach of the poor. Obeyesekere has described these rules as representing one way that Sarvodaya communicates a bourgeois ethos to the villages.[116] The rules also may be seen as a revision and reiteration of Dharmapāla's rules for Buddhists.

These traditionalistic and moralistic injunctions and tendencies, however, are neither surprising nor totally incompatible with Sarvodaya's reformist stance. Swearer's observation about the values of the Jayanti period is relevant to Sarvodaya also at this point: "The moralism stems from a critical stance toward the "materialistic" values of Western society; and the traditionalism is based on an idealization of a Buddhist heritage eclipsed by a long history of colonial domination."[117] Sarvodaya certainly critiques Western values in the strongest terms and turns to an idealized Buddhist heritage for options, as we have noted. Therefore, traditionalism and moralism represent aspects of its attempt to establish an alternative model for social and individual identities. This traditionalism and moralism also grow out of Sarvodaya's scripturalism, for it grounds all of these practices in texts containing injunctions for social life. Gellner, analyzing a similar reformist movement in Morocco, points out that scripturalism, which is based upon literacy, "makes possible insistence on rules and . . . a general puritanism." One of the features of a literate reform movement, he notes, is "a tendency towards moderation and sobriety."[118]

Overall, despite the traditionalistic tendencies, the intent of the ten basic human needs and other injunctions is to further Sarvodaya's reformist ideal of relating Buddhism's goals to the mundane context. Ariyaratne regards the basic human needs as an expression of the kind of integrated development that Sarvodaya seeks. They represent "an index to measure the spirituo-cultural quality of life," a corollary to Western development planners' Physical Quality of Life Index.[119] The teachings indicate the close relation between mundane factors such as housing and clothing and spiritual factors that lead to awakening. They reiterate the dual developoment model at the heart of all that Sarvodaya does. Stating these basic human needs in traditionalistic terms serves to "archaize" them and to give this reformism both authority and acceptability. They reflect a process that Singer notes in reforms in India: "Many of the revivalist and restorationist movements and their associated symbols turn out to have this Janus-like character—traditional from the front and modern from the back."[120]

The second example of apparent traditionalism comes from Sarvodaya's involvement with the *Sangha*. In view of the critical attitude held by many toward the *bhikkhus*, Sarvodaya's pro-*Sangha* position might appear to place it on the side of the neotraditionalists. The basic human needs handbook, for instance, advises the people "to see that a *Bhikkhu* conversant with the Buddha *Dhamma* . . . is resident in every Buddhist village."[121] Further, they are advised to ensure that the four requisites of the monks "are unfailingly provided" and that the temple is kept clean. These are not radical injunctions. Nor does Sarvodaya's close association with the *bhikkhus* and the temple in every village resemble the antimonastic sentiments of a group such as The Saddhama Friends Society. Nevertheless, Sarvodaya does not take a traditional stance vis-à-vis the *Sangha*. Its aim has been to reform or reinterpret the role of the *Sangha* just as it has reinterpreted the *Dhamma*, in pragmatic, world-affirming ways.

Throughout his writings Ariyaratne expresses criticism of the role that the *bhikkhus* had come to play in Sri Lanka. He says, "There are a vast number of Buddhist Temples in this country. . . . Now this is another centre for development action . . . that is not made use of. These places look after the souls of people after death. . . . We are not getting full use out of them."[122] Conducting a few rituals and helping the people earn merit that will accrue to their benefit in their next life, the *bhikkhus* had little impact on the social context, Ariyaratne feels. Sarvodaya points to the ancient and traditional role of the *bhikkhu* as "the active leader for social progress,"[123] The revival and reinterpretation of this role has been one of its major goals.

To accomplish this goal Ariyaratne again appeals to the Canon, noting that the Buddha admonished his *bhikkhus* to go forth and travel from place to place "for the benefit of the many, for the welfare of the many, out of compassion for the world."[124] Several factors conspired to destroy the influence of the monks, as we have noted. Although Sarvodaya frequently cites the colonial regimes and Western scholars as forces that sought to separate the monks from society, modernization may have played an even more significant part in making the *Sangha* irrelevant to the daily life of the people. The *bhikkhu*'s education and outlook remained the same even though sweeping changes in society, agriculture, and technology were occurring. As Ratnapala observes, the *bhikkhu*'s knowledge came to be "confined to subjects that had little relation to the enormous changes taking place around him."[125]

The Sarvodaya Movement's interest in reviving the ancient role of the *Sangha* stems both from its aim to reawaken society as a whole and its need for influential leaders in the villages. Clearly, resuscitating the *Sangha* is crucial to any plan to reconstruct a dharmic society. Sarvodaya depicts the ideal social order, derived from Buddhism but now termed a "Sarvodaya social order," to have three main components—the government, the people, and the *Sangha*—existing in a triangular relationship. If Sarvodaya is to build this social order, however, it needs a cadre of effective leaders at the village level. The *Sangha* seems ideally suited for this task. Ariyaratne wrote that "Sarvodaya uncovered the complex role that the monk played in our society in the past and interpreted it to suit the modern context of development, attempting in this way to harness the potentialities of a rural leadership that was not being tapped so far."[126]

From the beginning Sarvodaya worked with the *bhikkhus* and through the temples in each village. Ratnapala notes that "in almost every Buddhist village the monk became the local leader directing and guiding development activity."[127] It soon became evident, however, that the *bhikkhus* needed more training in order to be effective development leaders. In an interview Ratnapala explained that the *bhikkhus* needed to learn modern approaches to modern problems such as venereal disease, suicide, and exploitation. Convinced that the *Sangha* needed education for development, the Sarvodaya leadership founded in 1974 the Bhikkhu Training Institute at Pathakada. Accord-

ing to the learned and respected monk H. Gñanaseeha Thero, whom
Sarvodaya chose to head the institute, its mission was to train *bhikkhus*
in social service so that they may work for "not only the spiritual
development of the village . . . but also (for) the material development
of the community as well."[128]

Located in the rural hill country away from the heat of the coast, the
Bhikkhu Training Institute provides a peaceful atmosphere for learning. The buildings, erected with aid from the German foundation,
Friedrich Naumann Stiftung, comprise classrooms, a library, and dining and residential facilities for sixty *bhikkhus*. Initially the curriculum
included a one-year course, a six-months course, and shorter courses.
The one-year course was eliminated after the first year, however, and
the main course shortened to four months. Subjects taught ranged
from Buddhist philosophy and Sarvodaya philosophy to psychology,
agriculture, and health. With a mix of both theoretical and practical
subjects, the curriculum seemed well designed to turn the young *bhikkhus* into effective change agents. After a few years, however, the
leaders of Sarvodaya began to realize that despite a well-planned facil-
ity and a seemingly well-designed curriculum, the program was not
working as intended. Ratnapala did not overstate the situation when
he wrote in 1976, "There is no doubt that the training has been a limited success."[129]

The Bhikkhu Training Institute had two problems from the outset: it
had difficulty attracting well-qualified *bhikkhus* for the courses, and
many of those *bhikkhus* who took the courses did not go on to apply
their training in actual development work. The applicants to the Institute seem to have declined from around one hundred in 1974 to
around thirty in 1978. The Institute found itself competing unsuccessfully with the universities for the brightest *bhikkhus*. Those accepted
into the university preferred to go there rather than to Pathakada, and
others who came to Pathakada left if they later received acceptance
into the university.[130] Pathakada thus had to accept mainly *bhikkhus*
who had not qualified for the university, and this led to considerable
unevenness in the quality of the students. The first principal of the
Institute compared these *bhikkhus* to a set of "untrained buffaloes."
Another aspect of the problem was that even though the length of the
course was gradually reduced, the Institute had difficulty attracting a

full complement of students because the *bhikkhus* were unable to be away from their home temples for long periods.

Furthermore, those *bhikkhus* who completed the courses frequently did not apply their training by becoming the social change agents that Sarvodaya had envisioned.[131] Venerable Gñanaseeha explained that "the enthusiasm they cultivated during their stay amongst us dwindles gradually once they go back to their monasteries." Also, some of those who enrolled at Pathakada seem to have done so only as a stepping stone to careers other than village development work. Figures compiled by Sarvodaya show that in 1976 of those who had completed the full course at Pathakada, only 26 percent were "serving the community as expected by the originators of the Institute."[132] The *bhikkhus* who only did one of the short courses usually lasting one month had a somewhat higher service rate of 47 percent.

In recent years some steps have been taken to remedy the shortcomings of the Institute's program. Three "feeder" institutions were projected in 1978 to train novice *bhikkhus* prior to sending them on to Pathakada.[133] The current principal of the Institute said in 1985 that plans were being made to have a one-year training course for *bhikkhus* who had graduated from the university. At that time, however, the Institute still had not fulfilled its potential and had few students.

Despite the failure to produce a legion of trained social worker *bhikkhus*, Sarvodaya has continued to involve the *Sangha* in its programs, cooperating with temples and *bhikkhus* that have not gone through the training. Through its division of Bhikkhu Services and its Sarvodaya Bhikkhu (or *Sangha*) Association, the movement has tried more informal means of training monks to assist in development. Again, estimates vary as to how many monks are working with Sarvodaya as a result of this informal training. Macy wrote that "well over a thousand monks" serve Sarvodaya, "many on a full-time basis."[134] Leading *bhikkhus* whom I contacted said that "most *bhikkhus*" are working with Sarvodaya, in the sense of assisting with *shramadāna* campaigns and other occasional projects. When asked how many of these *bhikkhus* serve as full-time development agents, however, one leading *bhikkhu* replied that in the whole island "only a small number are actively involved." Another *bhikkhu* who served as the leader of a Sarvodaya *bhikkhu's* group in the southern part of the country said that in his district about one hundred and fifty *bhikkhus* worked with Sarvodaya, but only one-tenth of those were full-time workers. This seems to be the pattern today. Many *bhikkhus* are willing to cooperate with Sarvodaya, but they cannot be said to serve the movement on a full time basis.

How do the *bhikkhus* regard Sarvodaya's development activity and why do they ally themselves with it? Most of the *bhikkhus* whom I surveyed said that it is appropriate for *bhikkhus* to cooperate with Sarvodaya because social service represents the primary task of the *Sangha*. Again and again the *bhikkhus* cited the Buddha's admonition from the *Dīgha Nikāya (2.48)* that the *Sangha* should "wander for the welfare, the benefit and the good of gods and men." This seems to be a well-known proof text for the *Sangha's* engaging in welfare work. One Thera commented on this verse, saying that the Buddha did not tell the monks to propagate Buddhism but rather to serve for the good and welfare of the people. Given the belief that *bhikkhus* should do social service anyway, these monks felt that it was better to work with Sarvodaya because it has "organized the work well." Although monks can and do work in society on their own, they can be more effective working through Sarvodaya. "Not a single *bhikkhu* is opposed to Sarvodaya," one senior monk explained.

To gauge how extensively Sarvodaya has reformed the monastic role, one can examine the kinds of services the *bhikkhus* perform for Sarvodaya. A minority of those working with Sarvodaya, as the *bhikkhus* cited above explained, do so on a full-time basis. Those who do, serve as Sarvodaya's coordinators or organizers in the villages. Macy notes that fifteen *bhikkhus* serve on Sarvodaya's fifty-one member governing board, the Executive Committee, and one is a district coordinator.[135] The majority of the *bhikkhus*, however, serve in less formal ways on a part-time basis while carrying out the normal duties associated with administering a temple. The most common service that these *bhikkhus* perform for Sarvodaya is to motivate and inspire the villagers for development. The *bhikkhus* from Pathakada with whom I met said that although villagers are often apathetic and lazy, a *bhikkhu* can awaken and enthuse them. This opinion was confirmed by a district coordinator, a layman, who said that the yellow robes of the monk attract people to a *shramadāna* camp. The people will come to work for the monk.

Macy observed that *bhikkhus* are often the ones who introduce the goals of Sarvodaya to the village.[136] Even when a village layperson initiates Sarvodaya's work in that village, he frequently seeks the assistance of the *bhikkhu* in promoting and explaining what Sarvodaya has to offer. During a *shramadāna* campaign the monks not only encourage the people but also teach *Dhamma* during the "family gathering" sessions. Although the rules of the *Vinaya* prevent the *bhikkus* from doing actual construction work at a *shramadāna*, monks occasionally join in the work by doing such things as carrying bricks and passing buckets; but this kind of activity seems much less common than their acting as advisers and directors of the projects.

In addition to organizing and motivating the people for development, the *bhikkhus* also serve Sarvodaya by using their influence with government leaders and other important figures. The ordinary villager may have little clout with the government, but the *bhikkhu* necessarily commands the respect of government officers.[137] One Sarvodaya leader noted that the government agent or wealthy farmer might refuse a villagers' request to borrow his tools, but he cannot refuse a *bhikkhu's* request. The *bhikkhus* remain influential, especially in rural areas—the "top people," one *bhikkhu* said—and their support is vital to Sarvodaya's success in the village.

Do the people accept these changes, or have the *bhikkhus* been criticized for them? Most of the *bhikkhus* reported that their activities on behalf of Sarvodaya had been well received by the people. One elder *bhikkhu* commented that some people will criticize anything new, but if the *bhikkhus* "conduct themselves properly" and explain the projects carefully, the people will accept them. I was unable to verify this claim that no one objects to *bhikkhus* engaging in social service because I did not conduct a survey of villagers to ascertain their opinions. The *bhikkhus*, however, clearly believe that while some people are still critical, most approve of their new role. But fear of criticism by the laity probably has constituted a major factor preventing the *bhikkhus* from going any further in the direction of social work than they have.

Does serving as advisers, motivators, and facilitators mean that the *bhikkhus* have taken on a reformed role Have they become change agents for a Sarvodaya social order? Clearly, the *bhikkhus* believe that they are simply following the Buddha's injunction to serve for the welfare of the people. They feel that Sarvodaya has merely given new scope to this ancient role of the *Sangha*, and that Sarvodaya's form of welfare work is consistent with the Buddha's injunction. Not many of the *bhikkhus* whom I consulted thought that the Buddha's notion of the welfare of the people might have had a strictly spiritual connotation. One senior *bhikkhu*, however, said that social service constitutes a "reduced role" for the *Sangha*. They should be giving spiritual rather than social guidance.

The view that social service is the appropriate role for the monk, however, has been developed by reformist leaders in the Sinhalese Theravada *Sangha* in modern times. The Venerable Walpola Rahula, one of the *bhikkhus* who argued for the political involvement of the *Sangha*, also advocated the importance of social service when, in 1946, he began his book *Bhiksuvage Urumaya (The Heritage of the Bhikkhu)* with the statement, "Buddhism is based on service to others."[138] He went on to cite the above-mentioned proof text ("O *bhikkhus*, . . . wander for the welfare of the many") and to present a stirring argument for the *bhikkhu*'s involvement in social and political affairs. Other monastic leaders have taken the same line, establishing this viewpoint among the progressive *bhikkhus*. Thus, when Sarvodaya decided to involve the *bhikkhus* in social service, it found a ready audience among the *Sangha*.

Although the *bhikkhus* do not feel that they are doing anything outside their traditional roles, and see Sarvodaya's views as consistent with what these leaders in the *Sangha* have said, their involvement with Sarvodaya has nevertheless led to some important changes. The *bhikkhus* may have served as village leaders traditionally, but now they exercise their leadership to help bring development and appropriate technology to the village. Although they have traditionally led the people spiritually in following the *Dhamma*, now they are assisting Sarvodaya in bringing about the dual revolution: awakening the people and awakening society. So, while on the surface little appears to have changed in the way the monks relate to the people, actually a significant change has occurred in the goals to which the *bhikkhus* have commited themselves. The *bhikkhus* who work with Sarvodaya lead the people toward a reinterpreted understanding of both the Buddhist ideals and their application to society. In spite of the difficulties in establishing a full-fledged training program, Sarvodaya has done much to move the *Sangha* toward a world-affirming vocation. Even relatively traditional *bhikkhus* are usually willing to serve Sarvodaya when called upon and by so doing they gain new insights into the meaning of working for the welfare and awakening of all.

Conclusion

Sarvodaya has reinterpreted the *Dhamma*, applying it to social change and development. It has proclaimed a new middle path that avoids the extremes of spiritualism and materialism. As other reformers before him, Ariyaratne has appealed to the Buddhist scriptures and cultural traditions for the charter of this movement. This use of the Buddhist tradition to provide a new understanding of development has been described by Obeyesekere as "practical rationality." He observes that "the implication of the recent Buddhist reform movements is to make the point that practical rationality ought to be articulated to tradition and incorporated into the basic postulates of the religion."[139] In this way not only can modernization draw on tradition for values, but tradition can provide legitimation for the process of modernization. We have seen that Sarvodaya has followed this approach in formulating its philosophy of development.

One question that arises after examining Sarvodaya's theory of development, however, is whether the theory has made a difference in village development activities. In practice, does dharmic development actually have significant differences from Western development? Although I did not conduct a comprehensive survey of Sarvodaya's development activities in the villages, I can offer some insights based on observations and discussions with Sarvodaya's leaders and workers in various parts of the island. Basically it appears that although Sarvodaya has not effected the complete social revolution that it seeks, the movement has instituted significant programs based on its philosophy. The most obvious success in applying the philosophy has been the *shramadāna* campaigns. Here the movement has redefined the Buddhist ideal of *dāna*, sharing, giving it a practical application to the problems villagers face. *Shramadāna* has proved effective in bringing about Sarvodaya's dual awakening of both persons and society. Ariyaratne says that "the most outstanding contribution that the Movement has made to the social development of Sri Lanka, in my opinion, is the re-introduction of the technique of *shramadāna*.[140] Obeyesekere, although questioning Ariyaratne's claim that it is an ancient practice reintroduced, says that in the practice of *shramadāna* Sarvodaya has introduced "a concept of voluntary selfless giving of one's labour" and that this represents a "truly significant innovation."[141]

Although *shramadāna* has been the most visible application of the *Dhamma* to development, Sarvodaya workers cited many other ways that Sarvodaya's Buddhist values have made a difference in practice. They spoke about projects based on *ahiṃsā*, nonviolence, such as one village's dairy program which did not sell the excess cows and bulls for slaughter. At another center Sarvodaya was experimenting with various methods of organic farming both to protect the environment and to save on the expense of fertilizers and pesticides. The ideals of self-reliance and right livelihood are manifest in Sarvodaya's vocational training programs for youth in places such as Tanamalvila and Kandy. These programs are teaching young people appropriate technology for the village rather than preparing them to work on the assembly line of a factory in the city. Countless projects begun by Sarvodaya put compassion and concern for people ahead of profits and material gain. One center instituted a milk collection program that divided the profits equally among the producers, eliminating the middleman who formerly had taken a disproportionate share of the profits. At an urban center the director had great success with a criminal rehabilitation program because the ex-convicts were treated as equals by the Sarvodayans and came to trust them.

Time and again people told me that the philosophy or theory of development has filtered down to the practical level. One district leader said, "The work and the philosophy go hand in hand." Another said that "everything we do comes from the philosophy." The reinterpretation of the *Dhamma* not only provides values for development but also inspires the people's confidence in the movement and its programs. These programs seek to provide alternatives to materialistic development practices; they seek a simpler, more self-sufficient life with humane values.

Has Sarvodaya succeeded in these aims? This question has been asked frequently of Sarvodaya by its Western aid partners because evaluation is essential to Western development models. For Sarvodaya, however, evaluation becomes more difficult. Ariyaratne says that he has occasionally agreed to allow so-called objective measurement techniques in order to justify the movement to the outside funding agencies. The whole thrust of the Sarvodaya Movement, however, dictates that its approach to development cannot be measured by the same standards as Western or materialist development. The overall objective is awakening, not productivity or economic growth. While Sarvodaya's programs may not have turned Sri Lanka overnight into the perfect *Dhammadīpa*, they undoubtedly have created places in the country where the *Dhamma* can be both heard and lived. These communities facilitate the goal of a dual awakening, and we cannot doubt that at least mundane awakening has occured for many people. Ariyaratne says that "by personal experience I know that tens of thousands of our rural people have awakened to sacrifice their time, thought and energy through the Shramadana Movement to build up a better Sri Lanka."[142] "We build the road and the road builds us."

Sarvodaya has been criticized for this reformist understanding of the *Dhamma* which regards awakening as attainable by this-worldly asceticism. To be sure, Sarvodaya has departed from the traditional understanding of the path and the goals for laity. In the end, however, Sarvodaya does not go so far as to equate social reform and mundane awakening with *Nibbāna* in this life, *loka Nibbāna*. Burmese reformers during the first half of this century seem to have made such equations.[143] But as we have seen, Sarvodaya, ever optimistic about human potential, still regards the highest *Nibbāna* as supramundane, requiring many lifetimes to achieve. Mundane awakening is not *Nibbāna* in the traditional Buddhist sense, but leads to it. Mundane awakening represents a valuable spiritual, ethical, and personal consciousness raising that produces better individuals as well as better communities. Sarvodaya has reinterpreted the path and the goal, but not totally. It retains a notion of the path as gradual, even if the path now has this-worldly asceticism as its task; and it retains the ultimate goal of a supramundane *Nibbāna*, even if it also speaks of a mundane awakening. Sarvodaya has recognized the insights into the truth of the Buddhist tradition that Bardwell Smith expressed when he wrote, "The work of social welfare, even the reconstruction of society along more rational and just lines, is therefore crucial to the nirvanic quest, though not equatable with it."[144] Sarvodaya holds that the reordering of society in accord with the *Dhamma* represents an essential prerequisite for enabling people to attain *Nibbāna*. This agrees with traditional Theravada. Sarvodaya's reformist interpretation says also, however, that dedicating oneself to reconstructing society along these lines can serve as a vehicle for attaining both mundane awakening and—for some—supramundane awakening.

Another indication of Sarvodaya's success or influence might be the emergence of other groups in Sri Lanka that have started social service or development programs inspired directly or indirectly by Sarvodaya. For example, two of the most important Buddhist temples in the Colombo area, the Bellanwila Rājamahā Vihāra and the Gangaramaya Vihāra, have established successful programs of this sort. At Bellanwila the program is called the Community Development Foundation. Begun in 1981 by Venerable Dr. Bellanwila Wimalaratne, this foundation operates an extensive vocational training school and also conducts *shramadāna* work. Ven. Wimalaratne describes the aim of the foundation as providing technological education and training to youth in a Buddhist environment. The wide variety of courses in subjects as diverse as automobile repair and Oriental dancing are intended to equip the students for employment. The Gangaramaya Vihāra, a temple in central Colombo, sponsors a similar technical training school enrolling some eight hundred students.

These two institutions have clearly been influenced by Sarvodaya, yet they differ from Sarvodaya in significant ways. That the Bellanwila temple's Community Development Foundation followed Sarvodaya's example is manifest from its descriptions of its programs. Its brochures state that the courses were begun to teach technical skills "for development of human qualities and intellectual development" and to "promote a Buddhist religious atmosphere conducive to the promotion of spiritual development." Acknowledging the example of Sarvodaya, the foundation invited Ariyaratne to speak at its dedication ceremonies. Even the symbol or logo of this foundation resembles that of Sarvodaya.

Yet these two institutions have some important differences from Sarvodaya. The most obvious and striking distinction is that both are headed by monks and have their headquarters in temples. This contrasts with Sarvodaya, a lay organization in both inception and operation. We noted, however, Sarvodaya's involvement with the *Sangha*, and these monastic social service institutions might be seen as at least indirect outgrowths of that involvement. As we also noted, though, monks have been active in social service traditionally. These two examples then seem to represent a number of influences: Sarvodaya's activities; the old Protestant Buddhist expectation that temples and monasteries should perform social service; and the monks' own heightened consciousness about their true vocation. In addition, both of the monastic leaders who began these programs have lived abroad and were influenced by Western models. Venerable Wimalaratne said that he had the idea for the Community Development Foundation after he returned from a period of study in England.

These vocational training institutions are more pragmatic and less philosophical than Sarvodaya. They have not evolved an elaborate philosophy to support what they are doing, but that may be because they assume that the *Dhamma* which is the foundation of the temple also constitutes the foundation of their programs. They seek to promote the *Dhamma* through their programs, but without fanfare. The head of the Gangaramaya project replied that he carries out this work just because it makes him happy. Venerable Wimalaratne said that he did not teach *Dhamma* explicitly to the students except on holidays, but he tried constantly to teach them *Dhamma* by example. He hoped that the youth would come to appreciate the *Dhamma* by being exposed to the life of the temple where they attend their classes. Interestingly, these temple-based programs seem to stress this-worldly asceticism as much as, or more than, Sarvodaya. The head of the Bellanwila program, for example, expressed disinterest in teaching *vipassanā bhāvanā* because he felt that it is not necessary to retreat from the world to do meditation. Bellanwila's programs of training are very much world-affirming, but make no claims to constitute a this-worldly *Nibbāna*.

The youth represent the main reason these programs have sprung up. The technical training classes seek to address the serious problem of high unemployment among educated young people. This problem did not exist when Sarvodaya began, and although Sarvodaya too has sought to deal with it through vocational training, it has not been the determining factor for Sarvodaya as it has for these programs. Through vocational training the students can, it is hoped, find useful roles in society, roles for which their standard education did not prepare them. Although these two temple schools avoid explicit indoctrination in *Dhamma* and meditation, they view their programs of preparation in Buddhist terms. They express hopes that they can instill the spirit of service in the youth. The leaders of the programs also feel that by these courses and social actions they are putting the Buddha's teachings into practice.

Following Sarvodaya's lead, these temples have given the *Dhamma* a social gospel interpretation. Although traditional temple services and rituals continue to be conducted, a temple such as Bellanwila has entered a new era by promoting vocational training while eschewing meditation. Out of a new understanding of their identity, these monastic leaders have responded to the social context and needs of the present.

Notes

1. Robert N. Bellah, ed. *Religion and Progress in Modern Asia* (New York: Free Press, 1965), 207; Donald K. Swearer, "Thai Buddhism: Two Responses to Modernity," in *Tradition and Change in Theravada Buddhism*; ed. Bardwell L. Smith (Leiden: Brill, 1973); S. J. Tambiah, *World Conqueror and World Renouncer* (New York: Cambridge University Press, 1976); Bardwell L. Smith, "Sinhalese Buddhism and the Dilemmas of Reinterpretation," in *The Two Wheels of Dhamma: Essays on the Theravada Tradition in India and Ceylon*, ed. Bardwell Smith (Chambersburg, PA: American Academy of Religion, 1972).

2. Bellah, *Religion and Progress*, 210.

3. One scholar who has argued this is Gananath Obeyesekere, "The Economic Ethics of Buddhism: Reflections on Buddhist Modernism in South and Southeast Asia" (Unpublished paper, 1984).

4. Bardwell L. Smith, "Toward a Buddhist Anthropology: The Problem of the Secular," *Journal of the American Academy of Religion*, 36 (1968): 208.

5. Letter in *The Buddhist*, 37.4 (Sept. 1966); 97, cited in Donald K. Swearer, "Lay Buddhism and the Buddhist Revival in Ceylon," *Journal of the American Academy of Religion*, 38.3 (1970): 262.

6. Joanna Macy, *Dharma and Development: Religion as Resource in the Sarvodaya Self-Help Movement* (West Hartford, CT: Kumarian Press, 1983), 87.

7. Denis Goulet, *Survival with Integrity: Sarvodaya at the Crossroads* (Colombo: The Marga Institute, 1981), xviii.

8. A. T. Ariyaratne, *Collected Works*, ed. N. Ratnapala (Moratuwa Sarvodaya Research Institute, n.d.), 1: 48.

9. A. T. Ariyaratne, *In Search of Development: The Sarvodaya Shramadāna Movement's Effort to Harmonize Tradition with Change* (Moratuwa: Sarvodaya Press, 1982).

10. Ariyaratne, *Collected Works*, 1: 57.

11. Nandasena Ratnapala, *Study Service in the Sarvodaya Shramadāna Movement in Sri Lanka 1958-1976* (Colombo: Sarvodaya Research Centre, 1976), 16.

12. Ariyaratne, *Collected Works*, 1: 63.

13. *Ibid.*, p. 48.

14. Much of the information in this chapter I learned from Dr. Ariyaratne during interviews with him in Sri Lanka and Hawaii during 1984 and 1985.

15. Detlef Kantowski, *Sarvodaya, the Other Development* (New Delhi: Vikas Publishing House, 1980), 44.

16. Kantowski, *Sarvodaya*, 45.

17. Ariyaratne, *Collected Works*, 1: 106.

18. *Sarvodaya Annual Service Report*, Apr. 1983–Mar. 1984 (Moratuwa: Sarvodaya Publications, 1984), 34.

19. Tambiah, *World Conqueror*, 401.

20. Tambiah, *World Conqueror* 433.

21. Macy, *Dharma and Development*, 76.

22. Kūṭadanta Sutta in *Dīgha Nikāya*, ed. T. W. Rhys Davids and J. Carpenter (London: Pali Text Society, 1967), I: 127–48.

23. Sigālovāda Sutta, in *Dīgha Nikāya*, 3: ed. J. Carpenter (London: Pali Text Society, 1911), 180–93; Mahāmangala Sutta in *Sutta Nipāta*, ed. D. Andersen and H. Smith (London: Pali Text Society, 1913), 46–47; Parābahava Sutta, in *Sutta Nipāta*, 18–20.

24. L. G. Hewage, *Relevance of Cultural Heritage in Development Education*; paper presented to the Conference on Sarvodaya and Development, 1976, p. 31.

25. Winston King, *In the Hope of Nibbāna: An Essay on Theravada Buddhist Ethics* (LaSalle, IL: Open Court, 1964), 177.

26. Ariyaratne, "Introduction," Macy, *Dharma and Development*, 14.

27. A. T. Ariyaratne, "The Role of Buddhist Monks in Development," *World Development*, 8 (1980): 588.

28. Kantowski, *Sarvodaya*, 182.

29. Edward Said, *Orientalism* (New York: Pantheon, 1978), 10ff.

30. Walpola Rahula, *The Heritage of the Bhikkhu*, trans. K. P. G. Wijayasurendra (New York: Grove Press, 1974), 3.

31. Ariyaratne, *Collected Works*, 1: 132.

32. Obeyesekere, "The Economic Ethics of Buddhism," 3.

33. Obeyesekere, "The Economic Ethics of Buddhism," 54.

34. Ariyaratne, *In Search of Development*, 22-28.

35. Susantha Goonatilake, "Review of *Collected Works of A. T. Ariyaratne*," *Journal of Contemporary Asia*, 13.2 (1983). 236–242.

36. Ariyaratne, *A Reply from a Conduit* (Moratuwa: Sarvodaya Publications, 1981), 10–11.

37. Milton Singer, *When a Great Tradition Modernizes* (New York: Praeger, 1972), 383–414.

38. Obeyesekere, p. 33.

39. Ariyaratne, *Collected Works*, 1: 52–53.

40. Ariyaratne, *Collected Works*, 1: 133.

41. *Collected Works*, 1: 124.

42. Kantowski, *Sarvodaya*, 44.

43. Macy, *Dharma and Development*, 87.

The Buddhist Revival in Sri Lanka

44. Ariyaratne, "Introduction," Macy, *Dharma and Development*, 15.
45. Ariyaratne repeated this frequent assertion in my interviews with him.
46. The following quotations, unless otherwise noted, are from my interviews with these leaders.
47. *Collected Works*, 1: 47.
48. Kantowski, *Sarvodaya*, 77.
49. Ariyaratne, "Introduction," Macy, *Dharma and Development*, 15.
50. Macy, *Dharma and Development*, 49.
51. Nandasena Ratnapala, *Study Service in Sarvodaya* (Colombo: Sarvodaya Research Centre, 1976), 12.
52. Macy, *Dharma and Development*, 30.
53. This comment was made by Ariyaratne during an interview in 1983.
54. A. T. Ariyaratne, *Whence? Wherefore? Whither?* (Colombo: Sarvodaya Office, 1963), 3.
55. Kantowski, *Sarvodaya*, 74–75.
56. *Collected Works*, 1: 47.
57. *Collected Works*, 1: 49.
58. Ariyaratne, *In Search of Development*, 12.
59. *Collected Works*, 1: 73.
60. Kantowski, *Sarvodaya*, 68.
61. *Collected Works*, 1: 92.
62. Macy, *Dharma and Development*, 33.
63. Kantowski, *Sarvodaya*, 204.
64. Joanna Macy, "Buddhist Approaches to Social Action," *Journal of Humanistic Psychology*, 24 (1984): 122.
65. Goulet, *Survival with Integrity*, 80, 85.
66. A. T. Ariyaratne, *Collected Works*, Vol. 2 (Moratuwa: Sarvodaya Research Institute, 1980), 29.
67. *Collected Works*, 2: 76f.
68. A. T. Ariyaratne, *A Struggle to Awaken* (Moratuwa; Sarvodaya Shramadāna Movement, 1982), 4.
69. A. T. Ariyaratne, *Sarvodaya and Development* (Moratuwa: Sarvodaya Publications, 1980), 4.
70. Godfrey Gunatilleke, "Introduction," to Goulet, *Survival with Integrity, p. xii.*
71. Ariyaratne, *Struggle to Awaken*, 13.
72. *Collected Works*, 1: 85.
73. *Collected Works*, 1: 135.
74. Macy, *Dharma and Development*, 44.
75. Ariyaratne, *Struggle to Awaken*, 20.
76. *Collected Works*, 1: 167.
77. Heinz Bechert, "*Sangha*, State, Society 'Nation': Persistence of Traditions in 'Post-Traditional' Buddhist Societies," *Daedalus*, 102 (1973): 91.
78. *Collected Works*, 1: 133.
79. *In Search of Development*, 13.
80. *Collected Works*, 2: 78.

81. *Collected Works*, 2: 81.
82. *Collected Works*, 2: 98.
83. Ariyaratne, *Sarvodaya and Development*, 4.
84. Macy, *Dharma and Development*, 32.
85. Ariyaratne, *In Search of Development*, 36.
86. Bellah, *Religion and Progress*, 195.
87. *Collected Works*, 1: 26.
88. Ariyaratne, *In Search of Development*, 30.
89. An explanation of karma given by Ariyaratne during an interview.
90. Ariyaratne, *In Search of Development*, 16.
91. Macy, *Dharma and Development*, 36f.
92. Macy, *Dharma and Development*, 37.
93. *Collected Works*, 1: 50.
94. Macy, "Buddhist Approaches to Social Action," 126.
95. Macy, "Buddhist Approaches . . .," 126.
96. See *Visuddhimagga*, ed. C.A.F. Rhys Davids, (London: Pali Text Society, 1975), 499.
97. Macy, *Dharma and Development*, 32.
98. Macy, *Dharma and Development*, 33.
99. *Collected Works*, 2: 84.
100. *Collected Works*, 1: 50.
101. Ariyaratne, *In Search of Development*, 14.
102. *Collected Works*, 2: 79f.
103. Macy, *Dharma and Development*, 53.
104. *Collected Works*, 1: 119.
105. *Collected Works*, 2: 49-50.
106. King, *In the Hope of Nibbāna*, 183.
107. Macy, *Dharma and Development*, 77.
108. *Collected Works*, 2: 56.
109. *Collected Works*, 2: 78.
110. *Collected Works*, 2: 56.
111. Kantowski, *Sarvodaya*, 74.
112. Macy, *Dharma and Development*, 32.
113. *Ten Basic Human Needs and Their Satisfaction* (Moratuwa: Sarvodaya Development Education Institute, n.d.).
114. Hans Wismeijer, "Diversity in Harmony: A Study of the Leaders, the Sarvodaya Shramadāna Movement in Sri Lanka" (PhD. diss., University of Utrecht, 1981), 189.
115. *Ten Basic Human Needs*, 52.
116. Obeyesekere, "The Economic Ethics of Buddhism," 37.
117. Swearer, "Lay Buddhism and the Buddhist Revival," 263.
118. Ernest Gellner, *Saints of the Atlas* (Chicago: University of Chicago Press, 1969), 7.
119. *Collected Works*, 2: 80.
120. Singer, *When a Great Tradition Modernizes*, 400.
121. *Ten Basic Human Needs*, 51.
122. *Collected Works*, 1: 124.

123. Kantowski, *Sarvodaya*, 125.
124. *Vinaya Pitaka*, ed. H. Oldenberg (London: Pali Text Society, 1964), 1: 21.
125. Ratnapala, *Study Service*, 106.
126. Ariyaratne, "Role of Buddhist Monks in Development," *World Development*, 8 (1980): 588.
127. Ratnapala, *Study Service*, 111.
128. Kantowski, *Sarvodaya*, 125.
129. Ratnapala, *Study Service*, 109.
130. Ratnapala, *Study Service*, 109.
131. As to how many students actually completed the course, estimates vary. In 1976 Sarvodaya reported that 557 *bhikkhus* had been trained in either the full course or a short course. In 1985 a leader of the movement estimated that more than 2,000 *bhikkhus* had undergone training.
132. Ratnapala, *Study Service*, 107.
133. Kantowski, *Sarvodaya*, 129.
134. Macy, *Dharma and Development*, 64.
135. Macy, *Dharma and Development*, 65.
136. Macy, *Dharma and Development*, 66.
137. Macy, *Dharma and Development*, 70.
138. Rahula, *Heritage of the Bhikkhu*, 3.
139. Obeyesekere, "Economic Ethics," 51.
140. *Collected Works*, 1: 26f.
141. Obeyesekere, "Economic Ethics," 33.
142. *Collected Works*, 2: 47.
143. E. Sarkisyanz, *Buddhist Backgrounds of the Burmese Revolution* (The Hague: M. Nijoff, 1965), 125f.
144. Bardwell Smith, "Sinhalese Buddhism and the Dilemmas of Reinterpretation," 102.

Conclusion

These chapters have attempted to analyze the meaning and significance of the revival of Buddhism among the laity of Sri Lanka. Several sets of issues serve to illustrate the central dynamic of this revitalization process. First, the revival has been a process of tradition and interpretation. Interpretation is seen to be not only a means of understanding texts, but a living process by which people re-present an ancient religious tradition in modern times. Second, the revival exemplifies the necessary relation between social context and cosmology. Changes in the social context in Sri Lanka during the colonial period rendered traditional Theravada cosmology less plausible and meaningful to many Buddhists. Laypeople who had moved from the group-oriented context of the village to the individual-oriented context of the urban areas found the traditional Theravada ritual system and goals for laity no longer meaningful. The cosmology, or Buddhist world view, that had guided village culture did not offer the same edification to those who experienced the changes that had occurred in the political, economic, educational, and social aspects of their lives. The task of reinterpreting Buddhism for this new context fell to the new urban lay elite who emerged into positions of leadership during the colonial period. Although the Sangha had fired some of the initial salvos of the Buddhist revival through their debates with the missionaries at Pānadurā and elsewhere, the laity assumed much of the burden of reviving the tradition because in many ways the *Sangha* had lost both power and influence under the British colonial regime.

Finally, we have seen that the central issue of reinterpretation has been the dilemma of identity and responsiveness: the emerging lay elite who had been educated in English with a European curriculum sought ways to recover their traditional identity as Buddhists while still responding to the modern innovations shaping their world. Although the British colonial administrators and the missionaries had done all that they could to convey the impression that the Sinhalese people's Buddhist heritage had no relevance in a modern, scientific world, the lay Buddhists were unwilling and unable to give up their identities. The revival of Buddhism can thus be seen as an attempt on the part of the newly arisen lay Buddhists to reinterpret their heritage, to find adaptive strategies that would enable them to respond to modernity without becoming Western in their values and outlook.

This quest to re-present the meaning of the Theravada tradition has constituted a long historical process involving many influences and evoking varied interpretations. The diversity as well as the unity of the Buddhist revival among the laity can be seen in the four patterns of reinterpretation and response identified in chapter one: Protestant Buddhism; Jayanti period neo-traditionalism; the insight meditation movement, *vipassanā*; and the social development movement manifested by Sarvodaya. Certainly, these patterns do not encompass all of the interpretations that have emerged, but they do represent four of the most important and distinct patterns for laity in the spectrum of responses of the revival. These four responses exemplify two basic alternatives for reinterpreting the tradition: neotraditionalism and reformism. The revival among the laity began with the rational reformism of the Theosophists and Anagārika Dharmapāla. Dharmapāla, having mastered the rationalistic outlook of his Theosophist mentors, created his own reformist interpretation of Sinhalese Buddhism, which became the foundation for the revival. Dharmapāla's interpretation embodied the three elements that Bellah finds basic to reformism: an appeal to early teachers and texts, a rejection of much of the traditional cosmology, and an emphasis upon social reform and national regeneration.[1] In his writings and speeches Dharmapāla explicitly called on the Sinhalese to rediscover their identity as Buddhists; he assured the people that recovering their identity would be the best means of responding to the new challenges facing them. It was Dharmapāla who did the most to conjoin in the contemporary Sinhalese mentality Buddhism and Sinhalese nationalism. Although Dharmapāla proclaimed the value of their traditional Buddhist heritage, he reinterpreted it in a reformist fashion, rationalizing both the path and the goal and making them more accessible to laypersons than they had been traditionally.

The reformism of this Protestant Buddhism gave way, however, to neotraditionalism as the lay organizations that succeeded Dharmapāla opted for a more conventional and less radical view of Buddhism. Lay organizations such as the Young Men's Buddhist Association and the All Ceylon Buddhist Congress, while revering Dharmapāla, adopted an interpretation of Buddhism that was much more traditional than his. Their response to the challenges of modernization and Westernization was to return to the ancient values of Theravada. Both the lay leaders and the monastic leaders to whom they deferred proclaimed that the *Dhamma* constituted eternal truth, as relevant today as it was in the time when the Buddha declared it. When others suggested that the *Dhamma* should be reinterpreted because the conditions in the country and the outlook of science had changed, they responded that this was exactly why they should not reinterpret it; the *Dhamma* was the one unchanging reality amid all the change. They protested that they were not reinterpreting the *Dhamma* but merely reiterating its timeless truths. Of course, they actually were reinterpreting it, but in a neotraditional fashion that saw both the goal and the path in traditional ways. The goal of *Nibbāna* was for them still a remote goal to be sought only by virtuosos willing to renounce the household life. Although Dharmapala had preached universalism, opening the path to all, these lay Buddhists affirmed the traditional distinctions between the roles of the monks and the laity. They were content to follow the "preliminary course" of merit-making, updated somewhat for modern times.

This response flowered in the Buddha Jayanti period and produced a host of proposals and initiatives designed to restore both Buddhism and the Buddhists to their "rightful place" in Sri Lanka. The neotraditional response was undoubtedly the most appropriate one for many people who found support in its strong affirmation of their Buddhist identity and its restatement of familiar values. Even today this neotraditional response continues to flourish among many lay Buddhists. But while this interpretation may have satisfied the demands of the identity pole of the dilemma of interpretation, it does not seem to have constituted an appropriate answer to the other pole of the dilemma: responsiveness. The failure of so many of the proposals from the Buddhist Committee of Enquiry and the Jayanti period suggests that these attempts to return to ancient values and ways have not been the most effective response. For example, although the conjunction of Buddhism and nationalism may have been a necessary way to revitalize both the tradition and the nation after independence, it led to the tragic distortions that have resulted in the Sinhala-Tamil ethnic conflict.

In contrast to this neotraditionalism, two responses that have emerged in the post-Jayanti period have been characterized by the motifs of reformism. Just as lay associations promoted the neotraditional interpretation, so other lay groups have arisen to establish the reformist interpretation of the tradition through the *vipassanā* movement and the Sarvodaya movement. Like the neotraditionalists, these reformers grounded their interpretations in the Buddhist scriptures and found ample basis in the texts for their views. Sarvodaya, for example, found its charter in texts that showed that Buddhism was socially relevant; they rejected those traditional interpretations that lacked this social emphasis.

Both Sarvodaya and the *vipassanā* movement provided rational interpretations of the goal and the path of the tradition. Optimistic about the spiritual potential of the laity, the *vipassanā* reformers proclaimed that *Nibbāna* could be attained in the present. The Sarvodaya Movement, while stressing that awakening constituted an immediate rather than a distant goal for laypersons, also distinguished between a practical, mundane awakening and the traditional supramundane awakening. This reinterpretation of the goal was in keeping with the pragmatic character of reformism.

Neither Sarvodaya nor the *vipassanā* movement has accepted the traditionalist view that the householder's path represents a "preliminary course" of merit-making over many lifetimes. The essence of both of these movements has been to develop Buddhist forms of this-worldly asceticism. Advocating universalism and affirming this world, they have taught the laity to pursue the path in their daily lives. We have seen how the meditators have employed *vipassanā* to cope with the *dukkha* of existence and how Sarvodaya has established *karma yoga*, work in the world, as the means to self-realization.

These motifs of reformism indicate some of the ways that these two movements have reinterpreted the Theravada tradition and enabled people to reach a new understanding of their identities as Buddhists. These changes have been significant. As Michael Ames wrote, "Sinhalese religion is undergoing what has been defined here as structural change."[2] By enabling the lay Theravadins to recover their identity in these ways, the reformists have also equipped them to deal meaningfully with the issue of responsiveness, the other pole of the hermeneutical dilemma. The reformist movements have been more successful than the neotraditionalists in this regard. The reformists have fulfilled what some observers saw to be the outstanding agenda of the Buddhist revival after the Jayanti. Swearer, for example, wrote that "the progress of Buddhism in Ceylon will depend largely on the ability of Buddhist laymen . . . to help formulate appropriate ways for Buddhism to engage the contemporary world."[3] The lay Buddhists have played key roles in these reformist movements. Although they have worked closely with elements of the *Sangha*, the laity frequently have been the leaders in reinterpreting the Buddhist path for both monks and laypersons, as, for example, in Sarvodaya's proclamation of a social *Dhamma*.

Both Sarvodaya and *vipassanā* have grown and prospered because they have offered people meaningful ways to respond to the modern world out of a Buddhist heritage. Sarvodaya has set forth a new middle path avoiding the extremes of both a pure spiritualism and a materialistic social development movement. It has met the need that one observer pointed to when he said, "The development of a Buddhist social ethic and the organizational means to apply it to contemporary problems are the pressing requirements of the times. But it is still not clear how this social gospel is to be reconciled with the ideal of renunciation."[4] Sarvodaya has answered this with its *karma yoga* and its twofold awakening that links the liberation of the individual with the liberation of society. Acting in the world while renouncing attachment is seen as the way to correct the greed and selfishness that lie at the root of suffering, *dukkha*. Also, rather than accepting the Western parameters of modernity, Sarvodaya has employed its Buddhist heritage to redefine modern ideas such as progress and development. Similarly, *vipassanā* has enabled people to respond to their worlds. The meditators have found *vipassanā* to be, as Goenka called it, "the art of living."[5] Another meditator summed up the significance of *vipassanā* for this age when he wrote, "At the present time with our ever-increasing emphasis on material development, we are in fact getting more and more dehumanized. . . . Meditation is the only way for us and the sooner we get to it the better."[6]

Two comments by meditators whom I met provide a graphic contrast between the viewpoint of the neotraditionalists and that of the reformists. The first meditator was a young man in his twenties who recounted that he had grown up aspiring to become a monk. When he went to the temple, however, and told the senior monk about his desire to become a monk in order to seek *Nibbāna* through meditation, the monk discouraged him, saying that there is no point in becoming a monk to seek *Nibbāna* for it cannot be attained by either a monk or a layman in this age. After this incident, though, the young man met Anagārika Nārada and became an ardent lay meditator. The second meditator, whose comment illustrates the spiritual optimism of the *vipassanā* movement, was a member of the Getambe meditation group. When I asked him whether he thought *Nibbāna* was attainable today, he replied, "Of course *Nibbāna* is attainable. Otherwise what is the point of Buddhism?"

The Buddhist revival constitutes a spectrum of interpretations encompassing all of these viewpoints, from the spiritual optimism of this reformist at Getambe to the neotraditionalist interpretations that we have examined. Although some of these interpretations may seem more adequate than others, all have arisen as attempts by contemporary Theravadins to reinterpret their tradition for their particular contexts in the present. As we have noted, almost all of these viewpoints can be defended as legitimate interpretations grounded in the Buddhist scriptures. On this reading the Theravada revival constitutes a new gradual path with levels and goals adapted to the diversity of modern society. This metaphor of the gradual path helps us to understand how the various patterns of response that we have identified function and coexist in Sinhalese society. By virtue of the freedom that the laity have had to reinterpret the tradition, Sinhalese Theravada today exhibits a pluralistic character providing many options for people to define and develop their Buddhist identities. Yet, beneath the pluralism there is a unity, the unity of the meaning and goal of the *Dhamma*, just as in the traditional gradual path.

Notes

1. Robert N. Bellah, ed., *Religion and Progress in Modern Asia* (New York: Free Press, 1965), 210.
2. Michael Ames, "The Impact of Western Education on Religion and Society in Ceylon," *Pacific Affairs* 40 (1967): 37.
3. Donald K. Swearer, "Lay Buddhism and the Buddhism Revival in Ceylon," *Journal of The American Academy of Religion* 38 (1970): 259.
4. Donald E. Smith, ed., *South Asian Politics and Religion*, 509.
5. S. N. Goenka, *The Art of Living: Vipassanā Meditation* (Shelburne Falls, MA: *Vipassanā* Meditation Center: 1984).
6. Asoka Devendra, "Meditation in Day to Day Living," *Vesak Sirisara*, May, 1983: 127.

Bibliography

Aṅguttara Nikāya, five vols., 1885–1900. Morris, R. and E. Hardy, eds. London: Pali Text Society.

Allen, Joseph L., 1968. "Interpreting the Contemporary Social Revolution: The Revolution of Secularization," unpublished paper.

Ames, Michael, 1963. "Ideological and Social Change in Ceylon," *Human Organization*, vol. XXII, no. 1, Spring, p. 45–53.

———1964. "Magical Animism and Buddhism: A Structural Analysis of the Sinhalese Religious System," *Journal of Asian Studies*, vol. 23, p. 21–53.

———1967. "The Impact of Western Education on Religion and Society in Ceylon," *Pacific Affairs*, vol. 40, no. 1–2, p. 19–41.

———1973. "Westernization or Modernization: The Case of Sinhalese Buddhism," *Social Compass*, vol. XX, 1972/3, p. 139–165.

Ariyaratne, A. T., n.d. *Collected Works*, vol. I, N. Ratnapala, ed. Moratuwa: Sarvodaya Research Institute.

———1963. *Whence? Wherefore? Whither?* Moratuwa: Sarvodaya Publications.

———1980a. *Sarvodaya and Development.* Moratuwa: Sarvodaya Publications.

———1980b. *Collected Works*, vol. II, N. Ratnapala, ed. Moratuwa: Sarvodaya Research Institute.

———1981. *A Reply from a Conduit.* Moratuwa: Sarvodaya Publications.

———1982a. *A Struggle to Awaken.* Moratuwa: Sarvodaya Publications.

———1982b. *In Search of Development: The Sarvodaya Movement's Effort to Harmonize Tradition with Change.* Moratuwa: Sarvodaya Press.

306

Bechert, Heinz, 1966, 1967, 1973. *Buddhismus, Staat, Und Geselschaft, in den Ländern des Theravada-Buddhismus.* 3 vols. Frankfurt: A. Metzner, Wiesbaden, O. Harrassowitz.

———1970. "Theravada Buddhist Sangha: Some General Observations on Historical and Political Factors in Its Development," *Journal of Asian Studies,* vol. 29, no. 4, August 1970.

———1973a. "Contradictions in Sinhalese Buddhism," *Tradition and Change in Theravada Buddhism,* Bardwell L. Smith, ed. Leiden: E. J. Brill, p. 7–17.

———1973b. "Sangha, State, Society, 'Nation': Persistence of Traditions in 'Post-Traditional' Buddhist Societies," *Daedalus,* vol. 102, no. 1, Winter, p. 85–95.

Bellah, Robert, ed., 1965. *Religion and Progress in Modern Asia.* New York: The Free Press.

———1970. *Beyond Belief.* Evanston: Harper and Row.

Bloss, Lowell W., 1987. "Female Renunciants of Sri Lanka: The *Dasasilmattawa*," *Journal of the International Association of Buddhist Studies.* vol. 10, no. 1, p. 7–32.

Bodhi, Bhikkhu, 1978. *The All Embracing Net of Views: The Brahamajāla Sutta and Its Commentaries.* Kandy: Buddhist Publication Society.

Bond, George D., 1980. "Theravada Buddhism and the Aims of Buddhist Studies," *Studies in the History of Buddhism,* A. K. Narain, ed. Delhi: B.R. Publishing Corporation.

———1983. *"The Word of the Buddha": The Tipiṭaka and Its Interpretation in Theravada Buddhism.* Colombo: Gunasena and Co.

———1984. "The Development and Elaboration of the Arahant Ideal in the Theravada Buddhist Tradition," *Journal of the American Academy of Religion,* vol. LII, no. 2, p. 227–242.

———1987. "The Insight Meditation Movement in Contemporary Theravada Buddhism," *Journal of the Institute for the Study of Religion and Culture,* vol. 2, no. 4, p. 23–76.

Bond, George D., and Richard Kieckhefer, eds., (1988). *Sainthood: Its Manifestations in World Religions.* Berkeley: University of California Press.

Boulding, Kenneth, 1965. *The Meaning of the Twentieth Century: The Great Transition.* New York: Harper and Row.

Buddhagosa, 1975. *Visuddhimagga,* C. A. F. Rhys Davids, ed. London: Pali Text Society.

Buddhist Committee of Inquiry, 1956. *The Betrayal of Buddhism: An Abridged Version of the Report of the Buddhist Committee of Enquiry.* Balangoda: Dharmavijaya Press.

Carrithers, Michael, 1979. "The Modern Ascetics of Lanka and the Pattern of Change in Buddhism," *Man,* vol. XIV, p. 294–310.

————1983. *The Forest Monks of Sri Lanka: An Anthropological and Historical Study*. Delhi: Oxford University Press.

Collins, Steven, 1982. *Selfless Persons: Imagery and Thought in Theravada Buddhism*. Cambridge: Cambridge University Press.

Cone, Margaret, and Richard Gombrich, 1977. *The Perfect Generosity of Prince Vessantatra*. Oxford: The Clarendon Press.

Davids, T. W. Rhys, and W. Stede, 1921–25. *The Pali Text Society Dictionary*. London: Pali Text Society.

De Silva, C. R., 1972. *The Portuguese in Ceylon 1617–1638*. Colombo: H. W. Cave and Co.

De Silva, K. M., 1961. "Buddhism and the British Government in Ceylon," *Ceylon Historical Journal*, vol. X, no. 1–4.

————1981. *A History of Sri Lanka*. Berkeley: University of California.

————1984. "Buddhism, Nationalism and Politics in Modern Sri Lanka," unpublished paper delivered at South Asia Conference, Madison, Wis., November 1984.

De Silva, Lily, 1981. *Paritta: the Buddhist Ceremony for Peace and Prosperity in Sri Lanka*. Spolia Zeylanica, vol. 36, part 1. Colombo: National Museum.

Devendra, Asoka, 1983. "Meditation in Day to Day Living," *Vesak Sirisara*, May, p. 9–11.

Dīgha Nikāya, T. W. Rhys Davids and J. Carpenter, eds., 1889–1910. London: Pali Text Society.

Douglas, Mary, 1966. *Purity and Danger*. London: Routledge and Kegan Paul.

————1970. *Natural Symbols. Explorations in Cosmology*. London: Barrie and Rockliff.

————1978. *Cultural Bias*, Occasional Paper no. 35 of the Royal Anthropological Institute of Great Britain and Ireland.

————1982. "The Effects of Modernization on Religious Change," *Daedalus*, vol. III, no. 1, p. 1–19.

Dumont, Louis, 1970. "Renunciation in Indian Religions," in *Religion, Politics and History in India*. The Hague: Mouton.

————1980. "World Renunciation in Indian Religions," Appendix B in *Homo Hierarchicus: The Caste System and Its Implications*, trans. M. Sainsbury, L. Dumont, and B. Gulati. Chicago: University of Chicago Press.

Dutt, Sukumar, 1960. *Early Buddhist Monachism*. London: Asia Publishing House.

Evers, Hans-Dieter, 1964. "Buddhism and British Colonial Policy in Ceylon, 1815–1872," *Asian Studies*, vol. 2, no. 3, p. 323–333.

————1968. "Buddha and the Seven Gods: The Dual Organization of a Temple in Central Ceylon," *Journal of Asian Studies*, vol. 27, p. 541–550.

Fernando, Tissa, 1973. "The Western Educated Elite and Buddhism in British Ceylon: A Neglected Aspect of the Nationalist Movement," in *Tradition and Change in Theravada Buddhism*, Bardwell L. Smith, ed. Leiden: E. J. Brill, p. 18–29.

Fernando, Tissa, and R. N. Kearney, 1978. *Modern Sri Lanka: A Society in Transition*. Syracuse, N.Y.: Syracuse University Press.

Frauwallner, Erich, 1956. *The Earliest Vinaya and the Beginnings of Buddhist Literature*, vol. viii. Rome: Serie Orientale Roma.

Geertz, Clifford, 1975. *The Interpretation of Cultures*. London: Hutchinson and Co.

Geiger, Wilhelm, 1960. *Culture of Ceylon in Medieval Times*. Weisbaden: Otto Harrasowitz.

Gellner, Ernest, 1969. *Saints of the Atlas*. Chicago: University of Chicago Press.

Gokhale, B. G., 1973. "Anagārika Dharmapāla: Toward Modernity Through Tradition in Ceylon," in *Tradition and Change in Theravada Buddhism*, Bardwell L. Smith, ed. Contributions to Asian Studies, vol. 4. Leiden: E. J. Brill.

Gombrich, Richard F., 1971. *Precept and Practice: Traditional Buddhism in the Rural Highlands of Ceylon*. Oxford: Oxford Universitry Press.

———1983. "From Monastery to Meditation Center: Lay Meditation in Modern Sri Lanka," *Buddhist Studies: Ancient And Modern*, P. Denwood and A. Piatagorsky, eds. London: Curzon Press.

Goonatilake, Susantha, 1983. "Review of Collected Works of A. T. Ariyaratne," *Journal of Contemporary Asia*, vol. 13, no. 2, p. 236–242.

Goulet, Denis, 1981. *Survival with Integrity: Sarvodaya at the Crossroads*. Colombo, Sri Lanka: The Marga Institute, 1981.

Gunatillika, P. G., 1947. *A Biography of H. Sri Nissanka*. Colombo: Helvira Press.

Gunawardana, D. C. R., P. H. Wickremasinghe and D. E. Wijewardene, *Report of the Universities Commission 1962*, Sessional Paper XVI of 1963. Colombo: Government Press.

Gunawardana, R. A. L. H., 1979. *Robe and Plow: Monasticism and Economic Interest in Early Medieval Sri Lanka*. Tucson: Association for Asian Studies, University of Arizona Press.

Gunawardene, S., 1981. "Dr. W. A. de Silva: Pioneer Agriculturist, Patriot and Philanthropist," *The Buddhist*, vol. LII, no. 6, October, p. 7–11.

Guruge, Ananda, ed., 1965. *Return to Righteousness: A Collection of Speeches, Essays, and Letters of Anagārika Dharmapāla*. Colombo: The Government Press.

Hallisey, Charles, 1985. "Epithets of the Buddha," paper presented at the University of Chicago, November 1985.

Jackson, Carl T., 1981. *The Oriental Religions and American Thought*. Contributions in American Studies, no. 55. Westport, Conn.: The Greenwood Press.

James, William, 1960. *The Varieties of Religious Experience*. London: William Collins and Sons.

Jayatilaka, D. B., 1981. "Practical Buddhism," *The Buddhist*, vol. LI, no. 9, January, p. 2–17. (reprinted from *The Buddhist*, July 1901).

Jayawickrama, N. A., and W. G. Weeraratne, 1982. *The World Fellowship of Buddhists and Its Founder President G. P. Malalasekera*. Colombo: World Fellowship of Buddhists.

Kantowski, Detlef, 1980. *Sarvodaya the Other Development*. New Delhi: Vikas Publishing House.

Kearnry, Robert N., 1973. *The Politics of Ceylon (Sri Lanka)*. Ithaca, N.Y.: Cornell University Press.

———1979. "Politics and Modernization," chap. 4 in *Modern Sri Lanka: A Society in Transition*, R. N. Kearnry and T. Fernando, eds., Foreign and Comparative Studies, South Asian Series, no. 4. Syracuse, N.Y.: Syracuse University.

Kemper, Steven E. G., 1978. "Buddhism without Bhikkhus: The Sri Lanka Vinaya Vardena Society," in *Religion and the Legitimation of Power in Sri Lanka*, B. Smith, ed. Chambersburg, Pa.: Anima Books.

Kheminda, 1980. *The Way of Buddhist Meditation*. Colombo: Lake House Publishers.

King, Winston, 1964a. *A Thousand Lives Away*. Cambridge: Harvard University Press.

———1964b. *In the Hope of Nibbāna: An Essay on Theravada Buddhist Ethics*. LaSalle, Ill.: The Open Court Press.

———1980. *Theravada Meditation: The Buddhist Transformation of Yoga*. University Park: Pennsylvania State University Press.

Kotelawele, D. A., 1978. "Nineteenth Century Elites and Their Antecedents," *The Ceylon Historical Journal*, vol. XXV, no. 1–4, October 1978.

Lamotte, E., 1958. *Histoire du Bouddhisme Indien des Origines à l'Ère à Saka*. Louvain: Bibliotheque du Museon, vol. 43.

Leach, Edmund, 1962. "Pulleyar and the Lord Buddha: An Aspect of Religious Syncretism in Ceylon." *Psychoanalysis and the Psychoanalytic Review*, vol. 49, no. 2, p. 80–102.

———1973. "Buddhism in the Post-Colonial Political Order in Burma and Ceylon," *Daedalus*, vol. 102, no. 1, Winter, p. 29–53.

Macy, Joanna, 1983. *Dharma and Development: Religion as Resource in the Sarvodaya Self-Help Movement*. West Hartford, Conn.: Kumarian Press.

———1984. "Buddhist Approaches to Social Action," *Journal of Humanistic Psychology*, vol. 24, no. 3, Summer, p. 117–129.

Mahāvaṃsa, Wilhelm Geiger, ed., 1958. London: Pali Text Society.

Majjhima Nikāya, R. Chalmers and V. Tranckner, eds., 1888–1902. London: Pali Text Society.

Malalasekera, G. P., 1928. *The Pali Literature of Ceylon*. London: Royal Asiatic Society.

———1937. *Dictionary of Pali Proper Names*, 2 vols. London: Luzac.

———1969. "Fifty Years of Service," *Golden Jubilee Souvenir*, All Ceylon Buddhist Congress, p. 20–21.

———1971. "Buddhism in the Modern World," in *Vesak Sirisara*, Reverend K. Jinānanda Thera and H. P. Jayawardena, eds. Panadura: Sri Saddharmadana Samitiya Saranapalaramaya.

———1982. *2500 Years of Buddhism*. Colombo: World Fellowship of Buddhists.

Malalgoda, Kitsiri, 1976a. *Buddhism in Sinhalese Society, 1750–1900*. Berkeley: University of California Press.

———1976b. "Buddhism in Sri Lanka: Continuity and Change," in *Sri Lanka: A Survey*, K. M. De Silva, ed. London: Hurst.

Maquet, Jacques, 1975a. "Expressive Space and Theravada Values: A Meditation Monastery in Sri Lanka," *Ethos*, vol. 3, no. 1, Spring, p. 1–23.

———1975b. "Meditation in Contemporary Sri Lanka: Idea and Practice," *Journal of Transpersonal Psychology*, vol. 7, no. 2.

Mendis, G. C., 1963. *Ceylon Today and Yesterday: Main Currents of Ceylon History*, 2d ed. Colombo: Associated Newspapers of Ceylon, Ltd.

The Milinda-Pañha, B. Trenckner, ed., 1880. London: Pali Text Society.

Mills, L. A., 1948. *Ceylon Under the British*, Colombo: Colombo Apothecaries.

Netti Pakaraṇa, E. Hardy, ed., 1961. London: Pali Text Society.

Nyanaponika, Thera, 1962. *The Heart of Buddhist Meditation*. London: Rider and Co.

Obeyesekere, Gananath, 1963. "The Great Tradition and the Little in the Perspective of Sinhalese Buddhism," *Journal of Asian Studies*, vol. XXII, no. 2, p. 139–153.

———1966. "The Buddhist Pantheon in Ceylon and Its Extensions," in M. Nash, ed., *Anthropological Studies in Theravada Buddhism*. New Haven: Yale University Southeast Asia Studies.

———1972. "Religious Symbolism and Political Change in Ceylon," in *The Two Wheels of Dhamma: Essays on the Theravada Tradition in India and Ceylon*, Bardwell L. Smith, ed. Chambersburg, Pa.: American Academy of Religion.

———1976. "Personal Identity and Cultural Crisis, The Case of Anagārika Dharmapala of Sri Lanka," in *The Biographical Process: Studies in the History and Psychology of Religion*, Frank E. Reynolds and Donald Capps, eds. The Hague: Mouton.

————1984. "The Economic Ethics of Buddhism: Reflections on Buddhist Modernism in South and Southeast Asia." Unpublished paper.

Olcott, Henry Steel, 1931. *Old Diary Leaves*, vol. IV. Madras: Theosophical Publishing House.

————1970. *The Buddhist Catechism*. Madras: The Theosophical Publishing House.

Olivelle, Patrick, 1974. *The Origin and Early Development of Buddhist Monachism*. Colombo: M. D. Gunasena and Co.

Ondaatje, Michael, 1984. *Running in the Family*. London: Pan Books.

Phadnis, Urdmila, 1976. *Religion and Politics in Sri Lanka*. London: C. Hurst.

Poussin, Louis de la Valée, 1917. *The Way to Nirvana: Six Lectures on Ancient Buddhism as a Discipline of Salvation*. Delivered as the Hibbert Lectures of 1916. Cambridge: The University Press.

Premaratne, Bogoda, 1969. "The Social Welfare Objectives of the Buddhist Congress," *A.C.B.C. Golden Jubilee Souvenir*, All Ceylon Buddhist Congress.

————1984. "The International Center for Training in Buddhist Meditation at Kanduboda, Sri Lanka," a pamphlet published in 1984 on the occasion of the fourteenth General Conference of the World Fellowship of Buddhists.

Rachaka, 1958. "A Short History of the Y.M.B.A., 1898–1958," *The Buddhist*, vol. XXIX, no. 1, May 1958.

Rahula, Walpola, 1959. *What the Buddha Taught*. New York: Grove Press.

————1956. *History of Buddhism in Ceylon*. Colombo: Gunasena and Co.

————1974. *The Heritage of the Bhikkhu*, trans. K. P. G. Wijayasurendra. New York: Grove Press.

Ratnapala, Nandasena, 1976. *Study Service in the Sarvodaya Shramadana Movement in Sri Lanka 1958–1976*. Colombo: Sarvodaya Research Centre.

Reynolds, Frank E., 1972. "The Two Wheels of Dhamma: A Study of Early Buddhism," in B. L. Smith, ed., *The Two Wheels of Dhamma: Essays on the Theravada Tradition in India and Ceylon*. Chambersburg, Pa.: American Academy of Religion, p. 6–30.

Reynolds, Frank E., and D. Capps, eds., 1976. *The Biographical Process: Studies in the History and Psychology of Religion*. The Hague: Mouton.

Ryan, B., 1953. *Caste in Modern Ceylon: The Sinhalese System in Transition*. New Brunswick, N.J.: Rutgers University Press.

————1958. *Sinhalese Village*. Coral Gables, Fla.: University of Miami Press.

Said, Edward, 1978. *Orientalism*. New York: Pantheon Books.

Sangharakshita, Bhikkhu, 1964. *Anagarika Dharmapala: A Biographical Sketch*. Kandy: Buddhist Publication Society.

Sarkisyanz, E., 1965. *Buddhist Backgrounds of the Burmese Revolution*. The Hague: Martinus Nijoff.

Sayadaw, Mahasi, 1980. *Practical Insight Meditation: Basic and Progressive Stages,* trans. by U. Pe Thin and M. U. Tin. Kandy. Sri Lanka: Buddhist Publication Society.

Seneviratne, H. L., 1963. "The Äsala Perahära in Kandy," *Ceylon Journal of Historical and Social Studies,* vol. 6, no. 2.

———1978. *Rituals of the Kandyan State.* Cambridge: Cambridge University Press.

Seneviratne, H. L., and S. Wickremeratne, 1980. "Bodhipuja, Collective Representations of Sri Lanka Youth," *American Ethnologist,* vol. IV, p. 734–743.

Singer, Marshall R., 1964. *The Emerging Elite: A Study of Political Leadership in Ceylon.* Cambridge, Mass.: The M.I.T. Press.

Singer, Milton, 1972. *When A Great Tradition Modernizes.* New York: Praeger.

Smith, Bardwell L., 1968. "Toward a Buddhist Anthropology: The Problem of the Secular," *Journal of the American Academy of Religion,* vol. XXXVI, no. 3, September, p. 203–216.

———1972. "Sinhalese Buddhism and the Dilemmas of Reinterpretation," in B. L. Smith, ed., *The Two Wheels of Dhamma: Essays on the Theravada Tradition in India and Ceylon.* Chambersburg, Pa.: American Academy of Religion.

———1973. *Tradition and Change in Theravada Buddhism: Essays on Ceylon and Thailand in the 19th and 20th Centuries,* vol. iv, Contributions to Asian Studies, K. Ishwaran, ed. Leiden: E. J. Brill.

Smith, D. E., 1966. *South Asian Politics and Religion.* Princeton, N.J.: Princeton University Press.

Smith, W. C., 1964. *The Meaning and End of Religion.* New York: New American Library.

Soedjatmoko, 1965. "Cultural Motivation to Progress: The 'Exterior' and the 'Interior' Views," in R. Bellah, ed., *Religion and Progress in Modern Asia.* New York: The Free Press.

Streng, Frederick J., 1976. *Understanding Religious Life.* Encino, Calif.: Dickenson Publishing Co.

Sutta Nipāta. D. Anderson and H. Smith, eds., 1948. Oxford: Pali Text Society.

Swearer, Donald K., 1981. *Buddhism and Society in Southeast Asia.* Chambersburg, Pa.: Anima Books.

———1970. *Buddhism in Transition.* Philadelphia: Westminster.

———1970. "Lay Buddhism and the Buddhist Revival in Ceylon," *Journal of the American Academy of Religion,* vol. XXXVIII, no. 3, September, p. 255–275.

———1973. "Thai Buddhism: Two Responses to Modernity," in *Tradition and Change in Theravada Buddhism,* Bardwell L. Smith, ed. Leiden: E. J. Brill.

Tambiah, S. J., 1968. "The Magical Power of Words," *Man,* vol. 2, no. 3, June, p. 175–208.

————1970. *Buddhism and the Spirit Cults in North-East Thailand*. Cambridge: Cambridge University Press.

————1973. "The Persistence and Transformation of Tradition in Southeast Asia with Special Reference to Thailand," *Daedalus*, vol. 102, no. 1, Winter, p. 55–84.

————1976. *World Conqueror and World Renouncer*. New York: Cambridge University Press.

————1984. *The Buddhist Saints of the Forest and the Cult of Amulets*. Cambridge: Cambridge University Press.

Thamel, C., 1984. "The Religious Woman in a Buddhist Society: The Case of the Dasa-Sil Mänio in Sri Lanka," *Dialogue (Sri Lanka)*, New Series XI, 1–3, January–December, p. 17–28.

Thera, Kassapa, 1957. *Protection of the Sambuddha Sasana: A Collection of Articles on Meditation*. Colombo: Henry Prelis.

Thomas, E. J., 1927. *The Life of the Buddha as Legend and History*. London: Routledge and Kegan Paul.

Vachissara, Kotagama, 1961. "Välivita Saraṇaṅkara and the Revival of Buddhism in Ceylon," Ph.D. thesis, University of London.

Vajirañāṇa, P., 1962. *Buddhist Meditation in Theory and Practice*. Colombo: Gunasena.

Vijayavardhana, D. C., 1953. *Dharma-Vijaya (Triumph of Righteousness), or The Revolt in the Temple*. Colombo: Sinha Publications.

Vimalananda, Tennakoon, 1963. *Buddhism in Ceylon Under the Christian Powers*. Colombo: Gunasena and Co.

————1970. *The State and Religion in Ceylon Since 1815*. Colombo: Gunasena and Co.

Vinaya Pitaka, five vols., H. Oldenberg, ed., 1879–1883. London: Pali Text Society, 1964.

Weber, Max, 1958. *The Religion of India*, trans H. Gerth and D. Martindale. New York: The Free Press.

Wilson, A. J., 1979. *Politics in Sri Lanka 1947–1979*. London: Macmillan.

Wilson, D. K., 1975. *The Christian Church in Sri Lanka*. Colombo: Study Centre for Religion and Society.

Wiesmeijer, Hans, 1981. "Diversity in Harmony: A Study of the Leaders, the Sarvodaya Shramadana Movement in Sri Lanka," doctoral thesis, University of Utrecht.

Wriggins, Howard, 1960. *Ceylon: Dilemmas of a New Nation*. Princeton, N.J.: Princeton University Press.

Yalman, Nur, 1962. "The Ascetic Buddhist Monks of Ceylon," *Ethnology,* vol. 1, p. 315–328.

——1967. *Under the Bo Tree.* Berkeley and Los Angeles: University of California Press.

INDEX